United We Fall

The Crisis of Democracy in Canada

SUSAN DELACOURT

VIKING

VIKING
Published by the Penguin Group
Penguin Books Canada Ltd, 10 Alcorn Avenue, Toronto, Ontario,
Canada M4V 3B2
Penguin Books Ltd, 27 Wrights Lane, London W8 5TZ, England
Viking Penguin, a division of Penguin Books USA Inc.,
375 Hudson Street, New York, New York 10014, USA
Penguin Books Australia Ltd, Ringwood, Victoria, Australia
Penguin Books (NZ) Ltd, 182-190 Wairau Road,
Auckland 10, New Zealand

Penguin Books Ltd, Registered Offices:
Harmondsworth, Middlesex, England

First published 1993

1 3 5 7 9 10 8 6 4 2

Copyright © Susan Delacourt, 1993

Printed and bound in Canada on acid free paper ∞

Canadian Cataloguing in Publication Data

Delacourt, Susan, 1959–
United we fall: the crisis of democracy in Canada

Includes index

ISBN 0-670-85191-4

1. Canada – Politics and government – 1984–   .*
2. Canada – History – 20th century.*
3. Nationalism – Canada.   4. Referendum – Canada.
I. Title.

FC630.D44 1993   320.971   C93-093965-4
F1034.2.D44 1993

To the Honourable Men and Women of Politics

Acknowledgments

I am one of those lucky authors, who has many people to thank for helping me with this book.

The enormous contribution of all the people mentioned in this book, who offered all the insights and time they had, will be evident to any reader. This book is written on the premise that honour and politics are not mutually exclusive, and I hope that the truly honourable public figures recognize themselves on these pages. I thank Penguin Books Canada as well and the gifted editing of David Kilgour for all they offered to transform a constitutional obsession into a book.

There are other people involved in this book, though, whose names will not appear in the telling of Canada's constitutional history in 1992. But they are as important to me as the politicians and other constitutional crusaders.

First, my three pillars of support in this exercise: Ron Huizer, Ann Lawson and Jan Lounder, who held me up and fortified me with everything from food and shelter to love and warmth and encouragement. I owe these three people more than I can ever repay.

The Globe and Mail has also been a source of very professional and very personal backing, and I would be remiss if I didn't note here how proud I am to work for this newspaper. No matter where I have worked for the *Globe* in the past ten years, I have been able to bask in the company of special, talented people.

I single out for particular mention my bureau chief, Graham Fraser, who has taught me so much about the notion of respect; for him, for others and for myself. National editor Sylvia Stead has borne the weight of the nation and the *Globe* on her shoulders, and I am grateful and happy to call her my boss and friend. Sylvia, along with editors Kathy Mills and Jerry Kinoshita, are hugely responsible for any success I have had in writing about this national-unity business.

I have also borrowed heavily on the advice of Geoffrey York, who has a limitless knowledge of the important things in life — writing, human justice and fainting goats. Hugh Winsor is the brightest constellation in my life at the *Globe*'s Ottawa bureau, and Jeffrey Simpson has honoured me with his considerable wisdom, encouragement and a dance or two. My Ottawa bureau family also depends on the support of colleagues Maureen Harrison, Ross Howard, Alan Freeman, Jeff Sallot and Drew Fagan. Across the country, I have come to rely on the formidable skills of *Globe* reporters such as Rheal Seguin, Rick Mackie, David Roberts and Miro Cernetig. And I still evoke muses of the *Globe*'s "Mellowville" — Kirk Makin, Murray Campbell, Ann Rauhala, Lorne Slotnick and Stephen Brunt — when I need to remember why it's important to do a significant job at the *Globe* and keep a sense of humour.

Outside the orbit of the *Globe,* there are other friends whose support has been crucial to this book. My constitutional "brothers," the *Toronto Star*'s Edison Stewart and CBC Radio's Alvin Cader, made the national-unity mission into a wonderful, fun experience for me. My real brother, John Delacourt, along with Sabine Schmidt, are the two wisest people I know. I can't say enough good things about my lawyer, sage counsellor and friend, Richard Mahoney; and all the fellow travellers on the constitutional tour, 1992 — fellow brownie-lovers and people who understood a joke that featured the words "seven and 50."

I even have to mention Nell, my temperamental dachschund, who would probably exact some canine revenge if I didn't work a mention of her name into this book.

Last, but certainly not least — the official dedication of this book is to the honourable men and women of politics. But there are two supremely honourable people in this world, to whom all my writing has always been dedicated; whose faces flash before me each time I set any words to paper. To my Dad and Mom, this book is for you, too.

Contents

Introduction

In the sweltering heat of the Ottawa Civic Centre arena on June 13, 1993, the strains of Kim Campbell's song blasted from the rafters while more than 3,000 Progressive Conservatives were casting their ballots.

"Changing politics together; we can make our country better," the chorus rang, and the fuchsia-clad hordes of Campbell supporters waved their flags.

Campbell rode to power on a pink tide of promises about change, and the "new politics of inclusion." She persuaded Tories to see the looming political horizon through her own rose-coloured rhetoric about "changing politics by the way we do politics."

Campbell knew what every other politically astute person in Canada had recognized by the spring of 1993 — that the future of the Canadian political system depended on the will of the people and the politicians to restore their faith and respect in each other.

This book tells the story of how Canada came to realize the need for the new politics, and why the great constitutional debate of 1992 provoked this fierce drive for a brand-new era in governing.

It tells the story of the political year 1992 for what it was — the last days of faith in the old-style, traditional politics of Canada. I believe that only by understanding those last days can we understand what's ahead for this country and the "new politics" demanded by Canadians for the next century. Inside the story of those very difficult months of 1992 are lessons for the politicians and the people to rebuild their shattered relationship.

It truly is a relationship in tatters, and all the singing and party colours and talk of renewal won't help, until we start to understand what went so wrong when we tried to rebuild our constitution.

Yes, I know it's difficult to think about the constitution these days.

"Listen, I'm sorry to bring this up again, but . . ."

Thus began every conversation I have had about this book, whether it was with my interview subjects, my friends and family, or future readers. For many months after the referendum in October 1992, I felt that I was the only Canadian who had not been felled by the collective constitutional amnesia that afflicted the country.

"Let it go," my fellow constitutional reporters would joke. "Turn the page," said some of the people who lived the constitutional drama along with me.

For a while, I practised my book-writing trade like the lead therapist in a survivors' group, trying to make sense of the trauma of the constitutional debate, encouraging politicians to sit down with me and work through the disappointment and confusion they felt about the doomed national-unity enterprise.

There was a lot of ground to cover. The constitutional issue is now a subject you don't raise in polite company in Canada. But for a full five years before the fall of 1992, it was the priority item on the political agenda of the nation.

I was fortunate to be a traveller on this five-year odyssey. I didn't know in the spring of 1987, as I sat in my home in Milton, Ontario, absorbed in the unveiling of the Meech Lake accord reached by Prime Minister Brian Mulroney and the provincial premiers, that I would be drawn so deeply into the constitutional vortex. I didn't even recognize the first signs of my coming obsession later that fall, when I arrived in New Brunswick to cover the provincial election, and kept asking the Liberal leader, Frank McKenna, what he would do with Meech if he became premier.

All I knew in the spring of 1988, soon after my arrival at *The Globe and Mail*'s Ottawa bureau, was that I was determined to see former prime minister Pierre Trudeau testify before the Senate on his opposition to Meech.

Out in the hall for a break, I spoke to a stranger about the impressive arguments of Trudeau and my admiration for the way he made mince-meat of Senator Lowell Murray's arguments in defence of Meech. "We haven't been introduced," said the stranger. "I'm Norman Spector." I had just declared my antipathy to Meech to the architect of the accord, whose imprint was all over the doomed constitutional deal.

So began my coverage of Meech for *The Globe and Mail*. Graham Fraser, my friend and the bureau chief in Ottawa, and I covered both sides of the constitutional issue, both of us wearing our opinions openly and passionately on our sleeves. Neither of us believed that we could be dispassionate or subjective about an issue that carried so much emotion. The best we could achieve was fairness, and I believe we did accomplish that.

Emotion, believe it or not, was a huge part of the life of any constitutional reporter. No one who was present at the horrible week in June 1990 at the

Government Conference Centre could escape it; our normal reporters' defences were eroded by exhaustion and tension and stress. No one who travelled on the endless shuttle missions of Constitutional Affairs Minister Joe Clark and the national-unity negotiating road-show could treat this as just another story, another issue. When the subject was as important as the future of the country and fundamental changes in the relationship between the governed and the government, all the pressure of history descended on us. Like the politicians, we truly believed that we were part of something extraordinary. And the constitution had a way of taking over your life, removing you from your family and home for months and years at a time. It became your life.

When I was doing the interviews for this book, I talked to British Columbia's Moe Sihota about this phenomenon. Sihota came to the issue as I did, young and impressionable, determined to keep a balance between passionate participation in the job and calm, detached reason about the task ahead. His feelings about the year 1992, in retrospect, mirror my own sentiments in many ways.

"It's been a remarkable experience. It was a growth experience," Sihota told me. "For someone who's young and involved in this business, it's invaluable.

"You can look around the table there and quite often, you'd say to yourself, 'Well, now I understand what political success is all about.' There are a lot of people who have survived in that room, and you could pick out the qualities that got them there."

Before I start sounding too romantic about this exercise, however, I also have to quote another constitutional veteran of 1992, who gave one of the most eloquent summations of the personal perils in constitution-making.

On the morning of June 11, 1990, when the national-unity talks were on the verge of breakdown at the Lester B. Pearson Building in Ottawa, the negotiators were sitting down for another fruitless morning of discussion.

Saskatchewan Justice Minister Bob Mitchell, a kind, gentle man, trapped in the endless discussions, was offered a chance to make remarks at the table. He told Constitutional Affairs Minister Joe Clark: "Joe, I'm going to be brief. This has been just one godawful experience for all of us throughout the last three months. I am sure that there isn't a person in this room who would want to go through it again. It has just been hell.

"My friend, George Peacock, who is in our delegation, leaned over to me one day and said: 'The truth of the matter is that we were all killed in a car accident and this is hell.' He's right."

Indeed, much of the constitutional business was hell, and there was no happy ending or reward for the suffering. For any politician who did live through this particularly Canadian brand of torture, it was very difficult not to be bitter at the No vote in the referendum of October 26, 1992, the overwhelming rejection of their efforts by the Canadian public.

No one is apparently more bitter than Brian Mulroney. That's only my assessment of his disposition, mind you. For even though Mulroney proclaimed the national-unity effort as his most cherished interest in his nine-year term as prime minister, he did not agree to be interviewed for this book. To be fair, I was told that he was not against an interview on principle, or because of any antagonism toward me — he just couldn't find the time in the months leading up to his resignation and exit from power.

I cannot pretend that I know Mulroney well enough to peer into his mind or his motivations. In this book, he will have to be judged by the reader in the same way that I judge him — by his deeds, not his words. Only once before he left office in June 1993 did Mulroney actually lay out what he saw as his legacy on the constitutional file, in a speech at Ottawa's Chateau Laurier hotel. And it was an extraordinarily bitter performance, filled with recriminations and blame for Trudeau, and denial and self-congratulation for himself. Mulroney laid out the way he wants to be judged by history. He defended all his own efforts as right, and the public and his critics as wrong. This book, as one instalment in the written history of his national-unity bid, does not take that view.

In fact, I have to say that Mulroney's reading of his own history ignores the major lesson I've learned. If we are to have a civilized relationship between the leaders and the led in this country, we need one starting ingredient — respect. I've come to believe that any politician, including a prime minister, has to work enormously hard to respect friends and especially foes. Mulroney's fatal flaw was his lack of respect for his critics and his dismissal of their opinions. Similarly, I don't think the public or the media help the country by making any politician — even Mulroney — the object of hatred and disrespect.

I learned this lesson myself in writing this book. I supported the Charlottetown accord fervently, and during the referendum I had a very hard time listening to the views of No campaigners such as Reform Party leader Preston Manning or Judy Rebick, the leader of the National Action Committee on the Status of Women, or Deborah Coyne, the founder of the Canada for All Canadians committee. But once I started listening to them and their very real, very reasoned arguments about what's gone so wrong in this country, I realized that they had to be respected and heard — that we make a terrible mistake when we ignore the voices from the other side. We don't have to agree with everything or anything they say, but maybe it's time for the politicians and the people to start listening to each other again, with respect.

It's a lesson that Kim Campbell, Mulroney's successor, will have to learn herself, along with all the other politicians who aspire to represent a cynical and angry public in the years ahead. It's a lesson that will have to be pulled from the wreckage of the political relationships in this country, so damaged by years of recession and unpopular government.

Most of all, it's a lesson that has to be dragged out of the dreaded debate over the constitution, and what Canada learned about itself in all the wrangling of 1992. It starts, I suppose, when somebody says: "I'm sorry to bring this up again, but . . ."

United
We
Fall

1

Getting to No

The answer was "No."

Not "no thanks" or "maybe later." In the national constitutional referendum of October 26, 1992, the Canadian public uttered the one word that could shut down nearly every elected leader in the country.

Alberta's Premier Don Getty was sitting at home watching television that night, the converter in his hand. He had already told his voters that he wouldn't be around for another vote. After seven long years, the football player turned premier had announced his retirement from Alberta's top political post, just as the referendum campaign got under way in September. On the night of the vote, Getty was alone at home in Edmonton. He'd gone for a walk in the neighbourhood with his dog, Spirit, and mulled over the horrible mood in the country that had been unleashed by the referendum campaign.

Resigned politically and emotionally, Getty was not particularly looking forward to the night's television viewing. This was the last time that Getty would be watching votes being counted with a vested, political interest, the last time he would feel that nervous anticipation of the public verdict on his own acts.

The news was bad, just as he expected. Twice in his life as Alberta premier, Getty had put his patriotism on the line to make a constitutional deal. The Meech Lake constitutional accord, which bore his signature, died in June 1990. Now, in October 1992, another deal with Getty's signature was going down to defeat. It was a two-fisted assault on the Alberta premier's convictions about the need for compromise and accommodation in Canada's unity struggle. He had believed fiercely that an Albertan had a duty to make a deal with Quebec, and he was proud of the sweat and effort that had brought all Canadian politicians to two major constitutional deals in five years.

On the night of October 26, 1992, with the television listing the litany of No votes, Getty realized starkly that the public and politicians were miles apart in their view of the need for compromise. No one really cared what he had done, and no one really cared about all the emotion he had poured into the Charlottetown deal.

The No column just kept racking up the points on the television. Getty's Yes side was losing, badly. He aimed the converter at the television and switched the channel to Monday night football. If the public could tune him out, he could tune them out too.

"Here," these politicians had said to their voters that fall of 1992, when they handed their work over to the judgment of the people. "This is what all our politics and our beliefs and our energies have produced for you. It is a brand-new country, all fixed up, the way we think you'd like it."

"No," the Canadian public said simply. "No."

At Harrington Lake, Quebec, the private prime ministerial retreat of Brian Mulroney, the host appeared to be taking rejection well early that night. The No vote kept washing across the television screen, as waves of returns flooded in from across the country. Nova Scotia voted No, Ontario almost voted No, Manitoba and the rest of the West voted No. Natives voted No. Quebec federalists and separatists alike voted No. The rejection bridged every division in the country.

What was the question? It didn't matter. Canadians were saying no to a deal called the Charlottetown accord. But more importantly, they were saying No to the brand of politics that brought them this dreaded constitutional deal.

"Remarkable," the television hosts commented. "Devastating," they opined. But at Harrington Lake, for the first part of the night, at least, Mulroney stoically accepted the news, nodding solemnly, sometimes even joking.

Mulroney was surrounded by friends, family and advisers. Two cabinet ministers were there to watch the results with him. One, Quebec lieutenant and Health Minister Benoit Bouchard, was the embodiment of all the past and the emotion that had brought Mulroney to this point, late in his second and last term as prime minister. It was Mulroney's identity as a Quebecker that led him to pursue this quest, the attempt to make the French-speaking province a willing partner in the Canadian federation, a signatory to the 1982 Constitution.

When Mulroney finally resigned, on February 24, 1993, he would describe the constitution as his greatest passion and his all-consuming interest. It would be on page one of his list of government achievements, a thirty-four-page, autobiographical eulogy distributed with a thump at the final press conference. Under the title "Fostering Canadian Unity," the press release would call the constitutional mission the greatest effort of this prime minister. No mention would be made of the fate of the two unanimous agreements reached by Mulroney and other elected representatives. The pundits and the commentators filled in that blank. In their review of the Mulroney years, in all the retrospective commentaries that night, his abortive attempts at "fostering Canadian unity" would be described as Mulroney's greatest disappointment and greatest failure.

The other cabinet minister at Harrington Lake that night was Finance Minister Don Mazankowski, who symbolized the elusive future for the country. If this government, indeed Canada, was going to recover from this night, it would have to focus on two kinds of recovery: one would be economic, and that was Mazankowski's worry in these recession-plagued times; the other recovery would be a more emotional one. In Alberta, Mazankowski's home province, as well as the rest of the country, a mood of populist discontent had seized the public, an angry, simmering well of resentment about the state of politics. That mood had been seething and fermenting; now it was bubbling up to the surface.

The public was angry that this constitutional debate had spent Canada's dwindling resources, instead of adding to them. The public was angry that the politicians and the national opinion leaders had put so much time and effort into an exercise that made barely a dent in the ordinary person's life in Canada. And they were very angry that the basis of the country was being renegotiated through brokerage deals and political trade-offs.

Any political leader who wanted to survive the 1990s was going to be forced to grapple with the anger that produced this negative force. Deny it, push it aside, forget about it they might, but the anger would be back.

In the months ahead, the politicians would have to stop talking about Charlottetown, but they would all have to start talking about their dreams for a "new politics," a route to restore people's faith in their elected leaders. Prime Minister Brian Mulroney would be long gone by the time the country went to the polls again, but the bitter rift between the politicians and the public couldn't be bridged simply by his departure.

That night at Harrington Lake, two television sets were conveniently placed in front of the guests. One was showing a broadcast in French, one was a broadcast in English. The news was the same in both languages, though. For the first time in many years, English and French Canada had united in one voice, to say "No" to their elected leaders' offering. United, Canadians spoke. And united, the politicians fell.

The hardest fall was for Constitutional Affairs Minister Joe Clark, no novice at the game of losing in politics. While his boss was absorbing the results in his own enclave at Harrington Lake, Clark was — as usual — in a hotel room, far away from Ottawa. The past year had brought Clark to many hotel rooms in many cities across Canada, but this was the bitter end of the odyssey. In a large, corner suite on the fourth floor of Edmonton's plush Hotel MacDonald, Clark, his wife Maureen McTeer and sixteen-year-old daughter Catherine were coming to grips with the loss of the precious constitutional deal.

Clark worried about how Catherine would react to the defeat. This was the first time she was old enough to feel the real wounds of politics. Clark had been through losses before, and he was always praised for his grace in defeat. He knew, though, that the humiliation of political loss was often hardest on the family and friends in the wings, who couldn't step from behind the curtains to fight the battles themselves. He knew it was easier to be brave in defeat when the wounds were your own; much harder when you were feeling hurt for someone else. But on this night, Clark wasn't in the mood to be stoic.

"I was much more hurt than angry. I was hurt by it. Personally hurt by it. And people say, it wasn't about you. But in a sense it was, because I had been so much involved . . . You can't help but feel some of that."

Clark would also be gone from politics by the end of February 1993. He would announce his resignation just four days before his arch-rival, Brian Mulroney, stepped down. Throughout their political lives, the fates of these two men had been inextricably tied, even as they struggled against each other. From 1976 to 1992, Clark and Mulroney took turns scoring wins off each other. Clark beat Mulroney for the Tory leadership in 1976, Mulroney beat Clark in 1983. Mulroney would win the majority governments that Clark could never quite grasp. Clark would win Canadians' trust, respect and affection, in a way that Mulroney never would, in Mulroney's own passionate issue — national unity.

But in the end, they both went down together. Defeated in the struggle over the referendum of October 1992, they were effectively gone by February 1993. Such a monumental struggle, and both men lost. There would be much talk of how these two politicians gave their lives and reputations to the great Canadian national-unity mission. Nothing concrete would be left to show for all their efforts. After all their struggles over nine years of government, the Tories left the constitutional landscape the way they found it. Co-operative federalism never took hold; Quebec never did sign on to the constitution. A separatist threat still plagues the French-speaking province and English Canada is fragmented in cynicism and isolation against the central government.

Was all this consitutional negotiating really in vain? It seemed so, that night of October 26. It seemed a waste of time, a waste of talent, a waste of money. Days after the great democratic purge, too, it seemed all forgotten, a bad dream.

What happened to the country? Was it mass hypnosis? How could all of these politicians and all of their officials stumble into such a huge, almost inevitably no-win situation? What was the lure of the constitution, that it held so many political leaders in its thrall for so long?

Saskatchewan premier Roy Romanow has seen it happen twice in his political lifetime — once, as provincial attorney-general in the early 1980s, when he emerged as a key player in the constitution-building and patriation effort of Pierre Trudeau; the second time, in 1992, when the constitution once again sang its siren song and beckoned him to its perilous terrain. The first effort cost him his seat in Saskatchewan in 1982, and the second attempt, ten years later, put him on the losing side of an emotional referendum campaign. Why bother? Because the constitution is a temptation and a seduction. Make no mistake about that.

"I didn't think I'd ever be in politics to live to see it a second time," he says. It is easy to become enraptured with this demanding mistress. It seems so right, so noble, to devote your political life to an obsession that promises so few returns and no public gratitude. Romanow gazes away, almost seeing those television lights around him again.

"With the national media around you . . . you're talking big issues. You're talking issues of equality and fairness, and Canada, statehood. This is big, big stuff. And all of us get into public life because we want to do good things for people on day-to-day matters but we also want to, you know, change the world."

Never mind the feeling that people get when they

escape a bullet or walk away from a brush with death. In polite, constitutionally obsessed Canada, reaching a national-unity deal can produce the same rush of euphoria for a politician.

"When you achieve it, there's that flush of hubris," Romanow says. "I'm not sure if that's quite the right word, but something like that. That sense of invincibility; that everybody should see it."

It even grabs the political rookies. Moe Sihota, the British Columbia constitutional affairs minister, is a self-described new kid on the constitutional block. A young, smooth-looking, smooth-talking political hot shot in the fledgling New Democratic government of British Columbia, this was a man who seemed unlikely to be swallowed up by such an age-old drama in Canadian political life. This is a baby boomer's politician who seemed impervious to the obsessions of another generation of Canadian politicians. But he too would get swept up in the vortex of constitution-making.

Starting in March, a flying team of provincial politicians and bureaucrats, along with a planeload of journalists, federal politicians, bureaucrats and political aides, would spend the spring negotiating a new deal for Canada. They spent the summer trying to save the deal in Ottawa and the fall trying to sell the deal to the Canadian public. If time and fatigue were measures of commitment to the country, this constitutional industry, the travelling road show, was the ultimate exercise in commitment.

Sihota strode into the constitutional fray with almost a determined air of cynicism: his manner aloof, his eyebrows raised in an almost permanent expression of suspicion. He delivered his press lines to the reporters with a nodding, show-me kind of attitude; he could be counted upon to say that the emperor had no clothes, or, in this case, that Quebec was annoying everyone by staying away from the negotiations. But even if Sihota kept his arms folded in front of him, and his eyes firmly fixed on just surviving the constitutional mess politically, this rookie was drawn into the enchantment of the national-unity debate in the same way as the veterans around the table.

"It's not just tempting. It's totally seductive," Sihota says. Remember, he and many of these other people at the tables were lawyers in their previous lives, drawn by experience and interests to arcane discussions of weighty matters. "It was like going to law school again," Sihota says. "It brings you right back to your political roots because you can see how you can make certain political decisions and direct the course of the country in a very, very significant way."

Immediately after the referendum results poured in, politicians all over Canada would be saying that they had learned their lesson — never again would they be lured by the lights and the "big stuff" of the constitutional debate. Government had to focus on the more concrete worries of the people, not these lofty, law-school issues of constitution-making.

But that wasn't really the major lesson. What the referendum should have taught Canadians, the elected and the electors, was that a rift of enormous proportions lay between them, a rift dug out of disrespect and cynicism.

The country should also have learned the size of the chasm that existed between Quebec and the rest of Canada. Equally serious to the rift between politicians and the public, Canada was learning that it is very dangerous to put the potent Quebec chemistry of nationalism and federalism into the same simmering vat of English Canadian cynicism about politics. In this great exercise of conciliation between the two solitudes, the two would not learn much about each other.

Later in the referendum campaign, Sihota was to find out first-hand the perils of getting involved in a constitutional debate that always seems to pit the English against the French. To a few reporters in Quesnel, B.C., he said that Quebec premier Robert Bourassa had come to the national-unity bargaining table with outrageous demands and that the rest of Canada had stared him down. "Nine governments looked him in the eye and said No."

Those words were powerful fodder for a Quebec public just looking for another bit of evidence that they were getting shafted by the rest of Canada. Sihota's words planted few roots in B.C., but the seeds of the message blew into Quebec with gale force and boosted a No campaign that already needed little help.

It still sickens Sihota when he remembers the incident. "It never really bothered me, until I picked up *Maclean's* after the referendum and saw an article on the four defining moments in the campaign. And I was one of them . . . I've had great difficulty overcoming that.

"It wasn't the statement, and it wasn't dealing with the optics of the statement at the time, and it wasn't even the difficulty of stick-handling around the statement as we moved into an element of damage control. You know? You can handle all that."

No, for Sihota it was a self-inflicted blow to his very essence as a Canadian. This politician, proud of his East Indian heritage and one of the first of his culture to hold such a high post in Canadian politics, was disappointed in himself as a poor standard-bearer for diversity in Canada. This young cabinet minster, who still insists that his children speak Punjabi at home, felt a common cause with Quebec and its desire to protect its language and heritage as a different community in

Canada. Despite all his bluster at the press conferences about his frustration with Quebec, he was on a very personal mission to make sure that no one or no government in Canada felt isolation or alienation because of their love of their own culture.

"To this day, I feel terrible. Given the posture that I had taken all the way throughout the process, in terms of trying to do what we thought was right to bring the country together, and recognizing the role of Quebec in this nation . . . To have done that, and to have blurted it out . . ."

The politicians were not blinded by their obsession. They truly believed they had accomplished something remarkable and something important. How could the people be so casual or so dismissive of this euphoric sense of achievement?

The answer lies in the fact that the public no longer saw their elected leaders as representing them. It was a true crisis of representative democracy. Once upon a time, the public took part in the great debates of the nation on vicarious terms, through the politicians they sent to elected office. Now Canadians couldn't seem to accept that politicians were going through their decisions and angst on behalf of the voters. The culture of selfishness had made it impossible to believe that anyone could act in the best interests of anyone except him- or herself. Most of the constitutional negotiators didn't realize this, as they went through their torturous spring and summer of talks. They honestly believed they were at the table to get what their voters wanted and needed. They thought their experiences were the public's experiences. They believed their efforts were being made on behalf of the people who voted for them.

That's not the way it was in 1992. The constitution was not a shared experience between the voters and the

politicians. Just because a politician was euphoric
didn't mean that the people would be euphoric. Just
because the politicians had learned to respect each
other's convictions didn't mean that the public had
travelled the same learning curve. There was no public
sense that Bob Rae's agreement was the Ontario
people's agreement; that what the politicians decided
was what the public would have chosen to do. It's difficult to see the world through someone else's eyes when
you don't respect the person, or the politician. It's also
impossible for a member of the public to regard the
politician as a true representative when there are so
many other people — interest groups, experts, activists
— also claiming to represent them.

Manitoba premier Gary Filmon found this out in
London, England, of all places, in 1992. He thought
the Manitoba voters had come along with him on his
troubled but successful mission into constitutional
politics. This was a man who had been at the centre
of the storm over the Meech Lake accord, and who
had watched it die in his own province on June 22,
1990. This time, he thought, we've got a hardier deal,
one that can stand up to opposition.

At the end of September 1992, Filmon was in London
on a trade mission. He had taken a lot of heat for
leaving the country in the midst of the referendum
campaign. He was accused of fleeing the growing controversy, absenting himself rather than trying to defend
an indefensible deal.

That's not exactly right, says Filmon. He just had no
idea that things could go so wrong. He didn't realize
the magnitude of the abyss between the public and the
politicians. Filmon and his wife Janice were out pub-
hopping after the Manitoba premier had been through
a day of meetings with London finance-community
members. He was sitting in a tiny pub, just digging in

to a steak-and-kidney pie when he looked up and saw
his old fraternity buddy from the University of Manitoba, Glen Urquhart, a fellow Manitoban who had since
made his home in British Columbia. By some stunning
coincidence, Urquhart had stepped into the same
establishment, along with his own wife and another
friend from British Columbia. They started talking
about life back home in Canada, the state of politics,
the course of their lives. Filmon's old friend marvelled
at the way the Manitoba premier had been swallowed
up in the great Canadian national-unity debate. He
sympathized with him for the way Manitoba had been
thrown to the front lines, and Filmon with it. He shook
his head that an engineer from Winnipeg could be tied
up for so long in the intricacies of constitutional law.

"Well, what a life experience you've had in the last
nine months, or really, the last two or three years,"
Urquhart said.

Filmon nodded. Indeed, it had been a nightmare, a
tumultuous experience, especially for a man who
didn't even like or know the constitutional business
that well when all of it started for him in 1989. But it
was all over now — the Charlottetown deal had been
signed and delivered, Quebec was in agreement, and
finally the country would get on to the real business of
the economy. Filmon was already moving on, drum-
ming up investment in London with this trade mission.

Urquhart went on: "Incredible, this constitution —
but it's going down, isn't it?" The Manitoba premier just
stared at him, incredulously. He asked his friend to
repeat what he had said.

"God, I've just been telling all the people in the
finance community in London that everything's going
fine, and despite the controversy there's so many
people who support it." All that agreement — the fact
that so many of the traditional opinion-leaders were on

side with the politicians — had convinced the London financial community that the Charlottetown accord was a safe bet. Surely that same argument should appeal to Canadians, Filmon said.

"I mean, we have all the leadership of all the provinces, the three parties at the national level. In fact, leaders of the opposition in seven of the 10 provinces, territories are in support of it, the aboriginals are in support of it, labour's in support of it, you know, even environmental groups are starting to come out in favour of it. Business is strongly supportive of it. The public will be influenced by the strong consensus."

He shook his head, trying to absorb what his friend had said. Surely Urquhart was joking. Here he was, in London, England, listening to a displaced British Columbian paint a very gloomy picture of the Canadian landscape that the Manitoba premier thought he knew so well. So convinced was he that their forecasts were wrong, that he made a five-pound bet in favour of the Charlottetown deal.

He lost.

It's not as if the politicians couldn't sense what was happening. Indeed, by referendum night, most of them were cursing what their own radar had been telling them for several weeks. Roy Romanow calls it "the feeling in my elbow," a strange turn of phrase he uses to describe his political instincts. In the days before referendum day, out on the stump pushing his unpopular message of support for the Charlottetown accord, Romanow's elbow was starting to act up.

"I could feel, when I went to speak, I could feel the crowd in my elbow," Romanow says. He crooks his arm, points to his elbow, clutches it, as if trying to reconcile himself to this oddly placed political antenna. A veteran of the constitutional wars, and of politics, Romanow explains: "It's just the way they look at you, or the way they do not look at you, the way they react, the warmth, the spontaneity, the size of the crowd." He slaps his elbow, maybe in congratulation for its accuracy; maybe in reproach for its delivery of bad news.

"You could feel it. I mean, you'd be on a platform and you get a . . . You can feel it. I could just feel it."

Isn't this what the public wants of their politicians? The sensitivity, the instincts to perceive the people's discontent? Perhaps, but Canadian politics in the 1990s is not for the overly sensitive. To be a Canadian politician today, you have to have the instincts of a Roy Romanow and the resilience of Ontario premier Bob Rae.

Rae was at Toronto's SkyDome Stadium on October 26. It should have been idyllic — a wonderful day for Canada, its citizens and its baseball aficionados. Toronto was turning out in droves to herald the World Series victory, and the country was flocking to the polls to take part in a great democratic exercise over the unity and future of the nation.

Rae, indeed, is a baseball fan and he was in the stadium along with 50,000 other baseball fans to celebrate the October 24 victory. It was the first time a Canadian team had ever won the top title in "America's game." It was a profoundly important milestone in the ceaseless Canadian crusade to prove that this country is just as good as, even better than, the United States. This was a great moment in Canadian history, a time for a real celebration of Canada and Canadian baseball.

But the crowd soon let Rae know that he was not just a baseball fan — he was a politician. And even in their glee, their delight at this victory for Canada, this surge of patriotic fervour, the Canadians in that stadium drew a line between their love of country and their feeling for the country's politicians.

They booed Rae. They booed Toronto mayor June Rowlands. They cheered for mainly American-born baseball players who had represented Canada for a few glory-filled weeks that fall; they hissed at the Canadians who represented them every day in the nation's politics.

If that burst of anger hurt Bob Rae, or if it hit him in his political elbow, he will not admit to it. When you're a politician in Canada today, you can't afford to be too sensitive to the moods of the crowd; you can't let the feeling in your elbow make its way to your heart. Rae, in constitutional circles, would be known for his thin skin, his vulnerability to criticism. But by referendum day, he was starting to realize that being despised is part of the political territory.

"They were just kids, teenagers," he says, pointing out that boos and hisses are the price almost any politician pays for coming into a sporting arena. It's almost the 1990s version of throwing Christians to the lions. There was no respect for the Christians among the crowd. And there was little respect in 1990s Canada between the public and the politicians. Openly, in a public stadium, a politician could be held up to public contempt.

A basic, simple value such as respect had broken down. Maybe Rae had developed enough political shock absorbers in his bumpy ride as premier that he could ignore this display of disrespect in front of 50,000 people. But it was a large-scale illustration of the terrible relations between the leaders and the led in Canada in 1992.

Later, Rae would be spending the evening as his fellow premiers did, watching TV and taking in the results. These men were watching the television as no other Canadians were watching it that night. The distance between the elected and the electors showed up even in the way they watched the numbers piling up in the No camp. Any other Canadian would have viewed those numbers with sporting interest, as a contact-free form of Monday night football. The Yes and No forces, speeding down the field to a touchdown. Any other Canadian could watch this as a race, a fight to the finish. In this country where the politicians have ended up on one side, the people on the other, this was a game of tremendous symbolism. And the public seemed poised to win, taking home a trophy that gave them vindication of their anti-politician mood and a sense of superiority over those they had chosen to govern them.

But the politicians were hardly in a sporting mood. They were students of this lesson in adding and subtracting, and there was only one way to see these numbers — as a report card. They saw the rising No tide as confirmation of their disturbing instincts; an insight into the failure of their efforts. Like the student who knows that a failing grade is lurking in the future, the only comfort for these politicians was that at least they saw the result coming.

Signs of trouble for the Yes side had come very early to Bob Rae. Soon after the Charlottetown agreement was signed, the Ontario premier and the constitutional delegation pulled in some key people, about 100 representatives of interest groups and curious constitution-watchers, to advise them of the contents of the deal. Some were enthusiastic. But ominously, some voiced criticism. Rae heard that criticism and recognized its potential instantly.

As the groups filed out, the Ontario premier weighed the reaction. He couldn't stop thinking about some of the criticism levelled at the Charlottetown accord — the concerns of women, the concerns of special interests, the fixation on the cherished principle of equality. He thought to himself: "Some of this is going to have a lot of legs."

The Ontario premier was correct to see the equality issue developing "legs." Within weeks, those legs would carry the equality issue waddling into the referendum debate, knocking over much of the support for the Yes side. By the end of the referendum campaign in October, the politicians would be little more than the trampled victims of this equality march.

Rae's New Democratic colleague Roy Romanow had been knocked down before, after the national-unity travails in 1982. As we have seen, he marvelled that this fate could strike him twice in less than a decade. On referendum night, Romanow was in his office watching TV with a few advisers for company and pizza for sustenance.

"Damnit," he thought. "My elbow is smarter than my head." He had to think about strategy. He looked at his advisers quizzically. "Well, what do we do? Do we communicate: 'Oh well, end of the world'? Or do we communicate calm and reason?"

They decided that calm and reason was the best option. They put together a press release. Its key message revolved around platitudes. The people have spoken, let's get on with governing. It's not the end of the world.

"But I'm afraid I didn't carry that off very well that night," Romanow says. A number of his friends phoned him and told him he looked angry.

Rae resisted the impulse to anger. True to that very old Ontario, repressed style, he took a dim view of reacting personally to this defeat. He watched Joe Clark and marvelled that this consummate politician had chosen to reveal his personal, rather than political reaction to the defeat of Charlottetown.

"Clark's reaction was not a political reaction," Rae said. "It was a very human, personal reaction. . . . No one had obviously got to him and said this is what you've got to do; this is what you've got to say."

True. No one had got to Clark. But he was not going to go on television and pretend that he felt fine about this. His fellow politicians on the Yes team had been far too sanguine, too resigned about this massive rejection. So Clark stood up before the crowd in Edmonton. His daughter Catherine was angry and hurt, but she had come down to face the music with her father. As a last-minute gesture, more out of fashion than politics, she tied the Métis sash around her waist. Native people across the country were touched by Catherine's choice of wardrobe accessory. Her father had spent far too much time in the past twenty years showing grace in defeat. He was hurt, he was angry, and it was over.

"I naturally respect the decision of the people of Canada, and respect the clear result of rejection of this accord." He used the word "respect" over and over again; the virtue that seemed so absent in the Canadian political system of the 1990s. Though the politicians had learned over that spring and summer to respect each other, they couldn't seem to make the same leap with the Canadian voting public, and the people who opposed them.

"I want, however, to make a distinction. I respect the people's decision. I can't say the same for the arguments that were made by some of the people who led the arguments against this accord."

Clark couldn't stop thinking about his Alberta nemesis, Reform Party leader Preston Manning, who had capitalized on the anti-Mulroney sentiment to urge a No vote to the "Mulroney deal." The constitutional affairs minister put his finger on the issue that separated Yes and No. There was no respect.

"The accord is dead. There has been a No to reform of the Senate. There has been a No to a response to the claims for justice of Canada's aboriginal people. There has been a No to this particular response to the recognition of the distinct society. It's not at all clear to what Canadians said Yes."

For the Canadians who still had their televisions on that night, the image of a devastated, defeated Joe Clark would be the most enduring image of the wounds felt by the Yes side. He was the picture of the kicked, beaten politician in Canada in the 1990s.

"It was important to make it clear that this was something lost," Clark says.

If there were two politicians in the country who had a vested personal interest in the outcome of all that negotiating through spring, they were Rae and Clark. The Ontario government shaped the process; Clark invested his political life in overseeing those negotiations. But funnily enough, Rae did not share Clark's depth of despondency that night.

"It went further than I personally felt," Rae said. In fact, he had developed a fatalistic approach to the whole thing. And like a true politician, the Ontario premier looked for the political messages in these numbers. He found it was like the old joke: good news, bad news. Yes, the politicians had lost, but at least Ontario had voted in favour of the deal, with a slim, 56 per cent majority.

"I must confess that my own interests did sort of show, or the politician that's in me all the time, or the fighter that's in me all the time. I mean, I was really happy that we won in Ontario." But that was a small victory; nothing compared to the win of the No side. This unlikely coalition of alienated Westerners, old-style Trudeau Liberals and equality-seeking feminists had just united Canadians, in all regions, in a show of protest against their politicians.

Judy Rebick, head of the National Action Committee on the Status of Women, should have been happy that night. She should have been joyful that the No campaign, which she had helped to spearhead, had carried the day. As a participant in the parade of media reaction that night, she appeared as the victor. But as a spectator to the politicians' reaction, she felt as though she were one of the vanquished.

In a CBC studio, where she was positioned to deliver her instant reaction — a skill she has developed as a "media personality" — she saw all the politicians appearing on the larger-than-life screen behind the set. Their largeness behind her was daunting in itself. Rebick could report to her constituency the next day that she had seen the enemy and it took up about three square metres of screen space on the CBC set.

One after another, the politicians appeared to be saying the same thing. Like repentant sinners, they promised to ignore the unholy temptation of the constitution in the future and turn their attention to more legitimate interests: the economy, social justice. Rebick was devastated. "They hadn't learned, they didn't get it. And they just weren't going to get it."

Rebick would have liked the politicians to appear more chagrined. She would have liked them to recognize that the No vote was a judgment on their style of politics, not upon the issue they had decided to pursue. The public was angry that the great exercise in democracy and consultation had ended up as yet another example of politicians saying: "Here's our idea — take it or leave it." This wasn't just Canadians saying that politics was fixed upon the wrong issue; this was Canada's way of saying that their brand of politics had not worked. And yet the politicians seemed impervious to the message.

"I was distressed about the state of the leadership of the country," Rebick said. She was so despondent, in fact, that she ended up in her Toronto apartment late that night, on the phone, trying to be heartened by the jubilant Vancouver feminists who had helped her cause for the No side. Her Toronto co-combatants had long since abandoned their celebration and gone to bed. But the Vancouver feminists, three hours behind Toronto time, were just starting to exult over their success in the referendum. They were in a victorious mood; Rebick was open to their happy influence.

But she was destined to be blocked from any concrete demonstration of their jubilation. The Vancouver Rape Relief Crisis Centre tried to send her a gift of congratulations — a symbol of the feminist movement that comes from the song "Bread and Roses." Half a dozen red roses and a loaf of European, peasant-style bread was sent to the CBC studio where she was offering running commentary throughout the night. But the overzealous CBC security people would not allow the suspicious material inside their brand-new, shiny building on Front Street in Toronto. The package languished at the security desk. It was only the next day, when Rebick showed up to do an interview on the French network, Radio-Canada, that she was handed the symbolic bread and roses. By then, the bread was less than fresh and the roses were a little wilted.

But still, that giant No was sitting out there freshly in front of the nation, brazen and forward, for all to see. "The Answer Is No," proclaimed the headline in *The Globe and Mail* on October 27. It was such a negative statement, uttered with such force, that there was no misreading the bad mood of the nation. It seemed impossible to find something positive in such an overwhelming display of negatives.

Judy Rebick did see something positive, though, in that same CBC studio, where the larger-than-life politicians had dispirited her. In the audience, so-called "real people" were talking, and their words and insights heartened her.

"That's where I gained hope. That's where I gained hope through the whole referendum," she said. "What was different, and what I'd never seen in Canadian politics before, was how serious people were about learning about the Charlottetown accord, about finding out about it, about questioning, and about taking their own right to vote so seriously."

That phenomenon had taken hold all over the country. Canadians were hooked on the same constitutional drug as the politicians. One fall night in Wasketnaua, Alberta, Alberta's intergovernmental affairs minister, Jim Horsman, came to a local community hall to talk about the Charlottetown accord. Grease-stained and work-worn, the local farmers turned up to listen earnestly to the message of the "Honourable Jim." Their faces fixed in intense concentration, these farmers and other residents had brought their pencils and were dutifully underlining portions of the Charlottetown accord.

"Honourable Jim," they would ask, "what does this phrase mean on this page —?" Horsman had thrown away his more partisan rallying cry for a Yes vote when he saw that crowd and felt its mood. He had to be a teacher, an explainer, not a partisan politician. "Sometimes," he said in his car as he left the meeting, "you just have to get a read on the crowd. These people wanted to hear about the accord itself, not why they should vote for it."

All over Canada, the message was the same. The referendum had stirred up an intense desire to hear about the intricacies of constitution-making. Rebick was inspired. Meanwhile, Deborah Coyne, founder of the Canada for All Canadians committee on the No side, was experiencing the same renewal of faith in the people. All she could feel was relief, immense relief.

Coyne's loosely assembled band of No voters had installed themselves at the Butler House restaurant on the fringes of Ottawa, to test their conviction that they really did have the right to speak as "Canada for All Canadians." No one, at any point in the referendum campaign, had ever challenged Coyne to justify the sweeping confidence of her group's name. Coyne reaped the credibility borne of that vague, dull sense that somehow the national vision of Pierre Trudeau had to have a voice in this dispute. Coyne's closeness to Trudeau, the fact that she was the mother of his child, lent to the notion that she was somehow the spokesperson for the former prime minister.

Coyne thought her voice was larger than that. She was sure that she spoke for a powerful sentiment at the Canadian grassroots: Trudeau's legacy among the people who had grown up and come of political age during his 20 years of domination of Canadian politics. But she just wasn't sure whether it could overcome the politics of fear in Canada of the 1990s.

"I thought that people might go in and just be scared into voting Yes, or spoiling their ballot or something."

As she saw the No vote building across the country, this eternal optimist would be happy that her faith in the Canadian public was confirmed.

"If people had the courage to say this, despite all the pressures, and the fear-mongering, and so forth, there's hope for the future," she said. Coyne was doubly happy that Quebec and English Canada had stood together, united in the fall of the Charlottetown accord. It reminded her of the heartening experience of Meech Lake, when she believed the people had spoken through the acts of Newfoundland premier Clyde Wells. Quebec hadn't been part of that protest — this last time, the two Canadas were united in felling their politicians.

This was Canada's idea of a revolution. Though its most visible sign was a No vote, it nonetheless fit the definition of a populist uprising against the established class. The political people had tried to introduce a radical reform of Canada's system, but the Canadian nation wasn't in the mood for this type of radical reform. As one commentator on television quipped: "Only in Canada would they have a revolution for the status quo." Leave us alone, Canadians were saying. Stop messing with the balance of the federation. The status quo is just fine, thank you very much.

The status quo was not fine, though, for native leaders such as Ovide Mercredi and Ron George. As the head of the Assembly of First Nations, Canada's largest organization of native people, Mercredi was crushed by the rejection. Once again, Canadians had said No to the native people. There was no equality, though, in this rejection.

"We had an opportunity through the constitutional process to resolve our conflicts peacefully, without resorting to barricades. Canadians have said No to that."

Ron George was even more blunt about the threat to Canada's fragile relations with the aboriginal community: "Our people are dying on the streets now, under the status quo. We're not equal. We've got nothing to cheer about."

Later, these two native leaders would have to retract their vitriolic statements against the Canadian public. As it turned out, their leadership and their obsession were slammed in the same fashion as those of the leaders in English Canada. Most native people voted against the deal and all the efforts of their designated representatives, who had made history with their first-time presence at the constitutional table. The history of the moment was lost on the natives. They were united with the rest of Canada in voting No.

"I was hurt," said Ovide Mercredi. "Very, very hurt."

Some people would insist that Canada's "élites" had

been quelled, but that wasn't quite right. What was former prime minister Pierre Trudeau, except a member of Canada's ultimate élite? He had voted No. Deborah Coyne, Preston Manning, Bloc Quebecois leader Lucien Bouchard — all were products of Canada's established class. It was too easy to say this was an élite versus non-élite question.

What it was, in fact, was a repudiation of the elected politicians and their brand of politics. It was an utter breakdown in the respect between the electors and the elected. Like Don Getty, converter in hand, the politicians and the people had turned each other off. Neither one had much time for each other any more. Politicians weren't listening when people said they had problems with the Charlottetown deal and the referendum campaign. The people weren't listening all those months when the politicians kept popping up across the country to report on the progress of the constitution. "No," the people said. Or, as the Reform Party phrased it: "No more." On October 26, the people spoke and the politicians were saddened and angered by what they heard.

For two years, Canada's entire political system had been geared to deal with the national-unity mission. Quebec's problems had been identified as a problem, so had the aboriginal people's grievances. But the overwhelming issue for the politicians these past two years had been the crisis of confidence in Canada's political system and how to fix it. In the end, they were defeated by the very problem they had tried to solve. Their goal was unity, and united they fell.

2

The Two Ottawas:
Between a ROC and
a Hard Place

At a cosy little Greek restaurant in downtown Montreal in May 1992, Constitutional Affairs Minister Joe Clark had taken the unusual step of socializing with reporters.

About a half-dozen reporters, French and English, were feasting with Clark on an endless, multi-course array of seafood and Greek cuisine. Outside the restaurant, a warm evening had pulled Montrealers out onto the streets, and the laughing, noisy crowds passed by the window. With his elbows leaning heavily on the blue, checker-clothed table, his hands knotted together in front of him, Clark talked about the human toll of a national-unity crusade. There was no self-pity; it was an accounting of his personal state, delivered with the same, earnest dispassion he used to report "progress" at the end of each day in these discussions.

"It's not like anything I experienced as external affairs minister," Clark said. "There, you had protocol and bureaucracy and years of diplomacy to fall back on." He paused, trying to find the right words. "In this, you feel so exposed, so alone, so unsure what the next step is." Here was the man who had been given the task of putting the nation back together in 1992 — and he was alone.

It was a fitting symbol for the nation. Ottawa, once the busy, noisy hub of political life in Canada, was sitting quietly alone, watching the provinces and the interest groups make all the noise. The force of federalism was now in an uncertain drift towards the future. It was also a fitting commentary on the politics within Clark's Progressive Conservative government. Here was Clark, out on the road, drifting alone in the raging seas of provincial dissent, and his old rival, Prime Minister Brian Mulroney, was back in Ottawa, absent from Clark's side, physically and figuratively.

How had it come to this in 1992? What was Ottawa doing out there all alone when the country was supposed to be at stake?

It's not new, the idea of two different visions of Canada. In the 1940s, novelist Hugh McLennan coined the notion of "two solitudes." Even farther back, in 1838, Lord Durham reported to his British colonial masters that Canada was actually "two nations warring in the bosom of a single state."

As 1992 rolled around in Canada, a new description emerged. There was Quebec, and then there was the "rest of Canada," conveniently nicknamed "ROC." And they were both struggling for dominance at the very top reaches of the federal government in Ottawa. It was Constitutional Affairs Minister Joe Clark, captain of the national-unity negotiations among the other nine provinces, who came to embody the "ROC." It was Prime Minister Brian Mulroney, a Quebecker to his core, who spoke to that province and its needs, the "hard place" of Canadian politics in 1992.

Like the two parts of Canada itself, these two men were tied together, in an explicable tug-of-war. When Quebec tugged on one end of the Canadian rope, the rest of the nation would pitch forward. Then the ROC would pull all the harder in the opposite direction. When Brian Mulroney tugged on that heavy blue Tory cord that bound him to his rival, Joe Clark would pitch forward, and then tug back even harder.

In 1992, Quebec and the rest of Canada would tug so hard on the unity rope that both would lose in the national referendum. And similarly, both Joe Clark and Brian Mulroney would be thrown together in mutual loss. The great Tory-Canada tug-of-war was finally over in February 1993, when the two men resigned within four days of each other.

In the early days of July 1992, Clark and Mulroney were each pulling on the rope with every bit of energy they had mustered in their sixteen-year rivalry. The story of these two men and their tense times in these days is, in fact, the story of a country caught between the ROC and the hard place.

Late on the night of July 7, 1992, a weary Joe Clark walked out to face the battery of reporters at the Lester B. Pearson Building in Ottawa, site of the gruelling final stages of the constitutional negotiations that took place among all the governments in the rest of Canada — provinces, Ottawa, territories and aboriginal organizations. He proclaimed to the nation a simple message of victory on behalf of his fellow negotiators — they had done it; despite all the odds against it, they had actually reached an agreement about reshaping the Canadian federation. The centrepiece of the deal was an equal Senate, a huge win for the Western provinces and Newfoundland, which had fought so hard for this radical redesign of Canadian Parliament.

"I think this in fact was a historic day, and it's been a historic process. I can't recall another time, literally since Confederation, where there has been so much agreement on such a wide range of issues," Clark said.

Within hours, those remarks would come back to haunt the constitutional affairs minister. Within hours, it would become clear that the feeling of triumph was not shared so enthusiastically by Mulroney or the rest of Clark's cabinet colleagues. That "so much agreement" hailed by Clark had been achieved without Quebec at the table. Conspicuous by its absence all those many months, Quebec would soon be unnerved by how far the national-unity mission had travelled without Quebeckers' participation. The nation was about to get squeezed in the vise between Quebec and the rest of Canada.

Mulroney, in Germany for a meeting of the G-7 group of industrialized nations while the deal-making was being wrapped up by Clark, immediately damned the July 7 agreement with very faint praise.

"I'd be reluctant to qualify anything as a miracle," Mulroney told the Canadian reporters travelling with him. His enthusiasm only waned as the hours went on. Later in the day, he pointed out that premiers had reached agreement before, during the 1990 débâcle over the Meech Lake accord — and look where that got him. His cherished Meech Lake accord had died, despised in the rest of Canada, in June 1990.

"I had an agreement with premiers before, signed, sealed and delivered, and I said, 'Great, wonderful work,'" Mulroney said.

The shine was quickly fading on the July 7 agreement that had taken months to build in the rest of Canada. It would take an incredible amount of manoeuvring and pride-swallowing that summer before the deal could turn into a full-fledged constitutional agreement. And during those first few weeks of July, it seemed that the deal was in fact headed for the trash heap rather than the history books.

Back in Ottawa, the federal government's Quebec lieutenant, Health Minister Benoit Bouchard, was plainly and simply not impressed with the deal that had been carved out in his absence. Bouchard, fed up with all the wrangling over the Senate and aboriginal issues and other non-priority items for Quebec, had abandoned his seat at these negotiations on June 11. So he had to learn second-hand about the month of subsequent events that led up to this July 7 deal.

The day after his Pearson Building declaration, Clark pulled together the so-called unity committee of cabinet, a collection of eighteen ministers from all parts of Canada, to give them the details of the rest of Canada's triumph. After that encounter, Bouchard said publicly that the deal was "interesting," maybe even "encouraging." Privately, he was fuming that Clark had called the deal historic. He thought to himself: "I will quit this government rather than sell this unacceptable deal."

He wouldn't have been the first Bouchard from Quebec to quit over an unacceptable deal for that province. Lucien Bouchard, the prime minister's former best friend and confidant, bolted in May 1990, rather than tolerate the compromises being made on the Meech accord. That was a blow to the heart for Mulroney, and one which he would never be able to endure again. This time around, in 1992, Mulroney was going to walk very carefully around Quebec's interests. Clark was in for a difficult time as he tried to defend the rest of Canada's deal against this onslaught from the prime minister and Quebec.

It took about a week for Clark to get a glimpse of the full magnitude of this rift. Eight long, bewildering days after the July 7 deal, eight days of limbo for the rest of Canada, Mulroney was back in Ottawa after his European visit, and the full cabinet was set to meet. It was an unusually cool summer day, one of many in that strange summer that never really took hold in the nation's capital. On July 15, the wind blowing on Parliament Hill had almost a fall-like bite to it; tourists were wrapped in cardigans and windbreakers. Inside the Parliament Buildings, in the third-floor cabinet room, it was even colder. For almost a full day, Clark would find himself at what he described as a "very chilly" encounter with his cabinet colleagues and Mulroney.

Quebec cabinet ministers came to the meeting fresh from their own private session along with several other Quebec Tory MPs, and they were clearly not happy with Clark's "historic" deal. The week's press in Quebec had been filled with diatribes against the equal Senate. *Le Devoir* editor Lise Bissonnette had issued a stunning, one-word editorial in response to the July 7 accord — three big block letters filling the editorial box — "NON." Eloquent in its simplicity, it was a sign that the rest of Canada and its constitutional vision was being dramatically written off inside Quebec. The Quebec cabinet ministers were almost certain that this deal could not be sold in their own province.

Marcel Masse, the globe-trotting defence minister and an outspoken preacher for Quebec's distinctive culture, was the first to publicly state his disapproval as he entered the cabinet meeting.

"Sure, I'm disappointed in the sense that I would have preferred to have a deal by the nine provinces acceptable for Quebec, obviously. But it's not the fact. Now, we have to come back and find a new approach."

This was entirely the Quebec ministers' attitude as the summer began. Clark had made a mistake that had to be fixed. It wasn't simple, these Quebec ministers believed, but Canada and Clark would just have to forget about this July 7 deal and try something else.

They did not seem to understand that Clark was coming into this meeting with the rest of Canada behind him, and that if the federal government took a stand against the July 7 deal, it would be also up against the ROC.

Inside the cabinet room, around the table, an air of gloom prevailed. What had happened? How do we get out of this? Clark, outwardly, was a wall of resolve. Inwardly, he was stunned by their lack of support for him. He heard what they had to say, one by one, at that chilly meeting. But he simply refused to indulge the idea that the July 7 deal could be discarded.

There were few histrionics, and only a couple of long speeches about the perils of selling this deal in Quebec. There was pity for the constitutional affairs minister. Perhaps daunted by the scepticism of the prime minister, no one, not even from outside Quebec, spoke up in Clark's defence. A few Western ministers noted, without much vigor, that this was a tough issue out West and caution was needed. But key English Canadian ministers such as Finance Minister Michael Wilson had also thrown a bucket of cold water over the deal, openly and publicly challenging the new "economic union" in the constitution as too weak. So Clark sat there, in stubborn solitude, while the rest of the cabinet debated how to disengage from the July 7 deal.

"What surprised me," Clark recalled later, "was that no one from Quebec thought we had a chance. Everyone was very spooked by this. Every Quebec minister. Very spooked by it."

Every Quebec minister included Prime Minister Martin Brian Mulroney, the right honourable member of Parliament for the picturesque Quebec riding of Charlevoix. Soon after the July 7 deal was reached, the ground in Ottawa started rumbling, as the Clark–Mulroney fault line crumbled open. This rift in the cabinet is now recognized as one of the most serious divisions

ever to have hit the Mulroney government. Clark nods
when he is asked about this reading of the state of government in July 1992.

"It is true that the two most senior ministers of the
government had two very different ideas about how
things should work out," he said.

The political seismographs were jumping off the
scale as word leaked out of the prime minister's rage
against Joe Clark, and Clark's resentment for Mulroney's lack of support. Would Clark resign? That was
the question on everyone's mind.

Clearly, Mulroney was not happy with the deal.
Though Clark carefully insists that the resignation
threat was never raised with Mulroney, these were dark
days. He had to summon every trick he knew to maintain the fragile loyalty to his rival. All his training as
external affairs minister had taught him how to use the
diplomatic understatement. Yes, the prime minister
had some problems with the July 7 deal, Clark said.

"I think he hoped it could be brought back to something that would be more acceptable in Quebec," Clark
said. The reasons may have been understandable, but
the pure political fact was that the prime minister was
refusing to stand behind the work of his constitutional
affairs minister. For almost nine years, Mulroney and
Clark had been able to manage their tense, bitter
rivalry by keeping at a safe, constructive distance. But
this time, their paths were crossing and all hell was
breaking loose. There was no yelling, Clark says. "Most
of our battles have been waged in silence."

Tense silence was the mark of a severe rift in July.
Around the cabinet table on July 15, a rigid, deadly
serious Mulroney was presiding. And the rest of the
cabinet treated Clark to the worst thing of all — they
said they were sorry for him.

"There was almost a solicitous attitude in my regard

around the room, solicitous in the sense that they hoped I might move on it, or say that it could be moved. That would make the problem easier," Clark said. "They were worried that I had got myself and the government into some difficulty....We've got a problem here and don't know how to resolve this." The two solitudes, and the two men, had hit a point where the tugging had to stop. Clark sums it up this way: "The prime minister's instincts told him we couldn't proceed with this as it was. My instincts told me that we couldn't back off. So there was then a period of tension for us both, in which we tried to find some way in which we could move."

That "period of tension" was marked by ugly rumour about the way the two men were being discredited and ridiculed in each other's camp. Only one block on Sparks Street in Ottawa separates the offices of Joe Clark and the Langevin Block office of Prime Minister Mulroney. During those tense July weeks, it might as well have been a continent, a very chilly, unstable continent in drift.

Clark only got truly and visibly angry once in this time, and that was when a suggestion crept out that the constitutional affairs minister had "exceeded his mandate." The suggestion, he believed, had been carefully lobbed to the media, and the source, Clark believed, was someone inside the Prime Minister's Office. It probably wasn't Mulroney himself, but it was likely to be someone in his circle. If this person was looking for a way to enrage Clark, or a way to dredge up all the tense past between Mulroney and Clark, this was the way to do it.

This touches on the very essence of the deal between Mulroney and Clark, the delicate arrangement that has allowed them to function together for almost a decade in government. Clark explains it this way: "I gave him

a lot of loyalty; he gave me a lot of latitude." And whenever something came along to shake that arrangement,
like the July 7 constitutional deal, two parts of the
country, symbolized by these two men, are also shaken.
To delve into that arrangement between Clark and
Mulroney is to understand their thinking and how they
came to represent two very different streams of thought
in Canada in 1992. It also explains how the federal government, and Canada itself, sailed down a river fed by
these two streams for such a long time before they hit
the turbulence of the national-unity crusade.

Clark, of course, was the leader of the Progressive Conservative party who had run up against Mulroney and
won in 1976, only to be defeated by Mulroney in 1983,
after a nasty, back-stabbing campaign. Clark was an
Albertan who was able to take the Tories shakily to the
seat of power, only to lose it after a very brief time in
1979. Mulroney was the smooth, successful Quebec
lawyer who was the first Tory leader to truly tie French
and English together under the Conservative party
banner and two majority governments in 1984 and
1988. To accomplish this feat in Quebec, though, he
had to draw from the ranks of disgruntled Quebec
nationalists who, like him, had viscerally opposed
Liberal prime minister Pierre Trudeau. Clark, for all
his efforts, could never extend his reach that far into
the heart and soul of Quebec — he would always be the
Albertan with the careful, well-intentioned, but hard-
on-the-ear French.
    Their language skills told a lot about them. Mulroney
was the expert at French bonhomie; he was a hail-
fellow-well-met in both languages. Clark was an
awkward French speaker, who prefaced nearly every
French utterance with the three words "Je crois que..."
One reporter suggested that the staccato preface was

merely the sound of the ignition firing as Clark revved up his French. CBC television reporters and producers mischievously tried to insert those three words into every broadcast that featured Clark speaking French, before their inside joke was spotted by higher-ups and stopped. In English, however, it was Clark whose speeches could stir the emotions and evoke a rich, patriotic well of pride in his audience. Clark in 1992 was easily the most fluent Canadian in the language of the heart surrounding the constitution.

So it was apparent in 1992, by any measure, that the two men had come to stand for the different ideas of Canada. In July 1992, Mulroney, the Quebecker, was intent on getting his province to sign the constitution and become a full member of the Canadian family, at almost any cost. Clark, the Albertan, had delivered up a design of a new Canadian nation for Quebec to consider — one that included the cherished Western goal of an equal Senate. Clark and Mulroney clashed; Quebec and the rest of Canada clashed. What Canada was witnessing, in effect, was a face-off between Quebec and Alberta.

Clark was driven by the same forces that drove his province as it tried to find its place in the Canadian federation. His Alberta roots run deep in him, and he talks often about how his alienated, Western philosophy has shaped the politician that Canadians have viewed in so many roles since the mid-1970s — the loyal opposition leader, the ill-fated prime minister, the vanquished Conservative chief, the external affairs minister who soldiered on, the constitutional affairs minister who poured his patriotism and his life into keeping the country together in 1992.

Joe Clark is the son of a newspaper owner father and a teacher from the small Alberta town of High River, Alberta. He has vivid memories of the politics of his parents' era. His own member of Parliament, a Social

Credit MP, did not even know the Clark family, even though it ran three newspapers in his riding. He remembers that this MP only met the Clarks late in the 1950s, after encountering the young Joe Clark in Ottawa during an "adventure in citizenship" program for promising Canadian youth. It was Clark's first real taste of what Ottawa can do to isolate a politician from his constituents. After all those years, his MP had never met an important family in his riding, and it wasn't until one member of that family entered the realm of Ottawa that it was seen to exist.

That lesson has driven Joe Clark to spend as little time as possible in Ottawa. It was his own personal hobby horse, he says, and it carried him and the rest of the national-unity negotiators all over the country in a merry-go-round of talks through the spring of 1992. Clark simply refused to lock his politics up in Ottawa. He'd have been happy if he did not have to spend any time there at all.

But all the travelling away from Ottawa often also meant travelling away from Alberta, and the distance between Clark and his home often showed. For example, he does not share the basic Alberta suspicion about the wisdom of official bilingualism. He has embraced the notion to his being, and he has been forced many times to square off with his provincial compatriots over this trust in the French–English fact of Canada. In one memorable encounter in Barrhaven, Alberta, during the 1988 election campaign, the Liberal candidate asked how many of his fellow Albertans in the room had been forced to learn French to keep their job. Clark was the only one who raised his hand.

He was on the defensive as late as January 1992, when Alberta premier Don Getty openly and surprisingly challenged the federal policy of bilingualism. "Let Canadians choose," Getty said, playing into the Alberta lore that people were being forced to speak French. In Ottawa, one of the strongest voices against this Getty incursion came from a fellow Albertan, Joe Clark.

Always charitable, Clark sees this anti-French attitude in Alberta not as racism, but as an understandable fear of difference or a resistance to change.

"People really do think that this is more than language, that it's an attempt to change their way of life."

Clark tells a story from his mother's experience while teaching high school in Blackie, Alberta, a little town east of High River. Alberta's high school students had the choice between two options to get their diploma. Most of the students, knowing biology was tough, took French. But on the morning after the Official Languages Act was passed in 1969, nearly every student switched out of French class and into biology.

"The rationale was that they were not going to be pushed around, forced to learn French by Quebec." Even as a young Albertan then, Clark saw the stubborn foolishness in such a gesture. He would continue to portray anti-bilingualism as self-defeating stubbornness.

"We're into a very critical two months in the life of Canada," Clark said in response to Getty's dropped glove in January 1992. "We need to work very hard at finding those things which draw people together, and I think this sort of thing could be used by people who are driven more by anger than they are by patriotism."

It was a stand that would earn Clark plaudits in much of the rest of Canada, but not in the far reaches of Alberta. It marked him as a departed Albertan; as much as the snapshot that appeared in February that year, showing an awkward Joe Clark sitting uncomfortably on a huge bull that had been shipped in as a prop to the Calgary conference on Senate reform. The constitutional affairs minister was no cowboy; he rides herd on bureaucrats and his staff far more confidently than he rides wild horses or the bucking force of anti-politician sentiment in Alberta.

Clark is not surprised that his closeness to Ottawa and official bilingualism has worked against him in any effort to keep his link with Alberta, or that it has been seen as a milepost in how far he has gone away from his home province.

"If you grow up in Western Canada and Alberta, if your views are formed there, the great national debate is a debate that has, by and large, taken place elsewhere. . . . The central thing that it touched was your Canadian nationality, not your roots and identity — it touched the integrity rather than the identity of the country."

This is an important point that distinguishes Mulroney and Clark in their pursuit of the elusive national-unity dream. For Clark, the debate was all about the integrity of the nation. For Mulroney, it was all about the identity of Canada. Clark would judge his success by these questions: Does this new deal embrace the very essence of what makes this nation function? Is the integrity of the nation intact? Mulroney would ask these questions: Does this new deal embody the essence of who we are? Is the identity of the nation preserved?

Mulroney is a Quebecker, one of six children born to Benedict and Irene Mulroney in Baie Comeau. His life as a youngster revolved around the Quebec mill town; he was an anglo Quebecker thriving in a mainly francophone world. He would always be comfortable in both parts of the province. When he left Quebec, it was to be educated, briefly, in New Brunswick and one incomplete year at Dalhousie University in Halifax. His real education was at Laval law school and in Montreal, where he cultivated the friendships and the style that vaulted him to power, first as head of Iron Ore Company and then as leader of a new Progressive Conservative dynasty for the 1980s.

Mulroney's whole concept of national unity was wreathed in the need to make Quebec a full partner in the Canadian federation, to seal its identity as a full member of the Canadian equation. Quebec's needs drove him as no other province could. Back in 1984, when he was campaigning for his first term in office, it was his friend Lucien Bouchard who helped him write the famous speech in Sept-Iles, Quebec, that vowed to bring Quebec into the constitution with "honour and enthusiasm." By 1992, his friendship with Bouchard was over, but the promise and other Quebec friendships were still at the centre of his thinking.

Where most other premiers enjoyed a civil, if cool, relationship with the prime minister in the years after Meech, Quebec premier Robert Bourassa could count on his friendship with Mulroney to carry him through thick and thin. Together, Bourassa and Mulroney shared a love of Quebec and a sense of devastation over the failure of Meech. Politically, the prime minister was an ardent admirer of Bourassa's art of ambiguity, which allowed him to walk the delicate line between the separatists and federalists for so long in Quebec. Their frequent phone conversations were reported to be affectionate exercises in mutual admiration. Bourassa was a Liberal in name, but his alliance with Mulroney's Tories far outweighed any nominal ties he had to federal Liberals in Ottawa.

Even on the day he resigned in February 1993, as Mulroney was displaying the icy grudge he still held against Newfoundland premier Clyde Wells, he paused and warmed for a moment to talk about his friend. In these early days of 1993, all the old friends and allies from the Meech years were coming to grips with their own form of adversity. Bourassa was one of the few Meech-era premiers left in office, in fact, but he was undergoing a different, more personal struggle. On the very day that his friend Brian was bowing out of politics, Robert Bourassa was undergoing experimental treatment for his deadly skin cancer. Mulroney made it abundantly clear that he was not far from Bourassa's bedside.

"I've talked to him," Mulroney said. "He's got out of tougher things."

Clark, on the other hand, would be more adept at cultivating relationships with the other premiers and the other constitutional negotiators. Mulroney would be using his identity to build up his alliances. Clark would be using integrity to build trust. In fact, whatever Mulroney did in the interests of Quebec, Clark would be doing for the rest of Canada. Clark hit the nail on the head when he identified the division between them as one of integrity versus identity. It is probably the most apt way of summing up their differences, and the differences of the regions they represented in Ottawa. Whatever approach Mulroney took as a reflection of his identity as a Quebecker, Clark would be taking the rest of Canada's approach, a reflection of his integrity as an Albertan.

Look, for example, at their approach to politics in the 1990s — the real point of departure between Quebec's attitudes and attitudes in English Canada. Clark was moved by the same populist discontent that had seized the rest of the nation. He saw the crisis of government as a crisis of faith in politics. From his very roots as an Albertan, Clark sensed the new public ownership of the constitution. He knew that no deal would be acceptable unless the people felt a part of it. Even back when he had been the external affairs minister, Clark had been motivated enough by this public hunger to take a very active interest in the establishment of the Citizens' Forum on Canada's Future, the committee headed by Keith Spicer in 1990/91 to measure Canadians' fury towards government.

Mulroney, on the other hand, retained Quebec's

residual faith in politics and politicians. That was the faith that led Bourassa later in 1992 to fight for the National Assembly's right to choose senators, while the rest of the provinces prepared to establish Senate elections. Quebec's public accepted that the Legislature acted in the interests of the public; the rest of Canada would never accept more power in the hands of their politicians. It wasn't the Quebec press who exposed politicians to microscopic scrutiny of private lives, airline travel or the perks of power. That was an English Canadian phenomenon.

The prime minister, showing Quebec's faith in politics, was perplexed at the level of cynicism being directed at public institutions. So it wasn't surprising that Mulroney, as a Quebecker, would unquestioningly believe that politics and the existing political institutions in Ottawa — which he controlled — would rescue Canada from its national-unity crisis.

From the beginning, Mulroney had charted a path to national unity that depended on the heavy hand of Ottawa politics and the force of Parliament and federal government. His plan, once he had recovered from the Meech crisis of 1990, was to bring the country to a new national-unity deal through decisive leadership from Ottawa. There would be the public venting of rage in the Spicer forums. There would be a set of federal constitutional proposals, introduced with much fanfare in September 1991. There would be a grand "mother of all committees," the special joint parliamentary committee led by MP Dorothy Dobbie and Senator Claude Castonguay (later Senator Gerald Beaudoin) to study the proposals and issue a report in February 1992. After all these efforts, the strong hand of Ottawa would descend in April with a constitutional resolution to present to the House. Then there would be a debate and a national referendum, well in advance of

Quebec's own vote in October. This was the plan, and it all revolved around Mulroney's fundamental belief in strong, overarching leadership from the federal government.

It was knocked off course by Ontario and its insistence that the provinces be involved in any negotiations — a strategy that forced Ottawa into the so-called "multilateral ministerial conferences" of 1992. In the meantime, though, Mulroney was content to stand back and watch this process unfold, always keeping his plan in his back pocket. With true and absolute faith in the ability of politics to get the job done, Mulroney took very little active interest in the idea of involving the public or the provinces any more than they had already been consulted in his numerous committees and hearings.

Clark, though, knew that the sceptical public would want to keep participating in any attempt to build a new nation, no matter how many hearings they attended or how many constitutional conferences were televised. You can't come from Alberta and not hear the cry of anger and alienation from the public. He may not have been the one who thought of getting the provinces involved in that multilateral process of negotiations in the spring of 1992 — that was all Ontario's doing — but he, more than anyone else, came to be the personification of the noble effort to build respect and trust among the negotiators. This was a man who was not afraid to trust the provinces — another mark that distinguished him from his boss, Brian Mulroney. Nor was he blind to the breakdown of trust in Canada that had led to this place in the nation's political development.

"Our system of government has been one of responsiblity, to hold a person responsible. And that requires some trust that I don't think is there now. . . . I think the people do not want to be bothered making all the decisions themselves because they've got other things to do.

They'd like to have a system where they thought that their representatives would more or less represent them. They don't expect to have their views represented all the time. What they're worried about is they think the practice has become to ignore them."

Joe Clark, then, would not ignore the people. He would be there, listening to every word in the endless parade of words that were fed by the public into this national-unity crusade.

Canadians were treated to a perfect example of the struggle between the two approaches at the end of February 1992, when the Beaudoin–Dobbie committee was putting together its report. This huge beast of a committee had travelled around, listening to the public and all the experts and provincial politicians. But when the time came to issue its report, the recommendations were not simply a synthesis of all they had heard — as a Joe Clark perhaps would have put together. No, at the last minute, the political parties were locked in a mad struggle to insert their own expert suggestions about what was needed in the great Canadian constitutional trade-off: powers for Quebec, a social charter for the left.... This was very much an approach that Mulroney would have taken: yes, fine, the public has been heard, but there are political considerations that have to be met as well. Mulroney would always be tempted to jump in and steer the national-unity mission on a more organized, political path, but wisely, he decided to stay out of it for a long time. Clark insists that Mulroney's attitude was more "wait and see" than "show me."

"I think the prime minister was willing to let this go as far as it could. I think there were some people who were a little more eager... who would have shut it down earlier." Privy Council Clerk Paul Tellier was one of those people, Clark said.

For his part, Joe Clark would be content to go along

for the ride, to see what developed. He was, if nothing else, a remarkable listener, taking in every word spoken at those constitutional conferences and all his meetings. Just listening could earn a politician immense respect in Canada in 1992. Here is what his fellow negotiators have to say about Clark's facility for listening:

Moe Sihota, British Columbia's constitutional affairs minister, is fulsome in his praise.

"This thing couldn't have happened if it wasn't for Joe," Sihota recalled much later. "Watching Clark throughout this process, I began to appreciate what diplomacy is. I think that without his intelligence, I don't think we ever would have seen our way through it. He has a remarkable understanding of the country. He's passionate. There were times when he was passionate, eloquent when we were at breaking points. And there were many breaking points in this whole process."

Ontario premier Bob Rae has a long history with Joe Clark. As a young New Democrat MP, it was Bob Rae who introduced the motion that brought down the Clark government in December 1979. That was only the most visible example of the fact that Rae and Clark had spent years on opposite sides of Canadian politics. Still, Rae was an admirer of the way Clark handled the constitutional process that Ontario had essentially set up.

"Clark's strength is his incredible patience. Clark can sit there and take a lot . . . And he is enough of a detail person. He really did get into the words and the phrases and what was going to work. He really did follow the process, and has a clear sense of that," Rae said.

He was listening to every word, nodding, taking it all in. He appeared to have no other purpose in those days and months of negotiations. Clark's days were just one long constitutional discussion, from dawn until late at night. A typical day would find the constitutional affairs minister at a 7:00 a.m. briefing with his officials, an

8:00 a.m. encounter with the press, a full morning of talks, negotiations over a working lunch, talks all afternoon and evening, another encounter with the press and then yet another working meal in whatever city he was in. And yet, surrounded by approximately 400 people in the travelling national-unity industry, Clark felt alone. He had no confidants, no soul mates, no real friends to lean on as he pursued this mission.

The head bureaucrat, Paul Tellier, was closer to Mulroney in outlook and attitude. In fact, throughout the process, Mulroney would be getting one briefing from Clark, another from his friend Tellier. The prime minister addressed his chief bureaucrat as "cher Paul," and relied on Tellier for professional and personal advice. Both Quebeckers shared a fundamental suspicion about the other provinces, as well as a deep fondness for each other. Their friendship had been sealed during the difficult days of Meech.

Tellier was with Clark all the way through the negotiations, but it was widely rumoured that he was Clark's babysitter, not his helper. A vacant chair sat next to Clark throughout the negotiations; it was Quebec's traditional place at the side of Ottawa. Other provincial negotiators couldn't help but notice that Tellier often stationed himself there. Logistically, it made sense for him to be next to Clark. Symbolically, it showed that Tellier was at these meetings to speak up in defence of Quebec, and the Quebecker who served as prime minister.

The impression was explosively confirmed in early July, when the provincial premiers were at yet another brink of failure in their talks. But this was close to the end, and no one saw a deal in sight. At lunch on July 7, they were discussing the wisdom of convening a first ministers' conference to make the last gasp of this process into a public one. Premiers such as Saskatchewan's Roy Romanow believed that the public had to see every effort being made by the politicians on this national-unity disaster, and that first ministers had to be pulled in — regardless of the potential for failure. Romanow was in the middle of making this point, when all of a sudden, an angry voice popped up from the bureaucrats' table. Tellier was outraged.

"How could you ask Quebec to be there for another failure?" he shouted at Romanow. "They can't be humiliated again."

Tellier's aggressive, swaggeringly confident style was well known among the people who had been dealing with him since Meech. His closeness to Mulroney had seriously blurred the line between the Ottawa bureaucracy, which he headed, and the political structure, which Mulroney headed. Strategy was not his strength, but heavy-handed delivery was. The inside joke was that Tellier was remarkable at delivering the wishes of his political masters — and if a couple of schoolchildren happened to get run over on his delivery missions, well, so be it.

Romanow, on the other hand, had not been at the constitutional table since Trudeau's days, and he was stunned by the effrontery of this bureaucrat. In his day, the barrier between the politicians and the officials was heavily drawn. He barked back at Tellier: "Who do you think you're shouting at?" Such was the happy atmosphere around the table, where the chief bureaucrat was also one of the chief sceptics about involving the provinces. Tellier, later that day, would leave the Pearson Building under a black cloud of anger, even as Clark, his other boss, was praising the "historic" July 7 deal.

Clark had thrown himself into an exercise that Mulroney had not invited or wanted. Many times throughout those months, the other provincial negotiators would get the sense, just as Clark did, that he was making that plunge alone — that Ottawa was not the old, dominant presence it had once been. It was just Clark, being led along by circumstances, apparently without an overall strategy devised by his bureaucratic helpers.

He was tired, existing on no exercise and sustaining himself with the massive portions of food that were laid on by various hotel caterers. Newspaper gossip columns were starting to remark on the growing girth and fading colour of Clark. At lunch Clark would pile his plate with everything in sight, and then bolt it down as he discussed constitutional complexities with fellow politicians. He would never be sighted in the health clubs of the hotels. Prince Edward Island premier Joseph Ghiz would show up now and then for a swim, resplendent in a hotel bathrobe and black knee socks. It was not unusual to see Paul Tellier or Moe Sihota padding down the corridors early in the morning in their exercise gear, or Alberta's Jim Horsman and his exuberant young entourage heading out for an early tennis game. But not Joe Clark. His activities were limited to talking, listening, and more listening.

In Vancouver that May, the B.C. constitutional delegation had organized a little bonding ritual for the travelling team of negotiators. A box had been reserved at a hockey game between the Vancouver Canucks and the Edmonton Oilers. Welcoming the break in their tedious talks, the negotiators were happy to sit for a few hours in a frosty rink, taking in the action on the ice and the rallying refrains of the organ music. Jim Horsman was seated close to Clark, and was pleased to see him absorbed in something other than the constitution, if only for a couple of hours. At one point in the game, the constitutional affairs minister turned to his fellow Albertan and asked a question: "What colours do the Oilers wear when they play at home?" Horsman thought to himself: a real Albertan wouldn't have asked that question. He thought it important enough to note in his diary that night: "I don't think Joe Clark is a real hockey fan."

It would also be fair to say that Mulroney, conversant with the language of the locker room and the jocks, would not have asked such a question. Just one more difference between Clark and Mulroney. For Mulroney, often, politics was sport. For Clark, that year anyway, sport was only part of politics. Clark was not a cowboy, and he wasn't a jock, either.

The two Albertans, Horsman and Clark, did not have much in common, either in interests or constitutional philosophy. Clark, for all his grounding in the lore of Western alienation, was not driven to the religion of the crusade for an equal, elected and effective Senate, as Horsman was.

Late in March, not long after the first meeting of the constitutional ministers at the Pearson Building in Ottawa, Clark and Horsman were key participants at the annual meeting of the Alberta Progressive Conservatives. The main item on the agenda of this meeting, not surprisingly, was Senate reform. The divisions between the "real" Albertan and the "Ottawa" Albertan quickly emerged. Horsman publicly offered Clark some advice about Senate reform that sounded a lot like a threat. He told Clark to forget about getting elected again in Alberta if he turned his back on the Senate crusade in the West.

Clark's response was testy. "You can't get anywhere in this business if you say, this is my idea and unless everybody moves to me, I'm going to walk away. You can, I guess, if you don't care much about the country, but it's not a very successful way to keep the country together."

Later, Clark would concede that the federal government had erred in allowing the Senate issue to escape and grow so strong in Alberta. His legendary partisan-

ship, particularly fierce when it came to the Reform
Party threat in Alberta, was a major blind spot for the
constitutional affairs minister. The man famed for his
ability to listen would simply lash back at Reform Party
leader Preston Manning, rather than weigh any of his
arguments. Manning, who went head to head with
Clark in Yellowhead during the 1988 federal election,
would simply be dismissed viciously by Clark at any
opportunity. Manning, similarly, heaped nothing but
scorn on Clark, in public and private. In their mutual
contempt, they would not entertain even the suggestion of political insight on the other side.

That probably led to Clark's dismissal of the Senate
question, gripped so firmly as a grievance by the
Reformers. Nor would the federal government take
seriously the underlying motives in Alberta's quest for
Senate reform. Simply through neglect or carelessness
or incomprehension, Ottawa had failed to grapple with
the populist rebellion that was feeding the campaign
for an equal Senate out West. Clark now believes that
Ottawa languished unfortunately in those dying days of
the Meech Lake accord, while Alberta and Jim
Horsman were out laying the foundation for Senate
reform across the country, and while Preston Manning
was making political hay.

"If there was a failure on the Senate, it was probably
during Meech. And I've often regretted that I didn't
come back and take a more active role in those discussions at that time," Clark says. "I don't mean formally.
I just didn't take more of my time and attention to focus
on that issue." If Ottawa had tried to wrestle with the
Senate question, he said, it wouldn't have sneaked up
with such negative results late in the game in 1992,
when the equal Senate landed with a surprising thump
at Quebec's doorstep.

"It was surprising to me how shocked my Quebec

colleagues were that this was an issue. And by that time, it was too late to do anything about it."

Once again, the federal government got caught riding only one side of the see-saw between Quebec and the rest of Canada. The trick of governing such a two-sided nation, though, is knowing how to keep the see-saw rocking gently between both sides. Ideally, in its national-unity mission, Ottawa should have mimicked the action of a see-saw — it should have said, "we see the demands of the rest of Canada; we saw the demands of Quebec." See and saw, gently, back and forth.

But for much of the national-unity mission, it was only the demands of Quebec that Ottawa really saw. Though it could recognize the demands of the rest of Canada enough to crow about the necessity of a so-called "Canada round" this time, it could never embrace them with the same fervour as it did the needs of Quebec. The Canada round, for many in Ottawa, was just a device to make the real deal, for Quebec, tolerable in the rest of Canada. At the top of the federal government, there was little recognition of the idea of the ROC's grievances as equal in legitimacy to Quebec's grievances. And there was one simple reason for this. The prime minister, again, was a Quebecker.

"We're talking here about the perceptions and how you define issues," Clark explained. "This distinction about what's central and what's peripheral was really what was at issue here."

To Mulroney, the Senate issue was peripheral, as was the aboriginal issue. The central goal was to get Quebec to sign the constitution, with "honour and enthusiasm." Clark, however, came to see the Senate issue as equally important. That's what made Ottawa's national-unity mission work when it did, he said — Mulroney handled one side of the see-saw, Clark handled the other.

"We had a different view of where the great risks were

and we were both able to, for a long time, steer the adventure away from the great risks."

In July 1992, each man still continued to have a different idea of where the risks were. Mulroney was positive that Quebec was going to reject the July 7 deal reached by all the other provinces. Clark knew that Ottawa would have a huge problem on its hands in the rest of Canada if the federal government turned its back on the July 7 deal. This time, though, Clark and Mulroney's ideas could not work together in tandem — at least one side had to give. In the end, both sides gave a little. They went back to the deal that had ensured their political survival together in 1983. Clark offered some loyalty, Mulroney offered some latitude.

"We got that back together again. Not easily, but we got it back together. It took both of us finding a way."

Mulroney was on the phone almost ceaselessly in those days, seeing whether the July 7 deal could be undone. One of his key targets was Ontario premier Bob Rae, who was trying rather unsuccessfully to get some rest at his cottage just outside Ottawa.

Mulroney kept asking Rae: "Why would Ontario ever be interested in an equal Senate?" Repeatedly, he challenged Rae to explain why any Ontario premier could rationally give up that much power and influence in Parliament. Rae was not impressed with the subtext to this question. Mulroney seemed to be asking him, in no uncertain terms: Are you crazy?

"I mean, the pressure was on me in July," Rae said. "You had these Tories . . . these Tory MPs coming out of caucus saying 'Rae sold us out. What kind of premier would ever give in to an equal Senate? What is this nonsense anyways?' And I'm not dumb. I can read the writing on the wall," Rae said. What was apparent to this Ontario premier was that Mulroney was turning his guns on him, in a bid to get the July 7 deal undone. It wasn't mischief or malice, Rae hastens to point out. It was just that Mulroney, the Quebecker, did not believe the deal was good for his province.

Maybe it made sense inside this political orbit. But the view from outside these constitutional negotiations was not a pretty one. A prime minister was actually back-tracking on a deal made by his own constitutional affairs minister. B.C.'s Moe Sihota, after a long, devastating telephone chat with a depressed Joe Clark, was furious with Mulroney. He spoke out, asking: "Is Mulroney the prime minister of Canada or the prime minister of Quebec?" The sentiment was shared by many members of the Canadian public. The question was surfacing in more and more political commentaries. Just what was Mulroney's priority anyway? At one point that summer, Jim Horsman journeyed to Washington for business and a speech at the Canadian embassy. He was taken aback to discover that news of the Mulroney–Clark rift had travelled that far south. "The Americans are aghast at what Mulroney appears to be doing to Clark," Horsman wrote in his diary.

Slowly, very shakily, Clark and Mulroney were able to pull their loyalty–latitude deal back together, and get Quebec to the bargaining table. But, as Clark said, it wasn't easy. Nearly a full month after the July 7 deal was reached, the ground was ready again to pull the premiers in for talks in Ottawa. For months now, every constitutional development had been summed up in the headline: "Another meeting planned." It would be almost another month before this news would give way to the ultimate goal: "Deal reached."

Throughout these talks, the politicians had been forced to be all kinds of things at different times. In their arduous negotiations, they were lawyers, sales-men, crusaders, preachers, number-crunchers, mathematicians. Now they had to be trapeze artists too — they had to perform an act of political acrobatics that could keep the July 7 accord up in the air while Quebec swung over to join the troupe. And this was a high-wire act without a net. Quebec premier Robert Bourassa's political credibility rested on his commitment to hold a referendum in October. The rest of the premiers had a lot of pride invested in their July 7 deal. Mulroney and Clark had to find some way to allow both sides to preserve their integrity.

The feat was performed with some careful phrasing — using vocabulary, not tried-and-true political tactics. Prime Minister Brian Mulroney had summoned all the premiers to his retreat at Harrington Lake on August 4 to see what could be accomplished. As an event, this meeting was steeped in significance: Robert Bourassa had finally rejoined the constitutional table after a two-year absence.

As the crowds of reporters lined the dusty road to the entrance of Harrington Lake, the big blue cars kept pulling up, with their distinguished passengers peering out the windows. One by one, premiers pulled up to the gates, most of them hopping out to have a few words with reporters, or to soothe the temper of Ovide Mercredi and his angry group of fellow Assembly of First Nations chiefs, who had been excluded from the meeting.

Bourassa displayed his unmatchable talent for saying nothing, charmingly.

"The positions that are known now are showing an important gap." The mission was tense, he said, "because of the tight calendar, because of what is at stake for all Canadians."

If nothing else, this session and one the following week at Harrington Lake would prove to be catch-up sessions for Bourassa — a chance for the rest of Canada

to explain the roller-coaster ride of constitutional negotiations that had brought them to this lakeside preserve
in the middle of summer.

While the premiers dined on their Harrington Lake
garden salad, they all talked platitudes about how wonderful it was to be back together again. By the time the
steamed trout and sun-dried tomato risotto were on the
table, the talk had turned to the national-unity dispute,
firmly wedged between the ROC and the hard place.
Premiers such as Newfoundland's Clyde Wells laid it on
the line for the Quebec premier: "What you want, you're
not going to be able to get. You have to face facts."

Bourassa was giving as well as getting an education.
All the premiers were told, in stark terms, of the separatist threat that forced Bourassa to be very, very
careful. "You have to understand what I am facing at
home," he said.

It was at Harrington Lake, though, where the first
hints came that Clark and Mulroney were patching up
their problems. First of all, Mulroney took the unusual
step of telling Bourassa that he was being unrealistic.
Other premiers stared, their jaws agape. Was that really
Brian Mulroney, the Quebecker, distancing himself
from Bourassa?

Then there was Joe Clark, swallowing every bit of pride
he could, and declaring that a "misjudgment" had been
made about public opinion in Quebec towards the equal
Senate. Very, very carefully, Clark phrased it so that people would think *he* had made the political goof. Actually,
the misjudgment was Quebec's. Clark had been told by
Bourassa on July 7 in no uncertain terms during a telephone conversation that the Senate deal wouldn't be
much of a problem in Quebec. He turned out to be
wrong. But this whole national-unity enterprise rested
on the very precarious credibility of Bourassa in Quebec.
For Clark to have said there was a misjudgment on

Bourassa's part would have been disastrous. It would damage Bourassa — as his own officials could do so devastatingly during the referendum campaign.

All of this dancing around Quebec's and English Canada's realities really amounted to two questions, one for each side at Harrington Lake. The one question on the minds of the premiers from the rest of Canada: Do we have a deal or don't we? The one question on the minds of Robert Bourassa and Brian Mulroney: How much can this thing be changed to make it acceptable to us?

Alberta's Don Getty and Newfoundland's Clyde Wells were the most nervous guests at these luncheons. Back in June, they had been sure that the plan was to isolate their two provinces and get a deal without an equal Senate in it. Now that they had their equal Senate, they sensed once again the spectre of an agreement without them — that maybe their provinces would be cut loose to make room for Quebec at the table. The mere idea that they could get that close to an equal Senate, only to have it torn from their grasp, had them on their guard as they entered Harrington Lake.

Meanwhile, Mulroney's attempts to bend Rae had backfired. In the meetings at Harrington Lake, the Ontario premier would be one of the strongest voices for maintaining the pillars of the July 7 deal, and that meant the equal Senate. But he also knew that it would be fruitless to block any changes to the July 7 accord. A deal without Quebec was no deal at all. Wells was saying that nothing could be changed. Getty was saying that nothing should be changed. Others were trying to figure out a way out of this difficult impasse.

Bob Rae urged everyone to give a little bit. "Look, if you push this thing to the wall, it's going to blow up," he said. "But that all depends on whether you want to take it to the next stage." That was, in fact, the only thing on which these premiers could agree in August — "another meeting" was victory enough for now. And they got that trophy, with the use of some careful, weasel words about the July 7 deal.

"We had to come up with two acceptable sort of phrases," Rae said. "One was for Quebec's sake: we all agreed that we would say that the 'essence' of Meech was there, was protected. And everyone else would say that the 'framework' of July 7 was going to be respected as well."

True to their scripts, each of the premiers filed out of Harrington Lake, uttering their lines with precision and without much elaboration. The "essence" of Meech was there. The "framework" of July 7 was respected. Thank goodness for their long practice as politicians in the art of saying nothing. The master of that art, Robert Bourassa, was in the room to coach them, too, if they needed any advice. Never mind the impatient press, though, who were stunned that so little could come out of such a big meeting at Harrington Lake. The premiers, all of them, were on their way to the Pearson Building for — what else — another meeting.

If Mulroney was pleased about this development, he wasn't showing it. Those first few days at the Pearson Building in the dying days of August, he was positively hostile. Even Clyde Wells, who would have been expected to see the worst in Brian Mulroney during the Meech days, was surprised at the way Mulroney was carrying on, treating every debate as perfunctory, and obviously looking for a way to slide this process into oblivion.

"It was so strange that I found it out of character," Wells says.

On the eve of these meetings at Pearson, Mulroney

was at Harrington Lake entertaining a few reporters, who were trying to extract some information out of him about the prospects for the coming week. He was asked, bluntly: "Can the difference between Getty and Bourassa be bridged?" The prime minister's reply was equally blunt. "No."

British Columbia premier Michael Harcourt talks about the tension in that room at the Pearson Building on August 18, as Mulroney slid over to the chairman's seat, and Clark moved to the sidelines.

"He was terrible on the first two days of the first meeting in Ottawa. Because he had the flu, he was very tired. Mila had broken her ankle, she couldn't sleep, he couldn't sleep, and so he was in a savage mood."

The Senate dispute was the first order of business. That in itself raised suspicion — at these kinds of discussions Mulroney always dealt with the easy stuff first, then moved on to the intractable disputes.

The prime minister banged the gavel and established his mood immediately. He savaged the media, naming some reporters whose coverage he resented. He took a shot at Bob Rae and his NDP politics in Ontario.

"I don't need any lessons from the prime minister in managing the economy," Rae shot back.

Mulroney was obviously not interested in establishing any long-term relationships at this table. He seemed eager to get it over with, still digging in his heels and resisting an equal Senate. Citing John A. Macdonald as an expert, he talked about how the fathers of Confederation had been opposed to an equal Senate too. The message was loud and clear to all the premiers. Mulroney believed he was wasting his time. The talks dragged on for the first day and it didn't seem as if anyone was going anywhere. All the premiers had come out of the blocks early with their Senate positions, but the debate was simply being shoved off the table, summarily dismissed.

Midweek, Mulroney came out to issue a Clark-style report to the press. He couldn't have looked more unhappy. *Globe and Mail* Ottawa bureau chief Graham Fraser joked that the prime minister resembled captive American hostages in the Middle East, reading aloud the Hezbollah Party of God's manifesto to the national networks. The media pack buzzed with disbelief over Mulroney's obvious display of dismay. Hugh Segal, the prime minister's chief of staff, warned everyone not to read too much into Mulroney's demeanour. He had simply forgotten his glasses, Segal said. But Harcourt offered a different explanation for Mulroney's attitude problem these first few days: "He didn't expect it to succeed."

For Manitoba premier Gary Filmon, it was simply a replay of the hostile days of Meech Lake. Filmon had not been at the premiers' table either in a long time for constitutional negotiations — the talks all spring had been handled by his justice minister, Jim McCrae. Sitting beside Inuit leader Rosemarie Kuptana, Filmon could report to her that this was standard negotiating style for the prime minister. It came as a shock, Filmon said, to the people who had become accustomed to Clark at the table.

"They had been used to Joe's very gentle hand. . . . And you know, as was the case in my days in the latter stages of Meech, I know that the prime minister has never been, shall we say, a gentle hand at the gavel. He's always been an active participant and an interventionist chair of the meetings. And he always has the agenda and leads the agenda."

Kuptana, sitting to Filmon's left, watched incredulously as the prime minister snapped and barked at the participants. Harcourt thought Mulroney's attitude to the aboriginal leaders was "outrageous." He would demand speedy answers from them, then grow impatient with their cautious, deliberative style of negotiating. Filmon says he wasn't downright nasty, but he was very much in charge. "Well, in terms of meanness, I will only say that he was aggressive," Filmon recalls.

The Manitoba premier was correct to see the ghosts of Meech encircling the national-unity debate again. It was another very astute way to summarize the difference between Clark and Mulroney in this crusade, and many of the others who came along in the process. There were Meech vets, like Mulroney, and there were the novices, like Clark.

"I'm not sure there were two Ottawas, but I think there were two working definitions of the problem," Clark said. "Mine was that there were a number of important issues that had to be dealt with together. . . . I thought there were people who were feeling — call them the veterans of Meech — who would have preferred a more specific deal."

Mulroney was a Meech veteran, and much of his motivation was in trying to recreate the deal that he believed had been stolen from him by Manitoba, Newfoundland, the natives, Pierre Trudeau and a cynical public in 1992. On the day he resigned in February 1993, he would make clear, with stunning vindictiveness, that he was still agitated about the Meech fiasco — and specifically, Clyde Wells. His view of history is still distorted by the conviction that Clyde Wells lied to him by refusing to hold a vote on the Meech Lake accord on June 22, 1990, even though the facts would tell that there was duplicity on Ottawa's side during the dying days of Meech.

Mulroney, on his very resignation, would still be saying that Clyde Wells bore the blame for Meech's death. Forgotten in that raw, exposed nerve of memory was the fact that Wells had promised to hold a vote in the Legislature only after Ottawa had refused to extend the deadline to provide for a Newfoundland-wide referendum. His refusal to hold the vote came after an extraordinary, eleventh-hour move by Ottawa to extend the deadline for Manitoba, but not for New-foundland. His refusal to hold the vote was based on the firm conviction that Ottawa was trying to get New-foundland to kill the deal, so that it didn't have to take the politically risky step of blaming the natives in Man-itoba as well.

That should have been ancient history by 1992, but it was clearly not. The fact that Mulroney singled it out as the low point of his term in office showed that even by February 24, 1993, he still bore the scars of Meech, and that the emotion towards Wells was very raw. It would have been a disaster to sit these two at the same table for long in 1993.

But the prime minister wasn't the only one whose Meech war wounds made him unfit for this battle. In fact, anyone who had been around that table in 1990 was almost too scarred to take an active part in this process. Many of those people, such as Mulroney, chose to watch most of the action from the sidelines until the very end, during the summer of negotiations.

Newfoundland premier Clyde Wells handed the reins over to his justice minister, Ed Roberts. Mani-toba premier Gary Filmon gave the file to his justice minister, too. New Brunswick premier Frank McKenna made absolutely certain that he would go nowhere near the constitution again. He gave the job to Intergovernmental Affairs Minister Edmond Blan-chard. Interestingly, the NDP governments in Ontario, Saskatchewan and British Columbia were all new. Being new to this issue was a definite advantage, says Moe Sihota. It worked for Clark and it worked for all these governments.

"The people who started to exert leadership at the end of the day, well, throughout the whole process, were very much the people who weren't at Meech," Sihota said. "That was a very, very important aspect of what was going on." The Meech spectre was enough motivation in itself, he said. "There were times when you realized if you had Getty, Wells and Bourassa in the same room, you weren't going to solve it."

Over and over again, this proved to be true. Who were the people making progress at the table? The people who had not been at Meech — whether it was the native people, Joe Clark or Bob Rae.

Rae recognized quickly that the scars of Meech were keeping the prime minister well away from another constitutional obsession in 1992. "This was a guy at a human level who was very badly burned by Meech. He has also been betrayed, he feels, by a number of people — [Lucien] Bouchard foremost among them. He has no particular reason to like or trust any one of the first ministers. In fact, he can think of a million reasons why he shouldn't."

At one time, early in July, all the forces in the Senate battle were starting to rain down on Bob Rae. He was under siege from everyone, especially the prime minister. The Meech novice sent a letter to the Meech pro Clyde Wells. "Now I know what you felt like," Rae wrote to him.

But as those final negotiations started to come together in August, Mulroney, the old deal-maker, could smell a success in the air. Suddenly, it was no longer good enough to shoot for only an acceptable deal, one with just the minimum number of provinces' approval. He was going to go all the way — another unanimous deal. Lightning would strike twice in this national-unity mission of his. They said he couldn't win two majority governments — he did. They said he couldn't get two unanimous deals among all the provinces — he would, just watch him.

Filmon recognized it as the week was winding down and the provinces were coming down to a crunch on aboriginal issues. No one had really believed that the hard-line provinces such as Newfoundland and Quebec would be on side on the native question. Any deal this big would just have to be sealed with a few provinces off side on a few issues. But suddenly the prime minister was actively pushing Clyde Wells towards a deal: charming him, cajoling him, working on him to solve his problems with defining aboriginal self-government.

The native issues were being worked out in a small room off the main meeting hall in the Pearson Building, with just a few key players. It was Bob Rae sitting at a little Apple computer, Robert Bourassa with him and Ovide Mercredi. Suddenly, after these people had been negotiating for quite a while, Clyde Wells's presence was abruptly requested in the room. The message was loud and clear. Brian Mulroney wanted another deal with everybody on side.

"That was the day that showed me that he was going to do everything possible to have everybody bought into it," Filmon said. "And there's no question that strategy was the right strategy."

Clark was not merely standing idly by, either. He was using his form of gentle persuasion to do what he could. In essence, the federal team had a good cop–bad cop routine, and it was working. Clark's skills at being the quiet, good cop were finely tuned. Moe Sihota was standing around the delegation room one day with Harcourt, entranced, as they watched Clark use his good-cop skills. They stood, munching sandwiches, as a dogged Joe Clark shuttled quietly between Wells and Filmon and Getty; back and forth between them all. They watched Clark quietly talking to Wells, who was shaking his head. "No, no," Wells was saying. Back and forth, over and over again, Clark shuttled between Wells and other premiers, sometimes sending them over to talk to Wells, sometimes going himself for another try. Sihota and Harcourt stopped and looked at each other; their hypnotic trance broken. They turned around — they had eaten a whole tray of sandwiches.

Mulroney's style was far more direct and intense. Watching Clark's negotiating style is like watching a tennis game, mesmerizing for its continual motion. Watching Mulroney negotiate is like watching Wayne Gretzky, swooping through the defence to score goals. In fact, the intensity of Mulroney's style, his frequent shots on net, can stun a novice, as many provincial politicians have found.

"I mean, this is a guy from the Lyndon Johnson school of persuasion," Rae says. "He's just somebody who gets you in the room and stares you right in the face."

Clark believes to this day that the two approaches were needed in this atmosphere, and it was yet another example of how differences in approach can merge into a workable arrangement — not unlike the deal that resulted in the Charlottetown accord.

The days of intense negotiating, Mulroney-style, were an endless series of stiff, open sessions and long, private haggling among knots of premiers. In one of the final days at the Pearson Building in August, the sticking point was aboriginal issues and it involved only a few of the premiers, Wells included. So while these provinces sorted out their differences, mainly through meetings between Ontario, Quebec, Newfoundland and the aboriginal delegations, the rest of the provinces were left to wait — and wait.

A long day passed, the premiers passing the time, waiting for the endless series of tiny negotiations to end and the full conference to reconvene. Eventually, after hours and hours, Mulroney emerged, apologizing for the delay and thanking the premiers for their patience.

"I know it's been a long day and you've all been waiting a long time. You're probably upset at the long delay," the prime minister said.

"You're damn right," Alberta's Don Getty snapped.

The Charlottetown deal was reached on August 28, to very little fanfare. This meeting in the cradle of Confederation, which was supposed to symbolically stamp the deal reached in Ottawa the week before, had been bogged down in Newfoundland's problems with the Supreme Court and British Columbia's complicated snag over the Commons seats it would receive. It was time to get it over with, to return this deal to the track that Mulroney had prepared for the national-unity mission in the first place. The deal was a fait accompli — now it was time to move to a national referendum.

The minor miracle at this Charlottetown meeting was not so much the agreement — the groundwork had been laid for that deal back in Ottawa. It was that so many people, so many sceptics about the wisdom of a referendum, saw a national vote as the only option for the fall of 1992. One of the biggest sceptics was Clark himself. And true to form as a political pragmatist, he came to be convinced of the necessity of the referendum simply because three provinces — British Columbia, Alberta and Quebec — were committed to it.

"We weren't doing this in a vacuum. We were in a situation where there were already referenda. And I guess all of us thought if we had to have a referendum, better to be in it together on one side, than split."

It was certainly a sore subject for Joe Clark. Back in the fall of 1991, when he had stepped into the breach to try to introduce referendum legislation in the

Commons, he had faced near-mutiny from the Quebec caucus. Now, those worries had been soothed, mainly by the mere fact that Mulroney had turned to it as the only strategy. Clark explains how political life changed between that difficult November and the accepted wisdom of a referendum in August.

"It wasn't so much about a referendum," Clark remembers about his collision with the Quebec caucus. "It was about the perception in Quebec that a federal device was being used to intrude upon a provincial decision. . . . By the time we'd reached June, it was clear that we were not doing something that would go around Quebec . . . part of that may be a virtue of the reality that we had all these provinces with them."

Clark, too, was surprised that the decision was so easy that August. Provinces such as New Brunswick and Ontario, which had grave doubts about a referendum, were suddenly eager participants. One by one, premiers around the table voiced the same message: "Look, if we're going to do it, let's do it all together."

Ontario had analysed every single aspect of this national-unity effort. Virtually each night from March to August, some provincial bureaucrat was working on strategy papers, examining all possible ramifications of every tiny decision. But the decision to hold a referendum slid right by the province.

Ontario's deputy minister of intergovernmental affairs, Jeff Rose, the consummate strategist, marvels that a referendum was the one strategy that Ontario never fully thought out. Rose's boss and friend, Bob Rae, had always seen the referendum as a sword of Damocles hanging over the province's head — a threat of rash action in case Ontario's plan for multilateral talks didn't work out. Now, inexplicably in August, it seemed the only way to go.

"It's not the first time it's happened. It's sort of like

people who spend a lot of time writing a report . . . it's like a royal commission, and you forget about how the hell you're going to sell it, how you're going to deal with it," Rae recalls. "It's sort of a classic case, where everybody who's in that process is, first of all, physically exhausted. And emotionally we felt this was it . . . euphoria was strong; a lot of emotion in the room."

In Charlottetown, in the afternoon of August 28, 1992, the premiers were all lined up together behind a bank of room-dividers in the large ballroom of the Prince Edward Hotel. Each filed out to face the reporters, praising their historic agreement and hinting strongly that the country was about to face a referendum. Then Mulroney uttered the words that would galvanize thousands of No voters in the weeks to come; he would wake up the sleeping giant of public cynicism and distrust of politics and what Canadian politics had brought them.

"I know that there'll be fights and I know there are going to be challenges, and I know that the enemies of Canada will not be happy," Mulroney proclaimed.

"Pro-Canada crusade begins," *The Globe and Mail* announced on its front page as the Charlottetown deal was proclaimed. Mulroney had drawn the first ragged battle lines that would help defeat him on October 26, 1992, the day of reckoning for Canada's political leadership.

The more cynical among Canada's constitution-watchers believed that Mulroney had just displayed the real political pit bull that he was. The problem was that he was pitting himself against the Canadian public. His whole battle strategy in the national-unity war was to place himself on the right side of history and everyone who opposed him on the wrong side of patriotism. He had boasted to his caucus in the early days of 1992 that Canadians could be pulled into the pro-Canada crusade.

"Nine times out of ten, Canadians will choose Canada," the prime minister declared in one of his trademark, rally-the-troops speeches to the Tory caucus. The feisty eagerness for a campaign, the patriotic appeals, his us-against-them rhetoric had all worked their usual magic on the caucus. Doubters from Quebec, sceptics from the West — all their misgivings faded away in the face of this massive display of Mulroney confidence. Back in March, the prime minister thought he could simply magnify this approach and use it with the provinces. Ottawa above all, one for all — for Canada. The House of Commons would pass a constitutional resolution; the provinces, eager to be on the right side of patriotism, would follow its lead. Ontario had thrown a wrench into that plan, though, by insisting that the provinces have an equal hand in drawing up the battle plan. The referendum strategy veered off into the "multilateral" detour.

Still, Mulroney got the chance to use the us-against-them appeal again by August, once the multilateral force was spent. Now it wasn't the federal government against the provinces; it was Ottawa, the provinces and the aboriginal leaders against the public. For the "enemies of Canada" line would be snapped up quickly by an outraged public. How dare Brian Mulroney say that his enemies were the enemies of Canada? How dare he portray himself as the only one who could speak for Canada? Radio call-in shows, such as Rafe Mair's controversial CKNW program in British Columbia, were inundated with callers who were furious that their patriotism would be questioned.

The same outrage had seized provinces such as Ontario early in 1992, but their worries were assuaged. There was no possible way to soothe the anger of the public that was stirred up by this line. "We'll show him," many said. "We'll vote No, and see

who really speaks for Canada." It was a notion that
kept creeping up behind Mulroney all the way
through the referendum campaign.

In fact, midway through the campaign, the Prime
Minister's Office would take the unusual step of issuing
a clarification about the "enemies of Canada" line.
Let's get this straight, the release said. He was talking
about Quebec separatists, not the No voters in the rest
of Canada. But the press release simply threw Mulroney
out of the frying pan and into the fire. It showed that
this prime minister of Canada was obsessed with
Quebec, so much so that he was blinded to the realities
of the rest of Canada. As Moe Sihota had asked a month
or so earlier: Was this the prime minister of Canada or
the prime minister of Quebec?

While all this fuss was going on over the enemies of
Canada, Joe Clark took a suprisingly indulgent view of
his old rival's fiery rhetoric. He just saw the old Brian
Mulroney, staking out his ground for the campaign.
"Once he gets into a fight, he wants the issue to be
clear," Clark says. Clear it was. All the politicians were
united in their national-unity mission, and united they
would fall.

For all the fire and brimstone stirred up by Mulroney's
line in Charlottetown, and the one-for-all attitude that
had dragged the provinces into the referendum, the
real Yes campaign took a very long time to get under
way. And once it did, another rift would surface
between Clark and Mulroney, between their two very
different approaches to Canadian politics in the 1990s.

The constitutional affairs minister who had devoted
his life to this national-unity mission would suddenly
find himself out of the drama, relegated to a salesmanship job on the road, while the strategic decisions
were being made by a Star Chamber of Tory, Liberal

and New Democratic Party strategists on the so-called Canada Committee. This was the ultimate in political organization; a hybrid, tri-partisan team of strategists who oversaw the federal political Yes effort throughout September and October.

The Conservatives sent their well-respected operations guru, Harry Near, to oversee the Tories' interests in the referendum strategy. The Liberals sent Gordon Ashworth, a former principal secretary to Ontario premier David Peterson whose job at that time was heading up the federal Liberals' election-readiness effort. Like Near, Ashworth was chosen because the referendum was good practice for a forthcoming federal election. The New Democrats sent the chief of staff to Audrey McLaughlin, Les Campbell a young, political idealist who knew that the politics of confrontation were now a discredited force in Canada. Campbell, throughout this rare moment of three-party co-operation in Canadian politics, was moved by the fierce desire to bring honour and dignity back to public life.

Quickly, these three people and their political parties mustered every bit of talent they could find. They virtually had their pick of any political resource they could find in Ottawa. It was four years into the Tories' mandate and the political machine in Ottawa was idling, impatient for any action. Mulroney, thankfully, had fired a starting gun.

Pollsters, consultants and media strategists were immediately hurled into the world of campaign strategy once again. But it wasn't a huge political machine that was required in this delicate effort; it was a gentle, more old-fashioned tool, fashioned out of respect and trust. In all the frenzy to get the machine up and running, the strategists ignored the lessons that Clark and the others had learned on the constitutional learning curve. No matter what the opposition, no matter how intractable the dispute, you've got to respect your opponents and gently bring others into making a willing leap of faith. You can't call them enemies of Canada and browbeat them into a deal. It didn't work with Clyde Wells in 1990, it didn't work with any other provinces in early 1992, and it was destined to fail again in the fall of 1992.

Frustrated, Clark watched from a distance as a new style of politics took over in the national-unity mission. This was not the slow, tedious, respect-building process he had led for the many months before the referendum. This strategy was strong, pure politics. A big heavy machine had been dragged in to perform an operation that needed a very delicate touch. And it wasn't just Joe Clark who was relegated to the background when this machine lumbered in. It was almost every player who had carefully built the Charlottetown accord. It was as if Canada's constitutional drama had two acts, with two different casts. Clark and his supporting cast of provincial premiers and politicians were now bowing out, and the new actors were coming in. The new leading actor was Brian Mulroney and his "pro-Canada" team. Trust, tedium and respect were minor themes in this act. The careful and dull had given way to the exciting and the instinctive. The constitution was getting swept up in a torrent of political instincts, mainly those of Brian Mulroney.

It happened so smoothly, so quickly, that no one really noticed the transition had taken place. Just one meeting, at the Prime Minister's Office at Langevin Block in early September, sealed the end of the first act and the beginning of the second. That meeting would be the last real time that the provinces and Ottawa came together to co-operate in the national-unity crusade. From here on in, the politicians were out on their own, up against the most formidable opponent on the road to a new constitution — a cynical, jaded Canadian public.

The provinces, territories and aboriginal groups sent an official each, a tactician, to hear the details of referendum strategy. The federal team had come prepared with sheaves of data about voting behaviour and how to hold a referendum. The prime minister's chief of staff, Hugh Segal, finally took the lead and put Mulroney's hand at the tiller of this exercise. Clearly, Ottawa had been quietly dusting the referendum track while the multilateral process was going on. The feds were ready to wage their battle for Canada, the patriotic crusade. Instinct was about to prevail over political common sense.

But it wasn't just Brian Mulroney's instincts that crowded out logic at this stage. At the meeting, Tory consultant Bill Fox, a friend of Mulroney's, offered some advice about the referendum question itself. All the statistics showed them that the shorter the question, the worse the chances were for the success of a Yes. Too late. As the politicians in Charlottetown had been swept up in their emotion and relief at getting a deal, they were also swept up in the conviction that a short question was the best bet. Ontario premier Bob Rae had already said publicly that it had to be "short, sharp, direct, blunt and unequivocal." Quebec's officials feared that any long question would allow the formidable Parti Quebecois opponents to pick away at the Charlottetown deal. Fox's advice was politely heard and then ignored.

So the long question was shelved. Canadians were going to be asked a nice, simple, twenty-three-word question.

Do you agree that the Constitution of Canada should be renewed on the basis of the agreement reached on August 28, 1992?

Nice, simple words, with a positive feel to them. The

constitution was being "renewed." The words "agree" and "agreement" conveyed the happy tone of the Charlottetown euphoria. What patriotic Canadian would take issue with such a positive statement? Plenty, it turned out. Approximately 56 per cent of the Canadian population, as the results on October 26 showed.

Out on the road, still doing his never-ending tour of Canadian hotel rooms, Clark was confronting the fact that he was a bit player in the last act of the constitutional crusade. All the lessons he had learned about mutual trust and respect as the keys to political survival were forgotten or written off. And there seemed to be nothing he could do to change the course of events or reassert himself or his style. In the ceaseless tussle between Clark and Mulroney, between the rock and the hard place, Clark was definitely losing.

This time, it was a question of logistics. The ground couldn't shake because the fault line was moving all over the country. Clark was in one part of Canada, Mulroney in the other. Again, they were at cross-purposes.

"Most of the differences the prime minister and I have had get resolved when we sit down together, one way or another. And just the dynamics of the campaign had us in different parts of the country."

If Clark had his way, there would have been a lot less talk about Canada and whole lot more talk about the virtues of the Charlottetown deal.

"We sort of drifted into a particular kind of advocacy," Clark said. "We were hard sell in some cases. There was not a lot of talk about the agreement. There was a lot of talk about Canada." The miracle of Charlottetown, all the trust and respect that were needed to obtain that deal, was barely mentioned.

The problem, simply, was that the constitutional negotiators may have learned to trust and respect each other, but they were having trouble with the idea of trusting and respecting the Canadian public. The referendum campaign found the politicians slipping into a them-versus-us posture with the public. The rift was far more serious than any that would emerge between Clark and Mulroney or the rest of Canada and Quebec. This utter breakdown in the relationship between the leaders and the led is the fodder for revolutions. And Canada, in its own quiet way, was going to hold a polite revolution, where the final, battle-ending shot would be one word — "No."

Every battle has its marching band and this one was no exception. A song, "For Love of This Country," wafted into Canadian living rooms, over and over and over again through most of 1992, sung in a television advertising spot by a little girl whose hairstyle made her look like a young Mila Mulroney. Canada was celebrating its 125th birthday in 1992, and this television ad was a happy birthday song to the country. And the patriotic refrain didn't hurt the Yes committee in their pro-Canada mission. It didn't help either.

Nor did the half-dozen other commercials that showed up on television around this time, featuring all kinds of federal government departments celebrating the joy of Canada. The Department of National Defence put out a patriotic message about the country's peacekeepers. The Secretary of State showed Canadians dancing, singing, whirling, gratefully celebrating their citizenship. Canadian airwaves were flooded with these kinds of ads, all of them together shown about 150 to 200 times a week through September and October.

That was on top of the "real" campaign ads, which took a more direct approach. The themes? Baseball and young people. A very soft sell in a very hard market. In television ad number one, the camera opens up on a tight shot of a fastball catcher behind home plate. The umpire is behind him. A batter stands motionless as baseballs keep flying past him. The voice says: "We can wait for it to be absolutely perfect . . . With no compromises, no problems, everything just right . . . You know, everyone happy about everything, all the time." The umpire cries: "You're out." The voice comes back: "You're out." It was a clear message — Canada was up at bat and in danger of striking out. No mention of the Charlottetown deal. No mention of the changes in store for the country.

Similarly, the "Class Portrait" ad made no mention of the precise shape of the nation being handed to a group of smiling children, posing for a group photograph. The announcer says: "It is estimated by the time a child reaches the age of thirteen, he or she will have heard the word 'no' about 23,000 times. Isn't it time you said Yes to your children?"

In the meantime, reels and reels of homemade videos from the No campaigners zeroed in on the details of the deal. The No people weren't afraid to mention Charlottetown or the constitution. Canadians, the No committees reasoned, were not dumb. The referendum was about the constitution, not baseball or schoolchildren. They had the basement-produced appeal of "Wayne's World" and the grassroots credibility of shaky, home-video testimonials. One notable ad depicted the Charlottetown accord as a piece of old auto junk that was being sold by a bunch of used-car salesmen. Others featured normal, average Canadians holding forth on their concept of constitutional politics.

The Yes ads, put next to these homespun appeals, looked too slick and mysterious. Why were they talking about baseball and children? Why weren't they talking directly about the equal Senate, or the Canada clause, or anything about this massive overhaul of the

Canadian federation? The ads did little more than tell Canadians to vote Yes. They didn't really tell them what they were agreeing to.

Here was the crucial issue once again. The Yes committee's ads weren't speaking to the key notion of respect between public and politicians. In early October, something was starting to smell fishy to the Canadian public. The legal text of the Charlottetown deal had not been released, and the television ads weren't saying anything. For the cynical among the public, and there were many of them, it started to look like there was something to hide. Only the No voters seemed eager to talk about what was in the deal.

Of course, there was nothing to hide. Only months before, Canadians had begged their politicians to stop telling them about the constitution. Now they couldn't hear enough. The Canada Committee was still operating, though, on the assumption that people didn't want to be bored with the details.

Details, details. What did it matter what Brian Mulroney was really saying that day in late September, in Sherbrooke, when he launched into a tirade against separatists who opposed the Charlottetown deal?

On September 28, 1992, a huffing and puffing prime minister waved a copy of the Charlottetown accord in Sherbrooke, lauding its historic gains for Quebec. Dramatically, he held the paper in front of him, warning, in French: "If you vote No, you rip up all the historic gains Quebec has made." The message was reasonable, correct; the theatrics backfired with a bang. As was the case with many of the prime minister's flights of rhetoric through the years, the context would be forgotten and the dismissiveness remembered.

Premiers all across the country hunched their shoulders and winced. That's all they needed. A Mulroney display of bravado played right into the hands of the No forces, who had been accusing the Yes side of scare tactics ever since the "enemies of Canada" line. The polls, too, were showing that the public was getting edgy about the dire warnings of the Yes side, and the apparent conscription of the Royal Bank, which issued a report on the adverse economic consequences of a No vote.

Scaring the public was not going to work in 1992. In Ottawa, the Yes committee knew that. That very morning, as Mulroney was rehearsing his Sherbrooke speech for lunchtime delivery, the Yes strategists in the capital were talking about the importance of the high road. Hugh Segal told his troops: "We've got to stay on the high road, no matter what." If politicians were going to brave the cynicism of the public to wage this campaign, they had to be very, very careful about what they said. Talk about lofty principles, talk about patriotism, talk about historic compromise.

The archives of the Yes committee are packed to the rafters with strategy documents. Every tiny bit of political manoeuvring is documented and analysed. The campaign itself was to be dissected into three stages — the first, in which the Yes side frames the debate; the second, called the public "questioning" phase; and the third, during which the Yes side was to come in and "close the deal." History would show that the Yes forces never even got to the first phase. Strategists such as Les Campbell would boast bravely in the early days that the No forces had defined only themselves, not the debate. But that was all they needed to define. They were not politicians, they were not Brian Mulroney's friends, and they were not enemies of Canada. That was endorsement enough for a massive swing to No.

The Yes side thought they had anticipated every possible strategy of the No side. Their documents sketch out the three possible "campaign models." One would be to attack the Charlottetown accord as a sweeping change, stirring up all that Canadian fear of extremes. Another No strategy would be to go in the opposite direction — to present Charlottetown as okay, but not good enough. Yet another strategy would be to take the weakest link in the Charlottetown package and attack it for that. History would also show that the No side used every one of these models to great effect. And even though the Yes side anticipated the attacks, all the strategists money could buy did not seem to have any power to counter them.

While the No side had assembled powerful artillery of scepticism, separatism, cynicism and anger, the Yes side was fighting back with vague generalities. Strategists would file into their morning meetings at the new Save Canada headquarters in a shiny office tower on Metcalfe Street in Ottawa, sit around their boardroom table and sketch out only the most rudimentary style of campaigning to promote the Charlottetown accord.

"Everyone gets something," they would scribble in their strategy notes. "Everyone compromised," the pens would scratch away, furiously. "It's a package that allows us to move on." Maybe all of this was true, even noble, but in the politics of 1992, this was also deemed as very faint praise. Why were they so frightened to tackle the debate head on, to let the public in on the nature of the miracle of Charlottetown?

The answer to that is found in the respect issue. The public had no respect for the politicians, and the politicians were having a hard time respecting the public. The public was crying out for a chance to read the legal text of the agreement, certain that the politicians were trying to put one over on them. The politicians, in turn, were simply flabbergasted that the public would make this request of them. The message from the Yes committee's Iona Campagnolo, confirmed the political distrust of the public.

"These are the people who wouldn't even read the instructions on their VCR," she said.

Manitoba's NDP leader, Gary Doer, made a similar quip: "When was the last time you read the fine print on your rental-car agreement?" But Campagnolo and Doer are dyed-in-the-wool political people, with an abiding faith in politics to do the right thing for people. The public, on the other hand, did not have the faith. "Show us the text. We'll decide for ourselves."

The Yes side tackled the crisis of faith with window-dressing, pulling in Campagnolo and a slate of other non-elected "opinion leaders" to serve as the voice of real Canadians. On Tuesday, September 22, at a carefully chosen non-political site — an Ottawa high school — the seven non-politicians were unveiled to their fellow Canadians. There was the writer June Callwood; former Liberal cabinet minister Iona Campagnolo; former UN ambassador Yves Fortier; aboriginal leader Mary Simon; Ontario doctor Joseph Wong; Michel Bastarache, a New Brunswick business leader; and Ted Newall, an Alberta businessman.

"Look, no politics," the Yes committee seemed to be saying, its collective hands raised in innocence. But a campaign goof stole the show away. "Look, no French," said many of the reporters, pointing out that a huge "Yes" had been carefully installed on the stage, but no "Oui." What more proof did you need that English Canada and French Canada were still far apart?

But even if the Yes committee did have some problems saying in French what it said in English, it was capable of one type of simultaneous translation. One by one, the seven members of the Yes committee made an attempt to communicate with the public by saying exactly what the politicians were saying. It was the same faint praise as the politicians had been bestowing on the agreement. Compromise, not perfection; let's get this over with; our future is at stake. Their voices quickly faded away into the background, lost in the sea of debate. Here was the other problem, identified but not truly grappled with by the Yes committee. Rule number one of the Yes committee, etched into every move of the strategists, was "A referendum is not an election." It doesn't work the same way as an election; people change their minds, the vote is volatile, and only in the last days will people truly decide on their position.

The problem, though, was that the media did not have any experience with covering a not-election. One of the favourite puzzles for the Yes strategists was summed up in one line: "What do the boys on the bus do when there's no bus?" Well, they find any old bus. And it just so happened that Brian Mulroney had one handy. The prime minister, like the media he so resented, knew only one way to go about an election campaign and that was to throw himself into old-style speech-making and political fighting. In turn, he was going to set an example for his co-signers in the Charlottetown accord, who seemed to have vanished off the face of the planet.

Frequently through the two months of the campaign, Mulroney would glance over each of his shoulders, bewildered that he was out in front, apparently alone in his defence of the Yes side. For a prime minister who had come to support the deal very reluctantly, the same politician who had nearly come to blows with Clark over the July 7 multilateral deal, Mulroney was now, ironically, the lead spokesman, and he was being lacerated every day by the No forces.

The Reform Party produced an advertisement that took great advantage of Mulroney's unpopularity.

Preston Manning appeared on television, urging his fellow Canadians to vote against "the Mulroney deal."

For the people who had slogged their way through the multilateral process, building a deal in spite of Mulroney, not because of him, this tactic of Manning's was disgraceful. It borrowed on the public hatred of Mulroney, capitalized on the antipathy towards politicians and trivialized the achievements of the Charlottetown accord. All of Joe Clark's old Alberta Tory anger was unleashed on Manning. In a Christmas-time interview in 1992, after the dust of the referendum had settled, Clark was still steaming angry with Manning.

"Preston Manning for a long time has been pretending that he was a different species of politician, that he stood above the rest of us, that he had higher standards than anyone else did. And his conduct in the campaign demonstrated that he does not have very high standards," Clark told the CBC radio show "As It Happens."

"One of the consequences of the campaign is that it will be more difficult for Mr Manning to get away with the hypocrisy that he's patented for the last couple of years."

Manning, for his part, would later regret the move. For a leader whose positions are normally well articulated and defended, his defence of the "Mulroney deal" strategy was weak, almost apologetic.

"I didn't really think a lot about the 'Mulroney deal' phrase as being particularly emotive or being particularly significant. . . . Of course, in the commercials you had to have a shorthand label. What could you call this thing? . . . You know, what label did you put on it? And we ended up agreeing with using the adjective Mulroney."

Of course, Reformers knew that they already had a clever "Know More" Or "No More" campaign, capable of conveying public hunger for information and public fatigue at the same time. But it was too tempting to resist the opportunity that Mulroney was presenting them. Besides, said Manning, somewhat defensively, it was a lot better than the epithets that had been hurled at his group.

"Our own key people have been subjected to so much name-calling, like Reformers are fascists, Reformers are racists . . . The phrase 'the Mulroney deal' seemed so innocuous compared to the stuff that we've been labelled with that it didn't strike me as particularly heavy-duty." If the Reform Party had to do it over again, he said, the "Mulroney deal" would not have been part of the campaign. "I think, in retrospect, that given the reaction to that from some of our own people . . . we would not have used that." He joked: "If it had been called the Clark deal we probably would have had a phone call from 24 Sussex Drive protesting. Because he [Mulroney] worked pretty hard whenever it was, June and August there, to make sure that Clark wasn't the architect."

Right to the end, Clark and Mulroney would be doing their strange reluctant dance with each other — cheek to chin, locked in a clutch that was forced upon them by history, by their political alliance as Tories and their political enemies across the country. They would be the loyal Tory partners in the Yes camp, battling the Reformers and separatists together. But they would also be continually demonstrating their differences as they battled them.

Clark had figured out their differences in another context, when he reflected on the Albertan and the Quebecker — the Albertan, concerned with the integrity issue; the Quebecker, concerned about the identity issue. All through the referendum campaign,

Mulroney put his identity on the line to wage the battle for the Yes campaign. His was a larger-than-life identity, capable of overwhelming everything except the massive public cynicism towards him and all politicians. Clark, on the other hand, would put his integrity on the line. That, too, had assumed larger-than-life proportions, the constitutional affairs minister depicted as a loyal, dogged, trusted friend of Canada, forgiven his mistakes and weaknesses. Yet it wasn't enough, either, to overcome the cynicism.

On referendum night, they stood together again in defeat. All their efforts had won them only a No vote. But they did get to keep what they had put on the line in this referendum campaign.

Mulroney would keep his identity. On February 24, 1993, as he stepped down from politics, the farewells would be to the man himself, the Quebecker, the huge personality that had squeezed itself uncomfortably into the confining restraints of public office. All the tributes and commentaries would focus on the Mulroney identity that had made such a controversial mark on the Canadian nation from 1984 to 1993.

Joe Clark would keep his integrity. On February 20, 1993, when Clark journeyed out to his Yellowhead riding to say farewell to politics, the tributes and commentaries would all be focused on what this man did, rather than on who he was. He would be remembered as the man in constant motion, getting nowhere, but travelling with integrity intact.

In the House of Commons, on Brian Mulroney's resignation day, Clark slowly made his way over to his old rival's chair. Politicians and onlookers all paused to watch this last, symbolic clutch of hands between the Albertan and the Quebecker, the integrity and the identity, the rock and the hard place. The long struggle between them was finally over.

3

Ontario:
The Tug of Allegiances

There was once a time when Ottawa could count on its home province to act as the federal deputy. As Ottawa goes, so goes Ontario. But as 1992 rolled around, as Ottawa was locked in the grip of tension between the rest of Canada and Quebec, between Joe Clark and Brian Mulroney, Ontario slid away from Ottawa's side. New Democratic premier Bob Rae was not content to lead a province that served only as a mirror for the nation. Ottawa was locked in a tug-of-war between two interests; Ontario was involved in a struggle among a huge array of interests.

Bob Rae had an idea of his Ontario. It was big — as big as the largest province in Canada, as big as its deposits into the national coffers. It was as big as Ontario's population, as big as Toronto's skyscrapers and as big as the sweeping reaches of the province's north.

Now, Bob Rae was not the first Ontario premier to think big. His Liberal predecessor, David Peterson, had always said in national-unity matters that he wanted to do the "big" thing, whatever that was. And on the night of June 9, 1990, as Canada's first ministers sat around the table, congratulating themselves on their attempt to save the Meech Lake accord, David Peterson was praised as the "big guy" who offered Ontario's clout to the bigger cause of the nation.

But the New Democratic premier, who took power from David Peterson only a few short months after that ill-fated night, had a different idea of "big" when it came to Ontario. Rae's bid for the big would be called "inclusiveness" — it meant that Ontario was large enough to accommodate every interest that wanted to be a part of the NDP regime. Bob Rae's Ontario was supposed to be big enough to include everyone under the shelter of its left wing. The problem, though, was that all the interests pulled into Ontario's embrace were wrestling the province in different directions, tugging Ontario all over Canada's constitutional map. This Ontario, which would reach out to native people, Quebec, NDP allies in the West and the advocacy interests of women and labour, quickly found that all these diverse interests had a different idea about Ontario's destination.

Only one interest was not welcome in Ontario's world of inclusiveness. The federal government, once able to count on good old reliable Ontario as its loyal deputy, was not on the list of included guests in Bob Rae's big province. Prime Minister Brian Mulroney's Conservatives were in power, and Rae's NDP government was a big ideological opponent. So while Ontario struggled with all its warring interests on the inside, it had a more mammoth struggle on the outside. The old allies, Ontario and Ottawa, were now at odds, and their battle would shape the outcome of the national-unity negotiations in 1992.

Cast back to December 1991. Prime Minister Brian Mulroney was paying a rare call on the Ontario premier whose politics fell on the opposite side of the spectrum. Still, Mulroney knew that these were days in Canada's history where ideology shouldn't stand in the way of the practical need to get things done. Mulroney, graciously, had even taken the unusual step of meeting Rae in his own office.

The office, at the east corner of the main Queen's Park edifice in Toronto, has an imposing yet subdued elegance. And befitting the style of this Ontario premier, it is also clearly a working office. Amid the trappings of the top political post in Ontario, with the leather couches, the heavy-framed prints, there are sheaves of policy papers piled on the huge wooden desk. Well-thumbed political books line the shelves and sit open on the premier's desk.

Into this office came Brian Mulroney for a tensely cordial meeting with his most powerful ideological opponent. Mulroney may have faced off every day against his nemesis, the federal Liberals and Jean Chretien, and he may have looked the NDP in the eye every day in the House of Commons, but it was Bob Rae, as the NDP premier of Canada's largest province, who spoke for the most powerful left-wing opposition in Canada to this right-wing prime minister.

These were not happy days in the national-unity business. Mulroney's government was foundering in chaos, trying to figure out how to restart its stalled constitutional enterprise. The special joint Commons–Senate committee on the renewal of Canada had run off the rails. An attempt to blend town-hall style meetings with parliamentary hearings had flopped humiliatingly in Manitoba, and the committee had been forced to limp back to Ottawa to regroup. One of the committee chairmen, Quebec Senator Claude Castonguay, had quit, pleading an illness that bore a remarkable resemblance to "diplomatic flu." The Liberals and New Democrats were calling for the resignation of the other chairman, Manitoba MP Dorothy Dobbie, alleging she was incompetent and too partisan. Meanwhile, Constitutional Affairs Minister Joe Clark had tried to introduce referendum legislation in the Commons, only to be beaten into an embarrassing retreat by a near-mutiny from the Quebec Conservative caucus. All of this made Ottawa look like the Keystone Kops as they tried to invite public debate on their twenty-eight federal proposals, titled "Shaping Canada's Future." As a last-gasp measure, Ottawa had announced that it would be setting up a series of "Renewal of Canada" conferences, each to examine a different aspect of the federal proposals. But the widespread belief in the country was that Ottawa didn't know what it was doing.

It was against this chaotic background that a tense, stiff Prime Minister Mulroney walked into the office of Bob Rae that December day. The two men exchanged nervous pleasantries. It was only their second face-to-face encounter since Rae had assumed office nearly sixteen months earlier, and the first meeting, at Harrington Lake in August, had not exactly been the beginning of a beautiful friendship. Their ideological differences were just too deep.

Now, after a few introductory discussions, they turned guardedly to the most pressing issue for both of them — the state of national-unity negotiations. Rae's message to Mulroney was blunt: "You haven't told us what's going to happen. It's a complete mess." Mulroney's response was to turn icy and curt. Ontario was trying to figure out just where the provinces fit into Ottawa's whole national-unity escapade. Mulroney had no solid answers for Rae. He could only tell him what the premier had already seen in the papers about Ottawa's plans for the next crucial months before Quebec's referendum deadline of October 1992.

The two men talked about the forthcoming conferences for early 1992. They talked about Rae's demand
for a social charter in the constitution — an idea con-
spicuously absent in the federal proposals of September 1991. It had been studied in Ottawa that summer
and was widely expected to be part of the package of
twenty-eight proposals.

Following on the heels of the federal NDP leader,
Audrey McLaughlin, the Ontario government and Rae
came to see this social charter as the ideal way to put a
left-wing stamp on the constitution. Ideally, such a
social charter would guarantee Canadians the right to
basic collective values such as medicare, education,
housing and all the other social programs that con-
tribute to a decent standard of living in the country.
Europeans had embraced the idea of guaranteeing
these rights under the constitution; Rae wanted
Canada to adopt a similar notion. Ontario was mildly
distressed that the social charter didn't make the cut in
"Shaping Canada's Future."

Never mind that it was left out, though. That would
be fixed, or so it seemed. Rae came away from this
December meeting with Mulroney convinced that the
social charter would be on the list of subjects to be discussed at the Renewal of Canada conferences. Mulroney and Rae went out to face the media after their
meeting, putting the best face possible on their cool
encounter. Rae waited for Mulroney to make mention
of the social charter, and the assurance that it would be
discussed at the conferences for early 1992. There was
no word of it.

In the next few weeks, as Toronto and Ottawa were
swallowed up in Christmas festivities, the Save Canada
machine was busy in Ottawa. Under the able direction
of Arthur Kroeger, deputy minister of employment and
immigration, loaned to the Privy Council of Canada for

this exercise, the Renewal of Canada conferences were kicking into a much higher gear than the special joint committee had ever been able to reach.

Ontario's officials watched the agenda for the conferences churning out of Ottawa, in press releases and media leaks. They saw the list of subjects being prepared for a cross-country odyssey of weekend constitutional chatter. They saw the lotteries being organized — to choose the 200 lucky Canadians, ordinary and otherwise, who would attend these weekend national-unity retreats. No mention of the social charter. No one in the Save Canada exercise was putting Ontario's much-wanted social charter on the agenda for any conference.

By New Year's Eve, 1991, it was clear that the social charter just didn't fit into Ottawa's conference plan. Ontario's officials, baffled, realized that politics had overcome a promise. So the Ontario government collectively took a step back, folded its arms, and bided its time, waiting to pounce on Ottawa for its single-minded, centrally driven pursuit of a national-unity deal for Quebec.

In the next six weeks, Ontario would carefully build itself up as the representative of the provinces. The Ottawa–Ontario antagonism that had festered during Rae's tenure was about to pit the federal government not just against the country's biggest provinces, but against all the provinces — and the native people and the territories.

Rae lobbed the first grenade at Ottawa on January 13, 1992, when he appeared before the beleaguered special joint committee, now headed by Dobbie and Senator Gerald Beaudoin. If there was any doubt about the fact that Ontario was ready to square off against the feds, Rae dispelled it quickly. The message was carefully phrased, but the subtitles were clear. No more Mr Nice

Guy from Ontario. No more would Ontario be a simple handmaiden to Ottawa's interests.

"Let me say one last word to you about the process," Rae told the committee, gathered in the cavernous splendour of the West Block's Room 200 on Parliament Hill. "I am very concerned that there is still the illusion out there that this committee will produce a document which will go to the federal government, that the federal government will discuss it and maybe they'll make a few phone calls and a few airplane rides to different provinces and try to fashion something, present a resolution to Parliament and that that resolution will be the basis of what goes to the province of Quebec.

"I am doubly concerned when I read that there are now discussions going on between the federal government and the province of Quebec with respect to other changes in the package. I can tell you that as far as we are concerned, there have been no negotiations with the province of Ontario. None.

"And I can also tell you that until there are such negotiations with us and with other provinces, this is not the way we do things in a federal system. . . . I don't want anybody coming to me in May and saying: 'Here's the package, Premier. You know, take it or leave it, roll the dice, all the other metaphors, we are right up against the wall here, this is it.' "

Rae had just drawn the line in the sand. While Ottawa, and Mulroney in particular, were planning to do just what Rae had feared, the Ontario premier had called them out on their unilateralism. While Mulroney had been assuring Quebec that the plan was to introduce a House of Commons national-unity resolution in April, negotiate with the provinces and then call a June or September referendum for the rest of Canada, Ontario had just stopped him short.

Quietly, over the next two months, Ontario would

build its campaign to blunt Ottawa's single-minded-
ness. The big province was preparing the battleground
that in March would pit "unilateralism" against "multilateralism" — the constitutional version of the battle of
the titans for 1992.

Mulroney persisted in the belief that the provinces
were peripheral to the resolution of the national-unity
mission. Late in January, more than two weeks after
Rae's warning in Ottawa, the prime minister would still
be talking as though the provinces were consultants,
not participants. Mulroney would also reason that if
Quebec couldn't be at the table, no provinces could —
no first ministers' conference was better than a partial
first ministers' conference.

But there was some attempt to at least go through the
motions of consulting the provinces. On March 12,
1992, Constitutional Affairs Minister Joe Clark convened a meeting of all the constitutional ministers from
the provinces — except Quebec. The idea for the meeting owed its inspiration to another premier, Manitoba's
Gary Filmon, who suggested in his visit to the Beaudoin–Dobbie committee that a low-profile meeting of
ministers, not a grand-scale premiers' meeting, might
lure Quebec to the table. And so, in the midst of a March
blizzard, with several delegations still making their way
belatedly through the snow and wind to the meeting,
Clark banged the gavel and began what would be a long,
long, process of talking with the provinces.

Ontario arrived, ready to steal Ottawa's thunder. And
it did, armed with a simple, four-page document. That's
the weapon of choice in Canada's constitutional battles
— documents, memos and bureaucratic notes. Titled,
innocently enough, "Proposal for a Federal–Provincial
Constitutional Process," it was, in retrospect, a most
clever foreshadowing of the events to come over the
spring of 1992.

Jeff Rose, the veteran labour negotiator turned Ontario bureaucrat, ironically had hit the old federal labour negotiator Brian Mulroney where he lived. He and his government had presented Ottawa with a classic system for conflict-resolution, complete with working groups and committees and meetings. Really, Ottawa had no choice but to go along. What was the choice in March of 1992? Tell Canadians that the deal would be worked out by their federal Parliament and the three parties — who, incidentally, had not distinguished themselves with all their end-of-February wrangling over the Beaudoin–Dobbie committee report? Or tell Canadians that this would be a federal–provincial effort?

Ontario had just scored one big goal against Ottawa.

Only one key part of Ontario's plan was tossed out. In the Ontario proposal, all the various working groups were to be headed by an "eminent person," chosen from among the notable Canadians who spearheaded the successful Renewal of Canada conferences. Former Alberta premier Peter Lougheed was one name, Judge Rosalie Abella was another; former United Nations ambassador Yves Fortier would head up yet another working group. It was an attempt to link the surprising success of these conferences to the federal–provincial negotiations. But enough provinces rebelled to sink the idea. Alberta's intergovernmental affairs minister, Jim Horsman, argued: "We're elected people. We are the people who have been elected to represent Canadians, not these other people." Horsman didn't intend it that way, but it was one more brick in the wall between the public and the politicians — a wall that was not really evident to the politicians at this point in the national-unity travails of 1992.

Horsman's antipathy to the eminent-persons idea was fuelled by his simmering resentment of Ottawa's reliance on Lougheed. Every time Horsman turned around, it seemed that Lougheed was speaking up for Ottawa and against the government of Alberta. As chairman of Ottawa's Renewal of Canada conference on Senate reform in Calgary, Lougheed had pooh-poohed the idea of an equal Senate. That equal Senate, though, was the key objective of Alberta premier Don Getty and his loyal deputy, Jim Horsman. On page three of Ontario's proposal for the process, Lougheed is named as an eminent person to head one of the working groups. It is in the section titled "Public Legitimacy." There was nothing more illegitimate, in Horsman's view, than to replace politicians with former and would-be politicians. The idea was shelved.

But the eminent-persons proposal was not a must-have for Ontario. Rae and his officials were simply happy to force through multilateralism over unilateralism. The victory was political. But there was a personal element to this Ontario–Ottawa tussle as well, which can be understood from the histories of the key players.

First, there was the history between Clark and Rae. Canada is a huge country geographically, but it is a small country socially. Two men as immersed in politics as Clark and Rae are bound to have crossed paths in their past, enough to build up a fair assessment of each other.

Clark knew Rae as the young New Democratic MP who introduced the resolution that brought down his government in December 1979. Of course, that wasn't personal, and it wasn't Bob Rae himself who had had enough power to rise up and defeat the foundling Clark government — that was a job for the Liberals. But no New Democratic MP can sit in Parliament and not be aware of the fierce partisanship of Joe Clark. This eloquent parliamentarian and hapless, perennial victim of political bad luck is also known for his nasty catcalls across the House of Commons. Rae had heard the anti-NDP jeers of Joe Clark, and knew the intense Tory who uttered them.

On a personal level, Clark knew Rae as a fellow traveller in the same Ottawa-centred circles of Parliament Hill. The son of diplomat Saul Rae and a Rhodes scholar, Rae was not a New Democrat in a hair shirt. The less charitable among the New Democrats in the West would call him a "white-wine socialist," someone who talked a good game at cocktail parties, but a socialist who had no knowledge of the real human hardship that led to the crusade for socialism.

Clark's wife, Maureen McTeer, as rugged an individualist as Bob Rae, had run across him while both were doing their bar admission examinations for a law degree in Ottawa. Clark is not obtuse; he recognizes a smart person when he sees one. Rae's bona fides as a constructive, thoughtful spokesman on national-unity were well established with Clark's government. His contribution as a supporter of Meech Lake had earned him credibility with Mulroney. He had always stressed to the prime minister that regardless of their ideological differences, Ottawa could count on Rae when it came to the goal of making a place for Quebec in the federation.

So even if Clark did find the Ontario premier stealing the show away from Ottawa, even if there were deep, Tory–NDP differences, the constitutional affairs minister would be an admirer of Rae and his deportment through the national-unity mission.

"On the question of Ontario, this is not a paid commercial announcement, I found the premier of Ontario to be consistently helpful," Clark said. "I think sometimes Bob thought things could be made to occur that couldn't. But I didn't find any games being played. He came into this with some very understandable suspicions. . . . I mean, federal–provincial relations with Ontario have been pretty brutal, on both sides, budget-related and other things."

Rae was adamant that this kind of partisanship be kept out of discussion of the constitution. Yes, he may have pushed Ottawa against the wall, but once there, he would join his federal counterparts in taking every hit that was fired against that wall.

"I will have all kinds of arguments with them, on all kinds of issues, but on issues of language, on issues of civil rights, and on issues of the constitution — I think those are issues that are simply too important to be left to partisanship," Rae said. That was something Bob Rae had told former Ontario premier William Davis, back in the early 1980s, and Mulroney would hear the same message. He heard it that tense day in December 1991, when the prime minister paid a call at the Ontario premier's office.

Ontario, to be sure, was no shrinking violet in this round. Maybe the Ontario voters didn't care that much about the constitution, maybe they were more worried about the economy, but Rae was going to pour his heart and soul and all resources into the issue. Rae was certain that the Ontario people had put the constitution far down on their priority lists. He also knew that every time Ontario threw its considerable weight into a presence at the constitutional table, it risked looking like a bully. Rae and his big team of advisers shrugged. Ontario would put the constitution right at the top of its own priority list, and it would devote massive resources to the exercise. It was going to be the big province in this round. Small armies of Ontario bureaucrats would flood into the constitutional talks armed with memos that examined every twist and turn of every decision facing this massive province. Shall we put this clause in this section or that section? Ontario's politicians and bureaucrats could tell you the implications of each decision. But Ontario also had to show its sceptical population that an anchor had been thrown in the troubled economic seas of Canada. This would result in the very controversial, very new idea of "Ontario first."

Bob Rae saw an attitude change his province. He didn't think this new Ontario would be happy to be simply the friendly broker to Ottawa, as Ontario had always been in the past. Ontario was not feeling particularly friendly toward the Tories in Ottawa, and moreover, it couldn't afford to be a broker.

"My reading of things was Ontario increasingly has a sense of its own personality, character." Once, Ontario had been synonomous with Canada. Not Bob Rae's Ontario. He saw the Quebec Tories in caucus standing up for the interests of their own province, forcing Brian Mulroney's hand on economic issues they considered vital to their province. He never saw a revolt by the Ontario Tories. Who were they? What had they done for Ontario lately? Rae was outraged by the Mulroney government policies that had resulted in Ontario being burdened with Ottawa's inability to finance provincial-transfer programs. Describing the Tories as "absconding debtors," Rae adopted a brand of standing up for Ontario that quickly put it at war with Ottawa and made for some tense times between the two governments.

"It's the one region of Canada that's not allowed to speak its own name," Rae says. "If you do, you're accused of being a bully, of being arrogant." Those are precisely the adjectives thrown at Rae's *alter ego*, Jeff Rose. This Rose was chosen for the Ontario government because of his thorns, not for mere decoration.

Rose's friendship with Rae goes back to their days at

the University of Toronto in the 1960s. Their alliance as students was formed out of their mutually earnest, serious outlooks. They worked together on international "teach-ins" in 1966 and 1977 at University College. Their strengths and weaknesses fit together, interlaced. Rae was straightforward — too direct to plot strategy. Rose was happiest when he was running through the labyrinth of strategy upon strategy upon strategy. Rose, for instance, was watched closely by representatives of other provinces, who believed that his every move, every facial expression and gesture, revealed the Ontario position. Rose, unknown to these other provinces, was deliberately setting his face to bluff the others. It's like hockey, he would explain. Sometimes you look straight at the goalie when you have the puck, and then you shoot it off to a teammate on the side. Rae could be thin-skinned about criticism; Rose would barrel ahead, risking antipathy and anger from just about everyone he met. Nowhere did he risk it more than in his head-on clashes with Ottawa.

Rose arrived on the federal–provincial scene with a bang early in 1992. A dinner in Vancouver, at the final wrap-up conference of the Renewal of Canada series, was supposed to be a pleasant, get-to-know-each-other encounter among the top provincial and federal officials who had made their way to this sunny, hazy final meeting on the future of Canada. At a posh restaurant in the centre of Vancouver, a room was set up for all the provincial officials, and places were elegantly set for a crowd of a dozen or so officials. Not intentionally, Rose was seated at one end, Privy Council Clerk Paul Tellier at the other. The evening's idle conversation quickly dissolved, degenerating into a head-to-head match between Tellier and Rose. The other provincial officials just looked on, sliding into their seats as these two aggressive opponents tore strips off each other.

So it went, Ottawa and Ontario at opposite ends, at odds, but still, miraculously, at the same table. And so it was to go through the spring of 1992.

The "process" question was not the only issue that Ontario dominated in Ottawa on March 12, 1992. Rae's deep-seated belief in justice for native people resulted in another score against the federal government that day. But it was also one of the interests that would tug Ontario away from its other interests.

Explicit in Ontario's proposal for the "multilateral" process was the guarantee that native people would be at the table. As a gesture of inclusion to the native groups, Clark and Ottawa had invited the leaders of the four native organizations to breakfast at the March 12 meeting. They came, and thanks to Bob Rae and others, they stayed for the entire negotiations, right up to the bitter end. Clark willingly admits that it was Bob Rae who brought the native people into the process. Rae ventured into the zone where Clark feared to tread. Much to the constitutional affairs minister's surprise, Rae's feelings about native people's inclusion were shared by many of the people around the table. In fact, Rae's spirit of accommodation was shared by some people Ottawa believed to be the most unlikely advocates of native participation.

"Don Cameron thought it was unjust to leave aboriginals out. Joe Ghiz thought it was unjust," Clark said. Others were more eloquent in their silence. "Most people kept their mouths shut. That's what happened . . . In fact, Clyde Wells was the only person who sort of entered the debate on my side."

Ottawa and Newfoundland on the same side? Not likely — and not for long. Clark just didn't believe that all the provinces would be so open to the idea of including aboriginal people. He quickly left Newfoundland to its opposition, backed by a quieter dissent from Alberta, and joined the politically correct side of history.

"I always believed that there was going to be a point at which we had to bring aboriginal people in," Clark said. "I frankly thought, going into that meeting, that it was going to be too early to do it then."

Rae was the one person who had the iron-clad resolve to achieve native justice on his side, who was willing to take the political risk. It turned out to be not much of a risk, though. The Canadian public was bullish on the concept of redress for the native people. But it would be wrong to put this down as a case of Rae trying to curry favour with a guilty white public. It was not a matter of political expediency; the Ontario premier embraced aboriginal rights to his breast as much as he embraced the aspirations of Quebec. In the end, even more.

Rae's commitment to aboriginal people was unwavering and unquestioned, before, during and after this roller-coaster ride of 1992 constitutional negotiations. It reached back to his days as a University of Toronto history student, when he spent his summers at Fort Chimo, now known as Iqaluit, Northwest Territories. It reached back to his days as an opposition leader in the Ontario government, when he made extensive forays into the aboriginal communities once regarded as a political wilderness in Ontario.

"This is a very strong belief of mine," Rae said. He recalled those days in opposition, making official visits in the few short weeks of temperate weather in aboriginal communities in the far northern stretches of Ontario. It was a formative experience. "Every summer, I was going to reserves north of 50. I was the first politician, first leader of a government party, to be making official visits to all the communities on James Bay."

In 1989, Rae, then leader of the NDP opposition in Ontario, wrote a report for *The Globe and Mail* on his experiences during these trips. It is an emotional, very personal recounting of the events that shaped him on those visits north of the 50th parallel.

"The meaning of the phrase 'self-government' suddenly becomes very clear, and its historic parallels with the demands of other colonized people around the world are immediate and visceral. . . . Politicians come and go, bureaucrats come and go, plans are made and unmade. Negotiations are literally endless. No government is really interested in settling anything. There is no requirement, other than that of vague conscience, that governments should."

Those words are a powerful clue to the motives of the Bob Rae who showed up at the constitutional table. This would not be a government that came and went, making and unmaking plans. Rae's commitment was unwavering. A little over one year later, as the premier of Ontario, Rae's first speech in his new top job was to an Assembly of First Nations banquet at the University of Toronto. Again, he drew on his experiences in James Bay and northward.

"I say to you, that when I go north of 50, as a politician, I see communities which have been left, in a sense, in the same colonial status, with all those implications. Powerlessness, mistrust, people forced to speak English, destruction of native customs, destruction of native language, destruction of a native economy — destruction of a way of life that is no different from the destruction that is taking place everywhere where imperial power has been extended.

"And so, as a leader of this province, I tell you that in the time that is given to us, I am determined to do what I can, and our government is determined to do what it can, to see that we come to terms with this history." It was just one day after his installation as premier and Rae made absolutely clear that native rights would be a driving force for him.

"Yesterday I said that I was determined to make progress, and I am. And it was an interesting fact that, of all the things that I said, it was the only thing I said that received a standing ovation, a remarkable spontaneous ovation from the people who were in Convocation Hall yesterday.... I think that says something about where people are coming from. And to me it was a symbol."

Symbol it was. Rae would remain true to the aboriginal cause. In August 1992, it would be Rae, sitting at a borrowed Apple portable computer, who worked out the compromise wording for native self-government. It would be Bob Rae, in his Ottawa office, who told the four major native groups all the secrets shared when the first ministers held meetings without aboriginal people at Harrington Lake. For now, on March 12, the fight for native people's inclusion would be as natural to him as breathing.

"To me, it's not a philosophical point. It's a very practical one. And it's just a feeling I have about the country. I mean, we're not a European country. We are a North American nation in which the fact of our nationhood — who we are — flows from this meeting of different cultures," Rae says. "There were people who had been here for hundreds of years, and their situation and their place in our society is something that we've never come to terms with."

As a politican, Rae was not blinded to the political wisdom of this stand, even if it was new for an Ontario premier — or any provincial politician, for that matter. Ontario, after all, has more than 100,000 native people among its 10 million citizens; an estimated 60,000 in Metro Toronto alone. Moreover, Rae, an experienced ear to social trends, had heard the cry of justice for aboriginal people among the white population.

"The native constituency has huge support in the wider public, emotionally. And I believe that if they had been excluded from the process, or if people had said, 'Well, we'll get to you next time,' the thing wouldn't have had a hope in hell of getting off the ground at all."

Advocacy of native people's interests, though well-placed, did not sit well with many old allies of Ontario, especially Quebec. This was Bob Rae's fate. For every good turn he did for one ally, another ally would be angry. Such was the tug of allegiances.

Being the premier of Ontario is not easy, especially when you are an NDP politician whose politics have always rested on advocacy, not governing. Bob Rae would find that out in the countless series of scandals that beset his government, as inexperienced politicians found their brand of speaking up for the little guy was at odds with trials of governance. Peter Kormos, Shelley Martel, Evelyn Gigantes — the list goes on and on. Every time Rae turned around, another cabinet minister appeared to be in trouble. For some of his fellow politicians, these troubles stirred a sense of deep sympathy. How could you be a major political figure without running into this kind of trouble? Even his most staunch ideological opponents, such as Manitoba's Tory premier, Gary Filmon, were sympathetic to Rae's political plight.

"I can't imagine quite honestly coming home from being away for twelve days and finding out that another minister is gone," Filmon says. The Manitoba premier told Rae that he felt for him — the league of politicians in 1992 felt under siege from the public and the media, obliged to buck each other up in adversity, no matter what their ideological differences.

"Look, Bob," said Filmon to his fellow premier at one point in their constitutional travails. "I've got tremendous sympathy for you. If that happened to me, I don't know what I'd do."

But Rae's efforts on the national-unity crusade were not meeting with rave reviews all over Canada. In Quebec, the belief was that Ontario had finally let down its central Canadian partner. Privately, Quebec officials would whisper to reporters about this "boy scout" from Ontario who was screwing up the entire national-unity mission. Quebec premier Robert Bourassa was no fan of the great multilateral process that Rae had set up. In the summer, in fact, when Quebec finally rejoined the constitutional talks, it would insist that the table be set as Bourassa liked it — with just Ottawa and the provinces as invited guests. Quebec wanted no part of the bigger table that Bob Rae had painstakingly prepared for the rest of the country, with the extra six seats for native groups and territorial politicians. Similarly, Quebec was extremely displeased that Rae had acquiesced to an equal Senate. Quebec's officials were stunned. How could Ontario be so stupid as to give up that much power?

Rae wasn't stupid. Nor was he deaf to this murmured criticism that kept leaking out of Quebec and into the national media and constitutional circles. He saw the Quebec Tories in early July in Ottawa, streaming out of their meeting, obviously displeased with the July 7 constitutional deal and the Ontario premier who had let them down. But that criticism was nothing compared to the withering condemnations of Ontario contained in the famous leaked transcript of conversations between Quebec's bureaucrats.

"And the Ontarians, they are the worst sons of bitches that you can imagine," the transcript stated. Ontarians were also called hypocrites and harassers.

It was a supremely unfair and unjustified attack, even if Ontario had come to be somewhat overbearing at the multilateral talks. It cut Rae to the bone. He was proud of his constitutional advisers; he had braved all kinds of political risks in the past to support the dreams of Quebec. As an NDP opposition leader in Ontario, despite formidable anti-Meech sentiment in his party, Rae was a staunch ally of Meech. So was Rose, for that matter — one of the only labour leaders in Canada to support the Meech Lake accord from 1987 to 1990.

Rae's feelings about Quebec's place in the country are close to his core as a politician and a Canadian. He was the first truly bilingual leader of Ontario in many decades and the only premier from Ontario who was able to go into Quebec and campaign for the cause of Canada in French. But his affection was stretched by Quebec's impatience with his process, and frustrated over Quebec's preference for Mulroney's style of negotiations on the constitution, with Ottawa at the centre and provinces at the periphery.

Rae was famed and well-respected in other parts of the country for being direct and blunt. He did not spare Quebec any of this directness. He would say to Bourassa in their telephone conversations: "No one's betraying you, no one's stabbing you in the back. We're all in this process together. We're trying to work this thing through."

Neither Bourassa nor Quebec was placated by Rae's assurances. Behind his back, Quebec government officials condemned his multilateral exercise as a wasteful detour. To his face, Rae was told that his process was "very interesting, very democratic," or "Premier, you're very generous."

Rae wasn't fooled. He tried to tell Bourassa that a deal reached without the help of the other provinces would end in the same type of failure as Meech. "Look," he said. "This process has got to have credibility in English Canada. Whatever you're being told by the prime minister, it won't work in my province and you can't rely on that."

Wistfully, Quebec would get the word out, loud enough for Ontario to hear, that David Peterson had been such an understanding man, such a statesman. Quebec missed David Peterson. Quebec wanted Peterson back. Quebec wanted Meech back — not all these add-ons, courtesy of this new NDP premier.

Rae's response? "You may not agree with me, you may not like me, you may prefer to deal with another premier. I'm here, and I consider myself to be a good friend of Quebec's and I'm trying to give you good advice."

Indeed, Rae would feel vindicated by events. The multilateral track did work in the end — the premiers reached a deal that produced euphoria in the rest of Canada and an acceptance of Quebec. The referendum track, devised by Mulroney, failed dismally, and all of Canada was united in rejection. Rae truly believed that he had fought for the right course to preserve Quebec's place in the federation, and that Mulroney had not.

Rae was not a paragon of selflessness in the national-unity exercise. There were times, in fact, when he could seem positively self-absorbed, incredibly thin-skinned for the business he had entered. Among the people at the constitutional negotiations, his oversensitivity was legend.

In Edmonton, in early May, the heat from the smaller provinces was being turned up on Ontario. Out in front of the cameras, Alberta's Jim Horsman gave an anti-Ontario diatribe, specially prepared for home consumption in Alberta. This was, after all, Horsman's city, and he was going to make sure that Rae knew what he was up against, if Ontario was going to continue to block the Triple E Senate in these early stages of the negotiations.

"If it is going to be insistence of central Canada to maintain those strains, then the country will be put at risk in the long term."

Inside the meeting, as the negotiations got under way, Horsman received a note from Rae, angrily pointing out that Alberta should watch its rhetoric when it appeared in front of the national media. Horsman's ire was raised as he read the warning. Rae peevishly pointed out that only Ontario could speak for Ontario's beliefs and that Alberta had no right to attribute motives to his province. Furthermore, Rae told Horsman, there had been an agreement that only Joe Clark would do the talking for the constitutional exercise. Horsman's fury at Ontario was only fed by this dispatch from Rae. "Forget it," he thought, stuffing the note in with his other papers. "This is my province."

Alberta and some of the other provinces weren't above a little pettiness themselves. Clark would get notes from Alberta and Manitoba, for instance, protesting the fact that Ontario's Bob Rae was getting too much attention, too much time on the constitutional soapbox. Clark had to be careful, though. This was a premier, and he was owed a bit more, it seemed, for taking time out from premiership to sail on the multilateral boat.

This was another risk for Ontario. Rae said that the constitution was not a big priority for his province, yet he himself devoted the time to this exercise. Roy Romanow had been asked to stay away from the talks. In Saskatchewan, early in 1992, Clark himself sat on the couch in the premier's office, hands on his knees, and explained why it was better that premiers stay out of the multilateral limelight.

"Look, I've almost got enough premiers here," Clark told Romanow. "If you want to come, you can. But you understand the problem. I have a certain authority which I exercise as well as I can, but that authority becomes a little more difficult, the sense of balance in the room becomes a little more difficult, the more premiers that are there."

Romanow nodded. Okay, he would stay away. He would send Saskatchewan justice minister Bob Mitchell, who would emerge as the most liked, most trusted, most decent man in the constitutional exercise. Still, with no slight intended towards Bob Mitchell, Clark later regretted a request that could have been viewed as an insult by Romanow.

"I underestimated both the intensity of his interest in being part of the process," Clark said, "and how effective he could be when he got there. . . . He had been through all these things and he did bring a special authority."

Romanow, for his part, was surprised that his NDP colleague, Bob Rae, took so much time out from the day-to-day business of government to pursue the national-unity quest, which he knew the people of Ontario did not really want. Many would suggest that Rae was simply trying to escape the dismal life of governing Ontario in the recession to pursue life under the big lights, talking about the "big stuff" in the constitution.

For all the talk of the new NDP bloc in the country, all the bally-hoo in 1991 about the emergence of three NDP governments, controlling almost 50 per cent of the Canadian population, the alliance would be more imagined than real. Between Saskatchewan, British Columbia and Ontario, there was little cohesion among the socialists. In fact, they would have less in common than the Western provinces had in their alliance or even the Maritime provinces. History and geography separate these NDP governments more than their partisan politics could ever unite them.

Rae, as the head of the largest province, could lay a reasonable claim on the leadership of the NDP bloc. But the relations between Saskatchewan and Ontario are complicated on that issue.

Romanow explains: "New Democrats make a mistake in believing that all New Democrats are the same in their outlook on issues. And we are not...I think there's always been a belief that Saskatchewan was the motherland, it was Tommy Douglas's homeland...

"A prairie New Democrat comes from a different history. I mean, we've had a history of governance here. That means choices, and hard choices.... But Bob has not come from that tradition."

British Columbia, too, has its own history of governance and its own geographic and philosophical differences with its New Democratic partners east of the Rockies.

Together, these three New Democratic governments took three different positions on the most crucial controversy of the 1992 negotiations — Senate reform. Saskatchewan was a Triple E province, Ontario was in favour of an "equitable" Senate, and British Columbia was pushing its project for a five-region Senate, with itself as one region. The NDP bloc couldn't have been more fragmented.

On a night late in June, after the three NDP premiers had held a meeting with the prime minister and other first ministers at 24 Sussex Drive, they decided to dine together in the dark elegance of Ottawa's Le Jardin restaurant. Maybe these three diverse interests could come together. But what appeared to be a rare moment of NDP solidarity quickly degenerated into a battle of the socialists. Food as inelegant as a simple hot potato would never be served in the plush luxury of Le Jardin, and it certainly wouldn't be handled without a knife and fork. But the Senate issue was a hot potato this night, and these NDP premiers, plus B.C.'s Moe Sihota, kept trying to toss the potato into each other's hands as the night wore on.

"It's your problem," Romanow would say to Rae. "You're just putting Ontario's selfish need for power in front of the West." Ontario was the big hold-out, he said. "It's your problem," Rae would tell Romanow, "for getting on this ridiculous Triple E bandwagon." If Saskatchewan had abandoned the Triple E group, the country would have had a deal long ago, Rae said. "It's your problem," they would tell British Columbia's Mike Harcourt, because his province, by going to one side or another, could seal the fate of this dispute.

New Brunswick's premier, Frank McKenna, was at the dinner as an onlooker. He had been invited because he was well-liked by the other premiers. It wasn't over-looked, either, that McKenna had close ties to Mul-roney and Bourassa, and could be a conduit for some of that Ottawa or Quebec influence in the NDP circle. As the night wore on, the debate between Romanow and Rae became heated, beyond a mere friendly dispute among NDP partisans. The antagonism was building to a crescendo.

McKenna tried to lighten the mood. "Are you guys really from the same party?" he asked. "Is this what your conventions are like?"

The mood was lifted a little bit, but it wouldn't be long before Rae departed. He left so quickly and so abruptly, that the bill hadn't yet been paid. Add some NDP folklore to the social history of the constitution. Ontario walked out without paying the bill. Saskatchewan's Roy Romanow only had $20 in his pocket to pay for his share. British Columbia's Mike

Harcourt paid the tab for all his NDP colleagues. "We're the goose that lays the golden egg for Canada," Harcourt was fond of saying. The goose was the sitting duck that night, when it came to paying up.

"He stiffed us," the other premiers would say about Rae when they spoke to "The Journal" in two documentary programs aired in October. Later, they would proclaim jokingly that they didn't mind having Ontario as an absconding debtor — Sihota would joke that he was glad he had something to hold over Rae's head.

Rae was often the target of other politicians, even premiers, and he did not like the attacks one bit. Gary Filmon, for instance, found out that Ontario's premier paid a lot of attention to the way he was portrayed by others in front of the television cameras.

On July 3, at a meeting at Toronto's Airport Hilton Hotel, Rae was unprepared for the attack that Western premiers staged upon him on his own ground. Going into this very difficult meeting, Filmon and Saskatchewan's premier, Roy Romanow, accused Rae of being a stubborn hold-out on Senate reform merely because of his own selfish interests.

The first hour of that meeting was not pleasant. Rae was sulking, angry that he had been ridiculed in front of the national cameras. His thin skin was showing. But even so, he had come around to the idea of an equal Senate by the end of that day. Filmon, from then on, would regard Rae as a man of integrity at the constitutional table.

"From that point on, I would literally turn to Bob every time I felt that there was an issue upon which he could play a pivotal role."

Filmon had touched upon the point that would spell the difference between success and failure in the constitutional talks, and Rae respected him and the Triple E Senate group enough to bend his opposition.

As we have seen, respect, that vital component of political discourse, was largely absent from the national-unity debate between the politicians and the public in 1992. The public didn't respect the politicians and the politicians, in turn, didn't respect the public that so despised them. But, despite all the odds against it, respect did build among the politicians who were trying to shape the new national-unity deal. Rae showed that he respected the needs of his Western colleagues; they respected him in exchange.

Respect and faith were the important virtues in the national-unity debate of 1992, and their lack would be felt in the referendum campaign that pitted the public against the politicians.

It was only respect and faith, however — not conviction — that led Bob Rae to support the Triple E Senate religion. It was his respect for the plight and convictions of his Western colleagues, not his own conversion, that made Bob Rae into a supporter of an equal Senate.

Canada was grappling with three sets of grievances in the 1992 national-unity mission: Quebec's grievances were one problem; aboriginal people's grievances were another; the third was the cry of alienation from the West and from the smaller provinces. Rae would be a champion of the first two causes, sympathetic to and crusading for justice for Quebec and aboriginal people. He would never see the grievances of the smaller provinces as being on the same scale of importance.

The distinction is clear for him. Canada's native people, and Quebec, have been cast in the history books as the vanquished Canadians, overtaken by the victorious English Canada. Rae fervently believes that the road to peace in Canada must start with rewriting this erroneous history, to see these "conquered" Canadians as partners in the federation. On the other hand, in Rae's view, the West has never known the oppression of the vanquished. People in the West, though, would argue that the status of conquered provinces does in fact run deep in the blood of the Prairie provinces, and that an equal Senate would help rewrite that injustice of history.

For Rae, the most persuasive person on this argument was his trusted NDP colleague from Saskatchewan, Bob Mitchell. It was Mitchell, at the May meetings in Toronto, who spoke most eloquently and passionately to Rae about the historic injustice felt by the West. Angrily, Mitchell chided Rae for standing in the way of righting this wrong. Mitchell was outraged that Rae was pretending to understand the West. He told Rae about the sense of alienation and exclusion that pervades the mentality of Westerners. He emotionally recounted how a person growing up in the West was always made to feel like a second-class Canadian, left out of the decisions of the federation.

It would take more than a month for Rae to come to accept the idea of an equal Senate, but Mitchell's words had taken root that night. The depth of this Saskatchewan man's convictions stirred respect and admiration in Rae. Nor were there any hard feelings between Rae and Mitchell over this skirmish. The two continued to trust each other as honourable negotiators. Rae could be influenced by Mitchell because he respected him. But he would never, ever share Mitchell's deep convictions about the necessity of equality in the Senate. He simply accepted the fact that Mitchell and the other provinces needed it. That was as far as he could go — and it was far enough.

"I think there was a lot that was taken on faith," said Joe Clark. "And I guess that's what really has to happen." Clark himself, even as an Albertan, would never truly embrace the idea of equality in the Senate as a principle. "The leap was never made," Clark said. Not by Rae and not by Ottawa.

Many other times this happened during the constitutional talks. Many other disputes would have to be settled by someone saying: "I don't believe what you believe, but I believe what you say."

It's an important point — a crucial distinction. For the politicians devoted to the national-unity exercise in 1992, that concession, that leap of faith, was the "miracle" of their negotiations. As politicians, they knew how difficult it was to make the leap into accepting another person's view even if you don't share it.

But for the people on the No side, such as Reform Party leader Preston Manning, or B.C. Liberal Party leader Gordon Wilson, a leap of faith looked like an absence of conviction. A true constitution, in their minds, would be made up of all the shared convictions of the nation, the fundamental principles embraced by everyone. The best the politicians could do in 1992, though, was accept — not fully embrace — the fundamental principles of one another. It would allow Manning to dismiss the Charlottetown deal as "compromise upon compromise upon compromise." And the constitutional negotiators would just stare incredulously at this allegation. "Of course it is. That's what the national-unity business is all about."

If Rae wasn't worried about embracing the principles of an equal Senate, he still had to worry about politics. How on earth could he ever explain to Ontario voters that the number of Ontario senators had fallen to six from twenty-four? It seemed every time there had to be a price paid for progress in Canada, Ontario picked up the tab. No province had more to lose from changes to the status quo. Ontario had generally been well-served by confederation; it represented the old, established order, where people had grown up to respect politicians, and to think of themselves as Canadians before they were Ontarians. That was why Rae's Ontario-first policy was so jarring. Canada and Ontario used to mean the same thing. Now times were changing, partly because Ottawa and Ontario were political opponents, partly because Rae drew on some lessons from Meech.

When Peterson was hailed as the "big guy" from Ontario in June 1990, it was because he gave up some Senate seats in that doomed deal. In 1992, the "big guy's" Senate gesture loomed over Rae, like Marley's ghost in Dickens's *A Christmas Carol.* Peterson gave up Senate seats, and look what happened to him. The chains rattled noisily in the rooms where Ontario's small army of officials and aides planned political strategy. Even if Rae or Rose didn't really believe that this was the only cause of David Peterson's fall from grace with the Ontario electorate, they just weren't going to risk another loss for Ontario in the Senate. All around Rae, the political advisers were telling him: "Don't do it. Don't do what Peterson did."

Peterson's real mistake was not in giving up the Senate seats. It was in appearing far too cosy with Brian Mulroney and Robert Bourassa. That wouldn't be Rae's mistake — at least not until the very end of this exercise, when he joined their Yes crusade for the referendum. Rae believed that the cry of alienation from the West had more to do with politics than with history. To Rae, the anger stirred up in the West was not unlike his own, current antipathy to the Tories' political presence in Ottawa. Elections solved that kind of alienation, not constitutions.

This was also the line that he took with all the equality-seekers who began to clamber on the No bandwagon as the referendum campaign got under way. As a fervent devotee of the Charter of Rights and Freedoms,

Rae understood the hunger for equality that had risen up in Canada in the wake of the charter. He saw the legitimacy of the cause of women, of the disabled, of labour groups, of every interest that was demanding equality from the constitution.

Judy Rebick, head of the National Action Committee on the Status of Women, goes back a long way with Bob Rae. She was an NDP activist and a candidate on Rae's team in the 1987 Ontario election. She was reasonably positive that Rae was pushing for many of the same values she cherished, gender equality being her main goal. Reports came to Rebick that the Ontario premier was using gender equality as a bargaining chip in the Senate debate. She was grateful and relieved.

"Rae did fight. He fought on the gender stuff in the Senate and he fought on the Canada clause, changes to the Canada clause. Maybe not exactly what we wanted to see, but to strengthen it."

But after the talks were over, Rae came back to Rebick and told her that he hadn't been able to get everything.

"I fought," he said to Rebick. "But I couldn't walk away from the table over it. I didn't have support from anyone else."

Rebick did not feel betrayed by this. She appreciated the attempt and the candour. "I accept that. I mean, if I'd been there, I would have walked away from the table, because that was my constituency, right? But it's not his."

She would accept Rae's actions, but she would not accept the Charlottetown deal, putting her at odds with her old NDP ally. It was a break that had to be made, she told reporters, because the women of NAC simply "choked" at the idea of accepting what they saw as the offences against equality in the deal.

Rae believes that Rebick and her group were asking too much from the constitution. So are many of the country's equality-seekers, or the so-called Charter Canadians, who have come to see the constitution as a guarantee of absolute and wide-ranging equality.

"The constitution didn't give us medicare," says Rae. "You can't use the constitution as a substitute for political struggle. Or for collective struggle, whether it's at the provincial level or in other ways. The best you can get out of a constitution, it seems to me, is some protection and an expression of principle and another lever that can be used to advance a cause."

However, Rae's ideas of equality merged far better with Rebick's than they did with the other brand of equality championed in the referendum, by former prime minister Pierre Trudeau and his followers. Even if Rae was an admirer of the Charter of Rights and Freedoms, he was no admirer of Trudeau, its architect. He has nothing good to say about the type of equal Canada envisioned by Trudeau.

"Intellectually, I think his vision is completely inadequate as an expression of a diverse view of the country," Rae says.

Once upon a time, a young Bob Rae, a student and a voracious political reader, saw Trudeau as an ideological hero. During the late 1960s, when Trudeau was dreaming of his "just society," he fired up Rae's imagination as well. Arriving as a young MP in Ottawa in 1978, Rae finally got a chance to meet Trudeau. He was profoundly disappointed. First of all, Trudeau was haughty and cold. He couldn't have cared less about Rae or anyone else outside his own, tight little circle. Then Rae watched his performance in Ottawa, and found him a rigid-thinking demagogue, capitalizing on cute rhetorical tricks and clever devices instead of his intellect.

These were the very devices that Rae accused Trudeau of using during the referendum campaign, when the former prime minister waded in with his rocket-launcher of protest against the Charlottetown deal, as an offence against equality. Rae will never forgive Trudeau for inciting the anti-French element in Canadian society with his mention of Quebec blackmail.

"He made anti-French feeling respectable. For that I will never forgive him. Because he must have known, any responsible person would know, that to use the kind of arguments he was making, the language that he was using, would create that resonance."

Rae still seethes over Trudeau's foray. "Maybe it's some psychological thing with him. It's something going on inside himself . . . I disagreed with him about a bunch of things during my political life. But this to me was the worst."

Only weeks before Trudeau jumped, feet first, into the referendum debate, Rae bumped into him at the University of Toronto's Hart House. They were both there to hear a speech. Rae sauntered over to extend cool greetings.

"Hello, nice to see you," Rae said, shaking Trudeau's hand.

"Hello, nice to see you too," Trudeau answered.

Both men stood there smiling artificially at each other. There was an awkward pause. Then Trudeau said: "Well, now that we've told that lie, what else have we got to talk about?"

Rae's visceral reaction to Trudeau's intervention made for some of the most heated headlines from the Yes campaigners in the referendum debate. Only Brian Mulroney would be more outraged and angry and dismissive of the former prime minister. Rae, however, unlike Brian Mulroney, was not slipping comfortably into the campaign for Canada that was fuelling the Yes side. He still wasn't even sure he liked the idea of a referendum. Like many of the people who have sat at the first ministers' table, including Mulroney, Rae has been poring over the old Confederation debates, trying to use history as a guidepost for the future. Canada is lucky that the first Charlottetown deal wasn't put to a national referendum, he says.

"The same criticisms that people make of the Charlottetown accord were exactly what people were saying about Confederation in 1867. And the same defences were being made too." The fathers of Confederation were locked in debates over an elected Senate, and they went to the people with their deal, pleading their case of imperfection. For all the talk about the new Ontario, with its new personality as province in its own right, Bob Rae would make his province the voice of Canada in the talks, just as old Upper Canada had been in the Confederation deal.

This new Ontario would, in fact, act in the mysterious absence of Ottawa at times, overwhelming other provinces with sheer numbers and preparation. That used to be Ottawa's job. Rae, sitting at Mulroney's side in the final leg of negotiations, would be called upon to explain, to cajole, in the interests of Canada. For the final days, it would be Bob Rae, sitting at a piano, entertaining the other politicians while they waited for some issue to be settled; it would be Bob Rae, sitting at a borrowed computer, helping to work out a deal on native self-government. And when it was all over, Rae would be at Brian Mulroney's side, echoing the need for a national referendum.

In retrospect, Rae believes that the euphoria and relief of the politicians at Charlottetown in 1992 outweighed any logical consideration of the referendum. Ontario didn't even examine the strategic implications of a referendum. After all Ontario's dominance of the constitutional negotiations, the way it rushed in to fill

the vacuum created by Ottawa's absence, the referendum decision simply slipped by Ontario's strategic net.

Would he do it again? Probably not. Would he go
through the referendum campaign the way he did, with
Ottawa in the lead and provinces at the periphery?
Absolutely not. It was, in his words, "out of control."

"There was no collective strategy for the referendum.
After Charlottetown, we didn't have any more input.
We were out," Rae says. "Afterwards, we were just one
more voice crying, crying one way or the other, in the
wilderness."

The most plaintive of those cries came from Rae
himself, at the very end of the referendum campaign,
and it revolved around that delicate balance of trust
between the electors and the elected. It was almost too
delicate a message for the unsubtle headlines that
accompanied it — Rae appeared to be begging for
scraps of trust. He was actually saying something important about the nature of politics in Canada. Respect,
which breeds trust, works both ways in Canadian politics. And the country was never going to get its act
together until the leaders and the led in Canada
learned a bit about respect and mutual trust.

"I think it's time for all of us in public life to talk
about what it means in terms of the work we do, the job
we do," Rae told *Toronto Star* columnist Thomas
Walkom. "I really think it's important for us to restore
a sense of balance and a sense of trust as much as we
can. You know, trust is a two-way street. We're trusting
people in this referendum with exercising their sound
judgment."

The trust offered to the public by politicians such as
Rae was not the grudging type of trust; it was the trust
that grows out of faith in politics. And the loss of the
referendum would be a blow to that faith. Just as the
public would have to sit down and examine the nature

of the Canadian political system, so would the politicians. Bridges needed to be built, and the bridge-building had to start on both sides.

The public was going to have to show that it was making the first few moves towards restoring its faith in politics, just as the politicians were going to have to make those gestures too. But as some bridges were going up, others were coming down. The post-referendum era in Canada would find Ontario and Ottawa at loggerheads again. A few months later, Rae would bid farewell to Brian Mulroney the politician as a man who had done economic harm to the country. There were a few brief words of praise for the departing prime minister, his fellow Yes campaigner, and then Rae declared: "His whole concept of Canada's relationship with the American economy has deprived us of our own voice. We have lost under his leadership the capacity to speak truly as a country."

And inside the Ontario government, even as Mulroney was leaving office, Rose and the bureaucracy were cranking up to fight Ottawa again on the so-called "economic constitution," the battle of free trade and Tory fiscal policy.

Rae got his wish that Ontario be the big province. The failing of the national-unity mission, he said, was that it wasn't big enough. Ontario and Canada had reached out to pull as many people as possible into the constitution, but all the tugging in different directions left many people out.

"The whole thing was a big step toward inclusiveness. It could have been bigger. We could have done more."

But Rae had no intention of doing anything more on the constitution in the wake of the Charlottetown defeat. Instead, he had to turn his attention to the economic problems plaguing his province and the political price he was going to pay for tackling Ontario's deficit. The government that tried to be so inclusive in the constitutional process found in the wake of 1992 that its protective left wing could no longer encompass many of the interests it fought to protect. The Canadian Auto Workers ended their alliance with Rae's government; the public-sector unions were at war with Rae over his bid to cut jobs and bring in a "social contract" for provincial employees. In Ottawa, cracks started to appear in the once-solid friendship between the federal New Democrats and the Ontario New Democrats. Many of the federal NDP politicians, notably finance critic Steven Langdon, believed that Rae was headed down a path away from his socialist roots.

Rae got his wish in one way — this Ontario was not a captive of Ottawa's interests any longer. For while Ottawa was consumed by the Quebec question, its interests revolving around the balance between French and English Canada, those preoccupations were distant from Ontario's thinking in the early 1990s. The problems of Quebec might as well have been taking place in another nation.

4

Quebec:
A Problem of Translation

What does Quebec want?

For decades, this was the question that drove the never-ending debate over national unity in Canada. The answer to that question was supposed to be the cipher key, the Rosetta stone, in the quest to keep English and French Canada united. But in June 1990, as the Meech Lake constitutional accord was dying its spectacular death all over Canada, Quebec premier Robert Bourassa turned the question upside-down. He offered a translation, to be used by the country in the new constitutional politics of the 1990s.

"Since 1985, we've been asked what does Canada want and we are still waiting for their answer," said Bourassa, standing hollow-eyed in the Quebec National Assembly, just starting to absorb the depth of Meech's defeat. The challenge had enormous implications. With these words, Bourassa had set in motion a chain of events that encircled and captured Canada through most of 1992.

Bourassa had no idea what he was starting when he

asked Canada to redefine itself for the future; no idea just how much this challenge would be seized upon by other governments, in the West, in Ontario and in the Atlantic provinces. For two whole years, politicians from all over the country, aboriginal leaders and territorial leaders would pitch themselves headlong into the effort to come up with a reply for Bourassa.

Meanwhile, Quebec itself would continue to have no idea what it started; how the rest of the country was answering the question: "What does Canada want?" For while Bourassa had declared that Quebec knew what it wanted, the province spent its time from 1990 to 1992 in the same exercise as the rest of the country. Separately, in splendid isolation, the rest of Canada was figuring out what it wanted, while Quebec was struggling with a new definition of what it wanted out of the federation. Quebec asked the question of the rest of Canada, and then busily turned to its own problems while the country came up with a reply. Something serious got lost in the translation.

What did Quebec want after the death of the Meech Lake accord?

Most of all, it wanted Meech back. It wanted to pretend that the whole sorry incident had never happened. The Meech Lake accord, reached in 1987 by unanimous agreement, was supposed to make Quebec a full signatory to the constitution, a fulfilment of Prime Minister Brian Mulroney's promise to bring Quebec into Canada with "honour and enthusiasm." The death of this accord was a profound loss for Quebec. The magnitude of the rejection shaped everything that Quebec did on the constitutional front from 1990 to 1992. Meech's demise was paired with the events of 1981, when Premier René Lévesque had refused to sign the constitution patriated by former prime minister Pierre Trudeau. Both events, ten years apart, were uppermost in the mind of Bourassa's government when it considered its place in the Canadian federation. The death of Meech and the 1981 constitution were an illustration that Quebec just didn't fit into the rest of the country. But it desperately wanted to fit — Bourassa and his government made that clear, over and over again.

In the view of Quebec, every national-unity exercise in Canada had to be aimed first and foremost at righting the wrongs of these years, of finding a place for Quebec in the federation. So what did Quebec's government want in 1992? It wanted in; it wanted to fit. How did it intend to do that after the death of Meech? Quebec wanted Meech *plus*.

It took almost two years and hundreds of hours of hearings and debates to define *plus* in Quebec's constitutional language. The most intensive effort was launched by the Belanger–Campeau commission, a huge thirty-seven-member group of politicians and non-politicians; Quebec nationalists and Quebec federalists; federal members of parliament and provincial members of the National Assembly. Its major result was not "what" Quebec wanted, but "when" it wanted it. Belanger–Campeau decreed that the province of Quebec must hold a referendum on sovereignty no later than October 1992.

But Belanger–Campeau didn't entirely ignore the "what" question. The commission also gave the rest of Canada a bit of prodding about what Quebec expected to see in a national-unity deal. Yes, Quebec was interested in the timing of the offer from the rest of Canada, but it couldn't just be any old offer. There were certain minimum demands. Quebec was clamouring for the right to be a self-determining nation within Canada, with all the rights and powers that the federation could spare. From Belanger–Campeau to the ordinary citizen in the streets of Rimouski, every Quebecker was talking about the major demands to be made on Canada if the French-speaking province were to remain part of the country.

Of course Quebec wanted Meech back, especially the precious right to veto any major changes to the Canadian federation. The veto is a holy grail of Quebec's constitutional quest. It is the tool that carves out Quebec's place in the country as a partner in federation, not just one province among others. Quebec's view of the country is of two founding nations — English and French. The history of the country, from Quebec's perspective, is a struggle to maintain this balance. The English may have the French population outnumbered, but nothing changes the fact, in Quebec's view, that Canada is the result of a pact between two cultures. If there were to be any basic changes to the shape of Canada, Quebec wanted to make sure that its consent was needed. You don't change a partnership without the approval of one of the partners. Quebec needs a veto for any changes that might affect the partnership.

Back in 1987, when the Meech Lake accord was being negotiated, Mulroney and the other premiers knew that it would be impossible to give Quebec a privilege that the other provinces didn't have. Quebec may have seen itself as the French partner in Canada, but the rest of the country has tended to see it as one province among ten. Canada has been perpetually locked in this struggle over the federal "deal" — is it two partners, or ten equal provinces?

The Meech Lake accord tried to saw the problem right down the middle. If Quebec wanted a veto, everybody would get a veto. Do you want to change the Senate in the future? Quebec could say no, but so could all the other provinces. Do you want to let new provinces into the federation? Quebec could say no, but so could all the other provinces. Most changes in the constitution only require that seven provinces, representing 50 per cent of the Canadian population, say yes to any changes. This is the magical amending formula. Only a few basic things — the role of the Queen, adjusting the delicate formula to amend the constitution — require all provinces' consent. Under Meech, a few more things were added to that list of basics. Changes to the Senate and the admission of new provinces were the new items. Quebec got its veto, and in the interests of keeping the peace with the ten-equal-partners proponents, everyone else got a veto too.

Then there was the whole distinct-society question. If you asked any Canadian in 1990: "What was Meech all about? What did Quebec want?" the answer would be two words — distinct society. Quebec wanted the constitution to enshrine this idea of the province as the French partner in the federation; it wanted the courts to see that Quebec needed a special place to ensure its continued partnership in the pact.

In the rest of the country, though, this was another irritant to that notion that Canada is ten equal provinces, not two equal partners. "Distinct society" sounded an awful lot like special status for one province. Somehow, in the 1990s, Canada had to find a way to make Quebec distinct, but not special. This task was complicated by the fact that Quebec was figuring out even more ways to ensure its distinctiveness. While the rest of the country was busy deciding the answer to Bourassa's question, the province of Quebec was busy filling in a lot of blanks about what it meant to be distinct. The key to a distinct society was power — lots of it. If Quebec were really to be a distinct society in Canada, it would have to wrest some powers away from the dominant federal government. "Domineering federalism" was a popular catchphrase in Quebec, a shorthand way of cursing the forces that would deny Quebec's distinctiveness.

"Domineering federalism" was the phrase used in the famous report by the Quebec Liberal Party's own study of the constitution, headed by Jean Allaire. The Allaire report, as it was called, weighed into the national-unity debate in early 1992 with a huge list of powers that were supposed to guarantee Quebec's place as a distinct society in the 1990s, and end the domineering feder- alism. A staggering total of twenty-two powers were demanded by Quebec, ranging from internal, admin- istrative functions, such as marriage and divorce law, to huge powers, such as immigration and energy.

There was no question in 1992 that Quebec's major demand was power. It wanted Meech plus, and the plus was all about power. Unfortunately, however, the rest of Canada translated the "plus" in a different fashion.

For the first two years of the 1990s, the political debate over unity was like an updated version of the classic movie *It's a Wonderful Life*. Quebec was like the charac- ter of George Bailey, played by Jimmy Stewart in that film. Like George Bailey, the province of Quebec had come to the brink, mulling over a future that looked bleak and hopeless. Bailey had been thrust to the brink by a financial catastrophe; Quebec, in 1990, was pushed to the edge by the death of the Meech Lake accord. Bailey was sure that the future held nothing but sorrow and disgrace for him; Quebec was certain that a con- tinued life in Canada was filled with more humiliation and rejection.

In the movie, Bailey is pulled back from the brink by a glimpse of an imaginary world — a world without George Bailey in it. In Canada, from 1990 to 1992,

Quebec was treated to a glimpse of how Canada would look without the French-speaking province in it; how the federation would define itself without its Quebec partner. This was the world created in that travelling road show known as the "multilateral ministerial conferences." And just as the imaginary world unfolded in a dramatically different fashion for George Bailey in the movie, the absence of Quebec was keenly felt, and made a profound difference. The constitutional world without Quebec, the world with ten instead of eleven negotiators, looked a lot different from the kind of country that would have been created if Quebec had been at the table.

In the first place, the rest of Canada was intent on changing the Senate. Frustration with the Senate was definitely an English Canadian phenomenon, not a Quebec obsession. It was rooted in another big difference between Quebec and the rest of Canada, revolving around faith in politics.

Canadians outside Quebec were enormously cynical about their politicians. The world of politics was viewed as a shadowy underworld of deals and deal-makers. When politicians weren't preoccupied with abandoning their principles, they were feathering their nests with taxpayer-financed perks and privileges. The English Canadian media spent a lot of time chasing down scandals and poring through government business to find out where the taxpayers' dollars were being misused. Complicated stories about conflicts of interest, or details on cabinet ministers' travel, were given prominent display in the English Canadian press.

Quebec media, on the other hand, were not nearly as interested in such stories. Reports on the first-class air travel of cabinet ministers or the perks of public office were not seen much at all in the French press.

The difference in attitude showed up even in the way

that the French and English reporters performed their duties in the lobby of the House of Commons. Quebec reporters would spend a long time in the scrums, trying to get answers and rationales from the politicians. The exchanges between politicians and reporters were often more like conversations, or debates, and the object was to examine the motive behind the act, to present the debate in distilled fashion.

The English Canadian reporters, on the other hand, were far more likely to pursue questions as a means of getting a statement, or a quote, or an "official" word on an event. Politicians' statements would be duly recorded, then presented to the readers or viewers for their own interpretation.

Here is how that style ended up in the two very different media: Quebec's political stories revolved around what the politicians were doing; English Canada's political stories revolved around what the politicians were saying. This difference exposed the major fault line between English and French attitudes to politics in the 1990s. Cynicism and scepticism were rife in English Canada; in Quebec, faith in politics and the élites was more or less intact. It was a difference that divided the Albertan Joe Clark from the Quebecker Brian Mulroney. It was a difference that made Senate reform a hot topic in English Canada, and a yawning bore in Quebec. So, as the rest of the country prepared to answer the question: "What does Canada want?" it first had to wrestle with Senate reform. This was the first hint to Quebec that a world without the French-speaking province would look very different indeed.

It wasn't only that Quebec didn't care about the Senate, it was that its absence left its old partner, Ontario, all alone and isolated to fight against the campaign for an equal Senate. In the days when Quebec had been at the table, Ontario and Quebec could simply link up as Central Canadian allies, dominant in the federation, and say a quick and decisive no to any crusade for Senate equality. But without Quebec there, the dynamics of the constitutional table were changed. Ontario was outnumbered. It couldn't simply say no while the rest of the country was clamouring for changes. Without its old Central Canadian ally, Ontario was on the run from the Senate reformers.

Only much, much later, when it was too late, did Quebec realize how much its absence had affected the debate over the Senate. The Quebec government was shocked to find out, in July 1992, that Ontario had gone along with Senate equality. Quebec had merely assumed that its partner would wage the fight alone, but Ontario just couldn't wage the battle in isolation. Maybe Quebec didn't care that much about the Senate, but Ontario learned very quickly in 1992 that the rest of the country cared very, very much about overhauling the Senate. It had to acquiesce.

Even on issues that did matter to Quebec, such as the power question, the absence of Quebec changed the equation.

Not all provinces outside Quebec were big fans of strong, central government. The grievance against "domineering federalism" was being heard in the West as well, particularly in British Columbia and Alberta. B.C. premier Michael Harcourt had established a common cause with Quebec very early in the national-unity game, when he and Bourassa agreed that their two provinces wanted to be *maîtres chez nous,* masters of their own houses. Alberta was also sympathetic to the struggle for more provincial powers, especially over natural resources. Alberta was interested in keeping tight control of its oil; Quebec cherished the dream of hydro self-sufficiency, with its massive mega-projects in the Quebec North.

But even with British Columbia and Alberta as strong allies of decentralization, those forces were outnumbered at the table in Quebec's absence. B.C. constitutional affairs minister Moe Sihota often lamented that Quebec was not there to lend its strength to the power argument; he thought it was an ideal way to lure the French province back to negotiations *à onze* again. More deeply, though, he lamented that Quebec was not travelling on the same journey as the rest of Canada to define itself. It wasn't only the end deal that would change Canada, it was the process of reaching that deal. Like anything in life, the real learning and real changes take place on the way to a goal, not when the goal is reached. Sihota truly regretted that Quebec and the rest of Canada were going through their own educations alone, changing in isolation. He was sorry that while the rest of the provinces were learning to get along with each other throughout the months of the multilateral process, Quebec didn't have a chance to build that new friendship along with them.

"There was a genuine camaraderie that developed at the end of the day between B.C., the other three Western governments and the others. It's sad to see that Quebec, by being absent from the process, missed out."

In his trademark, West Coast language, Sihota explains how Quebec hurt its own cause by absenting itself. "They took a negotiating position which was out of step with the head space of the governments that were at the table."

Had Quebec been at the table, says Sihota, they would have learned directly about the other issues confronting the nation. Once they stayed away, they lost sight of the fact that other provinces had their own constitutional demands. Quebec, on its own, merely concentrated on its own needs, and didn't join the process that focused on all kinds of grievances — the so-called Canada round.

"They were intent on maintaining a position that was a hard-bargaining, in-our-parochial-interests position. Everyone else had chosen to rise above the fray and try to make decisions that were in the best interests of the country. And I don't know how many times in press conferences, I repeated that phrase, you know, we've got to rise above the fray, put aside our parochial interests. I must have said that a million times," Sihota said.

This is where the reality of Canada in the early 1990s parts company with the fiction of the movie *It's a Wonderful Life*. In that movie, the dispirited George Bailey stands by, an idle spectator of the world that unfolds without him. But in Canada in 1990 and 1992, Quebec was not much of a spectator. It was distracted by its own political obsessions, the delicate balance between separatism and federalism that was so crucial to the future of Bourassa and his government. Bourassa was trying to keep a lid on the conflict between Quebeckers who would accept a carefully crafted renewed federal deal, and the people who were agitating for a "knife to the throat" negotiating position with the rest of Canada. Bourassa was hardly a knife-wielder; but he was daunted by the bitter sentiments that could upset any attempt to make a deal with the rest of Canada.

By absenting itself from the multilateral talks, Quebec didn't have the opportunity to take part in the learning process over what Canada wanted. By focusing so much on its own difficult internal political struggle, it didn't have the time to watch as the rest of the country came up with the answer to Bourassa's question.

That's how Canada in 1992 came to have two different definitions of the word "plus" when it tried to come up with Meech plus.

The "plus" for Quebec meant powers and more powers. Constitutional Affairs Minister Joe Clark was constantly finding that the national-unity question, as it revolved around Quebec, was totally fixated on the idea of powers. Whenever the national-unity question was beamed through the prism of Quebec, the issue was refracted into a rainbow spectrum of powers. Everything was seen in this light. This in turn led to the difference between Clark's idea of the national-unity mission and Mulroney's idea of it.

"I'm not sure there were two Ottawas, but I think there were two working definitions of the problem," Clark said. "Mine was that there were a number of important issues that had to be dealt with together. And I think it is fair to say that other people who had been through the wars in Quebec ... had lived with that unresolved question for so long that power was the major problem."

In other words, Mulroney and the Quebeckers saw powers as the key to the question. Clark knew that the Senate, the aboriginal-rights issue and the problems of alienation from Ottawa were also crucial to the solution.

"That had to do with the way you viewed the issue. It was an analysis. And it had more to do with an analysis of the problem than it even had to do with the analysis of the solution."

Very early in 1992, a group of about 200 people from the rest of Canada put their heads together to come up with some kind of a solution to the powers issue. It happened in Halifax in January, at the first of the federal government's Renewal of Canada conferences. This one was devoted to the power question, and the dilemma was thrown on the table: Quebec is locked in the throes of decentralism, most of the rest of Canada embraces the concept of a strong central government.

The Halifax group came up with a surprising solution: asymmetry.

The idea of asymmetry would be to allow Quebec to have a different set of powers than any of the other provinces. If Quebec wants more control over language or culture or manpower training, hand them over, said many at the Halifax conference. That doesn't mean those powers have to be handed over to everyone. What's the big deal?

One of the converts to this cause was the NAC's Judy Rebick. She was sure that the Halifax conference was on to something that could be sold in the rest of Canada. She was sure that if she and other people at the conference could be convinced, other Canadians would see the light too. It just takes a bit of explanation, says Rebick.

"You can explain it," she says. "I spent two years doing it, so I know you can — to sometimes very hostile audiences.

"You can explain that Quebec is different. It's not that it's a distinct society. It's that Quebec sees itself as a nation, in a way that Alberta doesn't and Newfoundland doesn't.

"And you can talk very concretely about how that is — how they see the Quebec government as their government, not the federal government. How it is that they call their premier, the prime minister. . . . It's not only that they have a different language and a different culture. It is more than that. They see themselves as a nation. And it doesn't mean they're better than we are. It just means Quebec's different. And it explains why what they want is different."

The problem, though, is that the idea of different powers for Quebec often gets confused with the idea of different rights for Quebec. Rebick believes that the politicians could have separated the two ideas, with some careful work. In fact, she believes that the whole debate over distinct-society status got too wrapped up with the idea of different rights. Of course Canadians want everyone to have equal rights, she says, but does that mean absolutely equal powers too?

"If you explain that people in Quebec want more power for their province — we don't want that, we want a strong central government — it takes the emotion out of it. Then it becomes a rational discussion."

Joe Clark was as surprised as anyone else about Rebick's embrace of asymmetry at the Halifax conference. It was an idea that had simply been dismissed in cabinet in the summer of 1991, when Ottawa was coming up with the twenty-eight proposals called "Shaping Canada's Future." At a couple of those cabinet meetings, some of the Quebec ministers threw out the suggestion of different powers for Quebec, but most of the other ministers quickly threw a bucket of cold water over the idea. It wouldn't go anywhere, as far as they were concerned: the public just wouldn't take to it. Now here was a conference made up of all different kinds of Canadians, who seemed to be telling the cabinet ministers and Ottawa that they were out of touch with the public, that asymmetry could be sold. So after Halifax, Clark got on the telephone and talked to some other politicians across the country.

"I really thought we had something here," Clark said. "But I kept going around, and I could not find anybody . . . I went and talked to people, including NDP leaders in the provinces, and Liberal opposition leaders, Conservative opposition leaders."

The conversation was generally brief. "What about asymmetry? Could you buy it?" Clark would ask these politicians. Almost unanimously, they rejected it. "Well, maybe somewhere else but I'm not going to buy it."

Clark freely admits that the debate was political

rather than theoretical. "There may well come a time when people will say, that makes sense, and we've certainly done it several times before," he said. "But it's not a case I think is viable now."

The debate over asymmetry showed that Canada's politicians believed they had to be very, very careful about the way that Quebec's needs were handled in this national-unity debate. Mulroney's government firmly believed that English Canadians were opposed to Meech because Quebec got something and they didn't. It was a delivery problem; a marketing problem. Next time around, Mulroney decided, Quebec would get something; so would everybody else.

So, as the new constitutional enterprise was launched after Meech, Canadians were introduced to the idea of a "Canada round." Mulroney had no idea how deeply the rest of Canada would seize upon this idea and claim ownership of all kinds of terrain in the rocky constitutional ground. Ottawa was caught completely off guard by the demands that would be made of a true Canada round.

When Mulroney talked about giving everyone something in this 1992 exercise, he was assuming that Ottawa would be doing the giving, that the federal government would decide how much and what it was going to include in the new deal for Canada. Who speaks for Canada? Ottawa speaks for Canada. It was consistent with Mulroney's general approach to issues — strong, decisive leadership from the top, administered over, even despite, the voices of dissent. In Brian Mulroney's world of constitution-making, it would be Ottawa that ran the show called the Canada round. Other people would be consulted, of course, but the public airing of opinions would be only a prelude to a conclusive, federal-driven constitutional deal.

Here was his plan: Finish up the hearings of the special, joint Commons–Senate committee, known as the Beaudoin–Dobbie committee. Within six weeks of that report, pull together a constitutional plan, to be passed by the House of Commons. The key was to keep the three federal parties on one team to pass a resolution in Parliament — that would show Quebec that the country was speaking with one, welcoming voice. Then this resolution would fan out to the provinces for their approval, maybe culminating in a national referendum by the spring or early fall. The result would be a nice, festively wrapped package to celebrate Canada's 125th birthday, and a well-intentioned gift to Quebec in time for its October referendum.

In a letter to the premiers in late January, Mulroney made no secret of the fact that he wanted Ottawa in charge of this Canada round, and that his timing called for only perfunctory consultation with the provinces.

"After the joint parliamentary committee report is tabled, we will consult with all provinces, territories and the national aboriginal leaders on the format and the substance of any government response to be put before Parliament," he wrote. "I want to tell you that the federal government, and I know the federal Parliament, will remain flexible, open-minded and focused on an achievable consensus that can serve durably for generations to come."

Mulroney, the Quebecker, was showing his native province's faith in politics and political institutions to get the job done. It would not have occurred to the prime minister that there was anything illegitimate about Parliament presuming to decide the best interests of the nation. Quebec was making it known as well to the Tories, Liberals and New Democrats that the most effective message from the rest of Canada would be one spoken in a chorus of unity by the three federalist parties, in Parliament. That would be the symbol of welcome by the rest of Canada that Quebec wanted to see.

But out in the provinces and among the Canadian public, a powerful feeling of resentment was building over Mulroney's assumption that Ottawa and Ottawa alone spoke for Canada. The resentment was political: How dare a government that stood at less than 20 per cent in the polls have the nerve to say it spoke for Canadians? The resentment was also philosophical: Since when did the government of Canada define the national interest in isolation? Where did the provinces fit in? Where were the people's voices?

Nowhere was the resentment greater than in Ontario, the largest province and the largest ideological opponent of the Conservative government in Ottawa. Ontario's New Democratic premier was not about to simply nod in assent to any of Mulroney's plans for the Canada round. Ontario came up with a plan to involve all the provinces in the multilateral ministerial conferences, the MMC travelling show, that rolled throughout Canada in the spring of 1992.

This was not part of Mulroney's plan. Nor was it part of Quebec's plan. Quebec had been quietly reassured that its friends in Ottawa, led by Mulroney's government and helped by the federal Liberals and New Democrats, would take care of Quebec's constitutional needs. If Quebec had any doubts about this, it need only look to that mad scramble in Ottawa at the end of February, when the Beaudoin–Dobbie committee had turned political cartwheels in its final report to answer Quebec's demand for more powers. At the end of their hearings, even though the committee had heard no great call for more powers to the provinces, the Tories on the committee hastily pulled together a grab bag of powers to recommend for transfer to the provinces, especially Quebec. This seemed to be an enduring

picture of constitutional politics in 1992: the rest of
Canada madly dashing around, trying to figure out
what Quebec wanted while juggling its own national-
unity grievances.

For Ontario, the idea of "Meech plus" meant that the
provinces would decide the "plus" part. It also meant
that native people were part of the add-ons to Meech.
The Ontario scheme, presented on March 12 at a
meeting in Ottawa of the rest-of-Canada negotiators,
called for native and territorial leaders to be included
in the multilateral process, bringing the total number
of participants to seventeen.

In Quebec City, Bourassa heard about all these developments by telephone. His two senior bureaucrats,
André Tremblay and Diane Wilhelmy, were at the
Pearson Building as "observers," and what they were
observing proved spectacularly shocking to Quebec.

Bourassa was sitting in his office, the television
cameras of CBC's "The Journal" trained on him.
There, on camera, Bourassa's shock and dismay were
registered as he heard about Ontario's bold plan to out-
negotiate Ottawa. He counted aloud. "That's seventeen
there," he said in French. Then a long, agonized sigh.
"I didn't think the strategy was to multiply the players."
Bourassa told the "Journal" producers: "It was already
quite difficult to reach an agreement with eleven and I
thought that at seventeen it will be more difficult." It
harked back to his vow, made in the heat of rejection
when Meech died. He said Quebec would never negotiate à onze with the other provinces again. Now that
unacceptable figure had been boosted to seventeen —
an impossibly unwieldy number of negotiators.

Back at the Pearson Building, Alberta's Jim Horsman
ran into André Tremblay in the corridors, after the
phone call was made to Bourassa. "This is very serious,
to allow them in the room," Tremblay told Horsman.

"We couldn't do it with eleven. How can we do it with seventeen?"

That was only one sign that the universe was not unfolding as it should for Quebec in these days of March. At that same meeting, all the constitutional negotiators put their positions on the table. Another problem for Quebec made its multilateral debut that day — the Senate question.

Ontario thought that Meech plus amounted to provincial involvement and a whole range of new issues on the table. The native people were confident that they were a major part of the "plus" in Meech plus. After all, it was their grievances that had helped to kill Meech in 1990. For Alberta and some of the small provinces, Meech plus meant that Canada was going to have to grapple with the sense of exclusion felt by people outside Quebec. It wasn't only Quebec that felt adrift or alienated from the rest of the country — the West and the Maritimes had a perpetual sense of being on the outside, looking in on Confederation.

If this was going to be a true "Canada round," intended to give the country more than Meech, then Alberta was going to fight for its dream of an elected, equal and effective Senate. Alberta was ready to play hard politics on this issue too. It was ready to hold Quebec's demands to ransom for its equal Senate. Every province had to agree if Quebec was going to get its precious veto. But there was no way this time that either Alberta or Newfoundland were going to give Quebec the veto over changing the Senate until they got the Senate they wanted. Why would they allow Quebec to block a new Senate until they were sure that they had a new institution that they could live with?

After he left Ottawa, Horsman headed straight for a meeting with his old pal, Quebec's intergovernmental affairs minister, Gil Remillard. The two had developed a friendship of sorts during the Meech years. Quebec respected Alberta's politicians because they stuck by Meech through the withering storm of public antipathy to the deal out West in the late 1980s. Horsman paid his call on Remillard and served notice of the hard politics that were going to be played on the Senate question. Remillard listened to Horsman explaining the lay of the land after the March 12 meeting. He put both hands on the table.

"Let me get this straight. You get Senate reform; we get the veto."

Horsman flashed him a smile — one that he called his "Chauncey Gardener" smile. Mimicking the hero of his favourite movie, *Being There*, Horsman was trying to cultivate an aura of innocent insight; of being simultaneously wide-eyed but inscrutable. Horsman neither confirmed nor denied. He just sat there, and let the Senate issue sink into Remillard's thinking. But it never really did.

So the multilateral mission began without Quebec at the table, and despite serious misgivings about the whole plan from the Quebec government and Brian Mulroney. Joe Clark, ever the pragmatist, was willing to see this mission through, to see what developed. He even saw wisdom in the idea of such a process. But he was also determined that if this negotiation was going to take place without Quebec, it might be useful to insert periodic reminders about Quebec into the multilateral process. So, at the first stop of the talks in Halifax in early April, Clark invited everyone to dinner in an elegant, wood-panelled room in a nearby hotel, and treated the negotiators to a lesson in the realities of Quebec politics.

The tutors were former United Nations ambassador Yves Fortier and Claude Beauchamp, head of the blue-chip business group, the Regroupement economie et constitution. The two Quebeckers talked about the daunting threat of separatism in Quebec and the fragile balancing act that Bourassa had to perform between nationalists and federalists, in his province and in his party. They talked about the hard line of the youth in the provincial Liberal party; they drew a thumbnail sketch of the demands contained in the reports by Allaire and Belanger–Campeau. There was also a lot of talk about the influence of the Quebec media. Some of the provincial and aboriginal negotiators in Halifax came away from that dinner convinced that Quebec élites were overly spooked by the media, intimidated by the threat of negative press coverage.

All of this was intended to keep Quebec's concerns at the front of everyone's thinking in the multilateral process. There was no sense embarking on a Canada round without considering the needs of one of the major players, Clark thought.

"Obviously the most critical group with whom we had to have an understanding was Quebec," he said.

All of the negotiators believed they had friends in Quebec, special ties with Quebec, but Clark wasn't certain that all the people in the multilateral process were well-versed in the sense of battle fatigue and emotional politics plaguing Quebec in the early 1990s.

"I've been through a lot with Quebeckers sort of on their turf, and a lot of people haven't been. So what I was trying to get Yves and Claude to do is give some sense of where this was coming from."

It was a subtle way of getting the multilateral group to keep thinking about that perennial question: "What does Quebec want?" But from time to time, the Quebec government would make its wants known far less subtly. One of these occasions took place in late April, as the multilateral mission wound its way to Edmonton. Back in Quebec, Remillard stated flatly that his province wasn't interested in any deal unless it could get Meech back. "If we get something in substance, something like Meech, of course we will go back to the table and discuss the other points we have to discuss for complete constitutional reform."

Politicians such as Moe Sihota were taken aback by the demand being made by a province that refused to join the talks. It struck Sihota as the height of arrogance, and he made his anger known to the reporters.

"It seems to me that Mr Remillard should be coming back and engage in discussions here so as to be sure those points of view are reflected on the table. . . . He runs the risk or the peril that he won't even get what he's asking for if he's not here."

But in reality, the demand was made more with wistfulness than with arrogance. Quebec, with hopeful nostalgia, would often let it be known that it just wanted its old Meech Lake accord back in one piece. Bob Rae was constantly running into this demand, every time he engaged in a conversation with Quebeckers about the future of the unity mission.

"A lot of times, you'd talk to people and they'd say, 'Wouldn't it be better if we go back to Meech? Can we just go back to Meech?' " Rae's answer to all of them was the same: "No, we can't go back. No, we can't." Over and over, Rae kept telling Quebeckers, especially Bourassa, that they couldn't simply absent themselves from the process and wish for Meech's return. Do you want Meech back? Get in there and fight for it.

"I spent a lot of time trying to tell him [Bourassa], and trying to tell the Quebec delegation that their absence from the whole discussion was really unhelpful," Rae said.

At the same time, at the officials' level, Ontario's deputy minister of intergovernmental relations, Jeff

Rose, was also trying to lure Quebec back to the negotiations that Ontario had started. In Toronto one morning, he met Quebec's senior bureaucrat, Diane Wilhelmy, for breakfast. He laid it on the table — Ontario was not Quebec's proxy in this multilateral mission. If Quebec wanted Meech back, it should come back to the table itself.

Rose told Wilhelmy: "We're doing our best, but we're not Quebec." This was not a process to be negotiated at long distance or by proxy, he said. "You're in touch with everybody and everybody thinks they're your special friend. But nobody is Quebec. We are going to get a deal, and you're not going to be part of it."

With the brashness that has made him infamous in constitutional circles, Rose said: "Diane, the train has left the station."

Wilhelmy simply shook her head. The chances were almost nil that Quebec would return. Then she asked that plaintive question, the question that Quebec just kept asking of all the other provinces in the spring of 1992.

"Can't we just have Meech?"

In Edmonton, where the multilateral talks landed at the end of April, the rest of Canada tried to be obliging to this demand. At the end of the day on April 29, Clark came out to issue his daily progress report to the media, and immediately a pattern emerged. Just one day after Remillard had stated publicly that Meech had to be in place before Quebec's return, Clark and the others seemed to be rolling out the Meech welcome mat.

Clark didn't portray the day's dealings as an exercise in Meech revival, but there it was, almost each of the five conditions of Meech, checked off and reported complete for Quebec's approval. The talks had produced agreements on limiting federal spending power

— that was one item in Meech. The day in Edmonton had pretty well sealed the agreement to grant a carefully worded distinct-society clause to Quebec — another Meech item. They were all agreed that Quebec should be guaranteed its three Supreme Court judges — another Meech point. In essence, Quebec had talked and the rest of Canada had answered. But it wasn't enough to lure Quebec back to the table.

By the time the talks reached Saint John, New Brunswick, in early May, the people at the multilateral table were starting to despair that Quebec would ever return to the table. Moe Sihota got on the telephone and pleaded with Remillard.

"Listen," he said to Remillard. "The right place for you to come into the process is Vancouver."

"Why is that?" Remillard asked.

Sihota explained: "First of all, we are going to finally begin to deal with division-of-power issues. We've put it off until now, hoping you'd come back, but we have to start it next week." Sihota pleaded, in a long, long conversation, that he needed an ally on the power issues, he needed an ally on aboriginal questions, that he needed an ally to deal with the economic issues in the constitution.

"And it's going to be in Vancouver," Sihota said, "far, far away; perhaps the furthest removed you're going to get from Central Canada. It's the right point of entry for Quebec."

Publicly, Sihota made many of these same points, and he hinted that Quebec would be sorry in the end that it had not heeded his advice to be part of the crucial discussions over powers, the Senate and aboriginal issues.

"It can have a more detrimental effect to Quebec than it will to us. It just makes the process of negotiation on our part a little bit longer and a little bit more arduous and I think that's reflected in some of the frustration we feel today," Sihota told reporters in Vancouver. "I can't help but think that in Quebec they must be reassessing their decision not to attend, starting with these meetings."

But Quebec wasn't reassessing its decision. This multilateral process was not the process of Quebec's choosing, and it had no desire to join the bandwagon. Besides, it was almost certain that this unwieldy group of constitutional negotiators wouldn't be able to come up with a comprehensive deal — it already looked as if they were getting bogged down in Senate questions and the aboriginal issues.

Still, Bourassa and Remillard had decided by early May that it was time to step out of the bunker in Quebec and see what the rest of Canada was doing on the constitutional front. They decided to head out West for talks with the premiers and justice ministers. At each stop, they kept hearing the same message — this campaign for an equal Senate was serious.

In Alberta, for instance, Bourassa met with his old friend, Premier Don Getty. The Alberta premier told Bourassa that he was not bluffing with the demand for an equal Senate. Getty explained to Bourassa the reality of politics in the West. Yes, Bourassa had separatists breathing down his neck, but Getty had the Reform Party and populists nipping at the heels of the Conservatives. The Triple E Senate was a trophy for the Western populists, and they were determined that Alberta bring it home for them from the constitutional talks.

Bourassa nodded and listened, respectful of Getty's position. Bourassa explained to him: "We cannot have a Senate that is fully equal and fully effective."

Getty told him: "The three Es are linked together. You can't negotiate one without touching the other one."

Bourassa translated this in optimistic fashion. If all the Es are linked, that meant Getty was ready to trade away equal or effective. Getty, on the other hand, believed that he had said plainly that all three Es had to be part of the package. Yet another problem of translation. It had nothing to do with the French–English language rift, and everything to do with the difference in political approach between Central Canada and the West.

Clark, for his part, was just happy that Quebec was out travelling around the country, apparently renewing its interest in the question: "What does Canada want?" Certainly the Western premiers were telling Bourassa what Canada wanted, and a new Senate was high on the list. Asked about the trip, Clark told reporters: "It's a demonstration clearly that the government of Quebec and Mr Bourassa recognize that there are issues other than simply the Quebec issues that have to be dealt with. It's a clear demonstration that this is a Canada round, and that Quebec, like everyone else, is taking seriously the issues of the Canada round."

Indeed, Quebec was taking the Senate issue seriously — maybe for the first time. Bourassa and Remillard returned to Quebec City with a new appreciation of the West's tenacity about an equal Senate. This crazy idea just wasn't going away. Ontario, alone in its role as defender of Central Canadian interests, simply couldn't keep blocking the Senate reformers from the West and Newfoundland. And what kind of friend was Ontario anyway? Rae was the one who had started this multilateral process and put the native people at the table. There had to be some way to reply to this equal Senate without losing Quebec's influence or radically altering the province's power in the upper chamber.

It just so happened that one of the federal government's top constitutional bureaucrats, Jocelyn Bourgon, had filed away a plan for an equal Senate that might satisfy Quebec's concerns. This plan was first introduced through a February memorandum by Peter Nicholson, a vice-president of the Bank of Nova Scotia. In Edmonton, Clark made a cryptic reference to the plan, then known as the Nicholson proposal, saying that it was "being held very much in reserve."

No province had put forward this plan; the basis of it was to have an equal Senate, in which each senator would have a different number of votes. Senators from Ontario or Quebec, for instance, would have two or three times the number of votes as senators in Manitoba or New Brunswick. It was a strange hybrid mixture of an equal Senate and the population-based Senate that was in place. The aim may have been to take elements of each side in the Senate argument and merge them, but neither of the sides was holding it up for examination.

Clark's mention of the Nicholson proposal, though, was a clear sign that Ottawa was looking at some kind of back-up plan on the Senate. So was Quebec, it turned out. Through the labyrinth of channels joining Quebec and Ottawa in these days of the multilateral talks, the Nicholson proposal landed in Quebec City, where it was greeted with some interest. Remillard and Bourassa, who had heard about the equal Senate over and over again in the West, said maybe this was a type of equality they could live with.

The multilateral talks had finally landed in Montreal in the third week of May, and the negotiators were lining up to see Bourassa and Remillard. Quietly, out of the glare of the spotlights, they were meeting the various politicians. In the plush grandeur of the Ritz-Carlton Hotel, Remillard had breakfast with

Saskatchewan justice minister Bob Mitchell, whom he admired and liked. The two men chatted idly about the progress of the negotiations, and this whole Senate impasse. At this point, Remillard cautiously floated the idea of the Nicholson plan.

"What do you think about this idea of an equal Senate, with weighted votes?" Remillard said, explaining how it would work. Mitchell was mildly interested, but his mind was turned more towards building the force for a truly equal Senate. The Triple E people believed they had Ontario on the run. There was no need for a back-up plan yet.

Furthermore, the big issue in Montreal was the power question, central to Quebec's demands. As Clark explained it, it was the way to give substance to the symbolism of Quebec's distinct society. Big developments took place in Montreal on the power question, without too much controversy or rancour among the delegations. This wasn't a debate about centralism or decentralism, this was all about commonsense federalism.

"It makes so much more sense now in 1992 for the provinces to play a more active role," Rae said.

Within one day, a huge list of powers had been tallied up and handed over to the provinces. The so-called "six sisters" — tourism, mining, forestry, housing, recreation and municipal affairs — were "clarified" as provincial powers. For some decades prior to 1992, Ottawa had gradually been spending its way into influence in these areas. Now, in the new deal envisioned by the multilateral negotiators, Ottawa would have to ask permission to spend money in these areas.

Moreover, two other key powers were transferred to the provinces. Ottawa would maintain its sway in national programs such as the National Film Board, the CBC and the unemployment insurance program, but on general matters of culture and labour-market training, the provinces would be the rulers. Here, finally, was the answer to how far Canada would go in the issue so important to Quebec. Here was the gesture of English Canadian sincerity about meeting Quebec's demands. You got Meech back in Edmonton; now you've got "Meech plus" with all these powers. Or, that was the way it was intended.

The travel-weary veterans of the multilateral process had hoped against all hope that Quebec would be lured to the table by the Montreal talks. After all, they were in the neighbourhood — why didn't Quebec drop by? And after all, they were talking about an issue that was supposed to be crucial to Quebec. The bait was there to lure Quebec back to the table.

As a gesture of goodwill, Bourassa and Remillard decided to host a little cocktail reception at the Ritz-Carlton for all the negotiators from the rest of Canada. "Well, we'll not be at the table, but the buffet will be there," Remillard said. As the joke was told around this time, Quebec only ventured as far as the buffet line-up; it wasn't ready to rejoin the table. It was an elegant affair, complete with string quartet and dainty finger food arrayed on white linen. Politicians, bureaucrats and officials milled around in the jewel-box-like room.

This was a constitutional happening. Bourassa was finally in the midst of things again, and he was greeted like a film star. Cameras and reporters pressed in on him, looking for any hint of how he viewed the multilateral process that had landed in his backyard. Bourassa surveyed the situation, talked to premiers such as Newfoundland's Clyde Wells, and wasn't certain that he would be coming back to a successful process. He wasn't sure this multilateral negotiation was going to work. He had some serious misgivings about it, in fact.

"It's not a question of a lack of goodwill," he told reporters. "It's the question of being responsible. If I go back to the table and it's another failure, let's say on Senate reform, I don't think the political stability in this country will be reinforced. I have to have some guarantee that if I go back to the table there are important chances to succeed."

The meeting between Bourassa and Wells was another major event at the Ritz-Carlton Hotel that night. They had not sat down and talked together directly since the awful days of Meech's death in June 1990. Bourassa, like Mulroney, blamed Wells for the demise of Meech.

"I will not talk about the past. I don't think it's very useful to talk about the past," Bourassa said as he entered the meeting. But he did make the point: "If Meech Lake had been adopted two years ago, Canada now, in my view, would be a stronger country."

This time, with the Meech memories only partly consigned to the past, the Quebec premier wanted to know whether Wells was poised to block a demand of his province again. Would Newfoundland give him the veto he so needed?

"We'll see," said Wells. If he got the Senate he wanted, maybe he wouldn't be so concerned about whether Quebec could veto a future change. At this encounter in Montreal, the Newfoundland premier made it clear that he would not want to be the lone hold-out if the country wanted to give the veto to Quebec. That was the good news. There was also bad news.

Wells was the first premier in all this multilateral wrangling of 1992 to challenge the idea of giving Meech back to Quebec. While all the others had been talking about what kind of add-ons would be a sufficient Meech plus, the Newfoundland premier was questioning the *first* part of that equation, not the "plus." At the Ritz-Carlton, he said: "If the proposals, of the general nature of those contained in the Meech Lake accord, were not acceptable two years ago to the vast majority of the people of Canada, I have no reason to think that they would be any more acceptable now."

So while the rest of the negotiators were worried about adding those powers as an acceptable "plus" to Quebec, Wells was throwing cold water on the idea that Meech was a minimum.

More problems were lurking in Toronto. Maybe it wouldn't be so easy to just hand off all these powers. Maybe the "plus" was a big "minus" for some people. Culture groups were the first to stand up and take notice of this power transfer. Within a few days of the Montreal meeting, the multilateral ministers were in Toronto, getting ready to start their last week of talks with yet another reception, this time at Roy Thomson Hall.

Outside the hall, a scattered group of artists, actors and musicians were chanting: "Don't divide culture." Anyone in a suit approaching the hall was swarmed by this chanting group. They faced off with Joe Clark, who assured them that there would be no difference in how the arts were financed. Then they faced off with Bob Rae, who pointed out that cultural programs were always carried out by provinces and the federal government. "You're not opposed to sharing culture, I assume?" The noisier protesters stopped and considered this: "Okay, share culture, but don't divide it," they said. Rae managed to make this look like an exercise in semantics, and the protest fizzled. But in his own home province, among his old allies in the labour movement, trouble was also lurking on the idea of transferring labour-market training to the provinces.

Labour leaders were horrified that the federal government's $3.2-billion manpower-training program would simply be devolved to the provinces. At a time when all the politicians were talking about the need for big-picture policies on training, the unity negotiators were making job programs into a patchwork quilt across the country. By July, unions and key labour leaders had coalesced into a powerful behind-the-scenes force, prodding Rae, forcing Ontario to do some fancy foot-work with the legal drafting of the power agreement.

These were all warning signs for the multilateral negotiators; signs that the Quebec government wanted very different things out of the constitution than the general public in the other provinces. But the negotia-tors were more worried about the bigger obstacle looming right in front of them. The May 31 deadline for the multilateral talks was approaching and there was no agreement on the Senate. Soon now, this process was going to be tossed to the first ministers, so that they could put the political stamp on the techni-cal work that had been carried out throughout that spring. Suddenly, everyone started to worry about what would happen to the fragile deal that had been so care-fully built over days and days of arduous negotiations.

It was the question that Clark was asked continually at the microphone at the Royal York Hotel. The con-stitutional affairs minister stressed that this whole deal hadn't been negotiated in a vacuum; they had tried to take account of what Quebec would need. Clark also noted that Quebec had to be mindful of the fact that it had chosen to stay away from this process — a certain protocol decreed that it would be rude to rush in and change a deal they had shunned.

"I don't expect that Quebec is going to come back with a long list of things, saying change the principles here or change the punctuation there. I think that there is an understanding that their being away, their not being here for reasons that everyone can accept, has some consequences."

Clark made clear that he was expecting an atmosphere of goodwill to prevail in the country as the national-unity talks moved into this next uncertain phase.

"I have no reason to believe that Quebec would want to come back and pick at a loose strand. I don't think anybody would. I think Quebec, while they're not here, knows how complicated and sincere and genuine a process this has been."

A similar message came from Alberta's Jim Horsman when he was asked the same questions.

"We're prepared to listen to our colleagues from Quebec when they're at the table. But I'm telling you again, this process has been very seriously hampered by Quebec's refusal to be here and therefore, if they start to try to unravel what has already been accomplished, well, we'll have to deal with that."

Here they all were at the end of May, and Quebec had still not joined them at the table. It was all over, or close to all over, and Quebec wasn't coming back. The politicians from the rest of Canada were regretful but resigned. Quebec just hadn't seen enough to lure it back to the negotiations. The big missing element was the veto, the fifth of five Meech elements demanded by Quebec. And there would be no veto without a deal on Senate reform.

It was time for Quebec to play its card on the Senate issue. Suddenly Claude Beauchamp, the same man recruited to tutor the talks in Halifax, was wading back into the debate, trying not to make too many ripples in the troubled constitutional waters. He ventured into New Brunswick to see the affable Premier Frank McKenna. Ever since his days as Meech foe-turned-supporter in 1990, McKenna had tried to carve out a reputation for himself as an agent of compromise in the country. He liked to be seen as the great moderate,

the conciliator. All his efforts during the final days of
Meech had been aimed at placating and soothing both
sides. It was an approach that earned him scorn among
the hard-line opponents to Meech, but major goodwill
points with Mulroney and Quebec.

That reputation also made him an ideal candidate to
present a new compromise plan on the Senate.
Beauchamp, a tennis partner of Remillard's, arrived in
New Brunswick, armed with a plan that looked a lot like
the Nicholson plan. Remillard had pointed his political antenna into the air and detected that a Quebec-
sponsored proposal to break the Senate impasse was
not likely to sell in the rest of the country. He knew that
it had a better chance if it came from a neutral source,
and if it was transmitted to the talks through someone
like McKenna.

Beauchamp threw the "weighted-vote" proposal in
front of McKenna, who replied that the plan was interesting. A tiny wire story went out across Canada, offering only vague details of the new Senate gambit. But
among the people who were close to this constitutional
circle, it was clear that McKenna was acting as an agent
for Quebec. Maybe the wire story didn't say it directly,
but the New Brunswick premier was regarded as the
agent for Quebec-based compromise. This role was one
that would link Frank McKenna and Saskatchewan
premier Roy Romanow.

McKenna and Romanow shared a feeling of scepticism about the Charter of Rights and Freedoms. Both
premiers had received immersion courses in the idea
that individual rights were dominant in Canada's
liberal democracy. Yet both had grave misgivings about
the notion by 1992. McKenna had been sold on the
dominance of individual rights because he was an
adherent of the Trudeau doctrine of constitution-
building, a student and admirer of Trudeau's vision of

individual rights above all. Romanow had been exposed to Trudeau's ideas directly, as a co-signer of the 1981 constitution, but never bought into the concept of individual-over-all completely; he feared that the pursuit of individual rights would erode the underpinnings of Canada's collective "soul."

When Romanow and McKenna joined forces in 1992, it was as Charter sceptics. Both men had serious doubts about whether individual rights were all Canada needed in the politics of the 1990s. Together, and individually, the two premiers were ideal candidates to bridge the chasm between the individual rights craze of English Canada and the collective rights demand of Quebec. Not coincidentally, the two premiers were also friends. Romanow had replaced Ontario's former premier, David Peterson, as the colleague McKenna would choose for companionship after days of talks. In 1992, it wasn't Peterson and McKenna who were spotted in Ottawa restaurants, over a drink or a pizza — it was Romanow and McKenna. As the summer wore on, these two men were constantly finding themselves in the role of Quebec agents. They were the two premiers who could be counted upon to put forward the ideas that served Quebec's interests.

McKenna was an adequate candidate to put forward the Quebec compromise on the Senate in June; he had established his credentials as a compromise agent during the dying days of Meech. But Romanow was even better placed. New Brunswick had stayed pointedly removed from the fray of 1992 constitutional politics; Saskatchewan was a true, Triple E province, neck-deep in the dispute. It would be perfect if Saskatchewan were the province to weigh into the Senate debate with a Quebec-sponsored compromise.

And that's exactly what happened. Mitchell, running across the wire story about Beauchamp and McKenna

in a pile of press clippings, suddenly acted on the suggestion that had been planted in his mind by Remillard
a few weeks earlier at the Ritz-Carlton. He showed the
clipping to Jim Horsman, who started photocopying it
in massive numbers. That night, Roy Romanow was
brought in from New York to put forward the plan.
Quebec's Senate gambit had arrived — it had rico-
cheted from New Brunswick to Ottawa to New York,
and now here it was, safely in the hands of agent
Romanow. The Saskatchewan premier lobbed the proposal into the talks late on the night of June 10. But the
timing was off; the multilateral talks were drawing
quickly to a close.

No one was happier to end this process than the federal
government's Quebec lieutenant, Health Minister
Benoit Bouchard. He had been at Clark's side throughout these talks, and for him, it was an exercise in frustration. None of these negotiators, it seemed to him,
was keeping an eye on the major question — Quebec's
constitutional problems. Most of the time in these
meetings throughout the spring, Bouchard had sat and
watched, rarely offering a comment on the proceedings. When he did speak, it was to remind the rest
of Canada that Quebec was in a very, very difficult
position.

"Quebec is not going to go for this," he would say, as
they became embroiled in the Senate question. "I can't
sell this in Quebec," he would warn them, when the
constitutional train veered towards aboriginal self-government or strong central powers. The warnings
annoyed some of the other people at the table. "It was
too much bluster," said Sihota.

In Montreal, Sihota confronted Bouchard, and told
him he was tired of hearing what could and couldn't be
sold in Quebec.

"I mean, give me a goddamn break here," Sihota told him. "We're all making concessions here. We've all got to go out and sell this thing. We're all in politics. We understand in politics that one of the things we've got is that we're good communicators. And you've got to go out there, you've got to communicate to your people the strengths of the package as you can see it and try to downplay the weaknesses. That's our job."

But Bouchard was feeling his own brand of exasperation. The two years since the death of Meech had been a grinding, uphill journey, culminating in this terrible exercise of the spring of 1992. He had felt the high of emotion on a night long before, on June 9, 1990, when it seemed that the Meech Lake accord had been saved by the first ministers' marathon talks. Back in the anterooms of the Government Conference Centre, the politicians were giddy with delight. Among the giddiest were Benoit Bouchard and Frank McKenna, who with linked arms were dancing together. Bouchard, a consummate performer, was dancing the steps of a Quebec folk dance; McKenna was hopping about in the steps of an old Scottish folk dance. Miraculously, the two steps worked together. It was the last time for Bouchard that the French and English would work in such perfect step.

The death of Meech and the politics of the 1990s had disillusioned and saddened him. His immersion in the life of Ottawa had taken him away from his Quebec roots, and turned a nationalist into a federalist. It seemed that every step Bouchard took put him farther and farther away from the Quebec he loved. The distance was showing at these multilateral talks, where he had the lonely position of being the only Quebec politician at the table. And he wasn't even allowed to speak up for the province — he was a federal minister; he had to be careful.

By June, it was time to pack up and leave the multi-
lateral road show. He announced to the reporters at the
Pearson Building that he was fed up and was leaving.
Enough was enough.

Bouchard's relations with Joe Clark were never easy.
The Quebec lieutenant had been one of the angry
voices rising up in near-mutiny in November 1991,
when Clark had tried to introduce referendum legislation in the House. Bouchard, like his fellow Quebec
Tories, saw this legislation as a form of domineering
federalism, a sign that Ottawa was preparing to act
over Quebec's head. That mess had been sorted out by
the spring, with Bouchard and the other Quebec
Tories as converts to the cause of a referendum. It was
Bouchard's job to sit at Clark's side throughout the
multilateral mission.

That the two were awkward with each other showed
up at the first multilateral meeting in Halifax, when
Clark mistakenly referred to his Quebec sidekick as
"Lucien." An unfortunate blunder, it dredged up all
the old memories of Lucien Bouchard, the friend and
confidant of Mulroney who had quit the cabinet in
1990, with the Meech Lake accord in flames behind
him. Lucien Bouchard now sat petulantly as the
leader of the nine-member Bloc Quebecois in the
back rows of the House of Commons, a constant taunt
to Mulroney. The name Lucien Bouchard was a
synonym for betrayal in Tory circles. In Halifax,
Benoit Bouchard assured all the reporters that he was
not insulted. "That's wonderful," he laughed. "That's
just marvellous."

When, in June 1992, Bouchard staged his own
walkout — only from the multilateral talks, not from
the government — Clark also tried to be magnanimous.
He didn't say it was wonderful or marvellous, but he
did understand the exasperation Bouchard felt.

"What is extraordinary about the process is that more people didn't walk out," Clark said. "You see, what made it work was the sense that we were treating issues equally. And if you fundamentally believed that your issue was more important than everybody else's issues, all the rest of stuff was exceedingly irritating."

Aboriginal people had felt the exasperation, Clark said. So had Western Canadians. "For the Quebeckers to be faced with the absolute reality, day after droning day of talking about Senate and aboriginals and not them, this really proved that this was a Canada round . . . I think there's always a difference between accepting something intellectually and accepting it in your heart and your lives. I think that's what happened with Benoit."

Frequently, throughout the spring, Bouchard would pull Clark aside and warn: "I'm not that patient." Clark was simply happy that he was putting up with what he did.

"He did walk out a couple of times, but many more times when you know an awful lot of Quebeckers would have walked out, he didn't."

But when Bouchard finally did walk out, he missed the events that would prove so crucial to Quebec in early July. He was not there at the table to say: "I can't sell this," or "Quebec won't go for this," in those last stages of the multilateral process, when the deal finally came together.

For Quebec's perspective, the negotiators now had to rely on the frustrating tangle of confused messages that were being sent out through the telephone lines. Benoit Bouchard wasn't the only Quebecker who was half in and half out of this process. The Quebec government, whether it was the premier or the bureaucrats, was constantly sidling up close to the multilateral talks and then drifting away; planting one message and then inserting another contradictory idea. It was supremely frustrating for the politicians in the rest of Canada.

Several of the ministers at the multilateral table prided themselves on their relations with Gil Remillard. Sometimes, they could spend the good part of an hour arguing over what signals he had sent them on a particular dispute. Now and then they would run to the phone to talk to Remillard in the middle of discussions.

"He hasn't ruled out the equal Senate," Horsman would say.

"He doesn't want an equal Senate," Sihota would reply. "Quebec will buy into the five-region Senate."

Meanwhile, back in the delegation rooms, the provinces were locked in facsimile-machine races to see who could get the documents to Quebec first. Alberta's senior constitutional official, Oryssia Lennie, would be feeding papers into the machine, destination Quebec City. Meanwhile Ontario's or New Brunswick's bureaucrats stood waiting in line to fax the same information.

Premiers such as Ontario's Bob Rae and New Brunswick's Frank McKenna were happier to deal with Bourassa, and only Bourassa. He wasn't contradictory like Remillard — he was simply ambiguous. He would defer decisions, saying he had to read the text of an agreement, or he had to consult with his cabinet. But he could keep an issue in the air, merely by refusing to rule it out. This was how the other provinces were constantly measuring Bourassa's approval or disapproval. "He didn't say no," was translated as "yes" by many of the people around the table. But this was the essence of Bourassa. He didn't say no to anything. His history as a Quebec politician is dotted with significant occasions when he didn't say no.

Back in 1967, when a renegade band of Quebec Liberals were forming a separatist splinter group within the provincial party, the young MNA Robert Bourassa quietly sat and listened, not saying "no," as the then-Liberal René Lévesque argued the merits of the separatist case. In Bourassa's own basement, Lévesque and the other Liberal renegades plotted their internal party strategy, to steer towards a vision of sovereignty association. Bourassa never did say "no" to Lévesque when this band was turning away from the Liberals and into the foundation of the Parti Quebecois. He simply bowed out, saying the monetary issue needed to be studied more carefully. He needed to see the text.

Again, in 1971, in his first incarnation as premier, Bourassa couldn't say "no" when all the first ministers in Victoria, B.C., hammered out a new amending formula for the constitution. Bourassa said maybe when he left Victoria, but immediately backed down from the agreement when he faced a barrage of attacks from Lévesque and his fledgling Parti Quebecois. Bourassa buckled — he hadn't anticipated such a public drubbing.

Over and over, Bourasssa's history repeated itself in the constitutional drama. His two favourite non-replies were: "I have to see the text," or "I have to see what the public reaction is."

Very skilfully, however, Bourassa had been able to turn this weakness into a strength. He wouldn't be seen as indecisive; he would be seen as careful, shrewd. Where another indecisive premier might be accused of sitting on the fence, Bourassa would be praised for holding his balance there. Such was the miracle of image-making in politics in the 1990s. Bourassa was hailed as a consummate politician because of his elegant way of not making a decision.

By not making a decision, though, by refusing to say no, the national-unity mission hurtled through 1992 without him and his government's influence.

Bourassa, thanks to his friendship with Brian Mulroney, simply assumed that Ottawa would be acting in Quebec's best interests. The Quebec premier wasn't overly worried that the multilateral process was getting out of hand — he was being reassured constantly that Ottawa was looking out for him. But all this talk of Ottawa acting as Quebec's agent was a bit of an exaggeration, according to Joe Clark.

"You know, for a long time we had a big problem, though we were able to overcome it during the meetings. We had a big problem with the suspicion that the federal government was somehow acting for Quebec and that there was some kind of a deal in place," said Clark.

"One of the great advantages of the last several years has been the personal relationship between the prime minister and Premier Bourassa. But it created some suspicions. People assumed there was more contact than there ever was. . . . That isn't to say that we weren't talking to Quebec about various things, but it was not a conspiracy."

There was no question in the other provinces' minds that Ottawa was driven by Quebec's interests. Not only was Mulroney a Quebecker, but so were the chief bureaucrat, Privy Council Clerk Paul Tellier, and the top constitutional official, Jocelyn Bourgon. However, there were times when Ottawa couldn't stand up for itself and Quebec at the same time. In the tug-of-war over powers, Ottawa could hardly be expected to stand up for the provincial powers when it had the federal powers to protect. In Vancouver, Clark made clear that Ottawa had its role to play, and sometimes that was going to go against what Quebec wanted.

"Quebec seeks a lot of things that the government of Canada can't accept, just as other provinces do and that's part of the federal–provincial process. But I think it's understood by everyone."

Moreover, Ottawa could never be entirely sure of what Quebec did want. That perennial question, "What does Quebec want?" was still being asked over and over again in 1992.

On the whole thorny issue of the distinct-society clause, for instance, Quebec only made its wishes known at the last minute. At the eleventh hour, as the talks were headed towards their conclusion in Ottawa on July 6 and 7, Quebec suddenly made it known that the distinct-society protection should go in the "Canada clause" that was being drafted. This was a surprise — most of the other provinces thought that Quebec would demand distinct-society protection in several places of the new deal, dotted with exclamation marks. But Clark told the reporters that Quebec had made it clear that "distinct society" was to go only in the Canada clause. Still, no one was entirely sure about how this would be worded, or what the legal implications were. As the July 7 deal was announced with great fanfare by Clark, it was also announced that Quebec would be given three options to study on the distinct-society question. More text for Bourassa to study.

Quebec was a perpetual riddle. One of the main reasons for the enigma, though, was that the province was not sure how seriously to regard the multilateral process. Like Mulroney, the Quebec government was absolutely convinced that the multilateral mission was going to run off the rails, and Ottawa would ride in with a rescue package for July 15.

On Canada's 125th birthday, July 1, 1992, Remillard was out in Alberta on a hiking vacation with his son. He planned to be away for a week or two, taking in the Calgary Stampede, flipping hamburgers at a Canada Day rally with Premier Getty and heading up to Banff to commune with nature. On July 3, he was watching the news and saw that the multilateral talks had produced a deal of sorts at the Airport Hilton Hotel in Toronto. He got on the phone to Bourassa.

"Should I come back? Is there going to be a deal?" Remillard asked Bourassa.

"Relax," the premier told him. "I don't think this will come to anything."

As it turned out, Remillard did have to return. The July 7 deal was praised as "historic" by Clark. An equal Senate was part of the agreement. And Quebec got its veto — Wells had agreed to hand it over in return for the Senate deal. Never mind, though. This was not what Quebec had expected.

Horsman flew back to Calgary to see the Stampede on July 8, and he met with Remillard. By some stroke of bad luck, he had lost the copy of the July 7 deal, and he had no paper to show the Quebec minister. Remillard was suspicious, looking askance at Horsman, as the Albertan tried to summon up his memory of all the details of the July 7 agreement. Remillard's brows were furrowed as Horsman explained the equal Senate and tried to sell him on its virtues.

"And anyway, you've got your veto — your big demand," Horsman told Remillard. "We've given you what you wanted."

The Quebecker wasn't impressed. "What's the sense of having a goalie after all the goals have been scored?"

Out in the public arena of Quebec, the reaction was the same. The same French press that devoted so little attention to the Senate dispute were now filled with shock and horror over this new equal Senate. The editor of Quebec's most influential newspaper, *Le Devoir*, issued a huge, one-word reply to the July 7 deal. "NON," said the editorial, in gigantic letters.

Way back in Halifax, the multilateral negotiators had been warned about how the Quebec press "spooked" the government. Now, in July, Bourassa and Mulroney, along with the Quebec cabinet ministers such as Bouchard, were seriously spooked. The July 7 deal was not going over very well at all, and there seemed no other option but to cut and run from this agreement, just as Bourassa had done in 1971 when the PQ kicked up a fuss over the Victoria deal.

In the rest of Canada, though, the politicians were retracing their steps, trying to figure out how they had got so far away from what Quebec had wanted. They were certain that Bourassa had sent positive signals — after all, he hadn't said "no." A mood of resentment was starting to settle among some of the provincial politicians. Hadn't Bourassa or Quebec been paying attention? Wasn't this what Bourassa had challenged Canada to do, when Meech had died in 1990? Clark said as much at the July 7 press conference.

"We're answering the questions which have been asked by Mr Bourassa in the National Assembly two years ago. 'What does Canada want?'. . . Today, I think that Canada has answered and it's very clear."

Maybe the answer was clear, but the signals from Quebec were anything but clear. Clark had been on the phone to Bourassa repeatedly throughout those days in early July 1992. So had Tellier. What had they heard? "They didn't say 'No.' " Bourassa told Clark that he had to consult his advisers, he had to see the text, he had to gauge public reaction — all his standard non-replies, well-practised over the years. But as Clark tells it, Bourassa certainly saw what was coming. After all, Quebec hadn't really been too interested in the Senate debate all these months. From a weekend telephone conversation, Clark had no reason to believe that Bourassa would change his mind. But the public fury caused Bourassa to back away from that Senate deal with remarkable speed.

"He made an assessment that later events didn't bear out," says Clark, who also hastens to attribute only goodwill to Bourassa in this case. "He was not at all attempting to mislead anyone." The problem was that Bourassa was just a premier who couldn't say no.

He wasn't the only Quebecker Clark had to win over. Brian Mulroney, Bourassa's friend, was in Europe, and greeted the July 7 deal with surprise and scepticism. Clark had to go through a complicated tangle of time zones and telephone links to reach the prime minister in Germany. One of Mulroney's first questions was whether Bourassa had been told. "Yes," Clark was able to say. "And he didn't say no."

Mulroney didn't say no either, but he was enormously wary of how this was going to fly in Quebec. So was Benoit Bouchard. Back in Ottawa, Bouchard was toying with the idea of leaving the cabinet rather than selling this awful deal. Always a politician to keep his eye on the media, Bouchard knew that the July 7 deal was going over like a lead balloon in his home province. And meanwhile, Mulroney seemed to have forgotten that Bourassa and Clark had talked. He seemed firm in the conviction that Clark's process had proceeded in complete isolation from Quebec. Clark was beginning to get the sense that Mulroney was more intent on protecting Bourassa than protecting his own constitutional affairs minister.

Ontario premier Bob Rae was not pleased at this development. He had simply assumed that Quebec had been keeping up to date on this deal-making; all those facsimile transmissions had been headed for Quebec City, hadn't they? Now Quebec was acting shocked and horrified over a deal that they had been supposedly following.

"One never had the sense that they took those things terribly seriously," Rae said. "After July 7 one had the sense that they really hadn't worked through, absorbed it."

Bourassa and other Quebeckers were telling Ontario, "This Senate stuff, we really haven't thought very much about it. It really isn't an issue for us." Rae, a little miffed, was starting to get the feeling that Mulroney and Quebec had been humouring the multilateral negotiators, pretending to take them seriously, when in reality, they had actually thought the process was doomed. That annoyance on Rae's part was already starting to be felt before July 7, in fact. On that day at the Pearson Building, a simmering well of frustration spilled out at the luncheon among the first ministers. Collectively, they decided they were sick and tired of trying to divine Quebec's motives at long distance. B.C. premier Michael Harcourt said he was not going to negotiate any longer by reading sheep entrails, or dealing with Casper the Ghost. The final push for the July 7 deal was built out of frustration with the conflicting signals coming out of Quebec.

Rae was particularly annoyed that Quebec was now so cool and stand-offish about the all-important veto.

"Well, life is full of discoveries," Rae said sardonically. "My own view was that a lot of this stuff was impossible to tell until Quebec got to the table and that I was increasingly frustrated by this sense of shadow-boxing."

The shadow-boxing continued after July 7. Bourassa gave one of his virtuoso performances at balancing on the fence, and managed to hold an entire news conference without committing himself. He talked about reviewing the package, seeing it in context, examining the text, consulting more people — everything except where he stood on the July 7 agreement.

Reviewing his performance later, with the CBC's "Journal" cameras aimed on him, he joked to his press aide, Sylvie Godin, that he had actually said nothing in reply to one of the more pointed questions from reporters.

"Comme toujours," Godin laughed. "As always." And Bourassa laughed too.

To carve out a path back to the talks, Bourassa had to set up some conditions. The old wistful question returned: "Can't we please have Meech back?" All of July was taken up with an effort to prove that the Quebec government was going to get the substance of Meech in any new deal. There were problems, though. First of all, territorial leaders, such as the Yukon's Tony Penikett, were enraged that Quebec would simply parade back into the discussions and demand the return of the veto over the creation of new provinces. Back in Edmonton, there had been an easy agreement to allow territories to become provinces through a simple one-on-one deal with Ottawa. That had been the way other provinces got into the federation — why should it be different for the territories?

Quebec, though, was not happy about the prospect of being outnumbered by even more English-speaking provinces. The delicate balance of the French–English pact would be affected. The argument seemed to be holding sway in Ottawa; it was now assumed that the territories' gain would be one of the items jettisoned from the July 7 deal to make room for Quebec. It wouldn't be until later in August that this issue was resolved by compromise. In July, it was still a sore point for everyone and a sign of just how tough it was going to be, as the country tried to paste together some arrangement between the rest of Canada and Quebec.

The Senate was the big sticking point. Out West and in Newfoundland, the politicians were getting nervous. It was starting to look as if Ottawa was preparing to back off; the equal Senate was also going to be jettisoned to make room for Quebec. That was Mulroney's objective as he worked the phones, trying to get Rae to abandon this part of the July 7 deal. An angry mood was starting to bubble up in the provinces. Wait a minute, they were saying. Hadn't Bourassa told Clark he could sell this deal? Was it their fault if he was wrong? Why should we pay the price for his miscalculation? This problem of translation should not be allowed to scuttle the July 7 agreement.

As it turned out, however, Clark decided to take the fall for Bourassa's goof. To admit that Bourassa had made the error would be like throwing him to the wolves in Quebec; the premier's credibility had to be protected and shielded by Ottawa.

"I tried to be careful afterwards in saying that there was simply a misjudgment of opinion in Quebec. And I said it in ways which caused people to think it was my misjudgment," Clark said.

These political manoeuvrings, and the intense focus on Meech revival, were enough to persuade Bourassa to come to Harrington Lake in early August for a session at the prime minister's residence. It was a historic occasion. Finally Quebec was back to negotiating *à onze* again. And it was *à onze*: the extra six players — the four aboriginal leaders and the two territorial leaders — were kept out, in the interests of making Quebec comfortable in its return.

The Harrington Lake sessions were classes in political realities. All of the other premiers told the stories of what led to the July 7 deal. They talked about the symbolic importance of the equal Senate and aboriginal rights and the new power-sharing deals. Once again, they were running their own version of *It's a Wonderful Life*, showing Bourassa a picture of Canada without Quebec in it. This time, Quebec was paying attention.

Bourassa had his own script to read to the rest of Canada, too. He talked about his own political realities, his difficult balancing act, how hard it was to sell his province on all the things that were so important to the rest of Canada. Again, he raised that question: "Can't we have Meech back?" Premiers such as Clyde Wells simply said no.

"You're not going to get everything Quebec wants," Wells said. "That's just not possible."

"I'm telling you that if the July 7 deal is not the basis of an agreement with Quebec, including the equal Senate, then there's no sense in me sticking around," said Alberta's Don Getty. Bourassa saw Getty as a friend and a supporter. If Getty was telling him this, he had to respect it.

At two meetings, over two weeks in August, the first ministers tried to carve a road back to the negotiating table together. Everyone from outside Quebec was waiting for Bourassa to say he was coming back. Late in the second meeting, Mulroney turned to Bourassa: "If I call a first ministers' meeting, will you come?" Bourassa answered: "Yes."

He didn't say no! Around the table, all the first ministers sighed with relief.

"That was the magic moment," Getty said.

At the Pearson Building in the third week of August, the chances of a deal were still extremely slim. Everyone was still dug in on the Senate dispute. Quebec's return to the table was also prompting a wholesale review of aboriginal self-government and economic questions. The people who had been present at the multilateral talks were getting very edgy about the prospect of Quebec and Mulroney unravelling all their careful work. Moe Sihota was so disgusted that he left the talks. Saskatchewan's Bob Mitchell was annoyed that he was left cooling his heels, relegated to the spectators' booth along with veteran negotiators such as Jim Horsman.

Mulroney had predicted before this week began that there could be no way to bridge the gap between Bourassa and Getty. And indeed, that's how it looked one bleak night in late August, as Getty sat in his hotel room and contemplated the failure that seemed inevitable. He got on the phone to Bourassa; he tried to reach him at the Chateau Laurier, but the Quebec premier had checked out. Was it too late? Had he gone home? No, Bourassa and his delegation had simply moved across the river to Hull, to stay in their home province while these talks were under way. Bourassa answered the phone in his room at his new hotel. Getty told him of his angst over the impasse. "How can this end in failure?" he asked Bourassa. The Quebec premier was staring out of his hotel room at the park near the river, gazing into the distance at the lights of Ottawa twinkling on the other side of the border. Quebec and the rest of Canada seemed miles apart, too far apart.

"Maybe there will be a miracle tomorrow," said Bourassa.

And sure enough, a miracle did begin to unfold the very next day. But as with all miracles, there were a few strange apparitions that popped up along the way.

One of these was a strange list of powers that were being demanded by Quebec inside the negotiations. As a bargaining tactic, this was sloppy work. There was no way that Quebec was going to get everything on this list — it was huge, rivalling the Allaire report in its effrontery to the rest of Canada. If this was Quebec's opening bargaining position, it was folly to distribute it to reporters. For no matter what the deal looked like at the end of the day, reporters would be able to compare the list to the deal and make the calculation that Bourassa had lost.

Here was a foreshadowing of the problem that

dogged and defeated Bourassa in the next couple of months. In the eyes of his civil servants, he had lost. His assent to only a minor list of power transfers was seen as an utter caving-in by the bureaucrats. They would make that plain later, in an explosive telephone conversation that was leaked to the press during the referendum campaign.

If the list was intended to spur Bourassa to a tough bargaining position, it failed. Bourassa was starting to give signals that day that he was ready to close the deal. He showed his willingness the same way he demonstrated it at Harrington Lake — with a desire to attend another meeting.

"I want to go to Charlottetown," he told PEI premier Joe Ghiz, who was due to host the annual premiers' gathering in his home province in the last week of August. It was becoming apparent that this Charlottetown meeting would be turned into a full-fledged first ministers' meeting to seal the agreement.

It was at this point again that Quebec agents Romanow and McKenna flew in to the process to act on Bourassa's behalf. Besides the power issue, something had to be done to make Quebec accept an equal Senate. McKenna had come up with the idea to guarantee Quebec an additional flock of MPs to make up for its loss of senators. Romanow took that one step farther — why not guarantee Quebec a minimum of 25 per cent representation in the House of Commons, in perpetuity? Other provinces had similar guarantees; small provinces had certain minimum numbers of MPs and senators. It was a powerful incentive for Bourassa; a guarantee of the French–English balance. This he could sell.

Unfortunately, *he* could sell it but the rest of the politicians couldn't. It would turn out to be one of the most unpopular and hated parts of the national-unity deal when the referendum began. Romanow, reflecting on it later, pulled his tie up over his head, like a noose, and said: "Yep, I'm the 25-per-cent guy."

In addition, Quebec had won the right to choose its senators in a different way. Yes, they would be elected, following the spirit of the deal to put the E for elected into the Senate, but Quebec's National Assembly would do the electing. It would be a way to ensure co-ordination between the provincial government and the central forces in Ottawa. It was another sign, too, of the difference in attitude towards politicians between Quebec and the rest of the country. Quebeckers had more faith in the role of politicians; they could choose legitimate senators. The public in the rest of Canada believed that only they, not the corrupt politicians, should decide who sits in the Senate.

On August 21, Bourassa announced what he had accepted by way of a power-sharing deal with the other provinces. Buoyed by his win on the key Senate issues, he thought he had some room to manoeuvre. He believed he had a good list of wins to boast about to Quebeckers. "It's less than we'd hoped for, but it's real progress," he said, in the faint praise that was to become the hallmark of Yes forces in the referendum campaign. In the area of power transfers, not much was different from the agreement reached months before in Montreal. The only add-on, in fact, was the agreement to streamline telecommunications.

The Quebec reporters blinked in disbelief. Is that it? All this talk about powers, and Meech plus, and the "plus" turned out to be a smattering of small power shuffles here and there — nothing truly sweeping and substantial. Certainly it was nothing compared to the list they were holding in their hands. They looked at the list, looked up at Bourassa, looked back at the list. Was that it?

Bourassa was asked whether he believed he had enough ammunition to fight the Parti Quebecois in a referendum campaign. The old words of Trudeau were thrown once again in the separatists' face. "Just watch me," Bourassa said.

It was, in fact, just the beginning of the return of the Trudeau ghost, and the separatist spectre. A nasty fight was awaiting Bourassa — the final, losing battle of his political career.

It took no time for Bourassa's nationalist opponents to whip up the storm of opposition to Bourassa's deal. Their slogan had a clever appeal — it turned Bourassa's old "profitable federalism" back upon him. "At that price, it's No," the slogan said.

The two-party assault was a formidable force against the Quebec premier. Bourassa had to fight his own provincial opposition leader, PQ leader Jacques Parizeau, as well as Brian Mulroney's old friend Lucien Bouchard, the leader of the breakaway group of Quebeckers who now sat as the nationalist Bloc Quebecois in the House. Many had dismissed these two personalities as lightweights, lacking credibility against the estimable and elegant Bourassa. But their Non campaign blazed through the province, virtually unstoppable from the beginning of September. From a rally of 1,200 people at the beginning of September to a rally for 5,000 people in Montreal on October 24, 1992, the Non campaign multiplied in numbers and fervour.

At one point, these Non campaigners had been the same people to taunt Bourassa for abandoning a vote on sovereignty in favour of the referendum on the Charlottetown deal. Now, however, they were reaping the rewards of that Bourassa decision. "They asked us a simple question and they will get a simple answer," Parizeau said repeatedly throughout the campaign.

Quebeckers voting Non didn't have to commit themselves to sovereignty to be on the Parizeau–Bouchard team; they could simply use the Non vote to say the same thing as other Canadians — sorry, not a good enough deal. Polls at the end of the campaign confirmed this. Quebeckers were comfortable saying No to the Charlottetown deal; they were not so comfortable saying a flat No to renewed federalism. On October 27, once the referendum was over, it meant that it was still impossible to tell the lie of the land in Quebec — whether it was leaning towards separatism or towards federalism. That just wasn't the question in 1992.

Bourassa and Mulroney tried their hardest to argue that the Non campaigners were trying to lure Quebeckers down the road to sovereignty, and that the only logical vote for a federalist was a Oui on the ballot. But even key members of Bourassa's own party were having a hard time buying that argument. Even before the referendum campaign was truly under way, even before the first television ads appeared, Bourassa lost two major players to the Non team. Jean Allaire, the man who wrote the book on Liberal demands on national unity, bolted Bourassa's team to join the Non side. So did Quebec Liberal youth president Mario Dumont. The defections showed that Bourassa's support had eroded not just at the fringes, but at the centre of his political power.

For one brief evening during the referendum campaign, Bourassa appeared to have Parizeau on the run. In a televised debate, the Quebec premier stabbed the air, pointed at the PQ leader, in a tour de force of constitutional technicalities and detailed arguments in favour of the Charlottetown deal. Mulroney, glued to the television set to watch the performance, pronounced to his chief of staff, Hugh Segal: "Our guy's just taken home all the marbles."

But technical arguments weren't going to win the battle. A deeper, more visceral battle was being waged between Bourassa and Parizeau that had nothing to do with what Quebec got and everything to do with that perennial question: "What does Quebec want?" The answer, in the fall of 1992, was "not Charlottetown."

Bourassa had also tried to make hay of one misstep of the Non forces, when Quebec comedienne Diane Jules had said that the elderly were too afraid to vote Non. But the blunder was a minor sideshow in the keynote performances of the Parti Quebecois' allies. Parizeau diffused the damage by simply apologizing for any insult to the elderly people. Bourassa was back on the defensive the next day. Besides, Parizeau wasn't the only enemy that Bourassa had to battle, or the most dangerous adversary. The most devastating blow to the Yes side came from within Bourassa's own fortress, within the civil service.

In mid-September, just as the referendum campaign was beginning, a Quebec City radio station broadcast a promotion for their newscast. They had a bombshell; a transcript that would devastate the Yes campaign. The transcript was of a telephone conversation between the top constitutional bureaucrats, Diane Wilhelmy and André Tremblay. Bourassa's own advisers had taken the measure of the Charlottetown deal and found it wanting. The top constitutional thinkers in Quebec had accepted the No side's biggest argument — that Quebec lost a lot at the constitutional talks.

Wilhelmy rushed to court and obtained an injunction to halt publication in Quebec. But *The Globe and Mail* obtained the transcript and ran the story on its front pages, in newspapers circulated all over Canada — except Quebec. The picture painted by the bureaucrats was an ugly portrait of a weak, foolish Quebec government, put in its place by the rest of Canada.

"It has taken me three days to accept the fact that we have settled for so little," Wilhelmy said in the transcript. "I keep telling myself this can't be, this can't be. I probably don't understand. There must be a strategy behind all of this." The language of humiliation and rejection ran deep in the transcript. "We are walking on our knees, you know. I think they have holes in them. It just doesn't make any sense." As the conversation went on, they talked about Quebec being harassed and beaten up by the other provinces. "It is a heavy burden to carry, especially on the psychological level, with all these people against you," the bureaucrats said. "And the Ontarians, they are the worst sons of bitches that you can imagine."

The conversation backed up that sense of blinking disbelief felt by Quebec reporters back at the Pearson Building in August, when it seemed that Bourassa had accepted so little. Now these Quebec reporters knew that they weren't the only ones who were shocked — his own officials were not behind him. People began to utter the words that were unspeakable only a couple of months earlier — perhaps the Quebec premier was ill, weakened by the deadly melanoma that had sent him to the United States for treatment after the Oka crisis in 1990. Soon after the referendum, in fact, it would be announced that Bourassa was plagued with the spread of this cancer. In the transcript, the officials merely portrayed Bourassa's actions as weak and fearful. "He never wanted a referendum on sovereignty. . . . We just caved in, that's all."

Bourassa would spend the referendum campaign trying to quell the civil servants' mutinous attack on him. But he was like a punching bag, reeling from one blow, bouncing back up, and facing another knockdown punch. Just after he had pulled his Yes campaign together again and made a solid showing for himself in the debate with Parizeau, another transcript floated out, to *L'actualité* magazine. The message again was that Bourassa lost at the unity table. Nor did B.C. constitutional affairs minister Moe Sihota help matters when he declared in his province that Bourassa had been stared down to defeat by the other provinces. Another devastating blow, this time imported by a British Columbian.

Nothing Bourassa could do would save his campaign. Even his old friend Brian Mulroney couldn't deliver any rescue for him, no matter how hard he tried. And he did try. In an interview with *The Globe and Mail* at the close of the referendum campaign, the prime minister gave an animated, fierce defence of his friend, explaining that it was Bourassa's plight that put the unpopular Mulroney front and centre in the referendum campaign.

"This is a rough business. We had people like Parizeau and Bouchard calling Bourassa a traitor, a liar, a deceit, a weakling and a sellout. And I'm supposed to sit idly by and allow my allies in the fight for Canada's future to take this pummelling without a response? No way. My obligation was to get in there."

Mulroney had always known that the toughest sell for the national-unity deal would be in Quebec. Indeed, he often got swallowed up in his own obsession with Quebec's politics, forgetting that a political battleground in Quebec is very different than one in the rest of Canada. That's how he stepped into trouble with the No forces in the rest of the country, accusing his opponents of being enemies of Canada.

"I know that there'll be fights and I know there are going to be challenges, and I know that the enemies of Canada will not be happy," Mulroney declared. It was a challenge that was ignored by Parizeau and Bouchard, but one that was seized upon by the public outside Quebec. As we have seen, it was a quote that backfired spectacularly, a strategic error rooted in Mulroney's obsession with battling the separatists.

Even in that *Globe and Mail* interview in the closing days, Mulroney was agitated and angry with the separatists, still believing he could put them on the run. In his breast pocket, he was carrying a copy of remarks made by Parizeau the day before. He was sure he had caught Parizeau in a major blunder. He was sure in these last few days he could make Quebec's federalists think twice about casting their lot with the Non forces led by Parizeau. The proof of Parizeau's intentions? An escalation in the PQ rhetoric on Monday, October 19. Parizeau declared that sovereignty was the next logical step after a No vote in the referendum.

"This is an astonishing statement," Mulroney said. "It runs counter to every single bit of their strategy and they're all running for cover today."

At the headquarters of the Yes committee, the strategists were desperately trying to lash out at Parizeau and Bouchard as well. The closing Yes ad of the referendum campaign was a far cry from the faint, vague appeals of the early days. The last television ad went right for the throat. It depicted smiling PQ and BQ leaders, smug with victory. The ad asked Canadians: Do you want these men to be smiling after the referendum? Would you vote No and make these separatists happy?

But the message was lost on the Canadian public. So deep was the sense of French–English isolation in Canada in 1992 that the plight of Quebec or the spectre of Quebec separatism made scarcely a ripple in the rest of the country. Outside Quebec, the No forces had been prepared for the battle strategy that would try to paint them in the same corner as Quebec separatists, as enemies of a united Canada. That was the charge that was laid at the door of the Meech opponents during the late 1980s, and this time the No campaigners were ready to beat back that notion.

Manitoba Liberal leader Sharon Carstairs, vilified in Quebec for her opposition to Meech, put up with far fewer accusations of racism in the referendum campaign. She also noticed that those ugly undertones of racism were seeping away from the unity debate.

"One of the things that amazed me was the absolute lack of anti-French sentiment. Now, I mean, I've lived through the worst of this in Manitoba. Certainly it was virulent in 1983 and it was almost as virulent in 1987/88. I had often found myself writing letters saying, 'I'm not doing this because I'm anti-French,' and 'Yes, I do believe in official bilingualism.' I didn't have to write any of those letters this time around, because I didn't get any of that."

At the Reform Party's headquarters in Calgary, the strategists set up a 1-900 line, so that people could actually register the fact that the No vote was not a no to Quebec and that a No voter was not an enemy of Canada.

"What we did have to think about more was from the strategic standpoint of could we take the No position and communicate it in a way that didn't just allow us to be caricatured as anti-Quebec or anti-French or anti-Confederation, which you know was the box that the Mulroney people wanted us and the BQ to be in."

In the end, Manning was surprised that he didn't have to defend his No vote on these grounds. It just wasn't much of a factor, he said. But it was a factor in the bomb dropped by Trudeau in the referendum campaign, and Trudeau's words were used by Manning and others to demonstrate that they were not anti-French. In fact, though, Trudeau's words lit a fire under those people who had always suspected that Quebec, as a province, was looking for something unfair from Canadians — some would call that sentiment racist. Trudeau, with a rhetorical flourish, warned that the rest of Canada had made itself vulnerable to "master blackmailers" in Quebec.

Trudeau had told B.C. Liberal leader Gordon Wilson that he would only speak out in Quebec during the referendum campaign, even as Wilson pleaded with the former prime minister.

"That's where he saw his most effective role. Because Trudeau's feeling is that there's no Quebec politician, no francophone politician, federal politician, that has any credibility in the province of Quebec to be able to deal with that," Wilson said.

However, it wasn't in Quebec where Trudeau's words had much resonance. Quickly, almost effortlessly, Bourassa and Mulroney were able to tamp down any damage inside Quebec.

Bourassa said simply: "There's no evolution in his thinking. What he's saying in the 1990s, he was saying in the 1960s, in the 1970s and in the 1980s." Even Parizeau, also fighting for a No vote, dismissed the Trudeau talk of Quebec blackmail. "It's so abusive toward Quebec, so scornful that I think it will fade away rapidly. Many people will just shrug their shoulders," Parizeau said.

But in the rest of Canada, Trudeau's words picked up remarkable momentum. If a Quebecker could say that his province was a master blackmailer, why couldn't English Canadians say the same thing?

"He made anti-French feeling respectable," said Bob Rae. "For that I will never forgive him. . . . It's not just anti-Quebec, it's anti-French. And to play into that contempt and to go along with it — for the sake of what?"

Rae kept running into people during the referendum campaign who were using Trudeau's words to justify their anti-French sentiments. He was livid with

the former prime minister. "Maybe it's some psychological thing with him. It's something going on inside
himself. I don't know what it is. But what I do know is
that the political impact it had, in terms of stability in
this country, was completely negative."

There are others who will argue that the No victory
proved that Trudeau's idea of "tough love" for Quebec
is the one that should always prevail. Look how poorly
Mulroney fared in cultivating a special relationship
with Quebec; in trying to coddle it into confederation
with honour and enthusiasm.

Mulroney and Bourassa had argued that Trudeau
was a spent force in Quebec, that it was only outside the
province where his views held any credibility. But
Deborah Coyne, the lawyer and former Wells adviser
who served as the voice of Trudeau Liberalism in the
country throughout the referendum campaign, says
that his legacy has also sunk into his home province of
Quebec.

"He is not a marginal force," she said. "Look at all the
majorities he pulled in during the 1970s. There is obviously a legitimate current of thought in Quebec that
has no articulation right now.... The ideas he argued
for were not just his ideas, they were liberal principles
that a lot of us believe should be the basis for our political system." A resurgence of that view is just waiting to
happen in Quebec, says Coyne, no matter how much
the politicians of the 1990s may try to deny it.

Trudeau's ideas were not on display in the Quebec
marketplace of constitutional thought from 1980 to
1992, nor were they welcomed in the front door in
Ottawa; they sneaked up behind the politicians or
made their impact in the wings. Trudeau's idea of
Quebec was of a province that should be prepared to
fight head-to-head with the rest of the nation, on equal
turf with equal ammunition. Trudeau would say that

Quebec was strong enough to ensure its distinctiveness
in a bilingual nation, not one that put French in one
camp and English in another. This was not a view that
would be seriously entertained by anyone in Ottawa or
Quebec City in the years after Trudeau left office.

At the end of the 1992 referendum campaign,
however, the mood of the nation was shifting towards a
Trudeau-style face-off between the old Canadian partnership of French and English. In Quebec, the forces
that agitated for a Non vote were becoming more
emboldened in their campaign to put the real question
to Quebeckers: Do you want to stay in Canada or do you
want to separate? In the rest of Canada, the mood of
the No forces was registering the same sentiment: Just
ask the question; let's settle this once and for all.
Quebec and the rest of Canada did not arrive at this
attitude in tandem. They pursued their dreams and
their wants in exile from each other for two long, iso-
lating years. The referendum campaign was not an
exercise in understanding the other side. Quebec's referendum campaign and all its experience from 1990 to
1992 was an entirely separate effort from the giant multilateral mission to answer Bourassa's question: "What
does Canada want?"

In the wake of the failed national-unity exercise of
1992, the question would become more pointed: "Does
Canada want Quebec?" In Quebec, they asked: "Does
Quebec want Canada?" United at last in their fallen
national-unity missions, Quebec and the rest of Canada
were left with only more questions to ask of each other.

The pointed questions were not being asked inside
Quebec, however. For the short term, at least,
Bourassa's elaborate dance of ambiguity and political
caution appeared to have paid off in the wake of Charlottetown. He escaped from the post-Meech turmoil
without ever having to put the question of separatism

to the people, without really having to face off against the nationalists to determine Quebec's fate in the Canadian nation. Moreover, until Spring 1993 Quebeckers were more concerned about Bourassa's personal struggle rather than his political future. His battle with deadly skin cancer in the months after Charlottetown was a courageous one. His recovery after experimental treatment prompted a massive outpouring of emotion and affection from his friends and foes in the National Assembly.

5

British Columbia:
Against Its Will

The two British Columbia politicians were speeding along in a cab to Ottawa Airport, and one more long flight back home to their faraway province. This national-unity business was just too difficult for a B.C. politician. Too much travelling, too much dabbling in the Central Canadian obsession with constitution-making.

Moe Sihota, the B.C. minister of labour and constitutional affairs, could simply have been titled the minister of hard work in 1992. He was exhausted after months of negotiating in the multilateral ministerial conferences (MMCs), and fed up with the no-win situation for British Columbia. The drab Ottawa scenery flash past the window of his taxi. The bare landscape, the flat industrial sites and subdivisions on the way to the airport were nothing compared to the vistas from the window of a taxicab in British Columbia. But there in the Ottawa cab that summer day of 1992, Sihota turned and looked at his boss, Premier Mike Harcourt, and smiled. He recognized the signs as Harcourt talked.

"Mike, you know, you've just got the IV plugged in," Sihota told the premier. He recognized that gleam in Harcourt's eye, that need to talk about vetos and equality and power-sharing and context clauses. It was the constitutional intravenous machine, pumping its addictive substances into a politician who had strenuously resisted the powerful political drug. "And it will never come out," Sihota warned him.

British Columbia hadn't planned to put the premier or the province into the national-unity crusade. This was not British Columbia's battle, nor was it the government's intention to plunge these two politicians into the whirlwind of constitutional talks in 1992. They certainly knew that B.C. voters would not thank them for any extra efforts in the constitutional crusade.

In fact, there were only two rules governing British Columbia as it was pulled into the constitutional mission of 1992, two guidelines that served to explain nearly everything that British Columbia was to do in the constitution-making of the spring and summer, and in the referendum of the fall that year. Rule number one: British Columbians want the rest of Canada to know they are not flakes. Rule number two: British Columbians do not like being dragged into national-unity crusades, especially when they are driven by Central Canada.

With those two rules in mind, just about everything British Columbians did, whether the politicians, the public or radio-show hosts, could be understood by the rest of Canada. And with those two simple rules in mind, Moe Sihota, then a thirty-five-year-old political star, ventured into the national-unity business.

Rule number one was very big in Sihota's thinking. He was not going to see his province written off again as wacky or strange or eccentric. That had happened too many times before. His predecessor at the constitutional table was former premier William VanderZalm, a politician whose rise and fall was linked to the fortunes of his own theme park — Fantasyland. No jokes about the British Columbia government this time. No hints that this province was the class clown or the national village idiot. They weren't going to say about Sihota, as they had about VanderZalm, that he was only at the constitutional meetings to explain the hard parts to Alberta premier Don Getty.

So Sihota made the foray into constitutional territory, through the maze of cities that played host to the MMC negotiations. From time to time, probably a lot more often than other provincial negotiators checked their own credibility pulse, Sihota would monitor B.C.'s image. He would be flying home from one meeting or another, comparing notes with top B.C. constitutional bureaucrat Jack MacDonald. Sihota would ask: "So, what's the chatter about us?" All he wanted to hear was that B.C. was not being written off as a bunch of kooks or political lightweights. As time went on, the constitutional affairs minister would feel that he had obtained this one goal. "You know, Jack, at least we've got credibility," he'd say.

Looking back now, Sihota is still content with the reputation that he established. "We were kind of an honest player on this thing. We didn't go in with an ideological agenda. We were very practical. We just wanted the thing solved. We wanted to get it behind the country. And Mike and I were very, very practical."

Being very, very practical meant keeping Harcourt as far away from the constitution as possible. The B.C. team would shiver visibly at the idea of Harcourt in a group photograph with the modern-day fathers of Confederation, with Prime Minister Brian Mulroney at the centre of the snapshot. David Perry, a Victoria lawyer who had come on board to help out Sihota in the negotiations, joked that reporters shouldn't blink when Harcourt eventually did have to show up at the talks. He would be in and out of there so fast, Perry said, that there would hardly be time to capture a picture of him. If Harcourt were to spend more than five minutes with the national-unity mission, his political fate would be sealed. There was, after all, rule number two to consider: British Columbians hate being dragged into national-unity crusades.

So the unenviable job fell to Sihota, who would devote all his energies to the exercise in 1992. He would be so consumed by the constitution, in fact, that he would recognize that addiction when he saw it emerge in Harcourt months later, when the premier flew in the face of his political instincts and joined the national-unity bandwagon. For a few months before that, though, it would be Sihota's obsession.

Sihota was correct to worry about his reputation and about being seen as a flake. His colleagues in the West were perplexed by this young politician, difficult to read, whose speech was liberally sprinkled with words such as "like" and "you know." It was just like Sihota to describe a politician giving a diatribe as "going ballistic." In times of exasperation, it was Sihota who would utter the phrase: "Give me a fucking break."

Alberta's Jim Horsman, dean of the constitutional circle, referred to his bewilderment with Sihota at regular intervals in the diary he kept throughout the negotiations. The British Columbian's name pops up frequently in the early days of spring. Horsman found Sihota very "West Coast," very laid back and casual about the whole mission. At the first meeting of the Western delegates in Halifax, on a cold April night in Horsman's hotel suite, no one could figure out whether Sihota was an ally or not.

A real Western province would want to be part of

a Triple E Senate crusade, the Prairie politicians thought. A real Westerner would join forces with the other alienated, isolated provinces and play on the team against Central Canada. But the Rocky Mountains separating British Columbia from the centre of Canada also blocked B.C. from its closest neighbours in Alberta, Saskatchewan and Manitoba. Sihota, much to the amazement of the other Western politicians, was not going to be part of the team. Like his province, he was a lone wolf among the Western pack.

"We thought B.C. might come to us before Ontario would," Manitoba justice minister Jim McCrae said, recalling that first meeting back in Halifax. "We thought B.C.'s interests are obviously going to be well-served. If their so-called vision of an equitable Senate isn't on, they'll be the first ones to jump in with us.

"So I think we were trying to feel out what we could achieve with Moe. And this turned out to be a disappointment."

Horsman would describe Sihota in his diary as a "slender reed." McCrae also remembers the frustration in dealing with this province that had no vested interest in anything but surviving the constitutional ordeal.

"B.C. sat on the fence a lot. And I'm sorry to say that I think they could have helped us early on. We could have settled the issue of the Senate earlier than we did, if we could have got B.C. on side earlier."

But the Triple E Senate crusade was, if nothing else, a religion, and British Columbia was a confirmed agnostic concerning any constitutional creed. Sihota would always talk about being "very, very practical." For all the frustration that his Western colleagues felt about him, the word quickly got out in the wider constitutional circle that this man from British Columbia was the one to watch. He was able to cut through the bluster of other national-unity crusaders. He could see through the pretentious, the ostentatious and the ridiculous, and he was not afraid to speak his mind. In those early days, Sihota could be counted on to pull the meetings back on track. Maybe the previous British Columbian at the table hailed from Fantasyland. This B.C. minister was not going to let anyone, especially his own delegation, be dragged into the realm of the fantastic at the constitutional table.

British Columbia, in other words, would not be dragged away from its own priorities, which had to do with the economy and Asian trade. Take, for example, the dinner that British Columbia hosted when the travelling multilateral ministerial conference landed in Vancouver for its three days of meetings at the Radisson Hotel in mid-May 1992.

The bedraggled mass of politicians, bureaucrats and other constitution-watchers had spent the previous week in Saint John, New Brunswick, where it was unseasonably cold and snowy. Vancouver, warm and sunny and magnificent, spread out before them like a reward.

Dinner, however, was a lesson in itself about the priorities of British Columbia. The meal was a sumptuous array of Asian delicacies: a sixteen-course dining adventure of dim sum and other Pacific Rim treats. Harcourt, who was violating his constitutional quarantine to play host to this occasion, talked incessantly about trade opportunities in the Pacific Rim and the importance of British Columbia's reach abroad into that Asian circle. All the talk about the constitution was as foreign to Harcourt as the evening's cuisine must have appeared to many other politicians at the table.

There was no question that Harcourt had his eyes fixed on more distant shores than those of Meech Lake or other Canadian constitutional landmarks. The premier made no apology for being interested in other issues. After all, that's what British Columbians wanted.

"We were a new government in the first six, eight months of setting up...immense, ambitious goals," Harcourt explained. British Columbia's new government had listened to the people, he said, and they were not interested in the constitution.

"They wanted us on to the economy and we got on to that very quickly. The first trip I made was ten days after I got to be premier, and it was to the East. And by East, I don't mean Toronto or Montreal, I mean the important East, which is Tokyo and Hong Kong, to let the people there know that we're open for business."

Later, many said that Harcourt paid the price for ignoring the constitution as it crept up on his government. Despite the considerable efforts spent on being credible and constructive and "very, very practical," the B.C. premier would find himself, almost unbelievably, being singled out for ridicule and buffoonery at the constitutional table. It came as a shock to a government that had been so defensive about that very issue.

Harcourt spoke the language of trade well — it was the language that he used to build up a relationship with Quebec premier Robert Bourassa. Maybe he didn't share Quebec's fixation with the constitutional issue, but Harcourt did share Bourassa's ambitions when it came to trade and prospects abroad. On this foundation, the two premiers built up a quick understanding when they met at the annual conference of top politicians and economic thinkers in Davos, Switzerland, in early 1992.

"We hit it off in a number of ways," Harcourt recalls. "Personally, we hit it off." British Columbia wanted to expand its influence as a province into the Asia Pacific territory. Quebec had its sights set on a greater presence in Europe and among francophone nations. "What they wanted, we wanted for the same reasons. *Maîtres chez nous.*" Masters of their own house. Here was

where British Columbia could establish its constitutional priorities. Not in some crazy scheme to be an
equal province among others, like a Triple E Senate,
but to be one of the big players, with a huge presence
at home and formidable influence abroad. This was
also a strategy that could build a bridge between the
two very different extremes in the political spectrum in
British Columbia, the two extremes that make it so difficult to govern the province.

Sihota knew that his NDP government was sufficiently new and activist-minded that it could generally
count on the support of the left wing in B.C. It was the
right-wing Social Credit party, noisily making its way to
lowly third-party status in the province, that could be a
problem.

"We were very pragmatic," Sihota said, stressing once
again the B.C. strategy to put the practical over the
philosophical. "I wanted just more constitutional
power around economic issues. Which historically had
been what B.C. governments had always asked for. . . . I
felt that I could sell it in this province on division of
power, because the Socreds also understood that; they
had always wanted it, and I was proceeding on their
agenda around division of power. So I could always
develop a coalition between left and right on that, and
always got accolades at home from the right for working
on division of power."

It was true also, that this was a good way to link
Quebec and British Columbia in Sihota's thinking. But
it was more than just politics or economics that figured
in Sihota's mind as he tried to build common cause
with Quebec. Something far more personal was at work,
something that would provoke a visceral reaction in
Sihota whenever he felt that Quebec was in danger of
being isolated, or left to fend for itself in the large
Canadian nation.

"I grew up in this country as a kid, born a Canadian, born in Duncan, growing up in a little Vancouver Island community called Lake Elgin," Sihota explains. "Not being able to speak English until I went to school. Growing up in a neighbourhood that was predominantly East Indian, if not entirely. Knowing how important my own culture, my own language, my own religion is to me. You know, it doesn't take a giant leap to realize how someone from Quebec with the French language or French culture can feel alienated in this country as well.

"Now, I've never felt alienated, but I know how important it is to me to preserve that."

Sihota has two children, a daughter and son, four years apart in age, who speak Punjabi at home. He wants them to live in a country where they can be Canadian and enjoy their own culture as well. So when he tries to understand Quebec and its need to protect its differences within Canada, an emotional, very deep chord resonates within him.

"It's got very little to do with ideology or politics. It's got everything to do with me as an individual and how I feel about this country. And I honestly and deeply feel that Quebec has to be made to feel at home in Canada."

This was a politician, however, who could be counted on to administer some "tough love" when it came to his Quebec brethren. As the travelling constitutional road show got under way that spring of 1992, it was Sihota, blunt-talking as always, who would be the first and strongest voice to protest Quebec's absence from the talks. True to his reputation as the straight-talker among the politicians, Sihota was the one who portrayed Quebec's absence as petulant and self-defeating. Asked in Edmonton about Quebec's demands to get Meech restored in the multilateral talks, Sihota made no secret of his annoyance. "If you left it at irritated,

that would be a fair way to put it." Later, too, in a messy
referendum campaign, Sihota's straight-shooting
about Quebec would stir up a lot of trouble for his
province and for Quebeckers who wanted to stay within
Canada. But that was much, much later, long after
British Columbia had found itself deep in the reaches
of Canadian constitutional politics, against its will.

For the first few months of the multilateral negotiations, British Columbia coasted along quite well. Sihota
was building up a respectable presence for himself and
his province. Liberal leader Gordon Wilson, a hard
man to please in the national-unity business, actually
conceded that Moe was doing a good job, even if the
constitution didn't stir a fire in his belly. The British
Columbia delegation could be counted on to offer constructive advice about everything from power-sharing
to distinct society. Its five-region Senate, at many twists
and turns in the Senate debate, often looked like the
most reasonable proposal on the table. The sheer
refusal of British Columbia to get embroiled in the
staunch campaigns at either extreme in the Senate
debate earned the province some valuable points as the
voice of reason.

"We weren't on anybody's side. Everybody liked us. I
talked with everybody.... You know, in the months
leading up to Mike's entry, I was chatting with all those
guys around that table, building up credibility. There
were issues where I would back one government and
then not another. And then I'd back one that I didn't
back on another issue," Sihota remembers.

But things started going awry, in British Columbia's
view, once the constitutional stage moved to Ottawa,
and once the real political artillery started coming out
in the early days of June. As Sihota and the rest of the
B.C. delegation saw it, a prime opportunity existed in
early June to shut down the crusade for an equal

Senate, and to end the long negotiations. A deal, they believed, was within reach, if only someone had enough guts to reach out and grab it. Rule number two was never far from their thoughts. British Columbians hate being dragged into national-unity crusades, and this one was just lasting far too long in Ottawa. Any time at the constitutional table is probably too long from B.C.'s perspective, but this process was getting ridiculous by June 8 to 11 — or so Sihota thought. Cut it off now, before it's too late.

When Roy Romanow jetted up from New York on June 10 and put forward his plan for an equal Senate with "weighted votes," that was the time, B.C. believed, to swoop in and pull Saskatchewan off the Triple E crusade. The Romanow plan proved that Saskatchewan was not inextricably linked to the absolute principle of provincial equality in the Senate — they should have been pulled, there and then, into the plan for a Senate in which five regions were equal.

Sihota was stunned that Constitutional Affairs Minister Joe Clark simply decided to shut down the talks on June 11 without even trying to make one more bid to end the Triple E Senate crusade.

"I'm at a loss to know why it is that the federal government would conclude that the matter should be put to rest," Sihota told the reporters.

From that day forward, the constitution was a downward slide for the British Columbians. The talks had endured past the point of tolerance, and the province was being shaken too much out of its cool, distant attitude to this Central Canadian obsession. Sihota and Harcourt, in a few weeks, would still be scrambling to win the constitutional sweepstakes with their five-region Senate. As they came into Ottawa late in June, along with the other premiers, they were embroiled in a furious set of meetings and car trips back and forth between the politicians, desperately trying to get a team on side. Sihota and Harcourt were seeing a lot of each other in these weeks, on planes, in hotel lobbies, in the backs of cabs.

At the Westin Hotel in Ottawa, they filed into the room of Prince Edward Island premier Joe Ghiz, trying to figure out what could be done. New Brunswick premier Frank McKenna was there too. If they could just get Roy Romanow to buy into the plan, momentum would be running for these Senate pragmatists and against the Triple E gang. Sihota came to be clearly frustrated with Romanow during the summer of 1992. That meeting did nothing to foster good feelings. As Sihota remembers it, Roy Romanow came into the room "with his own game plan." It was no help to British Columbia.

"His own game plan was basically to make Mulroney look bad, to have the thing fall apart, and to blame Mulroney."

Romanow, indeed, was starting to get annoyed with Mulroney's insistence that Ottawa and the federal government had set itself up as the "voice of Canada" in constitution-making, that the provinces were dismissed so summarily. Sihota watched then as Romanow left the suite — off, he said, "to work on the Triple E boys." In turn, Harcourt and Sihota jumped into yet another car and made their way over to the Ontario government's prestigious headquarters in the World Exchange Building in Ottawa, where Premier Bob Rae was installed, perhaps open to some convincing.

"We tried to get Bob to buy into five-region. And he was, you know, amenable to it, far more amenable to it if Bourassa could buy in." There it was again — the issue that linked Bob Rae and Sihota in emotion and politics: Quebec would not be isolated by either of these two men.

That encounter with Ontario was not without a slap-stick moment. As Sihota and Harcourt were preparing to jump into the car and head over to see Rae, they turned around and saw the tenacious and aggressive BCTV reporter Mark Schneider right on their tail. This was supposed to be a secret mission by the B.C. politicians. A sighting of these two B.C. politicians, madly shuttling around Ottawa, would only distort that carefully constructed image of a government trying to be cool and distant about this whole constitutional mess.

Schneider, borrowing his script from an old movie, got into a cab and chased the B.C. politicians on their secret mission to Ontario's office. The car pulled up outside the World Exchange Building. Sihota and Harcourt stepped out of their cab, looking up at the imposing building in front of them. Schneider was hot on their heels. He darted out in front of them, shining his camera lights in their faces, and asking: "Why are you going up here? Why are you trying to meet with Rae?"

Sihota and Harcourt uttered something non-committal, and turned towards the elevator. But the camera lights were shining in their faces — they couldn't really see where they were going. They walked in the wrong entrance. Harcourt and Sihota, a little embarrassed, retraced their steps, walked into the right entrance and made their way up to Rae's office. "We were looking a little clumsy. We didn't know where we were going because camera lights were in our face," Sihota said.

It was a fitting initiation for British Columbia politicians, who kept finding the cameras making them look clumsy that summer. And clumsy was the last description they wanted to invite. They didn't even want to be part of this circus. Rules number one and two were in force: they were not flakes and they did not like being part of the constitutional crusade. What could be worse, then, than to have Mike Harcourt thrown into the pilot's seat on this bumpy trip? That's precisely what happened at the end of June.

At 24 Sussex Drive, the constitutional dispute was tossed to Canada's first ministers, many of whom had carefully avoided any dealings with the difficult nego-tiations. Now, Prime Minister Brian Mulroney was back in the game and the premiers had been summoned to rescue the runaway multilateral deal. Outside the prime minister's residence that warm Monday morning in June, the premiers stood around, blinking in the bright sunlight, laughing — maybe a little nervously — about finding themselves in Ottawa, talking about the dreaded constitution. Certainly, it had not been part of Harcourt's plan to get this involved.

Hours later, after receiving rather abrupt marching orders from the prime minister, Harcourt was not only involved, he was in charge. British Columbia was host province that year to the annual premiers' conference, so technically B.C.'s premier was the politician charged with herding up the other provinces and getting them together to solve this "provincial" dispute. At 24 Sussex, over a light lunch and some heavy conversation, the premiers had basically been told that the Senate dispute was theirs to solve. Go to it.

"We'd been tossed the ball by the prime minister. He took off to Europe and we were told to fix it." As Har-court describes it, the issue was "dumped in our lap."

Harcourt made his way out to the waiting throng of re-porters across the road from 24 Sussex and walked into his first rocky encounter with the Ottawa constitutional media. He wouldn't offer any opinions on the state of the Senate dispute, and the reporters interpreted his silence as obfuscation. In turn, he grew antagonistic and defensive with each question. It was a bad start, and an accurate forecast of the hostile climate that would de-velop that summer between Harcourt and reporters.

The premiers' repair mission was set to take place at Toronto's Airport Hilton Hotel, a central location that would allow all the politicians to zoom in and out, and, with luck, make a quick stopover deal. But the prospects didn't look so good, and Harcourt couldn't help thinking that he had been nominated to serve as the pilot on a plummeting airliner. From the windows of the Hilton, you can watch the planes taking off and landing, and the roar of their engines often reverberates through the corridors.

At the hotel that day on July 3, the travelling constitutional mission seemed to be skidding down the runway to a certain crash. It was neither taking off nor landing.

"It was pretty tense," Harcourt recalled. "But once it had been tossed over, I wanted to see it through to a successful conclusion." So Mike Harcourt, leader of the New Democratic government of British Columbia and former mayor of Vancouver, put on his cap as consummate chairman of a council meeting, and prepared to roll up his sleeves and treat this as any other difficult battle of wills.

His first trick was to pull the sniping premiers into the meeting room. His fellow NDP premiers, Bob Rae and Roy Romanow, seemed more content to while away the valuable minutes at the microphone, taking shots at each other for the national media. "Come on, Bob," Harcourt said, loudly enough for a camera to pick up the annoyance in his voice and attitude.

"Chairing the premiers was not as tough as chairing the city council in Vancouver," Harcourt joked later. "Chairing meetings was something I'd been doing for quite a while . . . trying to get a thread, a string you could pull on . . . That's what we did on a number of those issues, whether it be the Senate, the unanimity requirement or the veto."

Alberta's Jim Horsman would write in his diary that day about the remarkable skill of Harcourt in getting this meeting in order. Of course, Horsman was happy about the way the meeting turned out, because Harcourt, with some efficiency, simply whisked every proposal except the equal Senate off the table.

"Harcourt did very well that day," Horsman later recalled.

Sihota was looking on, pleased. There was no way the British Columbians could be dismissed now as idiots or lightweights. They had saved the day. Sihota was tapping his feet, waiting to go on vacation to Disneyland, of all places. He had flown in from British Columbia on a red-eye flight; his wife and children had shown up later in the day. Sihota was to go to the Airport Hilton meeting, grab some sleep and fly to Disneyland the next day. His holiday lasted precisely one weekend — his wife and children were left to fend for themselves in the Magic Kingdom along with Sihota's sister-in-law, her husband and children.

Cutting short the vacation was the bad news. The good news, though, was that Harcourt had been successfully able to pilot the constitutional problem into yet another meeting, to take place in Ottawa on July 6 and 7. It should have been a moment of satisfied triumph for the B.C. group, a moment to wipe their brows over the mere survival of this meeting. It was not to be. Harcourt had grappled with the complicated protocol of a premiers' meeting; the complex web of spinners and reporters was just a little too daunting that day at the Airport Hilton.

A pact had been made among the premiers, but the only agreement was to hold another meeting. No final decisions had been made about the Senate. Of course, the fans of an equal Senate were irrepressible. Alberta's communications official, Bill Gadja, was out in the media room early that afternoon, glowing with victory and lavishing his praise on the chairmanship skills of Mike Harcourt. As the premiers filed out of the Airport Hilton that afternoon, they all started their addresses with the correct line — nothing was agreed to; we're just going to have another meeting.

Yes, yes, the reporters replied impatiently. But everyone knew that the Senate controversy had been reduced to one proposal and that the equal Senate was winning. Some premiers, more seasoned in this game of spinning and counter-spinning, abandoned the charade of non-committal agreement. Manitoba's Gary Filmon, for instance, offered a few explanations about this finalist in the Senate-proposal contest. But Harcourt was sticking to the script. Sihota, in the wings, winced as he saw his boss doing the right thing with the wrong effect.

"We were going to announce we were having another meeting on July 6, going back to Ottawa. We weren't going to announce that we had essentially the contours of a Triple E deal. . . . It really put us in an awkward position in terms of our government. Because Mike had gone there and kind of skated around the issue of Triple E and basically said we've agreed to have another meeting. . . .

"Back home we had a political problem. Because Harcourt was seen to be fuzzy, after he had played a significant role in terms of getting the thing going. And we felt a little damaged, because you know it was in our political interest back home to get some credit for moving this thing into Triple E. If we were going to go there, we might as well get some credit and we didn't get any. In fact, Harcourt was seen to be evasive."

True, the enduring pictures of that encounter with reporters would feature Harcourt, standing in front of a horde of reporters asking: "Which proposal?" and seeming to play coy about the equal Senate. This was only minutes after Joe Clark and a raft of other premiers had come out and given details about the latest entrant in the Senate contest.

That was the way it was to go for the British Columbians as the long summer wore on. They wouldn't get in any serious trouble for the substance of what they did, but they would constantly be landing in political hot water over the way they measured up with the rest of Canada. Sihota says he knew all along that it wouldn't kill British Columbia to go for an equal Senate. But all that pressure from the West, whether in his own province or from the three Western negotiators he genuinely liked, could not outweigh his own reservations about the Triple E Senate, intellectually or ideologically, as an NDP politician.

"I'm a Western Canadian, and someone who was under enormous political pressure to go for Triple E . . . even before I met any of these guys, right? Because there was pressure on us as a government to recognize Triple E," Sihota said. "I always knew in the back of my mind that if a deal was produced with a Triple E it was not going to cause harm to our government. But I didn't think it was the right public policy option. And to a large extent, that's why I stuck to the position. . . . Eight of us were ready to abolish it. That came up on a few occasions. And whenever it came up, you know, there was no problem there, we were all ready to abolish it."

Abolition was just not an option, given all the fervent Senate reformers around the table. And slowly, Sihota became more open-minded about an equal Senate, as did Bob Rae, when the two of them sat in that room in the Chateau Laurier on the night of June 9 and sketched out an equal Senate plan with their friend Bob Mitchell from Saskatchewan.

So it was not a huge leap from June to those first days of July, when it came time to approve the equal Senate at Ottawa's Pearson Building. Joe Clark, for one, said he had always wondered whether British Columbia was against the equal Senate or just happier with its own, five-region alternative. By July 6, B.C. had decided equality was a politically viable option. Only a month earlier, at that terrible dinner at the Pearson Building, Sihota had made a speech about everyone needing a "trophy" to take home from the constitutional talks. Well, British Columbia didn't get the trophy that would make it a region on its own in the new Senate, but it was happy enough with the result of the July 6 and 7 meetings, when the rest of Canada came up with its version of constitutional renewal.

Harcourt again was prevailed upon to help head up the difficult talks on those two days, and he did it in tandem with Joe Clark. They were roller-coaster sessions. Even after they had come so far and emerged from the Airport Hilton with their deal, they still ran up to the brink of failure several times in those meetings.

Lunchtime on July 7 was bleak. Everyone was close to giving up. Sihota was enraged because Quebec just kept sending conflicting signals about what it would accept. They thought they had a Senate deal, then it was reported back to the meeting, in that mysterious, perplexing way, that Quebec wouldn't accept the Senate on the table after all.

"This is the first time that I've seen Moe totally — just like somebody had stomped on his back, had stomped on him," Harcourt says. It wasn't only Sihota who was fed up with hearing from Quebec at a distance. A slow, grumbling mood at the lunch gave way to outright annoyance with the inability to read Quebec. Rae, of all people, seemed at the end of his tether with Quebec's shadow-dancing. The rest of Canada just decided to make its own deal and worry about Quebec later.

Still, there were principles to be tidied up, deals to make, even after that decision was made. For six hours that afternoon, the room was a hive of negotiation. Sometimes it was Joe Clark, off in the corner quietly talking to Clyde Wells. Sometimes it was Harcourt, bouncing out of the chair to lobby Alberta's Don Getty. Eventually, the deal came through. It was Harcourt who first faced the cameras that night of July 7.

"We've reached a compromise package for Canada on constitutional change. It's a package that I can take back to the people of British Columbia," Harcourt said. "I think we're all aware of the difficulty we face, though, of not having Quebec at the table. There were several conversations over the last few days with representatives from Quebec, but they were not involved today directly in the negotiations. So this was a Canadian compromise from nine provinces, but it is a good package . . . No one gets everything they want, but it was a good day's work."

Those words are sealed forever in Harcourt's remembrance of how things could have been that summer of 1992. He still believes, indeed, that it was a package that he could have taken back to British Columbia, a package that would have passed the referendum that B.C. was required by law to hold. Now he believes that every time that package tried to pass Quebec's test for approval over the following weeks, its credibility dropped correspondingly in British Columbia. These may be two provinces that want to be different from the rest of Canada, but they were locked in a tug-of-war on different sides throughout that summer of 1992.

"July 7 would have been a tight vote, but I believe it would have passed," Harcourt says.

The night of July 7 was a celebration for the British Columbia delegation. About a dozen B.C. officials and politicians converged on Mama Teresa's restaurant in Ottawa to wash down their victory with some wine and good Italian food. They were there, sitting together celebrating, when a television camera crew marched in with Roy Romanow, preparing to film his province's celebration in another part of the restaurant. Sihota asked the "Journal" crew if they would mind keeping his province out of the limelight. It was a time for private contentment, he thought. And rule number two was still in force — don't make a big deal out of British Columbia taking part in the national-unity mission.

At some point that night, Sihota turned to Harcourt and said simply: "You know, Mike? We're a good government. You know? We've done a good job here." They were never to feel that good again. The downhill slide started the next day, when they realized that not every Canadian shared their triumph, least of all the prime minister. In the days after the heady experience of July 7, they watched with dismay as Prime Minister Brian Mulroney and the Quebec cabinet members distanced themselves from the deal. What was all that effort about? Harcourt wondered.

"Everybody else came to the table able to deliver and the federal government couldn't, for whatever reason. It couldn't count on the federal cabinet, it couldn't come representing its constituency in Quebec."

Sihota was equally perplexed in those days, as Mulroney and Quebec turned their backs on the July 7 deal. For the umpteenth time that year, he took a moment to deliver some blunt talk to Quebec and the prime minister who was championing the cause of Quebec. He asked publicly: Is Brian Mulroney the prime minister of Canada or the prime minister of Quebec? The reaction from Ottawa was swift and furious.

"Mulroney's one of those guys who must monitor news like crazy. I mean, it's just a constitutional minister out of B.C.," Sihota said. "And he's going ballistic on our government . . . He phoned Mike up and bitched about the fact that I had said that." Sihota, once praised by Mulroney in conversations with Harcourt for his national-unity contributions, was now a non-person in the prime minister's books.

So when the constitutional negotiations finally got back on track in Ottawa, after all the various comings and goings at Harrington Lake that summer, Sihota found the negotiations to be a much more hostile affair. It was that fact that led him to "pressing" international business in London during the last set of negotiations in August, and away from the issue he had come to care about so deeply.

"Once Mulroney took control of the process, I never felt as if I was part of the process. And I felt that I had contributed well all the way throughout and that Mulroney took it in a direction that I didn't think was the way to go."

People, such as Sihota, who had devoted all their energy to this constitutional exercise simply felt that the show was now out of control and that they weren't needed.

"We got burned," Sihota said. "Because at the end of the day, I think on the seventh of July we had arrived at a package, which we knew from our political instincts was one that could survive. We also knew from our political instincts that the one that came out afterwards was very hard to sell."

Definitely, the hardest sell was for British Columbia, and it all revolved around what had to be done to get Quebec into the constitutional deal. The B.C. government may have tied its provincial dreams of strength to those of Quebec, but among the British Columbia public, any evident pandering to Quebec was too much. The entire summer of 1992 appeared to be devoted to making Quebec happy with the rest of Canada's deal.

Harcourt recognized the trouble as it started to emerge that summer. Ever since his election campaign in the fall of 1992, he had walked a very careful line when he dealt with the Quebec question. To appear progressive and broad-minded, he had to be in favour of Quebec as a distinct society. As a British Columbian, after all, he could respect distinctiveness in a province. But he also drew the line at special status for Quebec. There is a parallel here, he says, between what happened between July 7 and the Charlottetown deal on August 28, 1992. In the first deal, Quebec was distinct, not special. In the next part, Harcourt believes, Quebec was seen to be distinct and special. And it all revolved around the question of seats in the House of Commons. This whole fuss, which involved British Columbia's seats in the Commons too, signed the death warrant for the constitutional deal in B.C.

The first order of business was a complicated feat of arithmetic; all of it aimed at making an equal Senate more palatable to Quebec. In essence, the idea was to give Quebec an extra sixteen MPs in the Commons to make up for the senators they would be losing in the new Senate. Quebec had twenty-four senators, and that number was dropping to six. So it would get the extra seats in the Commons. It was Ontario who had first put forward the idea of extra MPs as compensation for lost senators — it was their price for accepting an equal Senate back in July. Ontario premier Bob Rae had reasoned: if the Senate is supposed to be the home of pure equality of the provinces, then the Commons will be the home of pure equality of people — and that means more MPs for Ontario.

It also meant more MPs for Quebec, British Columbia and Alberta, who were all under-represented in the Commons. The problem, though, was that British

Columbia was only being offered four seats — not enough for a province with its sights set on massive population growth over the coming years.

If this all seems like far too much of a mathematical exercise, that's because it was. Suddenly, in August, with the negotiations back on track and Quebec finally at the table, the constitutional talks had turned into an accountants' conference. Everyone had their calculators out, scribbling down numbers and proportions and statistical forecasts for population and demographics.

"It was ugly stuff," Harcourt remembers. Veteran negotiators such as Horsman were appearing more frequently outdoors for walks around the Pearson Building, doing anything to avoid the tedium of political arithmetic inside. Statistics Canada officials were pulled in, as were Elections Canada officials. British Columbia's delegation locked heads with Ottawa bureaucrats to figure out what formula would best ensure that B.C. had enough seats in the new Commons in the decade to come. By the end of that week, as the talks were preparing to head to Charlottetown for a final session, the formula was still not worked out.

Maybe the math in this whole exercise would have been too complicated to really stir up a fuss in British Columbia. Probably it was — it was weeks, Harcourt believed, until the real numbers story made its way into print or the media. But it's difficult to convey complicated arithmetic in news-speak. Headlines don't revolve around plus and minus signs, long division or fractions. There's only one kind of equation, really, that makes its way to the front of the political headlines — and that's the kind that features the "greater-than" and "less-than" signs.

What the public made of all this arithmetical wrangling could be reduced to this: B.C.'s gains < Quebec's

gains. Quebec negotiators > B.C. negotiators. Those
equations made the headlines because of one other
important number — the 25 per cent guarantee of
Commons seats for Quebec — forever.

B.C. Liberal leader Gordon Wilson was no accoun-
tant, but he knew the difference between an equation
that features an "equal" sign and ones that involve the
< and > symbols. Equality is a major issue for Wilson —
he has serious problems with greater and lesser proportions. The fax machines in B.C.'s delegation office
started churning out the dire warnings from Wilson.
"This is never going to fly in British Columbia," Wilson
warned the B.C. negotiators by telephone. Frantically,
he sought any of the other Liberals at the talks to
point out their folly in guaranteeing Quebec 25 per
cent. He had long, painful talks with Newfoundland
premier Clyde Wells. He had a tense, angry chat with
New Brunswick's Frank McKenna.

Sihota was on the telephone too, from London,
warning the B.C. negotiators that this 25-per-cent stuff
would be a very hard sell in British Columbia. "I don't
know," he would tell Harcourt ominously. "I don't
know."

Harcourt made two mistakes. For whatever reason,
the word did not get out strongly enough that British
Columbia still had more work to do in the whole fuss
over Commons seats. The issue was not settled by the
end of the talks in Ottawa. But everyone seemed to
believe it was over and Harcourt had fumbled. His
second mistake, he believes now, was to head out to
Charlottetown early that next week, instead of staying
at home to deal with the sceptical B.C. media.

The premier was ridiculed, almost immediately, for
screwing up the numbers game against B.C.'s interests.
A political cartoon appeared showing a befuddled Harcourt returning to British Columbia, bags in hand,

wearing a T-shirt, reading: "I went to the constitutional talks and all I got was this lousy T-shirt." Uh-oh, it seemed Harcourt had violated rule number one — British Columbians looked like flakes. Harcourt was nicknamed "premier savant" because although the stories were legend of his political skills at the table, he gave no outward sign of political consciousness. The price was being paid, it seemed, for his self-imposed isolation from the constitutional front. The rumour was that he didn't know what he was doing.

Harcourt now remembers those days during and after the Charlottetown conference as a succession of nails being placed in the constitutional coffin. The critics were coming out of the woodwork to say what a dunce he had been. Even the federal Tories, who supported the national-unity mission, were picking on the B.C. premier. En masse, the twelve British Columbia MPs in the federal Tory government did an end run around Harcourt and protested his deal-making to Mulroney. Stan Wilbee, chairman of the caucus, declared to the media that the letter was drafted because the caucus felt that Harcourt had negotiated a weak deal for British Columbia.

Harcourt saw this protest as pure "treachery" and wondered how Mulroney could turn a blind eye to the caucus's stunning lack of faith in a deal that was signed by Ottawa too. No one in the media was reporting any big gains for British Columbia, even though Harcourt and other B.C. people had attempted to sit down and explain themselves to reporters, in private sessions. They wanted the news out that British Columbia now had six senators out of sixty-two, instead of six among 112 in the current Senate. They wanted the news out that British Columbia was getting seven more Commons seats by 1998, instead of the two more they were supposed to receive by 2002. Instead, the news was filled with suggestions that Harcourt had dropped the ball in the constitutional game, and that B.C. had lost.

Harcourt didn't help his own case, however, by hopping out of the province to give a speech in Los Angeles just as the referendum campaign was getting under way. It looked like he was fleeing an unpopular deal. He was too quiet. He was, as Vancouver's abrasive call-in host on CKNW Radio, Rafe Mair, would later say, "nowhere" in this all-important campaign.

The B.C. premier says in his defence: "It wasn't an election campaign . . . I really believed my role was to inform the public and to let them decide." He was frustrated, too, that the big machine in Ottawa couldn't grind out any information to get to the B.C. voters. He'd had his constitutional education, and now it was his electorate's turn to do their national-unity homework.

"The slowness in getting the information to them drove the eleventh and twelfth nails in. And it made it really hard to get, to deal with the half-truths and total lies that were being told about what was in the deal and what wasn't in the deal, when they couldn't get the deal in their hands."

More bad news for British Columbia came in mid-September when it became clear that it had been deemed the perfect site for Brian Mulroney's first stop in the referendum campaign. The prime minister wasn't wrapped in the flag on this first stop — he was wrapped in a Squamish blanket, and he focused his first appeal on aboriginal leaders. What he was doing, really, was talking about the easiest sell of the national-unity deal in the hardest-sell province outside of Quebec. His visit to British Columbia didn't help, though. In fact, his very presence there was baffling to politicians such as Harcourt, who knew that this prime minister could do more harm than good.

"I'm not being critical of Brian Mulroney because he

was campaigning hard on this," Harcourt said. But the reality, illustrated starkly by an Angus Reid poll, showed that for every person Mulroney persuaded to vote Yes, he persuaded two to vote No.

"You know what the figures were in B.C.?" Harcourt says. "Four to one. Four to one. That's a tough weight to carry around. When you're already twelve feet down in this agreement."

It was almost as if British Columbia had been waiting for this chance to tell Brian Mulroney and the rest of Canada to stuff their constitutional deals. A surge of No force burst forth in British Columbia, launched at the grassroots, on the streets and hurtled across the airwaves, especially by Rafe Mair.

Dr No was his nickname. His opposition to the Charlottetown accord quickly became bigger than the deal itself. Suddenly, feature articles began appearing in newspapers across the country, examining the influence of this former Social Credit cabinet minister turned radio host. Mair made no apologies for his No campaign on the airwaves and pronounced himself proud to wave the banner for the ordinary folk in Canada. He viewed the entire referendum debate as a colossal showdown between the politicians and the public, and in British Columbia he was the leading figure on the side of the public — a natural role for him, he believed, because of his day-to-day contact with callers to his radio show.

The people, in Mair's view, were saying "don't mess with us." The No vote was a chance to humble the politicians and restore the supremacy of the public's will. British Columbians responded viscerally to this perspective, and Mair was becoming a sort of anti-politicians' folk hero. His popularity was a sure sign that the Yes side was in serious trouble very early in the referendum campaign.

This storm of B.C. protest wasn't going unheard in the rest of Canada. It was reverberating and bouncing all over the country. In Ottawa, at the headquarters of the Yes committee, the political strategists were working on a line of defence very early in the referendum campaign. The message? British Columbia was a big winner; British Columbia was a big province. In other words, Yes salesmen were being told, if you want to sell this deal in B.C., tell the British Columbians that their province is a major player in Canada, just like Ontario and Quebec. It was a haunting echo of the whole strategy that Sihota and Harcourt had adopted — let's try to be a big player. It was also an echo of the criticism that Alberta's Jim Horsman had hurled at British Columbia back in May — B.C. just wants to be one of the obnoxious, domineering, big provinces.

In fact, in a strange way, British Columbia *was* getting to be one of the big provinces, by proving itself to be a big problem for the Yes forces and all the formidable political weight that was thrown into the Yes campaign. The provincial government that had hitched its wagon to Quebec's dreams as a distinct province was showing the same distinct difficulties in the Yes campaign. Early polls kept showing the Charlottetown accord holding its own in every province, except British Columbia and Quebec, where it was slipping and sliding out of the politicians' grasp.

Every little word that was floated in one province seemed to land with a leaden thud in the other. Then, for one disastrous moment, two very similar messages collided. While Quebec premier Robert Bourassa was trying to contain the spectacularly unfortunate leak of taped transcripts, which featured bureaucrats bluntly declaring how the province had "caved in" at the negotiations, Sihota offered an equally unfortunate confirmation.

This was the infamous incident in which he told reporters in Quesnel that Bourassa had come to the table with unreasonable demands and lost. "Nine governments looked him in the eye and said No." In Quebec, that was seen as the B.C. translation of "caved in." Just when Quebec thought it might be able to beat back the Wilhelmy controversy, Sihota offered the Quebec doubters a licence to say "I told you so." Sihota, unwittingly, helped the separatists in Quebec. British Columbia, in turn, was listening to how Bourassa was trying to say that Sihota was wrong — that Quebec had actually won. And in Canada, in 1992, this nugget of logic applied: If Quebec won, British Columbia lost; if Quebec lost, British Columbia gained.

It didn't help in B.C., either, that Prime Minister Brian Mulroney was making a big deal about Quebec's gains, listing them, counting them. When he launched into his fiery and excessive defence of the Charlottetown accord, ripping up the deal in Sherbrooke, Quebec, British Columbians were not amused. The translation of Mulroney's defence of Quebec's gains in British Columbia? The rest of Canada lost.

A document circulated around the Yes committee strategists on September 29, 1992, was called "Talking Points: Charlottetown Agreement and B.C." Its mere existence, relatively early in the campaign, showed that British Columbia was big, big trouble for the Yes team. In brief, the key points that the strategists thought they had to address were as follows:

1. British Columbia gets more seats in the House of Commons.
2. Moe Sihota says B.C. gets more seats in the Commons.
3. Moe Sihota says B.C. now is equal to Ontario and Quebec in the Senate.

4. The guarantee of seats for Quebec is nothing special for that province.
5. Quebec's guarantee of 25 per cent is merely a reflection of reality; Quebec will probably always have 25 per cent of the Canadian population.
6. Quebec's population is double that of British Columbia.
7. The provinces getting more seats are just getting their fair share, nothing more.

The Charlottetown accord, in legal-text form, filled fifty-three pages. But just one page of that document seemed to be the big threat in British Columbia. All of these "talking points" zoomed in on the controversy over how well British Columbia had fared in the negotiations, compared to Ontario and Quebec. All of it dealt with British Columbia's voice at the centre of power, in the Commons and the Senate. For a province that wasn't supposed to be interested in Central Canada, an unusual amount of attention was being focused on how much power B.C. had in Ottawa and Parliament. For a population that was cynical about politics, these voters were very vigilant guardians of the right to political power at the centre. Still, the Yes committee believed they could win the argument, on the above grounds. The idea was that British Columbia would accept this deal once the people realized they had gone to Charlottetown and won something away from the rest of Canada.

But Liberal leader Gordon Wilson believes that this was a serious misreading of the B.C. voters. They don't want to be big shots, Wilson says — they just want to be treated fairly. All of this talk about the big gains for British Columbia looked like sheer political puffery.

"British Columbians want their fair share. That's all they want," Wilson says. "What they want is strong

national programs. They want to have national programs. They want to have a central government that
recognizes that they want to get equal dollar back for
dollar given. . . . British Columbians are immensely
nationalistic, tremendously proud of Canada. This
notion that somehow British Columbians want to split
from Canada, and be independent and isolated
. . . Nonsense, absolute nonsense."

In these days of "family values," it's become quite
popular to compare the country to a family. Wilson uses
the analogy to explain British Columbia's place as one
of the "difficult children" in the federation.

"You know, often you'll find in the family that the
child that's the most wilful is the one that really wants
more attention and wants to be part of the family. And
so what we hear British Columbians saying is: 'Don't
ignore us. We want to be an equal partner.' And people
in eastern Canada have misinterpreted that to think
somehow that this looney-tune group out there, the
lotus-land set that doesn't keep pace with the rest of
Canada, really isn't interested too much in what's going
on in Central Canada. And that's the biggest mistake a
federal politician can make."

Late in September, as the Yes committee strategists
were confronting the real trouble in British Columbia,
the Viewpoints polling company went out to hear the
voice of real B.C. voters. A group of sixteen people were
pulled in, most of them undecided, half of them
leaning towards a No vote. When the results were in,
the Yes committee didn't realize what they had — the
canary in the coal mine. There, over seven pages, is the
first scent of the poisonous atmosphere that would
overcome the Charlottetown deal in the coming weeks,
all over the country. The poll produced the following
conclusions:

- The 25-per-cent deal for Quebec was a huge problem.
- People were frustrated over a lack of information about the deal.
- The "élites" were a big problem. In the words of the Viewpoints researchers: "Many participants perceived a patronizing attitude on the part of Yes supporters — a belief that ordinary people aren't sophisticated enough to understand the issues and that they should simply vote Yes because those who do understand such things agree that it is the right thing to do."
- One "élite" member was not shunned. Former prime minister Pierre Trudeau, who had not even spoken out yet in his famous Maison Egg Roll speech on October 1, was named as the expert that B.C. voters would heed.
- Another "élite" member was shunned completely, as Harcourt and the Angus Reid poll had shown as well. "Perhaps most worrisome of all is the widespread belief that the referendum is at least in part a personal vote for or against the prime minister," Viewpoints reported. "Several participants argued that a win by the Yes side would bolster the prime minister's political fortunes and make it more likely that he is re-elected in the upcoming federal election — an outcome which they clearly did not look forward to. . . . The consensus among participants was that voting No was a good way of sending a message to the prime minister. Both groups expressed anger at his hard-sell approach, notably his tearing up of the accord at a speech in Quebec earlier in the week."
- British Columbia believed that the safe status quo belonged to the No side, not to the Yes people. All the people who talked to the Viewpoints researchers believed that Yes was the "riskier" option.

• Viewpoints was not blind to the fact that trends are all-important in any voting behaviour. "There is almost universal belief that the No side has the momentum at this stage of the campaign."

Here it all was — nearly every reason that Canadians needed to vote No in the great national-unity referendum. The seeds of the Yes defeat were all deeply planted in British Columbia by the end of September 1992, and the gusts of the referendum campaign would send them out to take root all over Canada by the end of October.

The Viewpoints poll also noted another point, almost as an afterthought. "There was absolutely no mention of the provincial government or premier in either group."

The politicians who had sped along in that cab on that summer day of 1992, swept up in the national-unity vortex, were forgotten and dismissed by British Columbians. No matter what they did, they had run up against a rock of political will larger than the wall of the Rocky Mountains that shielded B.C. from the rest of Canada. The people were not listening to the politicians; they were listening to Rafe Mair and the gathering thunder of the No storm rumbling into British Columbia. It was time for the Yes committee in Ottawa to scramble, to figure out who could be a good salesman for the deal in British Columbia. The Viewpoints polling company headed out again, in a desperate quest to find out who held credibility in British Columbia. Who could turn this thing around?

Clyde Wells was number one on the list. Among males, aged forty-five to sixty-four years old, earning $30,000 to $40,000, the Newfoundland premier was seen to be a convincing politician. And apparently this demographic group needed to be convinced, much to the surprise of the Yes advocates. The No force had grabbed some of the key decision-makers, the "élites" who were supposed to be on the Yes side.

Gordon Wilson thought that he was headed into the lair of the Yes beast when he went to address the Union of B.C. Municipalities convention in Vernon during the campaign. But here were many of these people, older males, earning a good dollar, and they were giving strong No signals. "There was such a strong reception from municipal officials," Wilson said. "These are front-line politicians. These are people that the Yes campaign was supposed to have. And they weren't with them." Wilson entered the room, nervous, on edge because this was a Yes committee event. It had been organized by the Yes folks and it featured speeches by the major Yes campaigners, notably Brian Smith, the head of the B.C. Yes committee.

"Here were forty or fifty of British Columbia's senior executive officers, all on the Yes campaign, and they invited me to come and explain myself. Brian Smith got up and gave a bit of a speech. He had set it up so he had a retort, a rebuttal. I can tell you that when I had finished, I knew that I had at least 25 per cent of them thinking: 'Geez, this guy's got a point.'" Wilson felt the mood in the crowd. "Their responses, their body language — it changed. They started to listen and then they started to question."

A couple of the business people came up to Wilson after the event and said: "Hey, wait a minute, does the language actually say that?" Wilson, earnest, almost evangelical about his No crusade, pushed them to think for themselves. "Don't take my word for it, read the document." Then he would pick up his well-thumbed copy of the Charlottetown accord, and preach to them about the evils of this unholy political deal. He was stunned to find that these were the first words that many of these

Yes people had actually read in the deal. "It was the most amazing thing. Many of them hadn't even read it."

The Liberal leader had hit upon the point that would win a lot of support for No campaigners in the referendum campaign, and it got at the heart of the whole, tattered relationship between the public and the politicians. Wilson and others were telling the people: "We respect your right to make a decision. Don't listen to anybody, not even me. Listen to yourself."

Respect, the same simple tool that had helped Joe Clark and Moe Sihota and Mike Harcourt learn to work together around the constitutional table for the first half of 1992, had been claimed and captured by the No forces in the last half of the year. It was the No forces who assumed that the public could be constitutional experts, given the chance; it was the Yes people who drew in other experts to try to convince the public.

Maybe all those senior executive officers would have listened to Clyde Wells, and maybe he could have persuaded those forty-five- to sixty-four-year-old males to cast a Yes vote on October 26. But the Newfoundland premier was also employing a bit of respect for the public, and he wasn't going to brow-beat anyone into voting on his side.

Wilson wanted to debate Wells when the premier finally did show up in British Columbia. He was refused. "I knew Clyde was coming out to B.C. He'd said that he would come out to B.C," said Wilson, who talked regularly to Wells on the telephone throughout the negotiations and the referendum campaign. "I was very concerned that they would try to bring Clyde out to directly go after me. And what I wanted, and what I asked for — and I think it would have been really useful — I wanted to have a televised debate with him. I really wanted to debate Clyde Wells on TV. . . . He would not do it."

Wells was not interested in brow-beating anyone, on television or otherwise. He had put up with far too much of that during his Meech tenure. British Columbia would go on to defeat the referendum with an amazingly strong No vote — 68 per cent. And Clyde Wells would be happier that British Columbia got to vote on its own, with no pressure from him, rather than being harangued or harassed into voting Yes. He would be happy that British Columbia and Quebec — and the West — were united in their rejection. There would be no accusations in this constitutional round that anyone had been forced to compromise their principles, or that they had destroyed Canada, or rejected Quebec.

Yes, Wells made the trip to British Columbia to see what he could do. He even appeared on Dr No's show, where Rafe Mair asked him how badly his arm had been twisted to get on the Yes campaign bandwagon. But Wells didn't rise to the bait. His mission, even with Dr No, was to treat the people with respect. He had learned long ago, during the Meech débâcle of 1990, that the constitutional mission was absolutely dependent on the value of respect.

6

The True Grits

One picture would endure of that terrible week at
Ottawa's Government Conference Centre in June 1990
— of an exhausted, rattled Premier Clyde Wells being
jostled through the crowd as he left the building. Television cameras turned their high-wattage lights on the
pale, haggard visage of Wells; reporters and onlookers
shouted questions at him. Dazed, shell-shocked, Wells
had only narrowly escaped the political pummelling of
Brian Mulroney's hard bargaining style, through an
intense six days and nights in the drafty old former
railway station. It was finally over on June 9, and the
country's first ministers believed they had found a way
to save Meech Lake from the jaws of defeat. Wells's
advisers held on to his elbows as he shakily made his
way across the street to the Chateau Laurier. The Newfoundland premier, normally known for his articulate,
forceful statements of principle, could only say on this
night that he had not agreed to anything. He would put
an asterisk next to his name on the "deal" that was
reached on June 9.

This was the picture of true Liberalism in 1990. Beaten, battered and confused, up against the formidable assaults of a new kind of constitutional vision — a vision championed by Mulroney and the provincial premiers who were ready to put a Meech stamp on the nation that bore the imprimatur of former prime minister Pierre Trudeau. Wells, though, as the champion of this Trudeau-style Liberalism, would emerge victorious; a hero in the rest of Canada for his defeat of Meech Lake and the unpopular Mulroney deal on June 22, 1990. But just two short years later, Clyde Wells and Brian Mulroney would be on the same side of the national-unity referendum. And they would both lose.

The story is a lesson for those who want to take on the Trudeau idea of Canada. You can be an enemy of Trudeau, like Brian Mulroney, and try to contain or beat back the Trudeau vision. Invariably, you lose, as Mulroney did twice, in Meech and with the Charlottetown deal. Or you can be an ally of Trudeau, like Wells or even New Brunswick's Frank McKenna, and try to reshape the 1970s vision to meet 1990s reality. You will still lose.

Over and over again, the lesson is hammered home to Canadian Liberals. The dynamic, modern Liberalism of Montreal businessman Paul Martin was no match in the 1990 party leadership race against the Trudeau-era nostalgia of Jean Chretien. One word from Trudeau in the referendum campaign had more firepower than all the speeches of the country's politicians put together. If nothing else, the Trudeau vision of the nation has remarkable resilience, which can overtake friends and foes alike. In 1990, it was Clyde Wells who was doing the overtaking. In 1992, it was Clyde Wells who found himself among the overtaken.

Wells bristles at being described simply as a Trudeau

Liberal. The idea of Canada embraced by Clyde Wells and so many like-minded Liberals across the country is far broader than one politician's invention.

Rumours, though, of an unholy Trudeau–Wells pact have always swirled around the Newfoundland premier. It was said during the Meech years that Trudeau was like the phantom, stalking behind the curtains in the new constitutional drama, nudging his actor, Clyde Wells, to centre stage. It was whispered in the corridors of various constitutional meetings that Wells's key adviser, Deborah Coyne, was actually sleeping with Trudeau and infiltrating the Newfoundland camp with the former prime minister's influence.

The rumours were 90 per cent false. By June 1990, Wells could count on one hand the number of tête-à-têtes he had with the former prime minister, and they revolved around general subjects, not dark strategies to thwart Mulroney. Even two years later, after Trudeau and Wells had met in mutual, anti-Meech victory at the Liberal leadership convention in Calgary, and in several subsequent encounters, it would be stretching the imagination to suggest that Wells was Trudeau's agent. The Newfoundland premier was very much his own man.

"There was no relationship with Pierre Trudeau," says Wells. "Let me say, though, that there was and still is great admiration for the political, intellectual and constitutional integrity of the man ... history will record him as the greatest prime minister this country has ever produced."

There was that little issue, though, of the 10-per-cent truth factor in the rumours. A little over a year after the death of Meech Lake, a birth certificate for Sarah Elisabeth Coyne fell into the hands of *The Globe and Mail*. The mother was listed as Deborah Coyne; the birthplace, St John's, Newfoundland; the birth date, May 5,

1991. The father was the Right Honourable Pierre Elliott Trudeau.

A child does not a conspiracy make, though. Coyne and Wells, both intensely private people, never discussed Trudeau's place in Sarah's or Deborah's life. Wells's media adviser, Judy Foote, is the godmother to the child, and a close friend of Coyne. But the subject of Sarah Coyne and her father is not a topic that Coyne or Foote would ever broach with Clyde Wells. The Newfoundland premier is the same in private as he appears in public — direct, principled, straightforward, a puritan aura about him. Coyne's private life was her own business. Clyde Wells examined the issue dispassionately, as any lawyer would. Told the news of Coyne's impending motherhood, and Trudeau's fatherhood, Wells chose to adopt the neutral, legal safety of surprise. "I had no reason to feel disappointment or discouragement. I was surprised by it.

"Now, she may have talked to Pierre Trudeau all of the time. I didn't know. As a matter of fact, when I hired Deborah Coyne, I had no knowledge that she even knew who Pierre Trudeau was. . . . It was only well after June of 1990 that I discovered the extent of her relationship with Pierre Trudeau. And that's not to say that I might have done anything differently."

While she worked with him, and afterwards, Coyne would enjoy Wells's trust and respect. The Newfoundland premier had hand-selected Coyne as his constitutional adviser in June 1989. They first met in Toronto, after Wells got word of this young, former University of Toronto law professor who had helped organize an anti-Meech citizens' group called Canadian Coalition on the Constitution.

Wells asked some of his staff members to put together some information on Coyne: her prolific writings on the folly of the Meech Lake accord, and particularly an article in the magazine *Policy Options* that had caught his eye. Coyne showed up at the Sheraton Hotel in Toronto for her meeting with Wells, with even more sheaves of anti-Meech papers in her hand. "She was a prolific producer," Wells said. The two quickly established a rapport; Wells was struck by the fact that Coyne's anti-Meech arguments were so similar to his own.

"Would you like to come to work for me as an adviser?" Wells asked. Coyne had just taken up a job with the Walter Gordon Charitable Foundation in Toronto — she couldn't just leave. Politely, she declined. But a few months later, driven by the need to do something concrete to defeat Meech, she approached Wells again and asked whether the job was still open. He happily welcomed her to the fold in St John's.

Long before she joined Wells's staff, Coyne had established herself as one of the cries in the wilderness against Meech, in those years when opposition was just coalescing. In fact, it was Wells's decision to hire Coyne that sent a signal to the rest of the constitutional world — look out, this province and this premier are not just casual opponents of Meech Lake.

Coyne has an arresting intensity; her words and ideas tumble over each other in a frantic race to be heard. Her demeanour is almost pixie-like, but her gaze and her attitude are anything but playful. She is earnestly serious about the constitutional business and the legacy of Pierre Trudeau. When Coyne and Wells got together in Newfoundland to take on the Meech forces back in 1990, it was a potent mix of principled intensities.

They had disagreements — rifts that would later surface when they took opposite sides in the 1992 referendum — but as the adviser and the advised during the troubled Meech era, when all the political forces seemed to be raining down on Newfoundland, Coyne and Wells worked together as a team.

But just as neatly, in 1991, the ties were severed when Coyne left the employment of the Newfoundland premier to pursue a career in Ottawa. Wells would continue to refer to Coyne fondly and respectfully as "Debbie," but the two did not speak to each other through all the time that Wells started negotiating the 1992 national-unity deal that resulted in the Charlottetown accord. When asked about Coyne, Wells talks about the respect he feels for her and her opinions. The allegations of Trudeau infiltration stir up indignation. "To suggest that this was somehow arranged and I was in league with Pierre Trudeau . . . Well, that helps those people who can't intellectually deal with the arguments that are being put forward."

Coyne, when asked, says she regards Wells as a professional friend. "We are still friends in the sense that neither of us would deliberately malign the other." If you should broach the subject of Pierre Trudeau with Deborah Coyne, she has a simple answer, delivered directly but without rancour. "I have no comment to make — next question."

Private though the subject may be, the Coyne–Wells–Trudeau axis is an enormously symbolic way to look at the strains on Liberalism in the 1990s. It may have never been intended as a dark conspiracy, but the way in which these three people moved in and out of each other's influence shows just how complicated the choreography is, when you are a Trudeau Liberal in Brian Mulroney's Canada.

By the fall of 1991, Deborah Coyne had left Newfoundland, amiably enough, and Wells was starting on his own road to Damascus — in this case, the road to the Charlottetown national-unity deal. There were

conversions along that road. Wells gave the first hint of
his coming conversion when he turned his attention to
the twenty-eight "Shaping Canada's Future" proposals
that Ottawa put out in September 1991. He talked
about "three equalities" — equality of citizens, equality
of provinces, and equality of French and English. In
these three simple principles were the foreshadowing
of Clyde Wells's biggest victory and biggest concession
in the 1992 constitutional deal.

His unwavering commitment to equality of provinces
would get him his much-wanted equal Senate in the
Charlottetown deal. But his acknowledgment of the
need for French–English equality would lead him to
support a type of collective rights for Quebec and
special constitutional provisions for that French-speaking province. This acknowledgment would set him on
a course against Coyne, against Trudeau and against
many grassroots Liberals in the country. It would put
him on the losing side of the 1992 referendum
campaign.

Wells played down any suggestion that he had made
a great philosophical leap in this speech. But it was a
major concession to Quebec for Wells to temper his vig-
ilance about Charter rights in the interests of Quebec's
distinct society. Nothing momentous had happened to
change Wells's mind. This was always an issue on which
he was prepared to temper his principles. But its significance was not lost on the constitutional world.
Clyde Wells had been among the first to take one of the
many leaps of faith that would be needed in this bid to
unite Canada.

In fact, this was the issue on which Coyne and Wells
had waged their own battles when they worked together
in Newfoundland. The role of the national spending
power was one key area where they disagreed, but the
more serious disagreement was on rights. Wells was

never as strong as Coyne on the absolute opposition to any special measures for Quebec.

"On those fundamental issues we disagreed," Coyne says. "I don't believe in those issues he reflected the majority of Canadians."

This wasn't just a Coyne–Wells disagreement. It went to the very heart of what separated Wells from the Trudeau vision. On October 1, 1992, Pierre Trudeau chose a whimsically named Chinese restaurant in Montreal, La Maison Egg Roll, as the base from which to hurl his attack against the Charlottetown accord. The old gang from *Cité Libre*, the political pamphlet he founded, were gathered en masse in the upstairs rooms of the restaurant to hear the master speak. Downstairs, it was only his master's voice, and the occasional tinkle of the tableware, which resounded through the speakers in the crowded rooms where reporters were posted. Trudeau spoke as the champion of the Charter of Rights and Freedoms. He spoke as a constitutional law professor, not one of the breed of politicians so despised by the public. He spoke as an opponent of Clyde Wells.

It was the singular event of the referendum campaign. Pollsters later would be drawing their graphs of public support for the Charlottetown accord in those tumultuous fall days of 1992; a bumpy "Yes" line made its way across the graph from the start of September, right up until October 1, 1992. After that, the line took a plunge — the graph was suddenly a picture of a jagged, steep cliff. After Pierre Trudeau spoke, the Charlottetown accord took a dive to rock bottom.

Manitoba's Liberal leader, Sharon Carstairs, had looked upon Clyde Wells in the Meech years as her polar star, the politician she would follow to find her way through the sea of deal-making that engulfed them

all in those final days of Meech in 1990. Vilified in
Quebec for her anti-Meech stand, that strange, throaty
voice imitated and mocked by her critics, Carstairs will
always see those days as the nadir of her political existence. When she finally buckled to a deal, fearing that
Manitoba would stand alone, her long opposition was
branded as superficial. When she confessed that she
had turned to mild tranquillizers to conquer the stress
of these days, she was dismissed as a crazy person.
Carstairs was never the same after that week; she lost
her Liberal ground in Manitoba in the next election,
falling from twenty to just seven seats in the Legislature.
The lesson for her was never to brush close to a Mulroney deal again. From now on, the Charter of Rights
would be supreme in her national-unity vision.

"I had made up my mind when I finally came out of
my Meech fog that I would not deal with the Charter
and the diminution of the Charter again. And they had
dragged all of that out of me that they could get in June
of 1990. . . . I just simply wasn't going to be co-opted
ever again."

Carstairs had actually lost her Meech battle, even if
the deal was killed in Manitoba. By signing on to the
June 9 deal of the first ministers, the same deal that
bore an asterisk beside Wells's name, Carstairs had lost
her title as a Meech opponent. She was accused of
caving in during the very days that Meech lay squirm-
ing and dying in her own province and in Newfoundland. But for all Carstairs lost in these days, she never
lost faith in Clyde Wells.

There was a basic difference between them, which
was tiny in 1990 and huge in 1992. Slowly, over the
months and years of Wells's post-Meech negotiating,
the tiny difference, like a pin-hole in fabric, had been
tugged and pulled so much that it created a major tear
in the Liberal fabric. Carstairs, like Coyne, would never

allow anything to touch or change the Charter of Rights and Freedoms. For Wells, Charter rights were important, but they weren't everything. In the Meech Lake accord, the Liberals saw the offence against the Charter as so massive that Wells and Carstairs could stand up in opposition to it. In 1992, the impact on the Charter was more controversial. Wells would see it as not a big deal; Carstairs, Coyne and other Liberals were still offended.

"Clyde and I had always had similar positions but our emphasis was on separate issues," Carstairs says. "You see, he had always had this hang-up on the equality of all provinces, and I hadn't."

That's the other key difference between Clyde Wells's brand of Liberalism and the Trudeau form. Wells spoke for a strain of Liberalism that had blended with the alienation of the West — his idea of equality stretched all the way from individual equality rights in the Charter to provincial equality in the Senate. It is a position that puts him at some distance from the pure Trudeau destination, but still on the same road.

In British Columbia, then Liberal leader Gordon Wilson, a fierce Trudeau loyalist, had also made the link between the two kinds of equality. He applauded Clyde Wells's effort to win equality in the Senate. With a Trudeau-like shrug, he dismissed the discrepancy between the new Liberal passion for an equal Senate and Trudeau's outright apathy about the issue.

"No, he doesn't think it's a big deal. But I think he's wrong. I really do. I mean, Trudeau was not exactly a deliverer of great things for the West."

But where Wells would see the equal Senate as a fitting trade-off for the French–English equality he agreed to in the Charlottetown accord, Wilson would not believe it was worth the price. He now believes, in fact, that Wells was motivated more by fatigue than principles when it came to the Charlottetown accord.

"I think that he paid a very, very heavy price personally for Meech," says Wilson. "I think the prime minister in Ottawa really held him accountable and responsible for the failure of Meech."

The responsibility of Meech did indeed lie heavily on Clyde Wells's shoulders. Ontario premier Bob Rae spotted the scars on Wells: "He didn't want to be isolated again. Because I think every Canadian politician, not every one, but certainly most Canadian politicians who get involved in the process do feel something about the country and also are unsure about the risks that are involved. I don't think he was ever entirely sure as to what the consequences of the collapse of Meech really were."

Mulroney was only too happy, as well, to shove that burden onto Clyde Wells. On the very day that he resigned, on February 24, 1993, Mulroney would be asked about the low points in his term as Canada's most unpopular prime minister. A pause, heavy with history, descended on the Parliamentary Reading Room where Mulroney was delivering his swan song to the media. Mulroney bowed his head. Many thought Mulroney would mention the intense betrayal of his friend Lucien Bouchard, who abandoned his friend and boss when he bolted the government over Meech compromises in May 1990. Many thought Mulroney would speak in general terms of his devastation over the loss of Meech. Maybe it was now even the time to talk about his personal hurt, facing the hatred of the Canadian electorate almost each and every day of his life as prime minister.

Mulroney paused, haltingly pulling out the low point of his political life from the depths of his memory. It was a pure, white-hot attack on Clyde Wells; a sign that this prime minister bore a grudge that coloured every aspect of his political being.

"I suppose the failure to put it [Meech] to a vote in the Newfoundland Legislature was a very sad moment for me and my government and my family and the country. I would have no quarrel at all had it been put to a vote and voted down — no trouble at all."

The lash of the words snapped in St John's that afternoon. Wells responded: "The prime minister either has a terrible memory or he's attempting to rewrite history. It's too bad he has to resort to this kind of thing and didn't adopt a more statesmanlike approach."

The next day, in a Toronto hotel room, Clyde Wells joked about Mulroney's additional dig against him at the press conference when the Prime Minister said that he would have resigned in the fall of 1990 if Meech had been passed. "The Canadian public may forgive me for what happened to Meech, but they'll never forgive me for my part in keeping him around for another two years," Wells said.

The final days of Meech were like a swirling tornado; facts and events were uprooted and twisted in its wake. One of the persistent stories was that "Clyde lied." That's not the evidence, if one examines the key spots where the Meech tornado touched down.

1. On the June 9 document, an asterisk appears beside Clyde Wells's name, indicating that he would put the agreement to the Newfoundland people.
2. On June 10, Clyde Wells said he would prefer to hold a referendum.
3. On June 11, Clyde Wells asked for an extension of the Meech deadline, so that he could have time to hold his referendum. Privy Council Clerk Paul Tellier told him there was no legal way to extend the deadline.
4. On June 11, Clyde Wells telephoned Prime Minister Brian Mulroney and said the vote would have to be held in the Legislature, not in a province-wide referendum.

5. On June 21, Prime Minister Mulroney came to Newfoundland to speak to the Legislature, and was assured that a vote would be held.
6. On June 22, Manitoba was poised to kill Meech by refusing to vote on it.
7. On June 22, Ottawa announced that the deadline would be extended for Manitoba, but not for Newfoundland.
8. On June 22, Clyde Wells announced that if he could not get a deadline extension, he would not hold the vote.

There are dozens of other twists and turns in this tale: phone calls, warnings, angry exchanges. But these are the key points of the week. Wells would absolutely refute the idea that he killed Meech Lake or that he broke a promise. But if Clyde Wells wasn't going to bear this burden, another Atlantic premier would. Sheepishly, emotionally, New Brunswick premier Frank McKenna would be the Liberal who was personally sorry for the failure of Meech.

Neither Frank McKenna nor Clyde Wells would encourage anyone to compare their politics. They're both cut from the same cloth, as Liberal Atlantic premiers, but they have very different ideas and styles. The two men don't even like each other that much, though they prefer to reveal their antagonism with subtle gestures and digs, rather than blatant hostility.

McKenna slides easily into the boys' game of politics, the locker-room mentality, the snapping-towels type of camaraderie among politicians. His closest friend at the first ministers' table was the former Ontario premier David Peterson, whose ideas of a good time ran along the same lines as McKenna's. The New Brunswick premier who came into office as a foe of Meech was a convert in the end, building up a jovial relationship with Mulroney and Bourassa in the process.

"I won't call it guilt that I felt over Meech," McKenna says. "Call it responsibility. I was one of those responsible for Meech . . . I've done a lot of soul-searching since then."

On one of those soul-searching occasions during the summer after Meech died, Frank McKenna was paying a visit to his sister's house in a rural part of New Brunswick. The phone rang: it was for Frank. McKenna pulled up a chair in the kitchen and sat down for a long, heart-to-heart chat with Brian Mulroney. These were low days for Mulroney.

The New Brunswick premier hung up the telephone. "Who was that?" his sister asked.

"That was the prime minister. We were just talking about things."

"Well," his sister said. "I hope you two didn't discuss anything important, because you know I've got a party line and anyone could have been listening in."

Wells would never let anything like sentimentality or locker-room camaraderie invade his world of political principles. "Camaraderie impairs judgment," he says. Wells is not the kind of politician who could be back-slapped into a deal. A walk with Wells on the road to a decision is like a leap from stepping stone to stepping stone; carefully considered jumps from principle to principle.

There is a moral in the story of McKenna and Wells, and how they fared in Meech. It's a moral that stretches to other political allegiances too. McKenna was the Meech moderate who tried to introduce the notion of a "parallel" accord, to make a compromise between Meech foes and friends. His attempts to do just that were blown out of the water by another Liberal Atlantic premier, who argued that principles were paramount to deals — Clyde Wells.

It was the same in Canada's native community. Ethel Blondin, a Liberal MP from the Western Arctic, took the moderate route to find a solution for the anti-Meech sentiment running rampant among Canada's aboriginal people. She believed the two sides could compromise. Her efforts were blown out of the water by another, less moderate native politician — Elijah Harper. His principles were paramount to political deals too.

And even among the Quebec Conservatives looking for a way to save Meech in 1990, the same story unfolded. Jean Charest, MP from Sherbrooke and later a leading contender in the race to succeed Mulroney, headed up an effort to preserve Meech in face of the threatening opposition from the rest of Canada. His actions were blunted by the dramatics of a less moderate Quebec Tory, Lucien Bouchard, who bolted the government rather than compromise his principles.

The lesson, well learned in Meech, is that the constitutional territory is no place for moderates. Compromise is dangerous, inevitably defeating, when it collides with the "fundamental principles" that so many people bring to the constitutional issue. Clyde Wells would learn that story from the opposite perspective in 1992.

In McKenna's view, this 1992 version of Clyde Wells was the moderate product of three years' experience at the first ministers' table.

"When you sit in that chair, you come to understand the country. . . . I think Clyde Wells became tempered by the same chair I sat in." Others less charitable to McKenna would say that the New Brunswick premier wasn't tempered — he was co-opted, owned "lock, stock and barrel" by Mulroney and Bourassa.

"He was more concerned with the economic agenda of New Brunswick than Charter rights," says Carstairs, once such a strong ally of McKenna's that she jour-

neyed to Ottawa back in 1987 to see him testify against
Meech at the parliamentary hearings. That was a long
time ago, though, before McKenna became premier.
Now they do not speak to each other. Nor is there much
talk any more between McKenna and other Trudeau
purists such as Gordon Wilson in British Columbia.
During the final days of negotiating on the Charlottetown accord, McKenna was on the phone to Wilson,
trying to tell him that the deal was in agreement with
Liberal principles. Not only that, but the old Liberal
principles of purism were pitching the country toward
a breach with Quebec.

McKenna was exasperated, explaining to Wilson that
the country truly was at stake. "Do you think it's worth
breaking up the country?" the New Brunswick premier
pleaded. Wilson didn't take that as a warning — he took
it as a threat. He was infuriated further when McKenna
came to British Columbia during the referendum campaign and took similar aim against the opponents of
the deal; echoes of Brian Mulroney's "enemies of
Canada" rhetoric.

All the shouting ended, though, on October 26,
1992. An icy silence has fallen between new Liberals
such as Frank McKenna and Trudeau Liberals such as
Carstairs and Wilson. In that silence, though, pause
and listen to who was speaking out for Trudeau Liberalism in the country in 1992. Listen to where the words
and ideas were echoing. The voices come from Victoria, B.C., where Gordon Wilson built Trudeau-style Liberalism in a political wasteland. The very distinct voice
of Sharon Carstairs wafts over from Winnipeg. The
high-speed, staccato burst of Deborah Coyne's rhetoric
jabs the air periodically, finding its targets in provinces
such as New Brunswick. The measured, low voice of
Clyde Wells sounds in from Newfoundland.

The biggest irony of Canada's 1990s political culture

is that Trudeau's crusade for a strong central government has come from the provinces, not from Parliament Hill. All this talk of Trudeau's Liberalism was rising up in the provinces, not in the seat of strong centralism, Ottawa itself.

Gordon Wilson lets out a tired groan when he is asked about the Liberalism of Jean Chretien. "I don't know," he says, shaking his head, wondering why the Trudeau legacy has not taken hold in the federal Liberal party. "What we have to do is put roots down provincially, and the irony is that it will be a movement within the provinces such as British Columbia that will rebuild a strong central government."

Wilson had given up on the federal Liberals by the time of the referendum campaign. They had turned their back on Trudeau's type of Liberalism, he said, and headed down the road to a revised vision — one that has so far not worked. The federal Liberals reached that fateful fork in the road at a policy conference in Hull, Quebec, in 1991, according to Wilson. Their nine-point platform was really an open exit door for Trudeau's vision of the nation. Exit Trudeau Liberalism, enter new-style constitutional politics, inspired by people who followed Paul Martin and his Quebec-centred vision.

"The Liberal Party of Canada became badly derailed. They went off track," Wilson says.

Again, the silence at the centre was deafening. The federal Liberal party was meeting just across the river from its seat of former glory in Ottawa, and it was not championing the cause of strong centralism. No Trudeau appeared at the meeting to ignite the Liberals' fires; no great spokesmen for the Trudeau vision made their mark on this new rewriting of Liberal constitutional politics.

"Had there been a strong movement then, I think you would have found that the Liberal Party of Canada would have been on the right side of the referendum question," Wilson says.

Carstairs believes that Trudeau Liberalism had been sapped out of the Liberal party by the deal-making politics in Mulroney's Ottawa. It was more important in 1992, she said, for the Liberals to be balancing their Quebec interests against the rest of Canada's interests in an untenable deal. Gordon Wilson will never forget the sight of Jean Chretien in the referendum, campaigning side by side with Constitutional Affairs Minister Joe Clark in Drayton Valley, Alberta, in early October 1992.

"I have no idea who was advising him, but that had to be the epitome of bad advice," Wilson says. "Politically, from a straight, practical point of view, Chretien really missed it." He missed his chance, Wilson says, to consolidate the Trudeau Liberals with the unhappy Quebec federalists. He missed a chance to speak for the Trudeau legacy inside and outside Quebec.

Chretien, for his part, was spared the barbs of Trudeau's anger. Even if he was on the Yes side in the referendum, and Trudeau was on the No side, no one was looking for signs of mutiny in the federal Liberals, as they did when John Turner supported Meech Lake. This new Liberal leader simply rolled with the punch that knocked out the rest of the politicians, and Trudeau, meanwhile, offered a special dispensation to his former Quebec lieutenant. He said that Chretien had to be guided by the realities of politics.

Chretien made it look all too easy to part company with the Trudeau legacy. Almost noiselessly, the Chretien Liberals slipped out of the harness of their history and galloped off with the Tories. Clyde Wells, on the other

hand, made it look very, very difficult. Each step along
the way to the Charlottetown deal was an ideological
struggle between principles and pragmatism. This was
Trudeau Liberalism in 1992 — not brow-beaten, dazed
and confused as in 1990, but perplexed, anxious and
weary of the battles against Mulroney's Canada. Coyne
would spot the difference, so would Wilson. "I think he
was under a lot of pressure," they say forgivingly.

The change in Wells was also prompted by the role
he adopted in this round, compared to that he played
in 1990. During the Meech talks, Wells saw himself as
the politician who would serve as the voice for the
unrepresented at the first ministers' table — the Meech
foes, Trudeau-style Liberals. He saw his constituency as
stretching beyond the borders of Newfoundland.
Indeed, it was impossible to talk to Clyde Wells without
talking to him about his correspondence. It was
massive; letters of support and encouragement flooded
his office. New Brunswick's premier Frank McKenna
would say to him: "Come on, you know a lot of that is
from racists." Others would say that Wells was just
reaping the public mood to skewer an unpopular prime
minister. But Wells carefully sifted through his correspondence. He and Coyne put the intemperate, racist
letters in the infamous "bottom drawer," where they
were ignored. Still, he drew great political strength
from the legitimate letters in the Meech years, and used
them to bolster his credibility.

In 1992, he wasn't getting as many letters. Bigger,
economic worries were plaguing his province and the
country. Newfoundland was reeling, not only from its
Meech battering, but from the cod crisis that left thousands of the province's fishery workers unemployed;
from the collapse of the deals to get the Hibernia oil project under way; from the deep recession that was grinding have-not provinces into have-nothing provinces.

Clyde Wells had an awful lot on his mind in 1992. He took his seat at the table, not as a champion for a pan-Canadian view, but as one, lone premier among seventeen other negotiators at the table. Where once he was known for the phrases "totally unacceptable" and "fundamental principle," a tired Wells would be known this time for another, more resigned repetition: "If nine provinces and the federal government want to [extend the veto, hold a referendum, etc.], then who am I to block them?"

Still, no matter how weary he may have been, Trudeau-style Liberalism was not going to go down without a fight. Nor was it going to go out without a damn good explanation for why it had to bend. Wells would be stepping subtly away from Trudeau when he talked about his three equalities and when he helped drive the crusade for an equal Senate. When it got down to brass-tacks bargaining, though, Wells was a formidable negotiator. Neither Wells nor the Trudeau vision would be steamrollered on the way to a 1990s, Mulroney-style deal. This was the lawyer for the defence.

Take, for instance, the whole dispute over the Senate. Two distinct demands had seized the "A" list of the constitutional dispute in the 1990s. Wells and the West wanted an equal Senate. The new Canada would have provinces as equals on Parliament Hill. Quebec, on the other hand, wanted to make sure that it had a veto over any future changes to the Senate and other major monuments on Parliament Hill. Quebec had this agreement in Meech, and it wanted it again. It was a way to ensure that Quebec, as one partner in the federation, would have to assent to any reshaping of government. The rest of Canada, in Quebec's mind, amounted to another partner. French–English, one for one, none for all.

This was the ultimate Catch-22 situation for the

national-unity dispute. Hand over the equal Senate, Quebec demands a veto to block it. Hand over a veto, and the West never gets its equal Senate. The solution was found in "timing" — that old constitutional buzzword from Meech Lake. Wells would give Quebec its veto, as long as he got his equal Senate first. As long as the new Senate was in place, Wells would grudgingly grant Quebec the privilege of future changes to the Senate. Change would be impossible if one province could block Senate reform — better get the Senate you like, an institution that will last throughout an eternity of paralysis.

Wells made this clear in Montreal, at a historic May 1992 meeting with Bourassa. It was the first time the two premiers had met since the awful days at Meech. In the subsequent two years, with the help of Mulroney's rhetoric, Wells had been identified as public enemy number one in Quebec. The meeting, just prior to the Quebec government's reception at the Ritz-Carlton Hotel, was momentous for the mere fact that these two men were talking again. Wells added to the history of the occasion when he said, simply: "I think things are different today."

Newfoundland was not the enemy of Quebec, he said, emphasizing all the areas where the two provinces had their mutual differences with Ottawa. But the Newfoundland premier was pressed repeatedly on this whole Catch-22 situation between the Senate he wanted and the veto Quebec wanted. Wells made a remarkable concession — if the rest of the provinces wanted to give the veto to Quebec, he wouldn't stand in the way. He was using his own logic against himself. He didn't believe that any province had the right to block changes to the federation. So he didn't want Quebec to have the veto. But by the same token, if every other province wanted Quebec to have a veto, well, how could one province, Newfoundland, block it?

You almost needed a chart to understand it. After Clyde Wells gave this statement, reporters would stand around, silently figuring out the impeccable logic of it. "Okay," they would mutter to themselves. "Let's figure this out." Reporters were mentally ciphering in the air above them. Given: No province should have the right to block constitutional change. And given: Every province, except Newfoundland, believes that Quebec should have the right to block constitutional change. Therefore: ???

Clyde Wells could have gone one of two ways. He could continue to insist that Quebec had no right to veto changes for the rest of the country, or he could see himself as the obstacle to change. He chose to portray himself as the hold-out. Wells did not want to be a hold-out again. He would agree to the veto, as long as he got the Senate he wanted.

Ontario's Premier Bob Rae had not taken part in this logic exercise. It would be almost six weeks before he figured out that Clyde Wells would trade an equal Senate for a Quebec veto. At Toronto's Airport Hilton on July 3, as Wells was preparing to leave, Rae asked him the question. "If you get the Senate you want, will you give the veto to Quebec?" Wells, distracted by the cod crisis in Newfoundland, which was dragging him away from these talks, knew that he was about to commit himself. He made a snap decision. "Yes," he said.

"It just caught me suddenly," Wells said later. "I was quite unprepared for it . . . But for the first time, I felt the possibility that the Ontario government would agree with a Triple E Senate and I guess I made a snap decision."

Giving the veto to Quebec went against everything Clyde Wells had believed in, but this was the time to temper principles, the time to make the contract.

Over and over again, Clyde Wells would be one tough customer at this national-unity mission. He was smart and dogmatic, the most frustrating combination for other pragmatists at the constitutional table. Even during the referendum campaign, even after he had signed the deal, Clyde Wells would not be marching in lockstep behind the Yes banner. He would be dragging up behind, staring at his every step, trying to make sure he was doing the right thing.

Nowhere was this more evident than in the referendum fuss over a legal text. Slowly, the Canadian public had become suspicious about the absence of this text. Where was it? What were the politicians hiding? The hunger for a legal text was simply bewildering to the politicians on the Yes side. Canadians had never risen up in arms before to demand the text of any laws, not even abortion laws. These very same Canadians had been telling the politicians for two years now that they were tired of the constitution; that they didn't want to hear another thing about it; that they didn't want their newspapers and television news filled with stories about the constitution. Now, suddenly, faced with a referendum, Canadians were flooding the 1-800 numbers set up by the governments, angrily demanding the legal text of the Charlottetown deal.

The No campaigners fed the suspicion, nudging the public on: "What did they have to hide?" Every day that it didn't appear came to be seen as a sign of dark manipulation by evil bureaucrats, carrying out the trickery and sorcery demanded by their political masters. In fact, the constitutional drafting process was a long, boring exercise in clauses, sub-clauses and technical bickering. For the approximately eighty unfortunate people locked in Ottawa to do this drafting, the days were just long processions of arcane wrangles and stale sandwiches and coffee.

As the public cry for a legal text increased, this thankless task became a pressure-filled one as well. "Get it done," the premiers ordered their officials. "Fast." Except one premier — Clyde Wells — who would be saying: "Get it done — with precision." The eyes of the constitutional lawyer were fixed intensely over the shoulders of the Newfoundland bureaucrats. Wells was going to make absolutely certain that the legal text was letter-perfect, true to the agreement he had reached. And he was having some trouble on the way the new Senate was shaping up. He made the mistake of letting the Canadian public in on some of his worries. They were legal worries, from the lawyer. The public read them as political worries, from a politician.

There were political reverberations — Wells wouldn't agree to go on his trip out West, where his salesmanship was desperately needed, until he was satisfied that the text was in order. The public read this hesitation as one more reason to be suspicious about the Charlottetown accord. This whole fuss, though, is a direct result of Wells's tendency to make legal rather than political decisions.

"Sometimes he's too much a lawyer and not enough politician," says Coyne. Indeed, Clyde Wells was always a lawyer above a politician. If asked to give a political view, he would rely upon the safety of the law.

"Mr Wells, how do you deal with the fact that Quebec feels betrayed by you?" he was asked, soon after Meech died in 1990.

Wells's answer was legal, not political: "Who has made those allegations? Unless you or these persons are prepared to back them up, I cannot respond to them." But that's the basis of his appeal, too, in an era of anti-politician sentiment. The appeal wears thin, though, with fellow politicians who have to negotiate with him on politics, not the law.

"I grew to have a kind of respect and affection for Clyde," says Rae. But it's difficult, he says. "With Clyde you've got to get to the middle ground and then you've really got to persuade him that that's where he's got to come to. And you've got to show him that you can do that in a principled way."

The great constitutional question of 1992 was, How did the anti-Meech hero become an ally of the Charlottetown agreement?

Wells would demand legal precision in every issue that had to be solved in this massive Canada round. That's why he also had severe problems with the idea of native self-government. While other premiers were joining the crusade to provide justice for aboriginal people, Wells would risk being politically incorrect by saying: "Wait a minute. What are we getting into here?"

He would voice the words that Quebec would never dare say in public. The old Meech enemies were unlikely allies on the issue of native self-government. Neither Quebec nor Newfoundland were keen to give carte-blanche approval to the idea of self-governing natives. How would it work? Would aboriginal people carry around self-government rights in their wallets? Could they opt out of every law of Canada because they were self-governing? What would happen to order in Canada? What would happen to the Criminal Code?

Newfoundland's scepticism spoke to a powerful unease in Quebec as well. Quebec had been through crises over Oka, gambling and smuggled cigarettes on reserves, and was not as indulgent as others on the wisdom of natives governing themselves. The rule of law was high on the priority list of Newfoundland and Quebec. As we have seen, Bourassa, appreciative of irony, clearly enjoyed saying at these talks: "Clyde speaks for Quebec on this issue."

The aboriginal issue was not the only issue that

bridged the difference between Clyde Wells and Quebec. His stand on the distinct society, his leap of faith, had not gone unnoticed by Bourassa either. The cry of the staunch Meech opponents in 1990 was: "No distinct society." The less strident would say: "Okay, you can have distinct society, but you better define it."

Many Meech opponents would always choose to see Wells in the strident category. In fact, Wells always came down on the side of moderation. He would accept distinct society, as long as it was defined. In the Charlottetown deal, Quebec's distinct-society status had been defined. Distinct society was described as three things: Quebec's culture, Quebec's language and Quebec's tradition of civil law.

On this issue, Clyde Wells believed he had been heard and was satisfied in the 1992 round. The distinct-society status was now narrowed, and he was confident that the Charlottetown accord conferred no special status on Quebec. He could temper some principles — he always said he could. Look at my three equalities, he would say. There's the compromise we have to make, right in there. It's all well and good for provinces to be equal, for citizens to be equal, but French and English had to be equal too. So he could agree to a distinct society that nibbled at the edges of individual rights in Quebec. He could also agree to a 25-per-cent guarantee of seats in the House of Commons for Quebec.

"That was a tempering of principle of equality of citizens, beyond what was proposed at Meech Lake," he admits, "beyond anything I had ever agreed to support or speak in favour of in the past."

Was it so bad to "temper the principles," though? Wells doesn't think so. "Yes, to some extent, there was an extension of the tempering. I think that's true in Charlottetown, though some people call that changing

principles." Ever judicious, ever courteous to his detrac-
tors, Clyde Wells only says of this accusation: "Well,
okay. It's their word to describe it and I can't quarrel
with what they choose to describe it."

The anti-Meech forces in Canada were puzzled by
Wells's decision at this point to temper his principles.
If that was required, why hadn't he done so at Meech?
His answer forced him to indulge in a bit of semantic
self-delusion. In Wells's view, the 1992 national-unity
crusade hadn't produced a constitution, it had produced a "contract." The old lawyer, faced with a political dilemma, took the legal way out again. The
constitution was the embodiment of all the fundamental principles in the land — that wasn't in Meech and
it wasn't in Charlottetown. The contract was an attempt
to reconcile those principles — temporarily. The time
to sign the contract was in Charlottetown.

The idea of the national-unity contract was Clyde
Wells's way to mix his long-held principles with 1990s
politics, for the lawyer to become a politician. Ontario's
Bob Rae was right to spot a new uncertainty about Clyde
Wells, an unease about the political lie of the land
between Quebec and the rest of the country. If Meech
had done nothing else, it had taught Wells the emotional reality of Quebec politics. He may not have
believed what they believed, but he had to believe what
they said.

A real constitution, he said, would have been put
together in a slow, deliberate fashion. Clyde Wells's
method of constitution-building doesn't need leaps of
faith. It requires everyone to talk and think for so long
that they actually embrace the principles on the table.
If Clyde Wells had been building the constitution,
Ontario would not have agreed to an equal Senate until
it actually believed in the idea of equality of the

provinces. As Wells admits, Rae never did accept that "fundamental principle." But time has a way of forcing leaps of faith. Deadlines can be a spur to the great leaps. So can politics, especially the emotional politics that plagued the relationship between Quebec and the rest of Canada in the wake of Meech.

"In circumstances where we had raised the emotional level of the debate, we were no longer debating the issue in rational, clear-thinking terms," said Wells. "It was always in the context of emotion, probably because culture and language and economic position were involved."

That's no atmosphere in which to hold a constituent assembly, said Wells. So it was best to plunge into the emotion and politics of the issue and try to work out a reasonable "contract" that would hold the nation together until cooler heads prevailed.

"I saw the Charlottetown proposal as being that kind of emotional debate, which largely addressed most of those underlying emotional concerns. And even though it would not be in a perfectly acceptable way, we could at least do that, then go forward for at least ten, twenty, thirty years at least on an interim basis."

Wells is uncomfortable with emotion in politics and his personal dealings with people. He would be uncomfortable discussing how events made him feel, or how others felt, or the way he was affected by events or rumours. It would make him reluctant to answer political questions directly. It would prohibit him from any expression beyond "surprise" at the relationship between Coyne and Trudeau.

As his wife, Eleanor, once told a magazine interviewer, Clyde Wells likes to keep everything in order. His idea of gardening is to plant all the flowers in straight lines. Emotion does have a place in Wells's view of himself in politics. But in that orderly, legal fashion, he keeps it filed away. Actually, he used to keep it in his pocket.

During the Meech Lake crisis, the bursting mailbag in Clyde Wells's office was filled with tributes. A remarkable number of Canadians read Rudyard Kipling's poem, "If," and sent it to the brow-beaten Newfoundland premier. Wells, inspired and stirred by his supporters, would keep this verse close to him as he went through the national-unity business. Coyne called it his "pocket poem." It says much about the way Clyde Wells saw his job, and reveals why he seemed so impervious to the attacks of others, even on Brian Mulroney's final day in office, when he took a parting shot at his Meech nemesis.

IF

If you can keep your head when all about you
Are losing theirs and blaming it on you,
If you can trust yourself when all men doubt you,
But make allowance for their doubting too,
If you can wait and not be tired by waiting,
Or being lied about, don't deal in lies,
Or being hated, don't give way to hating,
And yet don't look too good, nor talk too wise,
If you can dream — and not make dreams your
      master,
If you can think — and not make thoughts your aim,
If you can meet with Triumph and Disaster
And treat those two impostors just the same;
If you can bear to hear the truth you've spoken
Twisted by knaves to make a trap for fools
Or watch the things you gave your life to, broken
And stoop and build 'em up with worn-out tools;

If you can make one heap of all your winnings
And risk it on one turn of pitch-and-toss,
And lose, and start again at your beginnings
And never breathe a word about your loss;
If you can force your heart and nerve and sinew
To serve your turn long after they are gone,
And so hold on when there is nothing in you
Except the Will which says to them: "Hold on!"

If you can talk with crowds and keep your virtue,
Or walk with Kings — nor lose the common touch,
If neither foes nor loving friends can hurt you,
If all men count with you, but none too much;
If you can fill the unforgiving minute
With sixty seconds' worth of distance run,
Yours is the Earth and everything that's in it,
And — which is more — you'll be a Man, my son!

Clyde Wells is a man who is far more comfortable with the word "fundamental" than "sentimental." Liberalism for Wells was more a question of principles for the future than nostalgia for the Trudeau years. He spoke, though, for a large section of the Canadian electorate who worshipped at the altar of the Trudeau religion, who felt persecuted and marginalized by the Mulroney years. Liberal principles, once the mainstream in Canadian politics, were thrown to the fringe by Conservative rule, and Wells became a spokesman for alienated, isolated Liberalism. He was also a powerful voice for the alienation that has fed the West and its discontent over its distance from the centre. The cry of isolation was perhaps the strongest cry of the constitutional battle of 1992 — it resulted in the Senate issue that stood at the centre of the debate over the future of the federation.

7

The Showdown at Triple E

No one will ever inhabit the Senate that was built in
1992. It stands empty, relegated to history books as an
interesting but useless piece of political architecture.

Such a lot of work went into this building. Dozens of
politicians, bureaucrats and academics laboured for
hours, days and months on every detail of its construction. Such a lot of energy was poured into its design.
This Senate was going to be a masterpiece of political
workmanship. This new institution was going to restore
people's faith in government. The people who built
this new Senate thought they had answered every perplexing question when they were designing it. They
believed they had figured out why other institutions
had broken down, and they were bent on correcting
every design flaw in the Canadian political system with
this new building.

But on October 26, 1992, the Canadian public
refused to issue a licence to that Senate. Its design was
admired by some, loathed by others. Design wasn't the
issue, though. The Canadian people decided that the

foundations were unsound. And now this Senate, elected, equal and sort of effective, stands like an empty, expensive skyscraper on the receding constitutional horizon. Before it fades away completely, however, there are some stories to be told about its construction. The product of the Senate reform work was rendered unusable, but the work itself taught the political architects some lessons about themselves, each other and their country.

The story starts in Halifax, in the brisk days of early April. The national-unity negotiators were taking the first tentative steps in their talks, just surveying the political landscape that brought them to this city and to these complicated discussions.

At the convention centre in Halifax, premiers and constitutional ministers, bureaucrats and justice ministers straggled somewhat hesitantly into their meeting rooms, looking quizzically at the signs emblazoned with the acronym "MMC." It would be several weeks before these three letters, short for Multilateral Ministerial Conferences, tripped easily off the tongue of anyone involved in the national-unity effort. This was all new to them, and they were just getting to know each other. No one really knew what they had got themselves into when they agreed to hop on the MMC bandwagon. They only knew that it was better than standing by and watching Ottawa and the unpopular Mulroney government figure out a new constitutional deal without the provinces' help.

Alberta's intergovernmental affairs minister, James Horsman, was an unlikely ringleader for a group. The initial impression Horsman leaves, in fact, is that he has landed in politics accidentally — not unlike the hero of Horsman's favourite movie, *Being There.* In that movie, Peter Sellers plays a sheltered, innocent gardener —

Chauncey Gardener — who is swept up into the highest reaches of national decision-making by uttering simple gardening tips. It's a parable for any politician who has found himself at the centre of an inexplicable vortex, the media hanging on every word, the trite becoming the significant. Horsman finds something new to laugh at in this movie every time he watches it, and he watches it a lot.

Horsman is a little bit like Chauncey Gardener. He's soft-spoken, yet almost innocently direct. His lips barely move when he speaks, and his face rarely betrays any expression. His strength was dogged loyalty as deputy premier to Don Getty. But it would be wrong to portray him as a naïve Albertan, swept up in something bigger than himself. Horsman has a biting, sharp sense of humour, an ear for the sarcastic and the ridiculous, and his tastes run towards the sophisticated in wine and dining. He was also the dean of the 1992 constitutional table. He had been around the block several times in this national-unity debate, immersed in constitution-making before, during and after Meech. That experience taught him that alliances were everything in negotiations. So his first order of business in Halifax, in April 1992, was to see about building a coalition for Alberta and the West.

It had been a long first day of talking in Halifax on April 8. There was to be no rest at dinner, either. It was part meal, part seminar, and the constitutional negotiators were treated to a discussion of Quebec politics at the dinner, courtesy of two Quebeckers invited to the social evening by Constitutional Affairs Minister Joe Clark. This was the dinner at which former United Nations ambassador Yves Fortier and Mouvement regroupement d'economie president Claude Beauchamp were the featured speakers, their mission to remind the negotiators of Quebec's phantom presence hanging over these talks.

Horsman slipped away from the dinner as soon as it was over to convene a meeting in his suite. His idea was to hold a little after-dinner tactics session with his colleagues from the West, a small get-to-know-each-other encounter for the traditionally alienated provinces.

"At the failure of Meech Lake here in 1990, coming out of the conference centre, Getty had moved a number of other people toward reform of the Senate," Horsman recalled. "But with the change of government in Ontario, Saskatchewan and British Columbia, we had lost a bunch of allies. So where were we going to go?" He started looking in his own back yard, the West, for a new alliance, even if it meant fraternizing with the New Democratic opposition.

Saskatchewan's justice minister, Bob Mitchell, entered the suite with his guard up. He and his government were acutely aware of their precarious position, as New Democrats wedged in the middle of the Prairies between two Conservative regimes — Manitoba to the east, Alberta to the west. Maybe it's a small thing, but Mitchell remembered that when the Saskatchewan NDP government took power away from Tory Grant Devine, letters of congratulation poured in to Premier Roy Romanow's office from every politician in the country — except two. No hearty greetings were sent from the Conservative premiers in Alberta or Manitoba.

It took very little time, however, for Mitchell to become a charter member of the Triple E group. Horsman's initial wariness about the Saskatchewan New Democrat quickly turned into admiration and true friendship.

"I think really Bob Mitchell, when he came into these discussions, had no real feel for the importance of Senate reform. But his understanding of our concerns built throughout the process. He became a very, very strong ally, a great ally. I have a great deal of respect for Bob Mitchell," Horsman says.

Mitchell, like Joe Clark, has earned a heroic reputation from every one of the people involved in the national-unity crusade of 1992. People talk of his kindness, his gentle manner, his way of holding to a conviction without becoming obnoxious. Even in Ontario, where Mitchell might have been viewed as a traitor to the NDP cause with his commitment to the Tories' Senate crusade, the reviews are positive. Jeff Rose, Ontario's pugilistic deputy minister, heaps nothing but praise on Mitchell. "He was a mediator bigger than the room. If only he had a moment to get his arms around the issue, everyone would be fine." Saskatchewan premier Roy Romanow had put his precious constitutional interests in safe hands; the hands of his former roommate, old and trusted friend, and easily one of the most quiet but influential people at the 1992 national-unity table.

Manitoba's justice minister, Jim McCrae, was eager to find common cause with the West. His province, after all, had been singled out, alone on the Prairies in its opposition to the Meech Lake constitutional accord. It had been vilified and condemned by Meech supporters, most notably Prime Minister Mulroney, who could not believe that a Tory government would let him down so crashingly on his national-unity quest. This made for uneasy relations between Manitoba and Ottawa, and not very profitable ties for a province that depended on Ottawa's kindness to keep its financial house in order. So McCrae, as Manitoba's representative, was in no hurry to be isolated; better to hitch the province's wagon to the stars of the West and follow that crusade this time.

The three Prairie politicians were to become solid allies and good friends, constantly seen together, enjoying each other's company as spring turned into summer. The meeting that night in Horsman's suite was an auspicious, if cautious, start to that friendship. As Horsman would write later that night in his diary: "My impressions are that we could build a Western alliance, despite the differences in political stripes." He recorded his initial assessments of his Western counterparts.

Mitchell, he said, is "quiet, feeling his way." Jim McCrae, "solid." It was British Columbia that no one could read. Typically, B.C. and its representative didn't quite fit into the Western mold that was being forged that night. Was British Columbia's constitutional affairs minister with them or not? Horsman had met Moe Sihota for the first time only a month earlier, at the Pearson Building, and pronounced him "very West Coast." At this Halifax meeting, Horsman's verdict on Sihota was that he was "mercurial."

A better way to sum up B.C. might have been to call it an outrageous flirt, at least in Horsman's eyes. In the view of the Albertan, Sihota was young and slick, playing politics to the hilt, keeping all his options open but committing to no one and no coalition. He flaunted his flirtatiousness in front of the cameras. He couldn't be pinned down on his ideology about the Senate question, but many times, for mischief and for sport, he would wear a Triple E lapel pin, just to tease his Western friends.

Sihota, who took the issue but not himself very seriously, enjoyed the tease. "Yeah, I joked around with them. I used to wear Triple E pins during the meetings," Sihota triumphantly reported later. "All those scrums and conferences we had. I would say, well, at one juncture, for a good couple of weeks, I had the little Triple E pin, that little lapel pin. . . . I was wearing it on my lapel. No one ever looked at it carefully." With a wink at his Western friends, Sihota would stride out before the television lights, smugly sporting the tiny pin on his lapel. It was a practical joke and a taunt. "I'm going to wear it and see if they pick it out . . . No one figured it out."

That night in Halifax, though, Horsman saw the potential for a Western alliance, with or without the presence of flirtatious British Columbia. And there was no doubt that he had established himself and Alberta as the leader of the group. "So far they defer to my experience and are prepared to listen," he wrote in his diary. Indeed, no one could question the fact that Alberta was the home of Senate reformers. Back in the horrible days of late 1989 and early 1990, when the Meech Lake accord was starting its descent into obscurity, Alberta had started making a lot of noise on the national scene about the Senate.

Alberta voters boldly elected a senator in the fall of 1989, the Reform Party's Stanley Waters, and brazenly demanded that Prime Minister Mulroney place him in the vacant Alberta Senate seat. Meech Lake was not yet ratified, but Alberta wanted Mulroney to follow the rules set out in that accord for naming senators from provincial lists of candidates. Alberta's list had one name on it — Stanley Waters — and they wanted him in the red chamber as the first of hopefully many elected senators. During the mad rush of marathon deal-making in June 1990, and that vain attempt to keep the Meech Lake accord alive, Mulroney had promised Don Getty that he would put Waters in the Senate. On June 11, 1990, not forty-eight hours after that marathon week ended, Getty phoned Mulroney at 24 Sussex Drive and demanded that he make good on his promise. Waters was installed as a senator later that afternoon.

Horsman had done his part for the Senate crusade in those days with a one-man, cross-country mission in the spring of 1990, laying the foundation for Alberta's cherished equal, elected, and effective (Triple E) Senate. It was to be the first priority after Meech Lake passed. It was the first priority anyway, even after Meech died. With the Reform Party nipping at the heels of Conservatives in Alberta, and Reformers' determined campaign for equality in the Senate, it couldn't be otherwise. The Triple E Senate was the West's holy grail, a political religion that prompted a farmer and political activist, Bert Brown, to plough the giant letters "EEE Senate Now, Joe" into Alberta's field of political dreams, a mission that sent dozens of people out to public hearings to convince Horsman that Alberta wanted an equal, effective and elected Senate.

In a time of recession and high unemployment, a vague, ethereal idea such as equality would hardly seem to be the stuff of populist revolution. But equality, whether it was through the ten-year-old influence of the Charter of Rights and Freedoms, or through saturation of American-style values into Canada, had become wedded to the cause of the people in 1992. Equality was a rallying cry, a supreme value. And it was the Senate debate that set the stage for Canadians to talk about their dreams of equality. Equality would be a notion that resonated through the referendum later, in the rhetoric of everyone from the women's groups to former prime minister Pierre Trudeau. The new Senate was supposed to embrace and enshrine the new Canadian penchant for equality.

But here was where the rest of Canada ran smack into Quebec. How can a country at one time be seen as ten equal provinces but also as a pact between two founding nations, French and English?

Alberta, true to its frontier mentality, wanted to stand at the vanguard of the new populist surge toward equality. Albertans wanted to lead the charge to a new

Canada, shedding the ancient ideas that had created two kinds of provinces — big ones, with everything, and small ones, with nothing. And this province, so far from the central Canadian French–English knot that bound the middle of the country together, was hard pressed to see the country as simply two cultures.

Reform Party leader Preston Manning, an Albertan and the voice of populist rebellion in the West through the early 1990s, wasn't surprised that the national-unity struggle was so dominated by the debate over an equal Senate.

"Of the three Es, the one that gets most to the heart of one of the most fundamental constitutional problems in Canada is this choice between two constitutional models. Is the route to unity and constitutional peace through the recognition of founding races and special groups and granting special status based on race, language and culture? Or is the route to unity through the equal treatment of all citizens, regardless of race, language and culture?"

Manning has two old political cartoons in his files. One is from a Toronto newspaper, showing the celebration of Dominion Day, as July 1 was then called. The cartoon from Central Canada shows two people singing together from two songbooks, one labelled French and Catholic, one labelled English and Protestant. A dual country, a dual celebration. Coincidentally, around that same holiday, a Western Canadian newspaper ran a cartoon with the same theme. But there were more than two singers, there were many, all carrying songbooks of other cultures — Ukrainian, Chinese, French, English, and so on. A country made up of many cultures, a celebration of equality through diversity. So the debate is hardly new, Manning says. "It's right from the very beginning, the two different conceptions."

In sum, equality was the issue running under so

much of Canada's never-ending debate over its identity. The old distinct-society clause for Quebec in Meech Lake attracted fierce antagonism because it pushed that hot button of equality. Now, in 1992, the politicians were about to tread into that danger zone again, but this time it would be a much bigger battlefield, with a bigger conquest in sight — a complete overhaul of Parliament to reflect that value of equality.

The other province clinging so tenaciously to the Triple E Senate was Newfoundland. Premier Clyde Wells, the champion of the Meech foes, who refused to ratify the deal in his own province, had the same evangelical fervour as Alberta about the Senate. Wells is a man most comfortable with "fundamental principles" and equality of the provinces is a top priority on that principles list. He, too, had come to symbolize the quest for equality and the refusal to make Quebec any more equal than other provinces, whether through distinct society or any other means.

Wells set out his mission for equality early in this post-Meech round. He declared that there were three equalities that had to be addressed in any renovation of the Canadian political system. Equality of citizens was one, and that was pretty well respected in the House of Commons. Equality of provinces was another — that wasn't doing so well, because it just seemed that big provinces got richer and small provinces got poorer, and the have-nots were always crowded out by the have provinces. A good, equal Senate would fix that, Wells believed. The third equality on Wells's list was French–English equality, and that's where things got complicated, again because of those two colliding visions of the nation. Quebec, on the one hand, was to be a province, equal to the others, in Wells's view. On the other hand, it was also the home of the French fact, so the balance between the rest of Canada and Quebec had to be respected — without making it a province more equal than others. That dilemma over the so-called "third equality" would haunt this debate over the Senate in 1992 and put Wells into a compromise that many of his followers found untenable.

And "haunt" is the correct term. Quebec, after all, was not at these talks, and it could only hover over the Senate debate. That left Ontario and Ottawa alone to fend off the cry for an equal Senate, and it paved the way for a formidable coalition to rise up as a challenge to the Central Canadian nay-sayers to a Triple E Senate.

Clearly, by mid-April, the idea of equality in the Senate was thriving. Joe Clark, in February, had joked to reporters at the Calgary national-unity conference that the chances of establishing an equal Senate in Canada were roughly the same as the chances of another "virgin birth." But two months later, as Clark repeatedly ran up against the stone-wall Senate cam-paign of Alberta, the odds for that kind of Senate were definitely outrunning those for the virgin birth. Just a few days before the negotiations stopped over in Ottawa for a brief session in mid-April, Clark gave an interview to *The Globe and Mail* in which he said that an equal Senate was looking more plausible. Collectively, constitution-watchers were taken aback. What had sud-denly happened, that an equal Senate was no longer some crazy fringe notion, but a distinct possibility?

A lot of it was stubbornness. Clark, no great ally of Don Getty, had gone out to Alberta around that time in April to see whether the premier could be shaken off his campaign for a Triple E Senate.

"He was very polite, very firm, not a lot to discuss," Clark recalled later. The Alberta premier had simply dug in and said he was not going to move. What could Clark do? "I guess that clearly demonstrated to me that Alberta was going to be hanging tough on this. I was making some speeches out there, saying, you know, Alberta could put all this at risk, and Don was quite prepared, it seemed to me, and I still think, to put it all to risk. Now that may have been clever bargaining or it may have been their real bottom line. But in any event, a lot of people assumed it was a bottom line."

At this point, Alberta and Newfoundland were linking arms in the Triple E struggle. Horsman huddled with Wells in April at Ottawa's Government Conference Centre in Ottawa, the site of the Meech fiasco of June 1990. It was the one and only meeting that would be held in 1992 in the place nicknamed "the scene of the crime." Even though it was the logical place to hold the meetings that took place later that summer, it had taken on a toxic aura for the first ministers. Wells, finding himself back in this building in April 1992, gave Horsman a forecast of victory as they talked Senate strategy. He told Horsman: "We'll get them elected. We'll get them equal. Then, damn it, we'll get them effective." Precisely, Horsman thought.

As luck would have it for the Triple E group, the next stop in their travelling road show that spring was in Edmonton. It would hardly be fitting to spit in the eye of the Senate campaign while they were in Alberta, Horsman's home. And so the Triple E Senate group lived and grew for another week in its friendly habitat. McCrae felt the momentum building when he was in Edmonton. He could barely contain his exuberance. He did not contain it, in fact. To reporters, as the Edmonton sessions were wrapping up, the very cautious McCrae appeared to abandon caution to herald the gathering strength of the Triple E group. There were now five on board, he said, though he left everyone guessing about who those five provinces were.

"I was excited," McCrae said. "I wanted to get the idea out there." It was clear to him that Nova Scotia was

poised to become their fifth, solid member, and that
Saskatchewan was firmly in their camp. So now there
were five — outnumbering the other four provinces at
the table. "That tells me there's a momentum moving
in that particular direction," McCrae boasted to
reporters.

There it was again. The unthinkable had become the
unstoppable. No one seemed able to slow the surge of
Triple E force — not even Ontario, which didn't seem
to be taking the idea all that seriously. By now, any
ridiculous Senate notion should have been swept off
the table. But this idea just wasn't going away. Because
they were in Alberta, the national-unity negotiators
kept being asked about Alberta's pet constitutional
project, Senate reform. The intensity of interest fed the
Senate debate like oxygen feeds a fire. An equal Senate
was not just looking plausible then — it was starting to
look like the front-running idea. And that's when the
seriousness of the Triple E bid started to make itself felt
in waves across the country. That's when the rest of
Canada started waking up to the fact that a dramatic
change was in the works for the dusty old red chamber.

Certainly Quebec got wind of the idea as April gave
way to May that spring. During the first week in May,
Quebec premier Robert Bourassa and his intergovernmental affairs minister, Gil Remillard, made a pilgrim-
age out of their province to test the constitutional
climate of the West. The constitutional group from the
West were primed to meet Bourassa, and eager to notify
him of the gathering strength of the Triple E crowd. At
each stop on the trip, Bourassa and Remillard got an
earful from the Western premiers and ministers about
the Senate question. There didn't seem to be any other
issue on the table worth talking about. The news
reports of that week's tour were filled with Bourassa
quietly but non-committally absorbing the Senate

obsession out West. The multilateral process was starting to assume a life of its own, and so was the Senate
debate. The next step was to solidify the Triple E
alliance, and that was due to take place in Saint John,
New Brunswick.

Ottawa had laid on one of its government-owned
Challenger jets to speed some members of the Western
group from its meetings with Bourassa to the site of the
next conference in Saint John. Horsman and Sihota
flew out together, comparing notes over their meetings
with Remillard. The Albertan tried once again to pull
British Columbia into the Triple E fold, arguing that
now Bourassa and Remillard were starting to take it
seriously. Horsman's evidence for this? Well, Quebec
had not said "never" to the idea. This, in the elaborate
shadow-dancing that became Quebec's bargaining
style in 1992, was about all that could be expected by
way of encouragement. As we have seen, when a
Quebec politician said: "I will not say no," in that spring
of 1992, it was loosely translated by others as "yes," or
"probably."

But Quebec wasn't the only province playing hard to
get or hard to decipher as the negotiations heated up.
Horsman could not read the tactics of his companion
on that Challenger flight either.

"I gave a good shot at convincing Sihota," he wrote.
"But he is hard to move or pin down."

In New Brunswick, Premier Frank McKenna hosted
a dinner for the travelling constitutional ministers.
Always one to wear his heart and alliances on his sleeve,
McKenna openly demonstrated that he shared
Ottawa's and Quebec's bewilderment — and frustration — with the Triple E crusade. McKenna had landed
at the first ministers' table in 1987 as a Meech foe and
a challenger to Mulroney's brand of constitutional politics. By 1992, he was widely viewed as the premier who

had given himself over almost completely to common cause with Ottawa and Quebec. He was known to be in regular and convivial touch with Mulroney and Bourassa. So when McKenna spoke at dinner about the futility of the Triple E Senate crusade, the group of five knew that they had grabbed the attention of the two men who stood in the wings, waiting to judge this multilateral effort. McKenna asked why so much energy was being poured into making an institution that would render premiers irrelevant. Why would Ottawa listen to a provincial government, when the provinces would have a stronger voice in the Senate?

Horsman saw this as turning up the heat, but the arguments fell on deaf ears. If anything, they were emboldened by the McKenna challenge. Other members of the Triple E group also saw signs that Ottawa was preparing to fight them, tooth and nail.

In Saint John, as attention revolved to the Senate question, another bid was made to knock the Triple E proposal off the table. But Ed Roberts, Newfoundland's justice minister, spoke up. "Give us some time," he pleaded. The Triple E group was going to pull together the only weapon that mattered in this kind of battle — some paper, filled with calculations and proposals. In other countries, wars are fought on the streets or over the airwaves. In Canada, constitutional battles are fought with memos, proposals and bureaucratic notes.

The Triple E group, now a firm five — Alberta, Saskatchewan, Manitoba, Newfoundland and Nova Scotia — needed time, that was all. But as the MMC train rolled into Vancouver in mid-May, all the negotiators also started to realize that time was not exactly on their side. After all, this road show was supposed to end on May 31, and, magically, a "best-efforts draft" would be produced. Now, though, it was starting to look like all the easy questions would be solved by this group and all the hard stuff would go to the premiers. Senate reform, of course, was part of the hard stuff.

Deadlines, deadlines; the need for a first ministers' conference. All of a sudden, this was starting to stir up disturbing echoes of Meech Lake. In their guts, many of them knew that a replay of Meech Lake negotiations would be political suicide for this constitutional effort. The man who voiced this fear was Jim McCrae. The description of this man by Horsman was apt. "Solid" was an appropriate adjective. Not given to outbursts or hysteria, he had a deep, authoritative voice, a calm, unflappable manner. But as he looked at his calendar in Vancouver, and as he checked the very limited progress to date in these talks, he suddenly realized that the Senate question could indeed be headed to a Meech-like showdown. The thought troubled him. So at their dinner in Vancouver, McCrae spoke up. Somebody had to stop this from turning into another Meech, he said.

"We ran the risk of only doing so much work, and turning over only the worst problems to the first ministers — one of whom was Brian Mulroney, one of whom was Clyde Wells. And we didn't really need to get back into that Meech Lake pressure cooker."

He told his colleagues that they had an obligation to get a whole agreement, even on Senate reform. He appealed to them to heed the spectre of the 1990 Meech Lake débâcle, and work on finishing this constitutional round in a dignified, orderly manner. "We have to do it all," McCrae warned the others at dinner. Joe Clark agreed. He had not been at Meech, but he recognized its scars. There was no way that the explosive issue of Senate reform should be thrown into a pressure cooker, he believed.

"What happened at the Vancouver meeting was that ministers who had been at Meech, or had been exposed to the scars of Meech, believed that first ministers just could not conclude it." It wasn't that this 1992 group thought they were smarter or savvier, Clark said. "It was simply that people who had been together in a room like that could not come together in a room again productively... It was very much the Meech experience."

Now, by this time, as McCrae noted, not much really had been agreed on the Senate issue. There were, in fact, a number of ideas floating around the talks, and three very solid ones. Each little camp was busy working and revising their individual plans, but the country as a whole was fractured between the various ideas.

First, as we know, there was the Triple E proposal, picking up momentum and allies. Then there was the "equitable" Senate, preferred by Ontario and Ottawa, which was more or less a reworking of the current system, to give big provinces more senators and smaller provinces fewer senators. Then there was the B.C. compromise bid, for a five-region Senate, in which each region of the country, East, Quebec, Ontario, the Prairies and — note well — British Columbia, would each have an equal number of senators.

Only some very basic reforms of the Senate had the support of everyone. Elected senators were a given. Everyone wanted Senate elections to end the patronage-ridden system of appointment to the chamber. No one wanted this Senate to have the power to block money bills from the House of Commons. And in Vancouver, much to the delight of the Triple E group, there was widespread agreement that any new Senate would be able to block a future national energy program. It was that NEP, brought in by the Trudeau government during the early 1980s, that so galvanized the move for an equal Senate in Alberta. In the eyes of Albertans, the NEP robbed them blind of their energy revenues, and

there wasn't a single thing they could do in Parliament
to protest the measure, because all their MPs were in
opposition, and the Senate was useless.

In Vancouver, the negotiators felt the clock ticking.
They knew their next stop was Montreal and it was time
to get down to brass tacks and tackle Quebec's all-
important questions about the division of powers.
Where were they going to find the time to settle the
Senate question in the next couple of weeks?

Again, the ball was in the court of the Triple E group,
and they chose Montreal to lob their piece of paper into
the discussions. Carefully, the complicated Triple E bid
was leaked to reporters, and the five provinces stood by
and watched as Ottawa and Ontario were forced onto
the defensive — forced to explain "why not" to an equal
Senate. For years, Ottawa and Ontario had always been
able to get the Triple E advocates on the run by challenging them to explain why they needed Senate equality. Now the tables were turned, and *they* had some
explaining to do.

Quebec's absence from the talks certainly helped
there. The old Central Canadian triumvirate of Ottawa,
Quebec and Ontario was no longer functioning as a
unit. Ontario and Ottawa were often at ideological
odds, warring on everything from fiscal relations to
constitutional strategy. Quebec was simply not there,
except as a shadow. But here the constitutional negotiators were, right in Quebec, in Montreal, in the lion's
den. And it was time to figure out where Quebec stood
on this whole Senate obsession.

Gil Remillard had been listening very closely to what
he heard out West; so had Robert Bourassa. This equal-
Senate thing — it was a stubborn bit of business. Remillard understood stubbornness; so did Bourassa. After
all, it was their persistent refusal to join the talks that
had resulted in this strange process travelling all over

the country. Now the process had landed in Quebec and it was time to send some messages out.

First, Remillard had a cosy little dinner with Horsman. Alberta wanted Quebec back at the table, and Horsman tried to use the lure of powers to get the province back.

"Look," Horsman said to Remillard. "We need you at the table. You need to be at the table." At this point in the national debate, the two men were known as buddies — "Jeem" and "Geel," as reporters would call them. "Important things are being discussed, on critical power questions. Come back and we can be allies, pushing for more control over natural resources, for example."

But it was to no avail. Yes, maybe this constitutional process was dealing with crucial matters such as provincial control over key powers, but Quebec was out, and Quebec was staying out. "Geel" would have to say "sorry" to his pal "Jeem." So much for that plea.

The next morning, Bob Mitchell embarked early from his hotel to try his luck with Remillard. They talked about Quebec's absence, about what was happening in the multilateral process. They also talked about an equal Senate. A hint was dropped; a signal that would prove to be very important in the next couple of weeks.

Remillard, very casually, asked Mitchell what he thought about a Senate that would have an equal number of senators from each province, a Senate in which each of these equal senators would have one, two or three votes, depending on the size of the province and the nature of the issue. In other words, Saskatchewan and Quebec could each have eight senators, but Quebec's senators would have three votes on most issues, compared to one vote for the Saskatchewan senators. Call it the "weighted vote" proposal; other, less charitable nicknames to describe this idea came later.

Mitchell heard this talk about the weighted votes, didn't think very seriously or very long about it, and then filed it away. He had his eye on bigger things — the release of the Triple E paper and the opportunity to outflank Ontario and Ottawa right there in Montreal.

That's exactly what happened.

Ontario premier Bob Rae had very studiously avoided giving any answers on an equal Senate all the way through the process. Sometimes he dismissed it as an Americanization of Parliament. Sometimes he talked about what was not in Ontario's interests. Sometimes Ontario would talk about the need to have more representation by population in the House of Commons, if the Senate was going to be the home of representation by province. The only concrete statement from Ontario, the one that kept surfacing as Ontario's position was gauged, was Rae's speech in February to the special joint committee of Parliament, the Beaudoin–Dobbie committee, which examined the constitutional question.

"A Triple E Senate, stated baldly, is not acceptable to Ontario," Rae had declared that day. There didn't seem much room for manoeuvre. But in Montreal, it was time to put the question directly to Ontario. What was the Ontario philosophy on Senate equality? Was it on or off? Was it wrong or right?

"The reality for us is this was always a bargaining question," Rae recalled later. "And it wasn't a card which we were about to play until we got a lot of the other things."

It was a raucous encounter with reporters in Montreal, as the Triple E Senate group appeared to have Ontario on the run.

"Reporters ... kept on asking me in different scrums, are you fundamentally opposed to equality or are you fundamentally opposed to effectiveness? Which is fair enough. I wasn't about to tell you. Because I'm not about to do that kind of bargaining in public," Rae said.

Ontario's mood was not improved in Montreal by the furor that came to be known as the "1-800-GIL" mix-up.

The negotiators were fiddling again with the superficial bits of Senate reform, steering clear of any real debate on whether it would be equal or equitable or how much real power it would have. The question in front of them was whether the new Senate should be elected along with the House of Commons, in simultaneous elections, or whether the Senate elections should stand alone. It was a side issue to the fundamental Senate debate, but an important political question. After all, a Senate elected at the same time as the House of Commons would probably look much the same, in terms of political parties' representation. Both the Senate and the Commons would be a snapshot of the political mood of the nation for four years. Undoubtedly, they would work in tandem. But if the Senate were to be elected on its own, say, midway through the usual four-year span of the House of Commons, it would be bound to be filled with people who had campaigned on an anti-government platform. Voters eager to send a message to a Tory government in Ottawa, for example, would probably fill the Senate with Liberals. And vice versa. For Ontario, the two different elections would be a recipe for deadlock. And deadlock was to be avoided at all costs.

But while this debate was going on in Montreal, Horsman slipped out and made a telephone call to Remillard. He asked which type of election Quebec would prefer. Horsman came back into the room and reported that Quebec was on his side — that gave the proponents of stand-alone elections enough force to squelch Ontario and its objections. Rae was furious at this shameless foray by Quebec into the negotiations it had shunned. He didn't mask his annoyance when he spoke to reporters.

"I don't like it," Rae snapped when asked about the phone call. "If you're there, you're there, and if you're not there, you're not there . . . We've got to play by a consistent set of rules, that's all. And I think that's now understood."

Yes, it was understood. A somewhat contrite Jim Horsman would write in his diary later that day: "Ontario clearly resents my call." Even Clark, Horsman noted, was not amused. Mischievously, Horsman noted also in his journal that he had simply been doing what Clark had always advocated: Get in touch with Quebec for yourself; set up a dialogue. Michel Auger, in his column for *Le Journal de Montréal,* gave this controversy its name. With biting wit, Auger joked that the constitution had come down to a reliance on Bell telephone technology. Need a position from Quebec? Call 1-800-GIL for details.

Only a day or two earlier in Montreal, at the fancy Ritz-Carlton reception for the constitutional negotiators hosted by the Quebec government, it had looked like Horsman and Remillard were bosom buddies. The elegant string quartet was playing its last strains as the crowd filtered out, and Horsman and Remillard were locked in amiable chatter, over to the side of the hall. Whimsically, the musicians struck up a chorus of "Turkey in the Straw." Remillard whooped, Alberta-style, and reached out to grab Horsman, as if for a swing around the room in a square dance. The two were laughing and joking with each other even as the musicians packed away their instruments and the caterers slid the trays of food away from hungry reporters who were picking through the leftovers of the cocktail reception.

One week later, in Toronto, Horsman would be asked, jokingly: "How's the hotline?" Deadpan, he would answer: "Very cold."

There was no mistake about it as these talks wound their way to Toronto for what was supposed to be the final session at the end of May. The big provinces were getting very edgy about the Triple E campaign. Ottawa wasn't happy either. Now, just as the negotiations were winding up, they had a David-and-Goliath battle on their hands between the small and the big provinces, all over Senate reform, and it didn't seem to be close to a finish.

The very mood of the meetings had changed. No longer was this a calm, orderly group of ministers, plodding away at their task of nation-building. Now they were in Toronto, headquarters for dozens of media outlets, and the press entourage had become a full-blown circus. Where all the action once took place inside the conference rooms, and then was dutifully reported to the handful of reporters at the end of the day, now different tactics were being employed.

The lobbies and corridors of the Royal York Hotel were literally littered with documents marked "confidential." Busy little knots of negotiators and bureaucrats huddled with reporters, plying the trade known as "spinning." Alberta had dispatched the exuberant young communications official, Bill Gadja, to circulate among the press. Ontario had sent deputy intergovernmental affairs minister Jeff Rose and Rae adviser Ross McLellan wading into the throng of information-starved journalists, who were installed in a small, glass-sided room resembling a terrarium in the basement of the Royal York.

So fierce was the spinning that week that people were

dizzy and giddy; the best joke of the conferences was uttered around that time by the *Toronto Star*'s Matt Maychak, when he declared: "I've been in the spin cycle so long with Ontario that I've got Ross McLellan's sock stuck to the back of my suit." People were trading their bits of paper on Senate proposals the way young boys would trade hockey cards. Ontario would appear with a document, Alberta would appear with another document. The piece of paper circulated by Ontario would make it appear that Triple E was losing ground. The Alberta paper would show that all options were still open.

It was a mess. It was also an ugly echo of those days of Meech Lake, when spinning and media leaks were the only method of dispensing information. This was not the way this constitutional machine had been running. The smooth, reliable, but quite dull vehicle named MMC 1992 was being traded in for the flashy but unserviceable roadster called Meech, which had crashed and burned in June 1990. And look who had climbed into that car as a backseat driver — Brian Mulroney. The politician who had stayed away from the process for so long had now quietly joined the trip, and the constitutional negotiators almost immediately sensed the effect of his renewed involvement.

Clark made no secret of the fact that Mulroney was on his way back into the process. The telephone, Mulroney's favourite political tool, was busy in the offices of the premiers, as the prime minister started to talk deal-making with the provinces.

"I can't get into the conversations, but the prime minister has been in touch with some of the premiers and undoubtedly will be in touch with others. And they are naturally comparing impressions of this process, but they are focusing, as we all are, on the questions of where there appears to be, where we don't yet appear to have an agreement," Clark told reporters in Toronto. That was his very diplomatic way of saying that Mulroney was lowering the boom on the Senate combatants.

Horsman definitely felt the reach of Mulroney-style politics while he was in Toronto. As the other members of the delegations headed out to Bob Rae's house for a barbecue, Horsman went out to dinner with his old friend, Canadian National railways chairman Brian Smith. Very quickly, Horsman sensed that his friend had been dispatched with a mission — shake this crazy Albertan off the Triple E crusade.

"He was trying to work on me, to wear me down, to ease my stand on Senate reform," Horsman recalled later. He suspected that Smith had been sent to talk to him by Clark and Mulroney. But Smith's relationship with Horsman as a friend soon overcame his role as an emissary from Ottawa. "The discussions were very brief on the subject. He didn't try too hard. There wasn't much use in trying too hard." The two went on to have a pleasant dinner, and Smith, to Horsman's delight, picked up the cheque.

The tactics in Toronto were getting silly, almost child-ish. One evening, Ontario's native affairs minister, Bud Wildman, was hosting a social dinner in Chinatown for everyone. Just to make a point, the key members of the Triple E group, represented that evening by Horsman, Mitchell, McRae and Roberts, arrived late. Make no mistake about it, they were telling Ontario. We are a team, and we don't dance to your tune.

All the action wasn't outside the rooms, though. Inside, a pivotal debate took place between Bob Mitchell and Bob Rae. Mitchell, impassioned, told Rae to stop blocking the legitimate desires of the West. He implored him to stop acting like a bully province and see the Triple E campaign for what it was — a true, heartfelt desire to end Western alienation. As these two Bobs from the NDP sparred, the two Tory Jims looked on. McCrae and Horsman knew now that Saskatchewan had got the Triple E religion, and its membership in the Western revival group was sealed.

As for the other Western province, British Columbia, well, the Prairies were less than impressed. At this point the Triple E people were truly disgusted with British Columbia and its refusal to be buffeted along in the prevailing Senate-reform wind sweeping the West. It was in these days that Horsman began to portray this battle as the strong against the weak in Canada. Vociferously, he declared at his encounters with reporters that the big provinces were grouping up on the small ones, and that British Columbia was acting in an unseemly fashion by trying to be one of the "big guys." The B.C. push for a five-region Senate was nothing more than a ploy to become as domineering as Ontario and Quebec, Horsman said. Rhetoric such as this only heightened the drama about the Senate controversy. Where once the story was relegated to the back pages of the newspaper and explained in chart form midway through the evening newscasts, now it was front-page news, top of the newscasts. Now Canada had a story on its hands. And now Mulroney and Ottawa had a problem on their backs.

Prince Edward Island premier Joe Ghiz, another Maritime premier who enjoyed good relations with Mulroney, was making a lot of noise about the danger of a Senate impasse. He kept telling everyone that no Canadians cared about Senate reform; it wasn't worth the rifts it was causing.

Rumours kept swirling around the Royal York that Alberta was preparing to walk out, or Newfoundland was getting fed up with the tactics to destabilize the Triple E campaign. The stakes were getting bigger and the drama was reaching fever pitch. Deadlines have a way of doing that to constitutional negotiations. So what did they do? They ignored the deadline. At the end of May, when the best-efforts draft was supposed to be produced, the MMC declared a time-out. And it was at this pause in the proceedings that the premiers, the head coaches, came into the game.

Now the Senate issue was truly getting interesting. Unfortunately, the debate was also headed underground, where the fights would be waged by telephone, by secret deals, by clandestine conversation.

It was also time for a few well-placed visits. Clark packed his bags and headed out to Alberta, Newfoundland and Quebec during the early days of June. In his dealings with reporters, he started sending some disturbing signals. Suddenly, all the old Meech-style talk resurfaced — about the intransigence of Clyde Wells and the possibility that he would be a hold-out. Maybe, Clark reported after this meeting, the rest of the country would have to go around Clyde Wells's personal objections and see whether his voters would endorse a deal in a referendum. The message was that a stubborn individual, not a stubborn province, was getting in the way. It was an echo of Brian Mulroney's antagonism to Wells as the man who would deny the country a deal.

Alberta, too, was portrayed as a problem. Aha, said many people watching at the time. So that was the tactic. Canada is going to get a new Senate, but without the endorsement of the two provinces who wanted it so badly — Alberta and Newfoundland. The isolation tactics appeared to have begun.

Jim Horsman, like most other Canadians, was relying on the news reports to figure out what was happening during this break in the constitutional discussions. Yes, the politicians' phone lines were busy, but no one knew where all these calls were leading. What would happen when the MMC got back on track? Horsman wrote in his diary about his "nagging doubt that a big buy-out is in the wings, on equalization, and regional development, of course." It seemed like a matter of time before the really crass bargaining began — money in exchange for principles.

Moe Sihota had been pleased that this tactic had so far not been employed. But he, too, got wind of the notion that Ottawa might be thinking of buying out Saskatchewan. If Saskatchewan could be pulled off the Triple E bandwagon, the group would fall apart — or Alberta, Newfoundland and Manitoba, the three provinces that didn't buy in, could be left to twist in the wind. Nova Scotia was not seen to be religiously committed to Triple E — the others in the group would find out later in June just how weak a partner Nova Scotia was. All Ottawa needed was seven provinces with 50 per cent of the population to put through a Senate that would make Ontario and the federal government happy.

"At one point, the feds actually considered the possibility of going to Saskatchewan with a proposal, as it was politely put . . . 'extra-constitutional,'" Sihota recalled. "I don't know that it was ever acted on. But I know that it was a consideration. I know that for sure. Because there were a lot of phone calls going on, back and forth."

Indeed, Saskatchewan was becoming painfully aware that it was being singled out in these early days of June, when it looked like the only solution was to bring in a Senate without Alberta, Newfoundland and Manitoba. Saskatchewan premier Roy Romanow could hear the worry in Alberta premier Don Getty's voice, in one of those countless conversations that were being carried on all over the country in early June.

"I just had a feeling at that point he was feeling more

and more the potential of being isolated," Romanow said.

About a week later, Getty would also find himself on the phone to Frank McKenna, trying to figure out what the heck was happening with another bit of curious shuttle diplomacy. This was probably the strangest, most shadowy development in the Senate dispute, and it would spook all the Triple E group.

Claude Beauchamp, always loosely linked to this process, whether through his talk at the dinner in Halifax, or through his tennis games with Gil Remillard, had suddenly shown up in New Brunswick in early June to talk to Frank McKenna about a new Senate proposal. The conversation must have sounded very much like the discussion held a couple of weeks earlier, when Gil Remillard had breakfast in Montreal with Bob Mitchell. Once again, the idea of "weighted votes" in the Senate was trotted out. Each province would have the same number of senators, but those senators would have a varying number of votes. And so it became the "Beauchamp" proposal for a while.

McKenna remembers that he gave tentative sounds of encouragement. Almost with a shrug, he responded, "Well, it's worth looking at." What really happened is that Frank McKenna had been asked to front for a Quebec-based proposal. A small news story went out on the wire, almost unnoticed by the rest of the constitutional world — for now.

It was time for another try at the Senate impasse, another kick at the can. No more travelling road shows, no more meetings with huge agendas and baby steps to "encouraging progress." Now it was June 8, time to pull the people into Ottawa's Pearson Building and get this Senate dispute settled.

On the evening of June 8, the *Toronto Star* went on strike at precisely 6:00 p.m., a walkout that would last well into July. Nevertheless, there was *Toronto Star* reporter Edison Stewart, along with the other constitutionally obsessed reporters, standing outside the meeting rooms on the second floor of the Chateau Laurier Hotel in Ottawa, waiting for the Triple E group to hold their pre-conference rallying meeting.

By now, the Triple E group had grown from five provinces to seven delegations. The Northwest Territories, for no other reason than common sense, had decided to throw their lot in with the Triple E group. The Métis National Council, because of their political reliance on the West, was also on board.

They held their dinner in a second-floor meeting room. It was a jovial, upbeat affair. Newfoundland justice minister Ed Roberts was handing out buttons for his forthcoming election. He had no seat in the Newfoundland Legislature at this time; Wells had appointed him to serve as justice minister and constitutional emissary on a basis of trust and confidence. Roberts did not let him down.

"The momentum is building our way," Horsman wrote in his journal that night. It was going to be tough, but the Triple E group still felt enough strength to wage a fight. The next day, Clark dropped the glove early for that fight. Uncharacteristically, he started the meeting with a speech, warning that Canadians would not tolerate failure in these discussions. Would they let it all go up in smoke over the Senate?

"The need for national leadership remains," Clark told the negotiators. "To pretend otherwise is to ignore the fact that our first priority must be to present Canadians with an approach that will allow this country to move on and face the challenges of the future united and strong. The country cannot fail simply because these discussions fail. This process is about principles and vision. If this meeting fails, our

previous successes will be rendered failures as well. No
new arrangement on powers and responsibilities.
No progress on equalization or regional development.
No new partnership with the aboriginal peoples. No
Canada round. And perhaps, no Canada."

That warning was taken as a threat by the Triple E
group, and it made for a less than constructive mood
in this meeting. June 9 was a day of slowly simmering
anger for the Triple E advocates. They weren't being
taken seriously. The question wasn't when or how they
would get their Senate — it was when they would wave
the white flag.

Discouraged, they made their way to their Triple E
lunch. They produced a new paper, the so-called June
9 proposal. In it, they delivered a significant compromise – they said that their new Senate would not kill
most Commons bills; it would just provoke a "joint
sitting" of two Houses. In other words, in cases of a
deadlock, the Senate and House of Commons would
get together as one giant Parliament and settle their
disputes. A very Canadian solution — mediation
instead of deadlock. A very interesting proposal, too,
to Ontario, which had floated the idea of abolishing the
Senate and making one huge House of Commons,
augmented with an equal number of extra people from
each province.

But the seeds of this compromise only took hold
later. For now, the Triple E people appeared to be up
against a stone wall. Inexplicably, Nova Scotia was also
faltering in its support; Premier Don Cameron fell out
of the group that day. Clyde Wells was the one who first
talked Cameron into the Triple E fold. The Nova Scotia
premier believed that Wells was absolutely right to
point out that the Atlantic provinces had no voice at
the centre of power.

"We just don't count. They ignore us completely,"

Cameron had said in a commiseration session on the phone with Wells. "And we should abolish the Senate." Cameron was in the midst of trying to scrape together a new method of governing Nova Scotia after the flamboyant reign of his predecessor, John Buchanan. That former Nova Scotia premier was sitting in the very Senate that Cameron wanted to abolish, plucked from the tides of controversy and scandal that were plaguing his government in 1990. Cameron was no fan of this red chamber or its image in Canada. It was a waste.

But Wells said: "Stop and think about what you've said. We don't count. Well, what better way to get influence than in an elected, equal and effective Senate?"

Slowly over the months, Cameron had evolved from a Senate abolitionist to a Triple E Senate crusader. Now he was gone. Wells phoned him on June 10.

"What happened? Why are you deserting us now?"

Cameron didn't have a lot to say. "Well, you know, I'm concerned about Canada."

The Newfoundland premier brought up all the old arguments he had used to get Cameron on the Senate bandwagon — the alienation of the smaller provinces, their perpetual status as have-nots, in money and power.

But Wells's persuasion was no match for the pressure of pragmatism that was being placed on the ultimate practical politician. McKenna was also making phone calls, pointing out to Nova Scotia that the Triple E campaign had become ridiculous, country-threatening.

Cameron had been persuaded to join the Triple E group because of practical politics. Wells's appeal hit him because it made practical sense. He wasn't a politician known to dance around principles and philosophies and deals. The Triple E Senate made sense — fine, he would support it. The Triple E Senate was starting not to make sense — fine, he would drop it. It was also fair to say that Cameron had bigger things on his mind. The Westray coal disaster in May in his own riding, which killed twenty-six trapped miners, had shaken him. After that, he was never the same when he did attend the multilateral meetings. He would seem distracted, far away, his mind obviously on the disaster of Westray.

With his defection, Nova Scotia, Prince Edward Island and New Brunswick would become linked together in what was disparingly called "The Hallelujah Chorus." Other provinces were convinced that the economic dependence of the Maritimes made their premiers merely the back-up singers to Ottawa's constitutional solos. Joe Ghiz's appeals started to wear on other provincial politicians; his lines appeared to have been penned by the federal government. Now Don Cameron had joined Ghiz's chorus. Publicly, he said little about his defection, and he skirted sheepishly around people such as Jim Horsman and Ed Roberts.

The effect of his drop-out was devastating on the rest of the group. They sensed that Ottawa was getting ready to lower the boom, and that Cameron had been just the first to get scared off. The storm clouds were moving in over the West and over Newfoundland. It looked like the best days of the Triple E campaign were behind them.

Nonetheless, the debate around the table that day was one of those great political debates — one for the history books. Sensing imminent collapse, the negotiators were pulling out all the stops, using every ounce of their political energy to debate the Senate question. This was a day that should have been opened up to the cameras, for then the Canadian people might have seen just how fervently these people wanted the new Senate to serve as the medicine for Canada's sick system. They had heard the people, they thought, and the reply to the public's frustration with government was a new Senate.

"Let's look ahead and let's listen to what people are saying to us as politicians," Alberta's Jim Horsman said. He talked about his cross-country odysseys on Senate reform over the years. "I became aware of a very major disenchantment with the political system, the parliamentary system itself. The requests, the demands, the representations in support of so-called direct democracy issues are very real. We would be kidding ourselves if we dismissed them as being of [no] significance, because they are out there.

"One political party has arisen in the West — the Reform Party — largely because they are appealing to that notion of direct democracy.... Quite frankly, those direct democracy approaches are a challenge to the current parliamentary system in a very major way. We cannot be blind to the wishes of the people, because that is the essence of democracy."

Prophetic words from a politician who would soon learn just how anxious the public was to use direct democracy to shut down the politicians. The No vote on October 26, 1992, was just as forceful, but far more concise.

Clark countered Horsman, pointing out that they were both Albertans, and had both heard the cry of alienation from the West: "There is no question that there is frustration and there is no question that, at least in our part of the country, part of that frustration has to do with a sense of exclusion, which is why there has to be this fundamental change, however we do it, that responds to the wanting in concept.

"But the other source of the frustration — and this is why this issue is so important to us — is that governments do not get things done. It is not just that television has come to the House of Commons, it is what has been there to televise that has done damage to the record of the House of Commons. It is all squabbling. It is not seeing people acting to get things done for Canada."

There was no doubt that politicians had poured their souls into this Senate campaign, or that this was to be their gift to the people, an offering to restore faith and populism and responsibility into government. Maybe it wasn't such a good idea, but Joe Clark decided that the best thing to do on June 9 was to carry right through, and let the proceedings move to a dinner. No one was in any mood for social chit-chat, but this problem had to be solved. Tired, grumpy and pessimistic, the politicians in the MMC group headed to their dinner at the Pearson Building.

Another mistake at this dinner was to let the wine flow freely. With their tongues loosened, their emotions not in check, civilized discourse broke down. Horsman was fed up. His anger whetted by wine, he blew up at the people blocking a Triple E Senate.

"Everyone's a little toasted and roasted and Horsman is hot," Sihota remembers. "And you can see he's blowing up. You know, he tried to contain himself all the way through this whole process. But the Senate stuff was never getting discussed, they were getting frustrated. We were never getting there . . .

"You could see what was happening. Horsman was ready to pop, and in fact, he did," Sihota said.

Horsman gave an emotional history lesson, giving full vent to all that angry Western alienation that had led to the Senate crusade. He rounded up all the familiar lore of this alienation: the Central Canadian dominance of every bank, board and federal agency; the national energy program; the axis of power in Ottawa that reaches only as far as Toronto and Montreal; even that oft-noted offence against the West, the fact that

CBC declared election winners even before the polls closed in Saskatchewan or Alberta. Now the spectre of alienation was facing the West again, in all the isolation tactics that were being whipped up against the Triple E group.

"If it's your view to isolate two provinces or three provinces, fine — you can do it," Horsman told them. "But don't forget the political consequences of that kind of action. That's not nation-building. That would be nation-destructive."

He readily concedes: "Part of the problem with that evening is that they'd been serving drinks. The idea was that it was to be sort of a social evening, we weren't going to get into heavy-duty negotiating." But all around that table, people appeared determined to put their deepest feelings out in the open, for all to see.

Bud Wildman, Ontario's native affairs minister, was holding forth, saying that his province would never, ever accept an equal Senate. Such declarations merely poked a sharp stick at the cranky Triple E group. Quietly, Bob Rae turned to the trusted Bob Mitchell, and said: "That's not Ontario's position." Across the table, Sihota was also giving signs to Mitchell that maybe he could look to his NDP colleagues to help him out of this jam.

"Look, you guys, everyone needs their symbol," Sihota said. "Alberta should get their symbol. We should give them their Triple E Senate and conclude the thing."

But Wildman was still saying "never" to the idea of an equal Senate. There was all kinds of debate over what was the right, "patriotic" thing to do for Canada. The people who were weary of the Triple E Senate group tried to use the lure of patriotism to push this troubled constitutional family back together again.

Horsman excused himself from the dinner to go to

the men's room. On the way back into the meeting, still steaming angry, he caught sight of the NDP group sneaking out the back door. Rae, Sihota and Mitchell were leaving in despair at the outcome of the dinner. Horsman went back into the room for a very short time, picked up his things and departed. He brushed by reporters on the way out, barking that it had been "a terrible evening."

Rae couldn't have agreed more. "That was awful. That was terrible. We all told Joe not to do it. Don't have a dinner...Oh God, it was awful. It was a mess. Jim Horsman walked out. We all walked out."

In the elevator on the way out, the three NDP negotiators, all from very different points on the Senate-reform spectrum, decided to see whether they couldn't put their left-leaning heads together and sort something out. "Look, you guys, you know, we haven't done this NDP thing much," Sihota told Rae and Mitchell. "We always talk with each other, but we haven't done this thing. Maybe we should just, you know, talk about this thing."

Like truant schoolchildren, the three NDPers sneaked down to the basement and out a side entrance of the Pearson Building. They made their way over to the Chateau Laurier, to Rae's room, and discussed what to do next. Rae pulled out a pencil and started to sketch out an equal Senate. Mitchell smiled to himself. Maybe this wasn't such a disastrous day after all. They were getting Ontario to move! Sihota, for all B.C.'s bluster about needing a five-region Senate, also knew he could live with the Triple E proposal. They were busily working away at their Senate ideas, Rae holding the pencil, the ideas flying fast and furious, when Jeff Rose, Rae's deputy and bureaucratic hit man in this whole exercise, walked in.

"We actually sketched out the details," Sihota said. "It

was basically a Triple E format." Again, like school-children caught in the middle of mischief, they explained to Rose what they were up to. Rae told his old university buddy how this equality issue could be sold to the voters of Ontario. Rose was very, very scep-tical. All three of the NDP politicians tried their hand at convincing Rose. It was three on one, but Rose was not budging. It just wasn't good enough. It wasn't saleable in Ontario.

The calculations continued for a little while longer, then Sihota and Mitchell decided it was time to turn in. They left the room, and started making their way across the Remembrance Day monument square across from the Chateau Laurier.

Mitchell was delighted. He couldn't wait to tell Romanow about the giant step Ontario had taken. Sihota kept thinking back to the distinct lack of enthu-siasm shown by Rose. He turned to Mitchell and tried to dampen his enthusiasm.

"Bob," Sihota said. "The rosebud's going to snip this thing." Mitchell could not believe that the interest had been so fleeting; that it would be gone by the next day. Sihota bet him five dollars that Ontario would back off the idea the next day. And sure enough, it did. The pro-posal just wasn't good enough to sell in Ontario.

A dejected Bob Mitchell was leafing through news-paper clippings the next day, June 10, in one of the side rooms off the conference room at Pearson Building. He came across that tiny newspaper story about Beauchamp going to visit McKenna a week or so earlier. Mitchell, perhaps remembering the seeds that had been planted at his breakfast with Remillard, pulled aside Jim Horsman. This could be a way out of the box, they thought.

Horsman telephoned Premier Getty, who in turn, telephoned Frank McKenna. "What is this thing?" Getty wanted to know. McKenna's ears pricked up — it sounded as if Alberta wanted a deal, maybe any deal.

McKenna put a phone call through to Prime Minister Mulroney's chief of staff, Hugh Segal, to tell him that Getty was nibbling at the bait of an equal Senate, with weighted votes. He asked to talk to Mulroney. No phone call ever came back. The next thing McKenna heard was that the prime minister was headed off to Rio de Janeiro for the world environmental summit.

But that wasn't the end of the issue. The "Beauchamp proposal" was about to get a new name — the "Romanow proposal." Spurred on by Bob Mitchell's interest in the wire story, Clark decided that now was the time to bring Roy Romanow into the discussions. The constitutional saga could make good use right now of that old Greek theatre device, the *deus ex machina*, the artificial contraption that is lowered onto the stage to magically set everything right. The machine in this case was a Challenger jet, and the person inside was Roy Romanow, summoned from financial meetings in New York to save the day at the constitutional impasse in Ottawa.

Romanow remembers the call he got from Clark this way: "They had reached a very critical point in the negotiations and it looked as though the ministers were on the verge of failure ... They needed some injection of new ideas or at least some new injection of will to keep this thing going." Romanow sighed. The last thing he wanted to do was drag himself out of New York, even if it was only a fifty-five-minute flight by Challenger. "With some reluctance, considerable reluctance, I agreed. Because I had not been briefed on it. I had not been part of the negotiating team and just the agenda made it awkward. But I agreed."

Mitchell and adviser Howard Leeson flew down to pick up the premier, to give him all the details so he could perform his act of intervention in this impasse. The Beauchamp proposal looked like the best thing going. They arrived at Clark's office on the fifth floor of the Heritage Building at the corner of Queen and O'Connor streets in Ottawa. It was dark, and the lights of Parliament Hill and Ottawa twinkled outside the window.

Romanow walked into the office and sniffed a set-up. There in the room were Clark, Rae, PEI premier Joe Ghiz and Nova Scotia premier Don Cameron. Immediately, Romanow was pounced upon, urged to abandon the Triple E crusade. Clark talked about imminent collapse. Cameron pointed out why he had left the Triple E group — it just wasn't worth the angst it was causing. Joe Ghiz asserted that it was simply damaging to the nation.

"I was the key. Saskatchewan was the key," Romanow said.

"Think of Canada," his fellow premiers implored. "Leave this Triple E crusade. We'll get a decent Senate and we won't break apart the nation to get it." Romanow was not to be moved. Okay, maybe he would look at a different idea, but how about giving this Beauchamp proposal a shot?

Well, it was something, anyway, as Joe Clark would later recall. "He brought forward this other proposal," Clark said, "that frankly, we didn't think would go very far that night." It was enough, though, to justify some further thought on the Senate question. Time to retrench again, go back to home base and see what could be figured out.

So with the Romanow proposal hanging in the air, and the Senate impasse still unsolved, Clark decided to shut down the meetings on June 11. Horsman chose to sing happy birthday that morning to a reporter celebrating her birthday at the Pearson Building, and said

little about the Beauchamp, now Romanow proposal.
McKenna got a telephone call from his delegation,
saying that the best way to sell this weighted-vote idea
was to have it come from a Triple E province. It was now
hanging out in the air, ready to be buffeted by the winds
in all directions.

The major goal for the Triple E group at this point
was to keep their fragile coalition together, even with
the loss of Nova Scotia, and despite the existence of this
strange Romanow proposal, which was now just a wild
card in a crazy game. The four Triple E premiers got
on the phone to each other for a conference call. Clyde
Wells was very edgy. He didn't like what he was hearing
from Getty or from Filmon and Romanow. They were
looking seriously at this weighted-vote proposal, which
Wells saw as an Ottawa invention, a trick against Triple
E. Actually, it was a Quebec-sponsored idea too, as he
would learn later.

As the call went on, the Triple E group seemed to be
reviving its go-get-'em attitude. They had no choice:
Wells would make them all look like sell-outs if they
abandoned the Senate team and he stayed on. Getty,
who had set his province up as the king of Senate reform,
could hardly hand over the crown to Wells without having to make a lot of embarrassing explanations.

By the end of the call, they were resolved that Prime
Minister Mulroney was not going to drag them off their
crusade. They knew that he was poised to re-enter the
constitutional crusade directly, and he did at the end
of June.

First, on June 28, the native and territorial leaders
were summoned to Mulroney's residence at 24 Sussex
Drive. As the native leaders emerged that Sunday afternoon to talk to reporters, the murmuring started again
— set-up, set-up, set-up. Here were the native leaders,
never very interested or engaged in the Senate dispute,

suddenly turning up the heat under the Triple E group. They went into their meetings with the prime minister to talk about their own issue of self-government, and they emerged convinced that their deal was in jeopardy because of stubborn old provinces such as Alberta and Newfoundland. It didn't help that Alberta and Newfoundland had also been among the most headstrong opponents of wide-ranging self-government.

"I would just like to add one further comment before I take questions," said Inuit leader Rosemarie Kuptana. "That is to say that if there is a failure in these constitutional discussions, it is not because of the aboriginal package. . . . If there is a failure on the constitutional package in this round, it will be because of deadlock on the Senate."

Native Council of Canada leader Ron George was even more blunt. "I'm not going to see the aboriginal issues go down because of the Triple E issue, which certainly doesn't seem to be something that's going to fly anyway." George was asked: Is that the message Mulroney gave you? Did he tell you that Don Getty and Clyde Wells were getting in the way of a deal?

"That's pretty much it, yes."

The next day the premiers were to meet for lunch at 24 Sussex. The Triple E group all got together in a room at the Ottawa Hilton, to high-five each other and seal the alliance before facing Mulroney's formidable persuasive skills.

The very seating plan at the lunch seemed to be a signal. Gary Filmon, who had not been at the constitutional table since the dying days of Meech in 1990, didn't think a whole lot had changed in Ottawa's negotiating style. There he was, down at the far end of the table, placed near Don Getty and Clyde Wells, and all the other "difficult" provincial politicians. Filmon looked around, cast his eyes far, far up to the end of the table where the prime minister sat, and then looked at his Triple E buddies around him.

"What's wrong with this picture?" Filmon asked his friend Wells. The Newfoundland premier just shook his head, sardonically.

The message at this lunch was simple. Mulroney essentially told the provinces: "This is your problem. Fix it. I'll be coming forward in mid-July with a constitutional proposal. You're either part of that plan or against it."

And so, once again, the story on the constitution could be summed up in those two words that carried the debate through the summer of 1992: "Another meeting." This one was to be held at the Airport Hilton Hotel, and as we have seen, it turned out to be pivotal, if not the key encounter of the entire Senate debate.

It's hard to believe that such a great meeting took place after such a hostile beginning. This was not a happy group that converged on the Airport Hilton on July 3. Newfoundland premier Clyde Wells was upset about the cod crisis that promised to throw thousands of fish workers in his province out of work. Saskatchewan premier Roy Romanow was miffed at the ridicule heaped on his Senate gamble, the gamble that dragged him away from New York and into the political hot seat. Manitoba premier Gary Filmon, borrowing a quip from his opposition leader, Gary Doer, told Romanow that the weighted-vote system in the Senate was an "Animal Farm" Senate, in which some animals were more equal than others. Doer was harking back to the George Orwell novel, in which pigs took over the farm under the guise of socialistic equality. Certainly Romanow didn't enjoy being the butt of a joke planted by his own NDP buddy Gary Doer.

Filmon and Romanow did not endear themselves to Bob Rae either as that meeting got under way. Heading into the meeting, they turned their guns on Ontario, accusing Rae of being the one who was blocking a deal to save Canada. If he is so patriotic, they asked, why was he holding out?

"We got nailed in the scrums," Rae recalled. "I was mad. I thought I was being set up and I didn't think it was helpful to keep doing this. I mean, there's an element in Western politics . . . or Maritime politics, where ritual denunciations of Ontario are just good politics." Enough was enough. It was time to get down to business.

B.C. premier Mike Harcourt was no expert at constitution-making but he did know how to conduct a meeting. He was having a little trouble getting the wilful premiers into the room to start the session. And at first, it looked like this was going to be just an exercise in political rhetoric. These were not the same people who had journeyed together throughout the spring and built up the bank of trust in each other, those who had travelled the learning curve on the constitution.

Sihota remembers that Wells just kept talking about cod. "On cod, right? Which was a little off topic." The Newfoundland premier announced he had to leave the meeting to get back and deal with the cod crisis. He had his briefcase in his hands, he was pushing his papers into the case and getting ready to leave.

Rae stopped him. He asked: "If you are satisfied on the Senate, if it is sufficiently in accord with your principles, would you give the veto to Quebec?" Clyde Wells also remembers that moment. For months, he had been telling reporters that this was a possibility. But there, on the spur of the moment, he committed himself.

Wells does not portray this moment as the crucial step in his evolution. Anyone could point to a number of statements he made before July 3 that indicated his answer would be yes when Rae threw the question at him about trading off the veto for the equal Senate. The Newfoundland premier says that the important step took place on Rae's side. After all, in Wells's view, it was the first time that Rae had opened the door, even a fraction, to the idea of the equal Senate. He had not been in Rae's room that night of June 9, when the NDP caucus did their scribblings. So it would be nice, in the interests of telling a dramatic story, to have the music swell at this point, with Wells and Rae facing off in the late-morning challenge at the Airport Hilton. But that's not really how these stories work.

Sihota points out that the ground was already fertile for a move to be made at the Airport Hilton. Remember, he said, that the meeting in the Chateau Laurier on June 9 had shown that everyone could be "elastic" on the issue. Clark, too, there as a very interested observer in this provincial bid to get the constitutional ball rolling, said there was no magic moment, with everything falling into place. It just happened.

"Whatever premiers Rae and Wells had said as Clyde was leaving, I think people thought we were a long way from anything ... The lunch [at the Airport Hilton] did not flow from the exchange between premiers Rae and Wells. It was almost as though that was one chapter, didn't get very far, and then suddenly..."

Another chapter was opened, thanks to the adept chairmanship of Harcourt. Much to the glee of the Triple E group, he simply kept sweeping the weakest proposals off the table, until there was only the one strong one left — the equal proposal, which contained so much sweat and effort. It was, simply, the strongest surviving idea on the table. Harcourt may not have known much about the constitution, but he did understand the dynamics of decision-making. The equal

Senate was the front-runner, so that was the one to work on.

So the "magic" of that Airport Hilton meeting, the gathering that allowed the equal Senate to take flight, got a little help from everyone. Rae was obviously ready to deal and to put his stock in equality, provided it did not cost Ontario too much. Romanow had been making clear that if his own proposal was knocked off, he would embrace wholeheartedly the equal Senate. There was no moving Saskatchewan. Wells was willing to offer payment of one of his principles — by giving Quebec the veto over future Senate reform. Everyone else was just fed up or saw nowhere else to go. And thanks to Harcourt, and the way he swept things off the table so effectively, the equal Senate had squeaked through as the last-ditch plan to a deal. It would go on to be part of the deal on July 7, and later the Charlottetown accord. There had been a showdown at Triple E and the West had won.

In the corridors of the Airport Hilton, Bob Mitchell grabbed Horsman in joyous victory. This was an unbelievable experience for Mitchell, a moment of true triumph for the West. And it wasn't just the victory of his side. Even later, Mitchell would recall this Senate debate as one of the most useful exercises Canada could experience. Every politician at that table learned so much about each other and the needs of their country. Everyone was talking about the need to give government back to the people. This was what politics was all about. As Roy Romanow said, much later, as he explained the constitutional obsession of politicians, this issue was what made statesmen out of people; solving it this way had sealed a friendship in the West that transcended political boundaries, had brought Ontario to a remarkable act of generosity and enfolded the Atlantic, and especially Newfoundland, warmly into the federation. This was truly a wonderful Canadian exercise.

But as Mitchell grasped Horsman's hand in shared congratulations, the Alberta veteran of these constitutional wars was not ready to be heartened yet.

"Mitchell grabbed me and exulted," Horsman wrote that night in his diary. "We're getting the Triple E ...Well, we shall see."

Horsman was right to be dubious about the chances for success. But he did not know back then that it would be the public who thwarted his crusade in the end. After years of believing that a new Senate would bridge the gap between old politics and new populism in the West, Horsman and the others found out that a Canadian crisis of faith had spread to every institution of government, not just the red chamber. The Senate campaign was stopped by the same forces of anger and alienation that drove the Triple E religion for so long. In the wake of the Charlottetown defeat, it was not just the Senate that was in need of an overhaul — it was the whole system of politics and government.

Months later, Mulroney had gone back to the old method of appointing senators in his final months in office. The Senate continued to function as the lame relic it had always been. The champions of Senate reform, whether in the Western-based Reform Party or among the newer converts in Saskatchewan and Manitoba, had set their sights on fixing the economy of Canada before the Senate question was ever tackled again. And the 1992 model of a new Senate sits empty, uninhabited, a haunted Upper House for the history books.

8

The Native People: Through the Rapids

Long ago, in the mid-1960s, in the turbulent waters of Manitoba's Grand Rapids, a fourteen-year-old Cree was shooting through the currents in a canoe. The young man was named Ovide Mercredi and he was making this journey with his uncle, Chief John Turner. This was more than a simple outdoor trek for the young Mercredi; it was a spiritual journey, one that would forever change his life.

Guided by his uncle, Ovide Mercredi discovered his native spirituality in the rapids. He had learned the practical lessons of being a native in Manitoba in the 1960s, experiencing discrimination everywhere from hospitals to movie theatres. The canoe trip taught him, though, that there were lessons of the spirit to learn as well. He felt his ties to the wilderness, his bond with the land and the water where the canoe travelled.

Years later, Mercredi would ask Canadian citizens to take their own spiritual journey through the rapids, to follow his example as they shot the spiritual currents of the unity debate, relying on elders for advice as he had

on that long-ago canoe trip. Most importantly, Mercredi and the other native leaders would be asking
Canadians to recognize that the constitutional odyssey
for aboriginal people was indeed a spiritual debate —
it wasn't about money, or new layers of government or
claims to land. The whole national discussion about
native rights and the constitution in 1992 revolved
around a far more emotional claim — on the heart and
the sense of justice of each Canadian citizen.

For years, Canada's native people had watched as
Quebec's issues had consumed the emotion and heart
of the national-unity debate, as Quebec's dreams had
fired up the great Canadian obsession. Aboriginal
issues had been laid to one side in 1981, when the constitution was patriated by former prime minister Pierre
Trudeau. Maybe next time, the native leaders thought
to themselves then. The country seemed far more preoccupied with Quebec's isolation from the great unity
exercise than it was with native people's exclusion. The
aboriginal leaders could only hope that one day Canadians would see Quebec and aboriginal people as
equally and disturbingly distant from the embrace of
the federal family.

But a little more than five years later, native people
were forced to bow out of the emotional limelight
again, when their own aboriginal-issues conference
broke down in 1987, and the new Meech Lake accord,
aimed at securing Quebec's signature on the constitution, rose less than six weeks later from the ashes of the
aboriginal defeat. Again, the native people were left to
picket outside the Government Conference Centre in
June 1990, when all of Canada's first ministers were
locked in their marathon and futile effort to keep
Meech alive. Denied security passes to get into the conference centre, the aboriginal people's mood started to
turn from resigned to bitter.

Ovide Mercredi, then a vice-chief with the Assembly of First Nations, was one of those holding a picket sign, parading silently around the fountain at the back of the conference centre in the unseasonably chilly days from June 4 to June 9, 1990. Early on the Sunday morning of that terrible week, as the first ministers were gathered together singing "O Canada" at 2:00 a.m. to celebrate their temporary success at rescuing Meech, Mercredi was leaning against a wall in a dark corridor in another part of the building, speaking with quiet, calm confidence about how the country would learn to regret this rude rebuff of native people. "We may have a way to stop this," Mercredi said, his voice barely a whisper. At his side was the Liberal Dene MP from Western Arctic, Ethel Blondin, wiping tears of frustration from her face. No more tears of sadness; the mood was turning angry.

Within days, that new mood would propel Manitoba's Elijah Harper to block Meech in the province's Legislature. As Mercredi had forewarned, native politician Elijah Harper was standing up day after day, eagle feather in hand, simply saying No to the passage of the Meech Lake accord. In the wings, Ovide Mercredi and the new guard of angrier, more bitter native people wore their serene half-smiles. Now they, too, were part of the emotional drama of constitution-making. Quebec would be devastated on June 22, 1990; native people would celebrate in a victory born of bitterness.

Never again would the aboriginal people allow Quebec to lay sole claim to the emotion and spirit of the unity debate. From 1990 on, their strategy was to tie together the dreams of native people and Quebeckers, to weave a strange rope of shared feelings of humiliation and rejection. Every time Quebec got up to speak its language of humiliation, aboriginal people did the same. Quebec was bitter about the rejection of Meech;

aboriginal people were bitter about their repeated rejection at the constitutional table. Quebec would hotly accuse the rest of Canada of wrongly treating Quebeckers as a conquered nation; aboriginal people would make the same protests. If 1992 was supposed to be the year when Quebec carved out its distinct place in Canada, then native people wanted a distinct place too. If the rest of Canada was ready to grant some collective or group rights to Quebec, then aboriginal people wanted their group rights too.

In February 1992, Ovide Mercredi had vaulted to the head of the Assembly of First Nations, Canada's largest organization of approximately 600,000 status Indians, and he was firmly in charge of the mission to twin Quebec's dreams to those of the aboriginal people.

"I want to make it clear that the First Nations are not adversaries of French Canadian interests," Mercredi told the 250 people attending the government of Canada's constitutional conference on rights and values in Toronto. "On the contrary, we are committed to the recognition of collective rights in this round of constitutional reform."

However, Mercredi said, "the constitution of Canada is based on a distortion of history. It is premised on the idea that there are only two founding nations — the French and the English . . . We are saddened by the fact that Canadians have an image of us which is tainted by this distortion. You do not know who we are and what we believe."

During these days, Mercredi was throwing down challenge after challenge to Quebec and the rest of the country. The simple message? Aboriginal people would not stand in line behind Quebec any longer. The challenge infuriated Quebec and widened the eyes of Canadians in the so-called rest of Canada. Just a few days after that speech in Toronto, Mercredi showed up at the hearings of the special Commons–Senate committee examining constitutional change. He produced a long list of powers that natives wanted to control in self-government — they were far broader than any provincial powers envisaged in the wildest dreams of Quebec nationalists.

The next day, Mercredi marched into the Quebec National Assembly and laid down the same rules to his constitutional rivals/soul mates. In an address to the Belanger-Campeau commission, examining Quebec's future in Canada, Mercredi said: "Unless the self-determination of the First Nations is fully acknowledged and respected by the National Assembly, there can be no legitimate self-determination for French Quebeckers. To deny our right to self-determination in the pursuit of your aspirations would be a blatant form of racial discrimination."

Relations were already bitter between the two groups in the wake of the angry stand-off between Mohawk Warriors and Quebec police and government and people at Oka in the summer of 1990. The charges of racism had flown fast and furious in those days, and ties between Quebec and the aboriginal people were further strained. Quebec and its native people were also locked in a struggle over the Great Whale hydro mega-project in the North; the dispute there was seen by Quebec as a sign that native people would forever block Quebec's road to becoming a great, self-sufficient power. The last thing that was needed in 1992 was to add to the antagonism between the two groups.

But it was as though Mercredi had seized Quebec as one stick, aboriginal people as the other, and was rubbing them furiously to make sparks. And the sparks were indeed flying when Mercredi told Quebeckers that they did not have the same right as aboriginal people to call themselves a nation. "Self-determination is not a right of a province. It is the right of all peoples. Are the peo-ple of Quebec a people in the international legal sense? The population of Quebec is made up of a wide range of racial and ethnic groups. It cannot be considered a peo-ple with the right of self-determination."

Back in Ottawa, Constitutional Affairs Minister Joe Clark was feeling the heat of this smouldering fire. These days of February were just one long series of back-and-forth declarations by Clark, Quebec govern-ment people and Mercredi; a tit-for-tat match on who was distinct and who wasn't. Clark was trying carefully to steer down the middle.

He told reporters: "Distinct society has, to my knowl-edge, not been used before with regard to aboriginal people. And to try to take a phrase that has a very par-ticular meaning regarding Quebec, [to] have people start a chorus of 'I'm distinct too,' has the effect of devaluating that concept as it applies to Quebec. It just isn't helpful."

Clark directed a warning to Mercredi and other would-be distinct aboriginal people. "I hope that they and he would reconsider because, among other things, what we have to do here is encourage the government of Quebec to be more forthcoming than they have been so far on the definition of self-government. And if abo-riginal people are on the one hand cutting away at something which is important to Quebec, and on the other hand asking Quebec to give something to them, they're not likely to make much progress."

Clark, though, was not blind to the spiritual nature of this debate. It was, in fact, the constitutional affairs minister who was the first to hear and heed this appeal from the native people to take the emotional journey, to see the spirit that moved them. He received this tuto-rial in spirituality in Morley, Alberta, in July 1991. It was a fitting spot for a first meeting — in a way, both men could claim it as their own turf. Mercredi knew the elders as members of his own Indian nation; Clark had known the elders as constituents of his own Alberta riding. For nine hours, Clark talked with Mercredi and native elders at the Stoney Indian Reserve on that hot summer day. The white politician and the native leaders shared their thoughts, their hopes and a peace pipe ceremony. Though the elders had decided in a meeting only a few days before that too many white people had shared the peace pipe with them, they made an exception for Clark. Afterwards, Clark and Mercredi took a long walk together, sealing a solid beginning to a true friendship. Mercredi waxed poetic about Clark's willingness to listen to the native people's plight.

"We have, in the person of the Honourable Joe Clark, a person who is willing to re-examine his own yester-days."

The memories of this encounter stayed at the front of Clark's consciousness, just as they did with Mercredi. Years later, any visitor to the offices of either man would notice that a special place had been reserved on the wall for the photograph of the Morley meeting. Both men have prominently displayed a framed snapshot showing Clark and Mercredi deep in conversation in Morley. Nearly every one of Clark's speeches began with a reminder of what he heard from elder Peter O'Chiese at this meeting: "We must lift each other up."

This was Clark's answer to Mercredi's plea. Canadians should listen to the advice of elders as they travelled down the rapids. Mercredi, too, took away some wise advice from that encounter with Peter O'Chiese. While this wise old man was telling Clark of the need for Canada to lift itself up, he was telling Mercredi why native people should stay very, very still. "You just stay where you are; hold your ground, don't walk away, and they will come to you," he told Mercredi.

On March 11, as Mercredi was ready to embark on the meeting that would relaunch the multilateral process, he was in Morley again looking for advice. He was treated to an extraordinary encounter. The elders placed a chair in the middle of the hall, and seated Mercredi in it. Then they gathered around and prayed for him. With a low, chanting hum, they encircled him, praying for his future success at the constitutional meeting. Some held his hands as they prayed; others loomed close and touched his hair. And then Peter O'Cheese reminded Mercredi that this journey was in fact a trip through the rapids.

Mercredi would use this symbolism to plead the natives' case the very next day. When he came to address the multilateral talks, he invited the provincial premiers and justice ministers to see the negotiating process as a trip through the rapids, not unlike the journey he took with his uncle many years before.

It was March 12 and this gathering was a watershed event in the lives of native people around the constitutional table. The original idea of the meeting was to pull together all the provinces, to come up with a unity deal that would be acceptable to Quebec before its October deadline for a referendum on sovereignty. It was to be a low-key event, a general update for the provinces on the state of the constitutional process. Along with the two territorial leaders, representatives of the four native organizations — the AFN, the Native Council of Canada, the Inuit and the Métis — were invited to a pre-meeting breakfast as a gesture of inclusion by Clark.

Very, very quickly, the dynamics of the meeting changed, thanks to Ontario and the plan it tossed on the table. Furious at the prospect of provinces being ignored by Ottawa in this constitutional process, Ontario had come up with a strategy for extensive multilateral talks, stretching right through the spring. It caught Ottawa completely off guard, unprepared for the assault, with no strategy of its own to launch a defence.

A key part of Ontario's plan would change the constitutional life of natives forever. There, in black and white, Ontario premier Bob Rae had declared that native people and territorial leaders must be full partners in all the discussions. In the open public session, Rae laid down his law for native people's participation. There could be no progress on the constitution unless it dealt with justice for aboriginal people.

Clark readily admits that Ontario caught the federal government at a disadvantage with this volley on behalf of the native people.

"I was very conscious of setting precedents for first ministers' conferences," Clark said. "I always believed that there was going to be a point at which we had to bring aboriginal leaders in. I frankly thought, going into that meeting, that it was going to be too early to do it then."

One by one, the premiers lined up behind Rae. One by one, they declared that this was an elemental part of constitutional justice. Prince Edward Island premier Joe Ghiz, who had taken the aboriginal cause to his heart, said it would be unjust to keep natives out. The ever-practical Nova Scotia premier, Donald Cameron, agreed that it just wouldn't be right to exclude native people.

Others were more nervous. Manitoba's justice minister, James McCrae, was going through a Meech flashback as this debate unfolded. McCrae had been the House leader in Manitoba in June 1990, and he had sat in the direct line of fire when Elijah Harper had blockaded the proceedings to help kill Meech. He couldn't stop thinking of how the native people were fond of using obstruction to get their way; McCrae was worried about a replay of the Manitoba Meech experience, on a grander scale. Even though Mercredi had been in the wings in Winnipeg during those days, McCrae had never seen him in action before. He was impressed; Mercredi, like McCrae himself, seemed like a man of quiet, calm reason. And even if McCrae was nervous about letting the native people in to this process, Meech had also taught Manitoba that it would be sheer political folly to buck the will of native people. He decided to sit back and let the rapids take him along.

Others in the West were also edgy, but they had similar political worries. Alberta's Jim Horsman, the dean of the constitutional table in 1992, had been around at all those aboriginal-rights conferences in the 1980s, and knew that his province and he himself were seen as adversaries of the native cause. Reluctant to be branded as an Alberta cowboy at war with the Indians, Horsman made only meek objections to the native people's participation.

Ontario had laid the groundwork for this strategy. Rae knew he was arriving at a very different constitutional table than the one set for first ministers in the Meech years. Ontario was now governed by a New Democratic government, as were British Columbia and Saskatchewan. Together, these three left-wing governments had a hold on more than 50 per cent of the Canadian population — a magic number for changing the constitution. Ontario and Bob Rae went into this meeting confident that the strategy would be backed by the NDP allies.

More than anything, this surge of strength, centred in Ontario, is what put the native people at the table. Joe Clark sees it that way, as a result of Premier Bob Rae's very particular and strong interest in the cause of native people.

"I don't think another government in Ontario would have brought forward the aboriginal issue to the degree that the Rae government would," Clark said. In the mind of this Conservative politician from Alberta, the Ontario premier had put the issue on the agenda because of his New Democratic, more left-wing sense of justice. "It's part of his approach to issues generally... that you give the benefit of the doubt to the victim," Clark said. "I think he considered the aboriginal people to be the victim.... It also has to do with a sense that it's futile to encourage people to improve themselves without giving them the means to do it."

Rae was motivated by more than simple left-wing politics, however. His view of native people had been shaped by his travels in the North, as a history student and as leader of the opposition in Ontario. He was even arrested for his participation in an Indian blockade in northern Ontario, at Temagami in 1989. The plight of Canada's native people had reached far deeper than pure politics in Rae's consciousness and had gone directly to his emotions. His commitment to the native people was unswerving and unchallenged. Ovide Mercredi was so confident of Rae's advocacy that he didn't even think it was necessary to lobby Ontario for the native cause. While Mercredi had been running around Canada, trying to plead his case to all kinds of provincial politicians in the months leading up to March 12, he simply accepted Rae's support as a given. Mercredi had been there in Toronto in October 1990, just one day after Rae had been sworn in as Ontario premier, and watched this politician make the first speech of his term to the Assembly of First Nations gathering.

Rae talked in this speech about his personal experiences with native people and made a vow to do right by the aboriginal cause in his term in office.

"As a leader of this province, I tell you that in the time that is given to us, I am determined to do what I can, and our government is determined to do what it can, to see that we come to terms with this history."

Words such as these marked Rae as a new-style premier of the 1990s when it came to aboriginal people. On the other hand, premiers such as Newfoundland's Clyde Wells were very much of the old, traditional school. Steeped in the view that politics and emotion should be separate, Wells was dismayed by this injection of pure, raw emotion into the constitutional discussions. Rae, he believed, was bringing baggage to the talks that had no place in a rational debate over principles.

"I didn't see that he had judged it on merit," Wells said. "He was absolutely emotional about it."

The Newfoundland premier also drew a clear line in his mind between elected, constitutionally sanctioned governments, and the loose-knit leadership of native organizations. One was legitimate in his mind, the other was not to be accorded all the same powers and privileges as the provincial governments. It was a view that had held in the reign of former prime minister Pierre Trudeau, and it was one that Wells would embrace too.

Wells argued on March 12 that constitution-making had to be conducted by elected people, relying on the advice of the non-elected. Native people could advise, but they had no right of consent. This was exactly the view that Native Council of Canada leader Ron George had expected to hear from most of the premiers. He arrived at this meeting as a veteran of constitutional discussions, an active partner in the debates of the early 1980s, when native people had pushed for a place in Trudeau's patriation of the constitution. George was a sceptic about the politics of provincial premiers and justice ministers. His experience told him that these white politicians didn't have a clue about native people's constitutional dreams. But that day, as he watched Wells on the outside of the move to put native people at the table, was the beginning of a voyage of discovery for George, in which he realized that maybe aboriginal rights were starting to be heeded and respected and heard in the rest of Canada.

Rae believed that he had the public behind him. Polls were showing a heavy weight of support behind the aboriginal people's crusade. The North American population was seized with a desire to soak in native lore. The movie *Dances with Wolves* was drawing huge crowds at the box office. Right in the centre of Ottawa, the National Gallery was giving new prominence to native art. Some called it a collective sense of white people's guilt; others called it a progressive step towards righting old wrongs. Rae, as a politician, understood that public opinion was an asset in his strategy.

"The native constituency has huge support in the wider public, emotionally," says Rae. "If they had been excluded from the process, or if people had said, 'Well, we'll get to you next time,' the thing wouldn't have had a hope in hell of getting off the ground at all." Certainly this view helped Ontario in its campaign to steer the constitutional process onto its own "multilateral" bandwagon. Maybe the other premiers and Ottawa could say no to big overbearing Ontario, but it was hard to say no to the powerless native people.

That week in March revolved around the idea of saying "yes" at last to the native people. Just one day after the historic March 12 meeting, aboriginal people held their own Renewal of Canada conference on their issues. Though the four native organizations had originally dismissed the idea of their own conference, the success of the previous Renewal of Canada conferences had fed an appetite for their own public discussion.

Native leaders were also dismayed that so much time at these conferences was taken up with declarations of support for Quebec and its desires; once again, they saw that Canadians' emotions were getting swept into Quebec's corner. It was time to sweep some of that goodwill over to aboriginal people.

So, on March 13, 1992, PEI premier Joe Ghiz and Mary Simon, leader of the Inuit Tapirisat of Canada, served as co-chairs of a conference in Ottawa on aboriginal rights. For three days in the West Block of the Parliament Buildings, Canadians were treated to a snapshot of the state of aboriginal people in Canada in 1992.

Symbols were everywhere. More than 200 of Canada's native people, many dressed in traditional costumes, milled about in the stuffy meeting halls and offices of power in the nation's capital. The aroma of burning sweetgrass wafted through the rooms usually inhabited by blue-suited politicians and paper-laden bureaucrats. Native people had come to Parliament Hill on their own terms, but were proving remarkably adept at playing the power games of constitutional politics.

Unlike many of the participants at the previous Renewal of Canada conferences, these Canadians did not need to spend a lot of time studying the big binder of background information that was distributed to each participant. The native people's constitutional campaign had long been fortified by an arsenal of facts and complicated knowledge. Native people had spent years absorbing their place in the Canadian federation with a thorough, detailed understanding of complex treaties and financial arrangements. The finer points of constitutional law are as familiar to many of the native activists as the TV guide is to ordinary people in Central Canada.

This was a conference intended to encapsulate the growing Canadian push in favour of justice for aboriginal people. All the Renewal of Canada conferences were supposed to complement the work of the special Commons–Senate committee, which had issued its report at the beginning of March. Along with a vague sense that Canadians were becoming immersed in native culture, the aboriginal organizations were also aware that the Commons–Senate committee had heard an awful lot of support for native rights in the cross-country hearings.

Clark may have been a late convert to the cause of native people's inclusion, but immediately after that historic step was taken on March 12, the constitutional affairs minister demonstrated that he was willing to use his own eloquence in public speaking to help the native cause. When Clark was asked to address the aboriginal-rights conference in Ottawa that weekend, he stressed that he was willing to grant native people more than symbolism in his thinking.

"Aboriginal self-government is not about feathers or folk dances or dancing with wolves. Aboriginal self-government is about the fundamental fact that that is the only way that aboriginal peoples — Métis, Inuit and Indian — will be free to build their own lives, their own communities, their own country called Canada."

For all the outpouring of generosity at this conference, though, there were two very important foreshadowings of serious problems to come on the native front. One problem surfaced among native women, who made it known here that self-government was not the be-all and end-all for every native person.

"We will not accept a regime of self-government without guarantees of basic human rights," said Gail

Stacey-Moore, of the Native Women's Association of Canada. Unless these women were guaranteed that their gender-equality rights under the Charter were safe in self-government, they were not going to follow their male colleagues in the crusade. The women and men eventually did part company on this issue, posing a formidable obstacle for Mercredi in later months.

Another problem was found in Quebec's conspicuous absence from the discussions. Clark was trying vainly at the weekend's discussions to point to the native issues as a sign that the country was moving rapidly along a track that Quebec should join. "Look," he was saying to Quebec. "Look how far we're moving without you in the process."

Clark was right to see this issue as a fork in the road on the constitutional travels. Quebec, maintaining its determined distance from the multilateral process, would not be travelling along the same learning curve towards a new constitutional deal. This whole move towards aboriginal rights would be as foreign to Quebec as the Senate crusade of the Western provinces. It would mark just how far away the French-speaking province was placed in relation to the rest of Canada.

Indeed, the rest of Canada was off and running in early 1992 towards a brand-new idea of the native people's place in the federation. A dramatic new accommodation was being made all over the country, except in Quebec. The new idea was sealed very quickly when the multilateral talks made their first out-of-town stop in Halifax in early April 1992. With remarkable speed and unbelievable consensus, the constitutional negotiators delivered their first big decision about their national-unity deal. Native people would be guaranteed the inherent right to self-government in the constitution, Clark announced in

Halifax. It wasn't a big development, measured from the March conference. But it was a gigantic leap from September 1991, when Clark and his government had unveiled the twenty-eight constitutional proposals called "Shaping Canada's Future."

In those proposals, native people had been offered self-government but not "inherent" self-government. This was a crucial distinction for native people. If Canada could not admit that native people had always had the right to self-government, that it had always been there, then the constitution was, in their eyes, a sham. If it didn't say "inherent," then Canada's constitution-makers were implying that they were granting the right. Native people, as the First Nations in Canada, wanted no part of a notion that the English or French founders invented the government. Canada's founding fathers had made a deal with self-governing nations, and that was the way it was to be put in the constitution.

Many of the months from September 1991 to April 1992 were taken up with the native people's persistent effort to get that word "inherent" into the constitution. It worked. By the time the Beaudoin–Dobbie committee released its report at the beginning of March, the inherent right was acknowledged. More importantly, the constitutional affairs minister had become a convert. In one of the important developments of respect and trust that animated the constitutional process, Clark changed his mind. He listened to the native people and answered their call for an inherent right of self-government. Mercredi would always respect Clark for changing his view; it would mark him as an honourable politician, held in high esteem by the native people.

Mercredi believes that Clark's view was shaped by his meeting with the elders, and that the constitutional affairs minister had heeded the advice to lift himself and others up. "I think that had a big impact on him as a human being."

By April 1992, Clark and all the other provinces spoke with one voice for the need for an inherent right of self-government. One Inuit leader, Zebedee Nungak, could hardly believe what he was hearing. Nungak had earned his own fifteen minutes of fame at the distinct-society conference in February, when he held up a map of Quebec, which showed that native people believed they held a claim to most of the province. It was like waving a red kerchief in front of a charging bull, another sore spot in the pained relations between Quebec and aboriginal people.

But at this meeting, with no Quebec there, the other provinces linked arms and embraced the inherent right of self-government for native people. Even the most sceptical premier, Clyde Wells, was on board. Nungak joked with members of the Inuit delegation. "It used to be that there were more Neanderthal provinces than progressive provinces. Now the Neanderthals are outnumbered."

Again, it was Ontario's premier, Bob Rae, who could claim a victory for his special cause in favour of native interests. "We're talking here about 500 years of colonial history in Canada and our finally coming to terms with the decolonization of that relationship."

This was the first major constitutional step taken by the rest of Canada without Quebec. Clark, though, was treading very carefully about the notion of building a deal without Quebec at the table, and as we have seen, to compensate, he invited former United Nations ambassador Yves Fortier and Mouvement regroupement d'economie president Claude Beauchamp to Halifax to provide a refresher course in Quebec politics.

Mercredi arrived late for this dinner, but he was immediately dismayed. Here was Quebec again, trying to capture an emotional hold on the national-unity debate. Even in the midst of native people's victory with self-government in Halifax, a troubling ripple of fear ran through the native people. The solution? Whatever Quebec gets, aboriginal people get too. If Quebeckers got to dominate one dinner, Mercredi was going to make sure that native people got a dinner too.

Even though native people generally felt that they had swept through these constitutional rapids with some ease, there was also a sense of frustration building. Yes, the inherent right was in place, but that was a symbol. They wanted to get down to the real nuts and bolts of self-government, but they just kept being pushed aside. The whole multilateral process was focused on getting the easy stuff done first. The practical questions of self-government fell into the category of "difficult" matters.

By the time the multilateral mission hit Edmonton, at the end of April, the four native organizations were getting angry that no progress was being made on their issues; they kept being deferred. This led to a fuss in Edmonton, which came perilously close to a native walkout. Midway through one of those long days of talks, as reporters were passing the time watching television news clips of the Los Angeles riots, a flurry of activity suddenly erupted at the door of the meeting room. The four native leaders, dragging their delegations along behind them, were beating a retreat from the talks.

The media room stirred into action. Were the natives leaving? Was this it? The native leaders were sending conflicting messages. Spokesmen for the Assembly of First Nations said that this was a walkout prompted by frustration. Inuit leader Rosemarie Kuptana demurred, saying this was only a native "caucus" to plot further strategy. "Nobody walked out," she said. Native Council of Canada president Ron George offered this explanation: "It looked like we walked out. I think maybe it was more like a saunter, or we ambled out."

What was clear, though, was that the native leaders were not happy. It seemed that every time the discussion turned to their issues, there was a brief debate and then it was on to the next subject. Native issues were being broken down into manageable little units — the traditional white people's method of negotiation. But the native approach is to look at the bigger picture, to take a holistic approach. They wanted the talks to look at their issues all together, in context.

The other negotiators took these concerns into account. Maybe they should have a whole day devoted to native issues. Maybe they should look at the whole picture. The native leaders won a promise for a full day and a half of discussions at the Vancouver meeting, scheduled to take place in a couple of weeks. Soon, everything was fine, everything was calm. Clark played down any suggestions that the talks with native people had come to the brink of failure.

"The frustration that's evident in the room is obviously going to leak out as well as be present in the room," he said.

Ontario premier Bob Rae offered similar reassurances. Though he had spent a lot of time behind the scenes in Edmonton, urging native leaders to make the most of this process, publicly he said that incidents such as this were a fact of constitutional life.

"Look, this is a negotiating process," Rae told reporters. "There are going to be caucuses, there are going to be meetings."

It was one of the few times that the four native groups actually acted together, albeit briefly. For the most part, the story of the relations between these four organizations was a complicated, often tense web of old history and deep-seated politics.

Mercredi's group was always the one that claimed the headlines and most of the attention, much to the annoyance of other native leaders. Mercredi himself had a bewitching charm, a combination of gentle style and hard rhetoric. He glided almost effortlessly into the white world, with his lawyer's degree and well-tailored suits, but he was also at home among the chiefs, dancing and practising the age-old rituals in traditional garb.

As a Cree in Manitoba, Mercredi had been through the gamut of experience of Canada's natives. He had immersed himself in native politics, along with Elijah Harper; he had lived the poverty-filled life of an urban Indian, when he was newly married and living in Winnipeg; he had experienced the wilderness through his uncle and all the other elders who influenced his life. By 1992, he was the natives' hammer in a velvet glove, the man who played hard politics with an aura of serenity. In addition to his charisma, he had the backing of a formidable organization. The Assembly of First Nations was also widely recognized by the media as the spokesmen for the "real" Indians — the 600,000 status Indians who lived in the 600 scattered Indian communities across the country.

The AFN's only true allies in the native cause were the Inuit. A strong bond had developed between the Inuit leadership and the AFN leadership, traced back to a real friendship between Mary Simon and Ovide Mercredi. The Inuit weren't always on side with the AFN, not always taking the hard line, but they voiced their differences in quiet fashion, working out their disagreements behind closed doors. Publicly, the AFN and Inuit were virtually indistinguishable in their positions, each feeding off the other's expertise.

Relations were far more rocky between the AFN and the Native Council of Canada. Ron George would often complain that Mercredi was treated as the only "real" Indian leader. His complaints went much farther than a mere hunger for the cameras. George represented non-status Indians, who had spent their lives trying to preserve their native identity off reserves, against incredible odds. George himself was extraordinarily articulate about the grief and hardship of the urban Indians, the native people who enjoyed no recognition. When the media flocked over and over again to Mercredi, portraying his views as those of all Indians, all the old resentments would fire up in George and his constituency. It was the story of their lives — "real" Indians live on reserves; urban Indians are illegitimate.

But if the NCC could be seen as the "illegimate" children of confederation, the Métis could be seen as the orphans. The Métis wore the badge of the wrongly conquered Indian people, the culture of mixed Indian-European people who belonged to no society. As far back as the nineteenth century, Canada's first prime minister, John A. Macdonald, portrayed them as people without a cultural home. "If they are Indians, they go with the tribe, if they are half-breeds, they are white," Macdonald said. The historic dreams of a Métis nation were crushed with the execution of leader Louis Riel, and the defeat of the Métis uprising in the late nineteenth century.

Only Alberta had assumed any direct responsibility for Métis people. In most other areas of the West, where the Métis were concentrated, the federal government and the provincial governments had spent years arguing over who assumed the jurisdiction over them. The Métis themselves were caught in the middle, recognized by no one, true orphans. In addition, other Indian leaders resented the Métis because they seemed so dependent, so grateful for any sign of recognition by governments. This was hardly the native mood of 1992.

The Métis leader, Yvon Dumont, was viewed sceptically because he was known to have close ties to Mulroney's Conservative government. Indeed, several months after the referendum was over, in early 1993, Yvon Dumont was appointed by Mulroney as the first native lieutenant-governor of Manitoba — a reward for his long Tory service, but also an extremely symbolic step on the road to erasing the bitter memories of Louis Riel's hanging. The 1992 constitutional deal-making was supposed to be another step on that road.

As the multilateral road show hit Saint John, New Brunswick, the native people were amassing more and more strength at the table. The native leaders and their delegations arrived a day early in Saint John, locking themselves in strategy sessions to prepare for the coming weeks of intense bargaining. Mercredi was remembering the advice given to him long before — just keep your ground, and they will come to you. The meetings in Saint John revolved around how to allow native people to keep their ground.

Mercredi was getting edgy about possible backsliding by governments. He was particularly angry with the conflicting signals he was getting from British Columbia. Though Constitutional Affairs Minister Moe Sihota was believed to be a friend of the native people, Mercredi saw him as a formidable opponent, rivalling only Clyde Wells as a potential problem for native people. In Saint John, Mercredi said this aloud, taking a swipe at Sihota as a hypocrite on native issues. The resentment was deeply personal — Mercredi saw this politician with East Indian ancestry as a living example of assimilation policies. He didn't see Sihota celebrating his differences; he saw a man trying to overcome his differences.

"There are two perspectives of ethnic minorities,"

Mercredi said. "The one perspective respects differences and the right to be different. The other perspective says, 'I just want to be Canadian,' and that's
where Moe is on that angle."

Sihota, for his part, wanted Mercredi to stop complaining and get on with the act of constitution-making.
To the native people, Sihota's impatience was a sign
that he was a joiner, not a conqueror of the prejudice-
filled relations between people of different cultures. To
Sihota, there was nothing more foolish than Quebec's
petulant refusal to join the constitutional talks, or the
native people's constant complaining about the provincial and federal governments. He saw the same language of humiliation and rejection being spoken at the
table by Quebec cabinet minister Benoit Bouchard and
native leader Ovide Mercredi. He didn't like either
diatribe.

"You know, I just don't have time for crocodile tears,"
Sihota said.

These tensions were a telling example of the larger
problems that plagued the unity debate. Sihota was
only one of the negotiators who had tired of hearing
that Quebec and aboriginal people were the aggrieved
peoples, demanding redress from the rest of Canada.
True to his citizenry as a British Columbian, Sihota was
exhibiting the trademark B.C. impatience towards
those who were demanding a special place in Confederation. For decades, British Columbia stood alone as
the only province that had refused to recognize any
Indian land claims. Its policy did not change until after
the Oka crisis in 1990.

Not surprisingly, the B.C. tension with aboriginal
people had strong parallels to the tension between
British Columbia and Quebec. British Columbia is one
key place in Canada where the nationalist language of
humiliation and rejection, perfected by the native

people and Quebeckers, is not tolerated. Gordon Wilson, then the Liberal party leader in British Columbia, and a strong voice on the No side in the referendum, said that the people in his province have a hard time with the idea of giving collective rights to anyone — whether Quebec or native communities. The whole effort to entrench self-government, he said, was dangerous territory for a country that is based on respect for individual rights.

"That really complicated the situation. Because to the extent that Canadians were ready to accept the distinct society in Quebec, British Columbians were not prepared to take that same kind of distinct society and make it applicable to the so-called self-government notion." In essence, Wilson said, self-government created a new kind of Canadian — "an immigrant with seniority." There was no way that British Columbia, a population steeped in the immigrant mentality, would accept that rights could be traced back to who was in British Columbia first.

"I have to tell you that British Columbians are not going to sit back and allow for self-government propositions to give aboriginal people the right to essentially revoke provincial law and replace that with aboriginal law, unless they understand how that's going to impact on them."

All the outstanding land claims in British Columbia, all the various treaties, just made this issue far too complicated, he said. Wilson made this clear to Constitutional Affairs Minister Joe Clark even before the multilateral process started. Back in February 1992, Wilson was travelling from a meeting with Trudeau in Montreal, returning to B.C. via Ottawa. He asked to see Clark and warned him about the B.C. antipathy to collective rights for aboriginal people. He told Clark: "If it appears that you're setting up laws in Canada that run with racial origin as a determining factor, it will not pass."

But Joe Clark was using another, more influential group of British Columbians to check the pulse of the nation on aboriginal self-government. Often, in situations when he reached an impasse or exasperation with Mercredi, Clark would seek out B.C. native chiefs such as the Musqueum tribe's Wendy Grant for a different perspective. He also attempted to recruit them so that they could exercise a moderating influence on the AFN. Mercredi did not take kindly to these efforts, especially when Clark used them to get some latitude on the question of distinct-society for aboriginal people.

In February, for instance, while the final wrap-up Renewal of Canada conference was being held in Vancouver at the convention centre adjoining the Pan Pacific Hotel, Clark darted across the road for a quick meeting with Mercredi and the B.C. chiefs, to hash out all the problems surrounding the call for a native people's distinct society. Mercredi was furious when Clark refused to start the meeting until Wendy Grant got there. "I am the national chief," Mercredi told Clark. "You don't need to wait for anyone else."

The constitutional affairs minister was playing very dangerous politics with this strategy. Although it is a famed Tory government tactic to recruit allies for gentle persuasion of opponents — CN chairman Brian Smith was commandeered, as we have seen, to talk to Alberta's Jim Horsman about the equal Senate — the structure of the native system was not open to this type of politics.

"At the beginning, there was an element of interference there...Because he knew he wasn't getting anywhere with me," Mercredi said. The B.C. chiefs had also been asked to play a large role in the Vancouver wrap-up conference, to serve as a moderate counter-voice to the angry words spoken by Mercredi and others at the Toronto conference on distinct society. Mercredi and other AFN leaders soon let it be known that they would speak with one voice — that Clark could not pit one side against the other.

"At one point in time he realized that there's only so much he could accomplish by going around my office," Mercredi said.

One of the B.C. chiefs was Squamish leader Joe Mathias, and it was on his people's land, in downtown Vancouver, that the multilateral process made some major progress on aboriginal rights in May 1992.

For two months, the multilateral negotiations had gone a long way on symbolism, but not very far at all on substance. Quebec's distinct-society status was in place, but no one had even broached the subject of powers yet — the method, as Clark liked to call it, of giving substance to the distinct-society symbolism. Similarly, the inherent right of self-government was accepted, but no one really knew how it would work. Once again, Quebec and the aboriginal people were enjoying the same experience in the constitutional talks — their symbols were in place, but the mechanics were not even designed.

In Vancouver, in mid-May 1992, it was finally time to get down to business on how self-government would work. This intense discussion was the result of that near-walkout in Edmonton, when the native people had demanded more time for a serious look at their issues. Yes, everyone accepted the inherent right of self-government, but what did it mean? Would there be a list of powers in the constitution, similar to the ones that were held by provinces and the federal government? Natives were adamantly opposed to this kind of list —

it was another way of saying that powers or government were "granted" by the constitution. If the constitutional negotiators really did believe in the idea of self-government, they said, then it also had to be accepted that natives have the right to define their own government too.

Newfoundland premier Clyde Wells had suggested the idea of a "negative" list, detailing all the powers that could *not* be exercised in self-government. But the natives were having none of that suggestion, either, especially because Wells's idea of a negative list would offer virtually no powers to aboriginal governments — they would be little more than trumped-up municipal governments.

Native people had seen the damage caused to their people when aboriginal life conflicted with white structures — education systems, justice and social welfare had simply not worked in their world. All these powers were important goals for native people in their quest for self-government. They wanted the right to govern themselves in every fundamental aspect of their lives. They also knew that some aboriginal communities would want more interaction with the white people's system; others would want less.

But the provincial politicians were not about to throw something that loose or wide open into the constitution. They needed to know how self-government would work. Native people, on the other hand, were saying that self-government means that aboriginal people didn't have to report in their powers to the constitution. It was an impasse.

The solution? A neat constitutional exercise known as the "context clause." This paragraph, to be inserted in the constitution, wouldn't precisely define self-government — it would just describe it. The Vancouver meeting saw the ushering-in of the context clause. Self-government was painted in broad brush strokes. It was summarized as the ability of aboriginal people:

> To safeguard and develop their languages, cultures, economies, identities, institutions and traditions; and develop, maintain and strengthen their relationships with their lands, waters and environments, so as to determine and control their development as peoples according to their own values and priorities, and ensure the integrity of their societies.

Originally, the word "distinct" was supposed to be part of this clause, but politics removed it by the end of May.

The Vancouver meeting was also significant for two other events, orchestrated by two different aboriginal organizations. Both were attempts by native groups to bring outsiders into the constitutional process; the two efforts produced very different results.

If there's one thing the Native Council of Canada understands, it's a sense of exclusion. For years, Ron George and others had the sense that they were on the outside of two communities; they were not part of the "real" Indian bands and they weren't part of the white communities where they lived. The NCC was determined that this constitutional process would not be an exercise in exclusion.

Now, most Canadians weren't beating down the door to get into these long, arduous talks. Most of the reporters covering the issue were faced with almost daily reminders that the Canadian public had stopped caring about the multilateral exercise; it would not be on the front pages of the newspapers or in the first few minutes of the newscasts. But some powerful interest groups were starting to mutter about exclusion. Organizations such as the National Action Committee on the Status of Women and the Canadian Labour Congress were complaining that this was the same old closed process of constitution-building that was discredited in the Meech years.

So the NCC took steps to end that exclusion, boldly inviting several interest groups, including the Canadian Labour Congress, NAC, the Native Women's Association and a handful of other representatives to serve as "advisers" to the native group. A wave of shock spread through the Radisson Hotel in Vancouver. Just what was going on? Since when were politicians inadequate representatives of the people's interests? Since when did the interest groups gain legitimacy as an add-on to the work of elected representatives?

Ron George put the fuss down to a clear lack of hospitality, saying that the others were just upset because this guest brought a few friends to the party. Judy Rebick argues that this fuss should have been a sign to the constitutional negotiators that they were getting too far removed from the people, that the politicians were veering far away from the voice of the public that had been heard over and over again at the Renewal of Canada conferences.

"For the whole first part of the multilateral talks, we didn't worry about it at all. We thought we had our say. We didn't expect them to accept everything. But we expected them to follow most of it," Rebick said. "And then what happened was the Native Council of Canada came to us. It wasn't Clark, it wasn't the NDP governments. No, the Native Council of Canada came to us and they said they were not comfortable with what was happening, with the other issues. And they had this idea for a monitoring group."

Rebick and others tried to use the monitoring group to wedge some of their concerns — especially about the

Canada clause — into the multilateral discussions. But it was to no avail. A couple of months later, Rebick would loudly proclaim at the microphones that women and other groups had been ignored in the mad rush to get a deal and the overwhelming obsession with the Senate.

The other outsiders to play a part in the Vancouver talks were some local B.C. chiefs, who came to talk one lunchtime about the importance of treaties. This was Mercredi's counter-strike to the Halifax dinner that featured Quebec speakers. The Assembly of First Nations chief decided he would engineer his own "sensitivity training session," as he described it. The constitutional negotiators would hear why treaties were such an important part of life for native people, why the constitution had to take account of treaties.

Clark wasn't convinced. It would take a couple of weeks to sell him on the need for treaty rights in the constitution. What happened later on the treaty issue was a very important development in the world of respect-building between the native and non-native populations in Canada. First, though, the multilateral road show was about to make a stop in Quebec.

The Montreal stop in the journey, in mid-May, was a corner turned in the process. All of the negotiators were now aware that time was running out in the bid to reach a deal by the end of May. The native people were starting to get nervous about the fact that they were headed into Quebec, back into the zone that always claimed such a hold on the emotion of the constitutional process. They were worried that all their progress so far would get eaten up by the perpetual, all-consuming interest in Quebec and its desires. So while other negotiators were quietly arranging little liaisons with Quebec government officials, Ovide Mercredi and

Rosemarie Kuptana arranged for their own audience with the inscrutable Robert Bourassa.

"You have no enemy at this table," Bourassa assured Mercredi at their meeting. Quebeckers, he said, are not the racists or the Indian-haters of popular myth. If the native people could be reasonable, so could Bourassa. Kuptana, for her part, did not learn much from the meeting with Bourassa. His mind was open, but so were his options. Bourassa closed no doors, but he gave no indication of which door he would take.

For most of the time at the Montreal meeting, the native leaders were content to bide their time, watching the others grapple with Quebec's key demands about power. This was not an overwhelming interest for the native people. At one point, one of the AFN chiefs walked out of the meeting room, running into Ovide Mercredi, who had slipped out of the talks to lounge around the corridors of the hotel.

Mercredi said to his fellow chief: "What are they talking about in there?"

The chief raised his eyes. "Powers," he said. Mercredi smiled, then drew a big circle in the air, poked the imaginary circle with his finger and then slid his hand outward. It was a mysterious gesture. The AFN negotiator laughed, and walked on.

Mercredi explained the joke behind the gesture. The Soviets, he said, once sent a monkey into space, which they were able to monitor with the use of a video camera. Through days and days of orbiting, the monkey kept making this gesture — a big circle, a poke in the air and a slide forward of the monkey's paw. No amount of scientific wisdom could decipher the monkey's message. Finally, the problem was conveyed to NASA experts in the United States. They were baffled too.

The NASA experts went out to dinner and mulled

over the problem. Sitting beside them in the restaurant was an old Indian man, who simply nodded and listened to them as they puzzled over the monkey's gesture. The Indian man approached their table. "What's the problem?" he said. The NASA people explained. "Oh, that's easy," said the Indian. "I'm an expert in sign language. The monkey is saying three words: big, fucking, deal."

The power issue, for native people, was just one big repetitive orbit of a globe that meant little to them.

Only one major step towards native issues was taken in Montreal. Finally, the Métis got their political accord, which provided for their recognition by both sets of governments. Ottawa would recognize the Métis as "real" Indians, the provinces of British Columbia, Alberta, Saskatchewan and Manitoba would take on financial burdens. A complicated process was set in place to enumerate Métis people and determine their land claims.

Yvon Dumont was jubilant; the agreement was simply the crowning glory in a year that had brought remarkable developments, righting the wrongs against the Métis. A sense of justice had arrived in Canada, pushed by the conscience of history — and a little bit of 1990 politics.

Even as the Métis agreement was being finalized in Montreal, the Métis negotiators were getting a bit of political advice from Clark. "Okay, now you've got what you want. It's time to get in the game," the constitutional affairs minister warned. What he was saying, in essence, was that he expected the Métis to act as a bridge, a conciliator, in the next tough set of negotiations on the nuts and bolts of self-government.

The Métis obliged Clark within one week. In Toronto, as the discussions over native rights were whipped up into a near-impasse, the Métis came forward with a compromise on one of the most crucial aspects of self-government — the role of the courts. In constitutional lingo, this was the old "justiciability" question. Many of the provinces were worried that putting self-government into the constitution would open up the floodgates to a wave of court cases by native people. On the other side, native people were apprehensive about provinces immediately running to the courts to test and limit the strength of self-government.

No one wanted to throw self-government before the courts to be interpreted right away. Time was what everyone needed, the Métis decided. So they busily hatched a plan to introduce a three-year delay for justiciability. Both sides would agree to keep self-government out of the courts for three years. In the meantime, disputes would be solved by an independent tribunal.

The plan was well-received and the constitutional affairs minister was impressed. As Clark entered the meeting rooms at Toronto's Royal York Hotel, he remarked to the Métis negotiators: "Boy, when you guys get in the game, you really get in the game."

But away from this small step of compromise, a bigger showdown was looming. It all rested on that issue of treaties; the same issue that dominated the "sensitivity training session" in Vancouver.

Mercredi is a politician as well as an Indian leader. Politics told him that self-government was an important philosophical point when he was dealing with non-native governments, but treaties, as the basis of the entire relationship with the rest of Canada, were the real bread-and-butter issues for most native people. If he was going to have a hope of selling this deal in his own community, he had to assure his people that treaties were protected.

Clark and most of the other premiers didn't understand the fuss over treaties. The Supreme Court of

Canada had been ruling in favour of respect for treaties; there was no need to enshrine treaties in the constitution. After all, Supreme Court rulings are part of the great "unwritten" constitution, the trail of tradition and legal precedent that holds as much weight as the written constitution. There was more to this opposition as well — provincial and federal governments were worried that putting treaties into the constitution would play havoc with issues such as natural resources and the control of them. Nobody wanted to put treaty rights in the constitution except native people — but native people wanted them badly.

Here is where one of the most important events took place in the series of huge leaps of faith that were needed to make a deal in 1992. The government of Canada, through Joe Clark, changed its mind. The native people were heard and heeded. Maybe Ottawa and the other provinces didn't really see the need for treaty protection, but they saw that native people needed it. They said that magic phrase that opened the door to so much compromise in the national-unity discussions: "I don't believe what you believe. But I believe what you say."

The person who helped build this bridge was Saskatchewan justice minister Bob Mitchell, who enjoyed immense respect on all sides in the multilateral exercise. The Prairies thought of him as one of their own, because he embraced the crusade for an equal Senate. The governments of Ontario and British Columbia saw him as a respected ally. The native people felt a special link with him. Mitchell's great-grandmother was a Sioux Indian, and his one-sixteenth native heritage is a powerful part of his family's lore. Through this connection, and his work as a lawyer on the Nunavut land-claims case in the Arctic, Mitchell held a special understanding of native dreams, and a special way to communicate those dreams to his fellow politicians around the table. His speech on the need for treaty rights in the constitution was one of the most heartfelt addresses he made, rivalling another one he gave in Toronto that week when he told Bob Rae about the realities of Western alienation. The treaty speech, however, was about the realities of native life.

Whether it was Mitchell's appeal, or all the ground-work laid by the native negotiators, Clark did change his mind. A near breakdown of the talks in Toronto, featuring banging drums and cries of native protest in the halls of the Royal York, quickly gave way to cele-bration. Mercredi remembers this as one of the most important developments in his evolving respect for Joe Clark and this constitutional process.

"It was a point of celebration in the process, a spon-taneous one, when we agreed to implement the treaties . . . there was spontaneous applause in the meeting. What he did was he changed his position, and that was the first sign of flexibility from the federal gov-ernment, on an issue that I'm sure Joe had no mandate on," said Mercredi. "I realized that this guy is making a decision that he's going to have to sell to his cabinet . . . And that's when I came to the conclusion that he's not an adversary. He's really one of those rare politicians that is trying to do what is necessary for the country. So from that point on, I gave him the benefit of the doubt in anything he said or did."

One night that week in Toronto, Bob Rae invited all the negotiators back to his house for a barbecue. The negotiators filed in, filling up the house, relieved to have a break from their talks. The room was packed; Mercredi had taken up a position on the floor, cross-legged, compact, watching everything. Clark, large and imposing, wandered over to him. He looked at Mer-credi, bent like a pretzel, and lowered his bulk to the floor beside the Indian chief. "How do you do that with your legs?" Clark asked Mercredi. He tried in vain to mimic the cross-legged position. But he stayed on the floor beside Mercredi, much to the delight of other negotiators, who knew what a good portrait this made — Ottawa and the Indian leader, side by side on the floor of the Ontario premier's house.

At the end of that week, as the multilateral talks ended without agreement on the May 31 deadline, Mercredi had to be out of the Royal York early in the afternoon and back in Ottawa for his daughter's dance recital. Clark, in a generous mood, waived the rule that the federal government had to speak first at the microphone so that Mercredi could depart a couple of hours early. The Assembly of First Nations chief was still happy about the treaties; still relieved and grateful that all the elders' prayers appeared to have been answered. He flashed an OK gesture to the cameras, smiling broadly as he left. He did not know then that his troubles were really only just starting.

In the first place, he left before he had a chance to throw a compromise plan on the table, intended to meet the concerns that native women had been expressing about self-government. Until 2:00 a.m. the night before, negotiators for the Assembly of First Nations and for the Native Women's Association of Canada had been putting their heads together to come up with a compromise. Mercredi was supposed to table that plan the next day. But he left, the interests of his young daughter overtaking the interests of the native women. He was sure the compromise plan would be tabled by one of the chiefs.

It never was. The Native Women's Association of Canada, insulted by this amazing oversight, would go on to join forces with Judy Rebick in their opposition to the unity deal. They would mount one of the most forceful challenges to self-government and the leadership of Ovide Mercredi.

What Mercredi also didn't know as he left that meeting was that the opposition to the multilateral process was just gathering force, even as the process was ending. The next couple of months in the summer of 1992 would be an intense struggle by everyone just to preserve the hard-earned gains up to this point at the Royal York Hotel.

When Ron George exited the meetings at the Royal York, he was sporting a sweatshirt, provided to all the people who attended the barbecue at Bob Rae's house. The shirt read: "I survived the MMC."

Of course George and the others had survived the multilateral ministerial conferences. But like his fellow native leader Ovide Mercredi, he had no idea of the troubles looming. Like most of the other people involved in the MMC process, he had no idea that the learning curve they had travelled in their marathon talks had not been travelled by the Canadian public. Their victories were theirs alone; the public held no vicarious sense of triumph over the progress so far.

George talked to Don Newman of CBC's Newsworld about the new state of relations between aboriginal and non-aboriginal people in Canada. He traced the history that had brought things to this new era.

"It started back in the 1980s when we were included in the first ministers' conferences," he said. "The education process started there, where average Canadians were able to witness for themselves on TV as we debated with the prime minister and the premiers of the country. . . . For the first time, they were starting to hear the issues."

George truly believed that Canadians had been listening; and that the lessons of the native stand-off at

Oka in 1990 had provoked a new understanding between natives and non-natives.

"Oka got my job ahead by ten years, because it would have taken me ten years otherwise to catch up or get Canadians to catch up with history.

"I'm not too sure whether guilt has much to do with it. I think just simple justice that people want to be proud of in Canada . . . It started for us in the last few months with the policy conferences that started in Halifax to Calgary, Montreal and Vancouver, and finally ours in Ottawa, and that's where I really think the awareness and the support of the non-aboriginal Canadians came forward."

These were optimistic words. Many people had not been following along on the road to a new education. Many of these people were rank-and-file, ordinary Canadians weary of the constitutional wars. Others were in key positions of power. Quebec, for instance, had not been at the talks. Nor had Prime Minister Brian Mulroney. Nor were some officials at the Department of Indian Affairs and Northern Development, where the prospect of a radical change to the status quo was rattling the old federal empire that had ruled native people for so long.

Mysteriously, during the early days of June, a story leaked out of the Department of Indian Affairs and Northern Development about the staggering cost of self-government. The report, attributed to strange, nameless` officials, estimated that self-government would cost Canadians a whopping $5 billion a year. Clark was angry. This was nothing more than empire-preservation from bureaucrats, he thought, and it was decidedly unhelpful in these difficult times. He told CBC television interviewer, Don Newman: "What it assumes is that we'd be extending to every person who called himself or herself a Métis the same services that

go to status Indians. That has never been envisaged."
Inside the meeting rooms, Clark assured the negotiators that the leak had come from DIAND, and that it
was being tracked down. But this was more than a
problem with bureaucrats, he told Newman.

"Our problems are not with the deputies at Finance.
The Finance Department has taken a look at this kind
of thing and they understand there are costs, and they
understand there are advantages to it. Our problem is
that there could be a lot of Canadians who'd look at
this, and they'd say: 'Whoa, what's going on here?'
They're worried about self-government, what does it
mean, what does it cost, other things . . .

"They are tough questions. Anyone who remembers
Oka, anyone who's ever been to a reserve, anybody
who's ever talked to, gone to Métis communities, as I
have in Manitoba, and seen the rate of unemployment
there, the problems with kids, anybody who's seen non-
status Indians in Toronto or Vancouver or in any other
urban centre knows that we have big problems now.
We've got a system that doesn't work. Sure, people are
afraid of the idea of self-government and they're
worried about the costs that are involved."

However, he added, could any new system be any
worse?

Clark was very much aware of the delicate image of
native self-government in the country as a whole.
Maybe the multilateral talks had solved the issue, but
the Canadian public still had to hear about all the complexities. One wrong move and the deal could be in
trouble with the general public. Yes, the polls showed
strong support for self-government, but it was the symbolism rather than the substance that enjoyed the real
support. Canada was in a recession and any new
expense, even for important symbolic reasons, could
prove hugely unpopular.

But at the end of June, there were only two major players who needed immediate convincing — Mulroney and the province of Quebec. Before self-government could be sold to the general public, it first had to be sold to these two players who had stayed outside the multilateral talks. On June 28, the native leaders got their first chance to talk to Mulroney, when he invited them for a discussion at 24 Sussex Drive.

Mercredi arrived at 24 Sussex Drive along with two chiefs. The prime minister graciously invited them all in to his study, to the left of the entranceway, where Mercredi's entourage conducted a prayer ceremony. For five minutes, Mulroney and the Indian leaders were locked together in the study in native prayer. In the elegant, book-lined room, the native people burned sweetgrass, to "purify" the discussions and to ensure an openness of mind from everyone. Then Mulroney led Mercredi up the stairs to a second-floor lounge, where the three other native leaders waited. The prime minister asked Mercredi's companions whether they would like refreshments while they were waiting. One of the chiefs mischievously played on the prejudices about natives. "Got any whiskey?" he asked. Mulroney had not touched a drop of alcohol in over a decade.

Upstairs, in the lounge, Mulroney took one chair, Clark took another. Across the room, on an L-shaped couch, sat the four leaders of the native organizations — Mercredi, Ron George, Rosemarie Kuptana and Yvon Dumont. The prime minister opened the discussion with an overview of the status of support for aboriginal rights. He warned the native leaders, "Some support is slipping," and urged them to look closely at Newfoundland and Alberta, where the deal could be in trouble. Coincidentally, Newfoundland and Alberta were also the two most hard-line provinces on the need

for an equal Senate. Together with Quebec, these were
also the provinces that posed the most serious challenge to native self-government. Mulroney, ever the
strategic thinker, was linking the troublesome Senate
provinces to the self-government issue. If Newfoundland and Alberta could be pulled off the equal Senate,
Quebec would be more likely to return to the talks.
Mulroney was no fan of the equal Senate himself. He
wanted to end the crazy Senate crusade. If the native
people could be recruited to help in that effort, all the
better. Then he turned his attention to the importance
of getting Quebec back to the table. "Without Quebec
at the table, there's no progress," Mulroney said.

This was Mercredi's first meeting ever with the prime
minister. All he could think was that it was too soon to
call it quits for the multilateral process, too soon for the
Mulroney to lower the boom. The prime minister was
threatening to pull the plug by July 15 and introduce
his own proposal for Quebec in Parliament. Mercredi
thought this would be folly. So did many of the provincial politicians.

"I was very much a supporter of the process by then.
I was convinced it could work. I was afraid that if Joe
didn't have the opportunity to carry on with it, if it was
taken from him too early, it could break down ... certainly bog down ... So in my first meeting with the
prime minister, when he started to tell me there's some
slippage in terms of support, I wasn't sure how to take
it."

Ominously, the prime minister also painted a picture
of how self-government would appear in a resolution
designed solely by Ottawa.

"The deal will be different," Mulroney said. (Indeed,
it did turn out to be different anyway, by the time the
summer was over.) "You may not be able to get
all ... But there's some slippage, and if you get 90 per

cent, I think you should be satisfied with that . . . Because you've done very, very, very well."

Mercredi couldn't stop thinking about the fact that Newfoundland premier Clyde Wells and Quebec premier Robert Bourassa would be at the table — the two provincial premiers who seemed so dead-set against native self-government. It was an ironic joke of Bourassa to say of Wells, the Meech-slayer: "On native issues, Clyde Wells speaks for Quebec."

Once the native leaders came out to face the press, they seemed to have been mesmerized, coached into saying the same thing — the Senate crusade was endangering self-government. Alberta and Newfoundland were bad provinces to be holding up the progress of the constitution.

That prodding had very little effect. Alberta and Newfoundland didn't back down, and they got the Senate they wanted. The multilateral deal was intact; the progress of native rights was on track. But even though the Senate impasse was solved, and the multilateral ministers did come up with a deal, the native people ended up losing three big items in the mad rush to make a deal on July 6 and 7 in Ottawa.

The biggest and most unexpected loss was the context clause. In the heat of the meeting on July 6, Alberta announced that it would not support the context clause. It was too broad; courts could interpret it in a sweeping manner. This was a surprise from Alberta, which had always insisted that self-government be defined. Suddenly, it was saying that no description at all was better than the context clause, which was originally intended as an appeasement to provinces such as Alberta. Mercredi and the other native leaders were taken aback. What, no description at all? Just the recognition of the inherent right would be in the constitution? They shrugged. Fine, it was gone.

The native leaders also had to buckle under pressure to extend the three-year delay in justiciability to five years. Again, they could live with that. And thirdly, they had to drop their demand to have financing arrangements enshrined in the constitution. That was a matter that would be worked out later in a political accord.

Individually, none of these changes were major setbacks. But together, they spelled a trend — every time the self-government discussion came back to the table, the clauses were made weaker and weaker. Its impact was ebbing with each touch-up. So it was time to seal this deal before anyone else fussed with it. The native leaders could sense that provinces such as Manitoba were getting nervous. Bob Mitchell had taken Jim McCrae out of the room to get reassurances about how the independent tribunal would work in settling self-government issues out of court. McCrae wanted Filmon to make the final decision, and Filmon offered his approval early the next morning, before the first ministers came back to the table to hammer out their July 7 deal. Manitoba had been the most forceful province in the bid to keep the lid on the costs of self-government; Manitobans were among the people most spooked by that June leak from the Department of Indian Affairs and Northern Development. Still, Filmon was sure by July 7 that the agreement was solid, and would stand up to even the toughest critics of self-government in the West.

It was at this point in the multilateral process that the native leaders sat back and marvelled over what they had accomplished. Doubting provinces such as Manitoba and Alberta had actually embraced self-government. A whole new relationship had been shaped between native and non-native Canadians, and it had taken place because the provincial politicians had been willing to take a giant leap of faith.

On that final day, July 7, as the talks were getting bogged down in near failure by the Senate problem, Mercredi appealed to the politicians to make the same leaps of faith with each other that they had made with the aboriginal people. If they were capable of that kind of spirit in one debate, surely it could be transferred to the Senate dispute. Once again, the native people had been able to harness the forces of spirit and emotion for use in the national-unity talks. Mercredi's appeal had self-interest too — he remembered Mulroney's warning at 24 Sussex. They had come too far to see their deal disintegrate in a unilateral act by Ottawa in mid-July.

Those fears only magnified as the summer wore on. Native leaders saw the same thing that every other Canadian witnessed that July. Quebec did not like the deal, neither did Brian Mulroney, and the whole arrangement was in grave danger.

The long, uncertain days of summer also demonstrated just how big an opponent Quebec was going to be in the self-government issue. Bourassa was still put off by the native people's presence at the table. How on earth was he going to accept them as full partners in the federation when he didn't see them as full partners at the talks?

"It did spook Quebec," said Clark. "And not only did it spook Quebec, it set in place a set of assumptions in Quebec about what was on the mind of the rest of us." The native people's presence only fuelled the suspicion that Quebec was no longer important to the rest of Canada, he said.

By the time Bourassa was ready to come back to the bargaining table in August, it was apparent that Ottawa would grant his demand to put only 11 people around the table at Harrington Lake, not 17. The joke was that this was the "Dallas" scenario — like the far-fetched plot line that brought the character of Bobby Ewing back from the dead after a whole season of broadcasts in 1987–88. When he came back to "Dallas," Bobby Ewing had to be placed in exactly the same circumstances as he left; any other plot developments over that year had simply been a dream. Quebec, in 1992, was also pretending that all the developments over the past two years had been a dream — the constitutional table would be returned to exactly the same condition as the way Quebec left it. No native leaders were allowed at the table.

Mercredi was furious. So were the other native leaders. Mercredi boycotted his post-meeting briefings with the prime minister and staged a noisy demonstration outside Harrington Lake as the talks were going on. But it made no dent on Mulroney. If anything, Mulroney was even more opposed to the native people's presence than Bourassa. Gary Filmon explained the difference: it was a political decision by Bourassa, but a theoretical decision by Mulroney.

"Bourassa had a political problem. He didn't think he could go back with these other people at the table. He thought it would be tough enough to convince his people that he should go back with nine other premiers, let alone have the territories and the aboriginals there as well.... His hope was that he wouldn't get politically slaughtered by doing it, whereas I don't think the prime minister really thought that it was necessary to have them there at all."

The premiers all promised that they wouldn't talk about native issues at the Harrington Lake meeting. Or, if they did talk about them, they wouldn't negotiate anything. Bob Rae also promised the native leaders that he would deliver a full report to them after the meeting, which he did. The four native leaders were worried.

Quebec and Mulroney were going to cause problems for self-government. That was obvious.

The day after the first Harrington Lake encounter, Mulroney invited the native and territorial leaders in for their own session, also to keep them up to date on what was happening. Mercredi didn't go to the briefing. Neither did Yukon leader Tony Penikett. But inside that meeting, Mulroney still managed to get an earful about his decision to exclude these four native leaders and two territorial leaders from the meetings. A very interesting dynamic made itself evident at this meeting — women were making a strong showing for themselves. For the first time in his entire political dealings on the constitutional file, the prime minister had to reckon with the strong leadership of women — women such as Inuit leaders Rosemarie Kuptana and Mary Simon, and the government leader of the Northwest Territories, Nellie Cournoyea.

Mulroney had always been more comfortable with men. His negotiating style was rooted in the rituals of male camaraderie. Women such as Kuptana and Cournoyea were a different challenge for him; he couldn't make them part of the team or the men's league of negotiators. Cournoyea, for instance, announced to Mulroney that she would be telling the press that the prime minister refused to confront questions in public. Kuptana came out of Harrington Lake and made it clear that she too had been unimpressed with Mulroney.

"I think there are some hidden agendas and some shallow promises are being made," Kuptana said. Women, unlike male politicians, were demonstrating that they were far less likely to emerge from a meeting with the prime minister voicing empty platitudes.

Meanwhile, that morning, Mercredi awoke angry and bitter. He thought to himself: "Mulroney is an

Indian giver and Bourassa is an Indian fighter." Did he dare say these words in public? Well, he thought, why not? And so, to reporters, he threw out the accusation, and it was immediately seized upon by the media. It was a battle cry of a quotation, fighting words.

"I used them deliberately," said Ovide. "And I thought, maybe this is the one time I can get away with this — but I didn't get away with it."

The resumption of talks at the Pearson Building in mid-August began with a forty-five-minute harangue by the prime minister. Most of the speech was devoted to a history lesson, about Quebec's place in Canada, the experience of Meech, the wonder of Bourassa's leadership and the evils of the media. Then Mulroney turned his guns on the native leaders, accusing them of leaking transcripts of the July meetings to the media, and condemning them for their unhelpful escalation of the war of words between native people and Quebec.

Mercredi looked over at Yvon Dumont. The Métis leader, a Tory and an ally of Mulroney's, had played it very cool when native leaders were kept out of the Harrington Lake meetings. While Mercredi was raging, with fists clenched, Dumont said the exclusion was no big deal. "The sky isn't falling," Dumont told reporters. Here at the Pearson Building, as they watched this extraordinarily angry diatribe by Mulroney, Mercredi scribbled a note to Dumont. "I think the prime minister is saying that the sky is falling," he wrote. Dumont glanced at the note and laughed.

Novices at the constitutional table, such as B.C. premier Mike Harcourt, or Inuit leader Rosemarie Kuptana, were shocked by Mulroney's rude and abrupt manner towards everyone, especially aboriginal leaders. He had no time for their slower, more deliberative style, no patience for their long speeches and frequent breaks to consult advisers. There were several tense moments between Mercredi and Mulroney on this issue, but a couple of times they were resolved with jokes and laughter.

At one point, Mulroney read out the list of people who would have the floor for speeches. Mercredi's name was on the list. The AFN chief thought he had enough time, however, to duck out to the washroom before he spoke. Unfortunately, he was next up. Mulroney started to offer the floor to Mercredi, but he wasn't in his chair. The prime minister saw red — he thought Mercredi had walked out on the meeting.

"Relax," said Chief Joe Mathias, who also sat in the AFN delegation. "He's just in the bathroom." The other negotiators chuckled like schoolchildren. It was such a human outburst.

On another occasion, the prime minister was trying to seal the difficult self-government deal between the problem provinces of Newfoundland and Quebec. It had been a long, hard day of negotiation, and they were almost there. Mulroney was going around the table, asking everyone if they were part of the deal. Yes, said Ontario, Yes, said Quebec, Yes, said Newfoundland. It was Mercredi's turn. "No," said the national chief. "Not yet." He pleaded for some time to consult his elders. Mulroney told him he had five minutes; Mercredi returned in about fifteen minutes. The slow burn of Mulroney was starting.

"Well, what is it?" Mulroney said. "Yes or No?"

Mercredi borrowed from an old joke about Moses and the Ten Commandments. "I've got good news and bad news for you," he said. "The bad news is that we have some rules for you to follow. The good news is that we've got them down to ten."

The room erupted in laughter. Even Mulroney chortled. Soon after this, the deal started to come together. It was becoming clear that the native leaders and

Quebec had a very similar style of negotiating — slow and careful. While the prime minister was familiar with Bourassa's consultative style, he didn't know how to react when he saw Mercredi and the others using the same methods. Many of the provinces noted that Quebec got a lot more latitude than the others, especially the native leaders, when it came to time and consultation during negotiations. The big question, though, was how well the natives' approach and Quebec's approach would work together when it came down to the substance, not just the style of negotiation.

Some people had speculated that the hard-line provinces such as Newfoundland and Quebec would simply opt out of the deal to entrench self-government. Most believed that it could be done with the consent of seven provinces with 50 per cent of the population, and that Newfoundland and Quebec, maybe even Alberta, would be out of the deal. But late in the week at the Pearson Building, a remarkable set of events took place. It was as if suddenly the world had been turned upside-down. First of all, there was Bob Rae, the friend of the native people and opponent of Mulroney.

Suddenly, Rae took on a job that made him Mulroney's friend and the adversary of the native people. Ontario, which had vowed not to serve as handmaiden to Ottawa in any national-unity deal, was being pulled in as a broker for Mulroney in resolving the native-rights dispute. The prime minister had dispatched Rae with a mission — to find a way to bridge the difference between Newfoundland and the native people, to get a unanimous deal.

For several people, this was an odd assignment. No one seriously expected Wells to come on board on the aboriginal deal. His objections were far too profound. Manitoba's Gary Filmon said to himself, "Aha. We're trying for unanimity now. We're going all the way." Bob

Mitchell wondered what was going on. For six months now, Newfoundland had not been able to convince one person at the table that its objections to self-government had any merit. As Mitchell saw it, Wells's objections were stubborn and dogmatic. And besides, Newfoundland didn't have a large native population.

Throughout the months of negotiations, as Newfoundland perpetually raised its hand in dissent over native rights, Mitchell would turn to Wells or Justice Minister Ed Roberts, whichever was representing Newfoundland at the time, and say: "Listen, don't try to take care of me. I'm the one with the native population, and I'm not worried about this. I don't need you to look out for me." He would dismiss Wells's objections, saying that the Newfoundland premier was getting all worked up over the prospect of what would happen if one self-governing native person happened to drop a beer can on the streets of St John's. Mitchell could not understand why Rae was now turning cartwheels and taking apart the native package to appease such unreasonable objections.

Outside the room, Romanow was aghast. He told Mitchell: "Ovide's getting beat up in there. Why aren't you in there too? Why is Rae doing this?"

The answer was simple. Mulroney wasn't worried about whether Wells would buy into the native package — he was worried about Quebec. Wells, unwittingly, was acting as the point man for Quebec. If Rae could solve Wells's objections, he would solve Bourassa's objections too. Mulroney knew that Bourassa had to come away from the Pearson Building with an entire deal; he couldn't opt out of key parts. The Parti Quebecois would eat Bourassa alive in a referendum campaign over a partial deal.

Wells said he was simply the only premier who had enough guts to speak up in politically incorrect fashion

against self-government. Privately, he said, other delegations would thank him for expressing what they
could not say. Bourassa was particularly grateful.

"On this issue, you're expressing our concerns,"
Bourassa told Wells.

"Why don't you speak up about it?" Wells asked
Bourassa.

"It is very difficult to say it," Bourassa told Wells. The
scars of Meech, the long antagonism between Quebec
and aboriginal people, especially the Oka incident,
were all on his mind.

"He was very sensitive about the situation that
occurred at Oka. And you know, I could understand
that," Wells said. "In the end, when it came to working
out the final compromises [for] aboriginal approval of
it, I ended up trying to persuade Quebec that what was
being proposed should not be unacceptable."

This is precisely what Mulroney had wanted. Wells
could act as the bad guy, and Bourassa could get the
whole deal he needed.

Mercredi, for his part, was a little stunned at the
whole development. He had arrived late at the
meeting. He had stopped at a large Catholic church on
Sussex Drive on the way to the meeting at the Pearson
Building, and he had prayed for guidance. Once again,
the native leader was hoping to harness spirituality for
his efforts. This time, he sought the spirits of the
Catholic world. He prayed for help in getting through
the next difficult stage of negotiations.

When he arrived at his delegation room, a message
was waiting for him. "Joe Clark wants to see you," one
of the security people said. Mercredi joked that he
would see Clark when he was finished chatting with
the chiefs. He ambled up to a room, only to walk in
and find Mulroney, Bourassa, Wells and Rae sitting
there.

Mulroney said: "Everyone who has the power to resolve this issue is in this room. Go to it." And he left.

Wells and Bourassa were worried about the thorny issue of "territorial integrity." They wanted to make sure that native self-government wouldn't violate the established order of the provinces, whether it was borders or the rule of law.

"Any recognition had to be clearly confined to aboriginal lands," Wells said. "I wanted to make sure there wasn't an aboriginal right to self-government that walked around everywhere in the country. That's a recipe for chaos. I wanted to make sure there was a clear recognition."

Rae sat hunched at a portable Apple computer supplied to him by the Native Council of Canada. The other three aboriginal delegations had more or less turned over the deal-making to Mercredi. It wasn't an abandoning of their responsibility — everyone simply knew that the AFN was the toughest nut to crack on native issues. If it bought into a deal on this issue, everyone would likely go along.

The Ontario premier tapped out a phrase that had particular resonance with the old constitutional lawyer Clyde Wells. Aboriginal self-government would be put in place, consistent with the federal responsibility for "peace, order and good government." This "POGG" clause, as it's known, is a relic of the old British North America Act, and it has been used to justify sweeping authority by the federal government. Wells could live with that clause. Mercredi was less sure.

"POGG did gut self-government," he said. Their only hope was to put in another phrase saying that nothing in this agreement derogates from the legitimate rights of self-government. It wasn't perfect, but the chiefs in the AFN delegation gave a tentative thumbs-up to the new phrase. But once again, the native people had tangled with the self-government issue, and once again, their rights were weakened.

That last little bit of erosion, however, started the landslide that culminated in the native people's large No vote in the referendum. Self-government had just been weakened too much for some chiefs. Even though they gave initial approval, they were soon appalled by the influence of the POGG clause. The context clause was back, but this new provision had them worried.

"If there had been no changes to those clauses, I don't think I would have had some of the opposition I had," said Mercredi.

The first chief to speak out against the changes was Billy Two Rivers, from the Mohawk community of Kahnawabe, south of Montreal. Two Rivers was an elected chief, but he had close relations with the Mohawk Warrior Society, which provoked the Oka standoff in 1990. The Mohawks held the hardest line on native self-government, bristling against any dalliance at all with federal or provincial authority. Most of the Kahnawabe Mohawks do not vote in national elections, nor did they see themselves as wards of the Canadian state. They see themselves as self-governing.

Two Rivers showed up on the doorstep of the Pearson Building the next day with some angry words for Mercredi and his compromise. The Mohawks would not be supporters of the Charlottetown deal and they were particularly angry at the peace, order and good government provision. (In the Mohawks' decree on the Charlottetown accord, issued midway through the referendum campaign, the POGG clause was called "repugnant, paranoid and paternalistic.")

"I assume he got the marching orders from someone back home," Mercredi said. "Probably the Warriors."

But the internal struggles of the native groups were

only half of the problems lying in wait for Mercredi and others as they faced the referendum campaign. For months, several of the thoughtful native officials around the table had begun to worry that the multilateral negotiators were just too many steps ahead of the Canadian public on this issue. And in the general public, the voices of dissent were making clear that the politicians had gone too far with self-government. Canada was just not ready, said many powerful voices in the fall of 1992.

The aboriginal people had asked to be treated the same way as Quebec was treated, and that's what they got during the referendum campaign. In many reaches of Canada, special treatment for native people was just as objectionable as special treatment for Quebec.

The No forces in the referendum, just as they had when they were speaking out against Quebec's special status, tried to very carefully steer around the accusations of racism. Reform Party leader Preston Manning, whose base of support is in the West, is constantly running into accusations of racism when he puts forward his argument for a "culturally neutral" constitution. But in the West, he says, where relations are rubbed raw between the native and non-native population, the self-government question has to be handled very carefully.

"We say there has to be some kind of a new deal," Manning says. And the Reform Party is going to have to bend a bit on its adamant opposition to race-based provisions in the constitution if this new deal is to work, he admits. Throughout the referendum, he said, Canadians had a few basic questions:

- Would these governments be democratic and accountable?
- Would self-governing native communities be

> co-operative or competitive with other govern-
> ments when it came to hunting, fishing and
> resource rights?
> • Who would pay and how much would it cost?

"Now, if the answer to those questions is yes all the way along: yes, they'd be accountable; yes, there'd be a co-operative approach on division of powers; yes, it couldn't cost more than what we were doing now; and yes, you would be moving closer to some model of equality, it might be acceptable," Manning says. "It wouldn't be perfect because the basis of this is still a racial criterion. But it would be closer to it than where we are now. Then I think the majority of Canadians would go along with that concept. . . .

"But if the answer to those questions is no all the way along, then I don't think you've got a ghost of a chance of carrying the judgment of your non-aboriginals, whose judgment you've got to carry to get the law changed."

Out in British Columbia, the self-government pro-posal whipped up a flurry of concern and anxiety among the non-native population. The Liberal leader, Gordon Wilson, who also fought on the No side, said he was accused of racism as well for asking these basic kinds of questions about the implications of self-government.

Wilson was giving a speech during the referendum campaign, emphatically stressing that self-government was a violation of the notion that everyone was equal. A native woman in the crowd stood up and declared: "We are not equal to you. You are a racist. Because if you say that every Canadian is equal to every other, you don't acknowledge that the first people are in fact superior."

Wilson shot back: "You're right, I don't. I don't acknowledge that you're superior. I recognize that there is a history and culture and tradition that must be protected, enshrined and you have a language and you have a right to self-determination like every other Canadian. That I understand. But I won't acknowledge that there's a superiority. And I won't acknowledge that certain rights have to be accorded to individuals simply on the basis of their racial origin. We can't as a society live that way anymore. That may have been something that was true in the 1860s. But it isn't true in the 1990s."

Wilson's constitutional soul mate Clyde Wells is stirred to righteous indignation when people call him a racist for speaking out against self-government. Nothing would make him angrier during the constitutional process than when Ron George or Ovide Mercredi levelled their accusations of racism against the Newfoundland premier. Unless someone is willing to say out loud what seems politically incorrect, he said, aboriginal people will be fooled into believing that they can claim special status in Canada. Wells does not believe they can.

"A lot of decisions were made around that table and the aboriginal people themselves were misled as a result of that. The greatest harm was being done to the aboriginal people. . . . They were coddled — everything you want, just name it, and no one would speak against it." If Wells did speak up, Mercredi and George were quick to accuse him of racism. "The only racism I saw was coming from Ovide Mercredi himself, with that kind of approach, and the intolerable comments of Ron George, accusing me of wanting to continue apartheid in Canada. What they're proposing in fact is more akin to apartheid than anything else. And the Canadian people want to see everyone as Canadians."

Manning believes that Canadians could accept some special status for native people based on the fact that they were here first — that is more palatable to the public than the idea of race-based laws. They would think of it as squatter's rights, he said, once an honourable legal term to grant privileges to people who arrived on the land first.

Years ago, Manning was in charge of a project to improve native employment in the energy industry. Easy enough — simply set up an affirmative action program for native people. But Manning believes that this stirs up more problems than it solves. Why weren't native people being hired in the energy industry? Mainly because, according to him, their chronic problems on the reserves had left them without the education or skills they needed. So what's the solution? Here was how affirmative action would work in Manning's world.

"Look, we're going to provide special help to everyone with less than a grade six education because you can't make it in a modern economy without grade six. Now the guys who will end up in the program are exactly the same guys as affirmative action. So they're going to get the help whether you do it my way or your way." It's more than just a marketing solution, he said, it goes to the heart of Canadians' sense of fairness. "If you're going to give people special help; whether it's women or aboriginals or immigrants . . . don't tie it to immutable characteristics that can't be changed, like race or gender."

Race and gender problems were at the heart of one of the most serious challenges to native self-government, from aboriginal women themselves. They weren't just fighting the Charlottetown deal in the streets or over the airwaves — they were fighting their battle in court.

Late in the summer, just as the multilateral talks were winding down at the Pearson Building, the Native Women's Association of Canada scored a surprising win against the four main aboriginal organizations. The Federal Court of Appeal ruled that the native women's constitutional rights to freedom of expression had been denied by the fact that they were excluded from the multilateral talks. The other four native organizations were not adequate representatives for their interests, the court ruled.

From that day forward, the native women pressed the case that the Charlottetown deal was illegitimate, and that the referendum should be cancelled. They headed back to Federal Court, looking for an injunction to stop the national vote and trying to halt the legal drafting that continued through the fall in their absence. High-powered Charter lawyers such as Mary Eberts joined their case. The native women's opposition was a huge umbrella for all kinds of complaints, vague or well-defined, against the idea of messing with individual rights.

The native women's biggest backers on the No side were the National Action Committee on the Status of Women, which supported its native sisters in the interests of feminist solidarity. Their court victory over exclusion spoke to a powerful feeling that NAC shared about being left out of the process. Judy Rebick was also firmly convinced that the constitutional deal-makers made a remarkable oversight against all women and equality-seeking groups when they failed to protect them from the collective rights that were inserted in the Canada clause.

Rebick, unlike Trudeau, was not against the concept of aboriginal rights or collective rights for anyone — she just didn't believe they were put in the constitution properly. But she was saddened by the fact that the referendum put her on the opposite side of the native cause that she so fervently believed in as well.

"You know, even though we supported the native

women, and their concerns, nevertheless, it seemed to us aborginal self-government was a huge gain for aboriginal people and it was really hard to go against it," Rebick said.

Mercredi doesn't accept her chagrin. During the referendum campaign, he ran across Rebick in Montreal. He told her: "Look, you have gender equality. We have nothing. If it's not perfect, don't stand in the way of our rights, because we can always perfect it later." His warning fell on deaf ears, he said. "She was a voice, she thinks, for women's rights. But from our perspective, she was a voice against Indian rights. And no amount of talking from her or reflection on my part will alter that conclusion."

Many, many people would hurt Mercredi in the national referendum of 1992, but none would wound him as deeply as his own chiefs. Towards the end of the referendum campaign, a huge group of chiefs converged on Vancouver to huddle and discuss the constitution. There were deep signs of trouble. Many of the same chiefs who had supported all that manoeuvring at the Apple computer in August had now turned against the deal.

A vocal group of these chiefs were making themselves heard at this meeting, and Mercredi reacted as a 1990s politician, not as an Indian leader — he refused to give a vent to their dissent; he refused to hold a vote. As the reports of this meeting filtered out to the public, the message was clear — even aboriginal people, who stand to gain so much, are not in favour of the Charlottetown accord. It was one of the major lethal blows to the deal.

Mercredi's desire to avoid dissent was a mark that distinguished the politicians all over the country in 1992, starting at the top with Brian Mulroney. Mercredi's reaction to dissenting voices confirmed some of the murmurings among the dissidents at this meeting —

he had been bought off by the non-native politicians, co-opted by the process; he wore too many suits and not enough traditional Indian garb. Mercredi was facing the same crisis of representation plaguing the old, established governments and politicians in Canada.

"I made a mistake at that meeting by not forcing a vote," says Mercredi. "I was concerned about the wrong thing. I was concerned about unity, which was not the thing to be concerned about there. In retrospect, a vote would not have destroyed the organization. Most of the people who came there were prepared to vote in favour... The ones who were opposed were against the treaty provisions. I still don't understand why."

Somehow, the chiefs on the No side had decided that the Charlottetown accord was too paternalistic, too domineering. It didn't demonstrate adequately that the natives and non-natives should enjoy a nation-to-nation relationship in Canada. Mercredi thought he had taken care of that in the treaty issue, that long-ago day in Toronto. But that other day of negotiations, at the Apple computer, planted the idea in many reserves that the Indian nations were actually going to be hurt by that sweeping authority of peace, order and good government. This was certainly the sentiment that whipped through the Prairies. Saskatchewan's Bob Mitchell heard it over and over again.

The Assembly of First Nations chief rejects the idea that the negotiations got away from the people, that the flurry of talks put too much distance between the leaders and the led in the native community. He disputes any suggestion that the native leaders were so busy convincing the non-natives about the aboriginal people that they forgot about convincing their own communities.

"There's no doubt in my mind that I was doing what the people wanted. I don't question that. What I recognize now is that we need a better way of getting information to people, so that they're better informed."

He takes this lesson from his old allies, the Inuit, who did manage to pull off a decisive Yes vote among their people. The Inuit, perhaps more than any other native organization, had a well-planned strategy in place to get the message out to the people. Good communication is a tool that the Inuit have developed by virtue of the vast distances between communities in the North. Rosemarie Kuptana was a broadcaster. Mary Simon, for her part, was the only one of the famous Canada Committee, the umbrella organization, to have played a leading role in all three major steps of the constitutional process — she was a chairperson of the Renewal of Canada conference on aboriginal rights; she was a negotiator at the multilateral table and she helped steer the Yes strategy. The coordination paid off; Simon was able to deliver the votes of her people.

Mercredi, like his friend Joe Clark, was personally hurt by the result of the October 26 referendum. The two men spoke on referendum night, in fact, and both decided that they would broadcast the message that something serious was lost.

"I was disappointed more by the backsliding in my own organization, by the leaders who supported the Charlottetown accord. And when the time came to explain it to the people, they didn't do it. They had all the information. We gave them in the course of eight months over twenty-two updates and reports, so it wasn't as if the chiefs didn't have the information.

"These are my friends. These are people who have worked with me for a long time. They didn't keep their word. In Indian politics, your word is everything. Consensus doesn't work if you don't keep your word. I think that's the part that dismayed me the most. I mean, I can live with the results of the Canadian people. I can understand it. We allowed our prejudices to prevail. And when I say we, I mean the native people. On our own side, some people have a certain opinion about treaties based on their own prejudices."

Only 22 per cent of the native population on the reserves actually voted in the referendum, but more than 60 per cent of these people voted No. Mercredi believes that the No vote came from prejudice, but it also came from fear. It was said that the Indians were the people who couldn't see the referendum as a rational choice between radical change and the status quo. The status quo was just too awful to contemplate as a rational choice. But Mercredi heard a lot of his people talking about the fear of change.

"Some people voted because they found security in the status quo," he said. "The Indian Act is to them the foundation for their education, their housing and their social assistance . . . The Indian Act is the foundation of all these services. Perception is everything. So they were afraid that the inherent right meant not just political liberation, maybe the end of these programs too, the end of their safety net."

The status quo held no safety net for Ron George and all the off-reserve Indians who came so close to a new recognition in Canada. On referendum night, George made no secret of his devastation.

"Our people are dying on the streets now, under the status quo. . . . We're not equal. We've got nothing to cheer about. I'd like those people who are celebrating the No victory to come and see what it's like to live on the streets. Come and live under the bridges with some of my people and see if they have something to cheer about."

All the way along, the native people had asked Canadians to see their journey as a voyage of the spirit. And when the loss came on October 26, it was a spiritual hurt felt by them all. The trip down the rapids ran into the rocks of prejudice and a country that just wasn't ready to make a new deal with aboriginal people. Their search for equality continues, but their dreams of equality have had to take a place well back in the long Canadian queue of equality-seekers in the 1990s.

9

Lost Among Equals

Ask any Canadian about the dream of the nation. It is like a beauty pageant, where every contestant lines up and says the same thing: "All I want is world peace." In the Canadian constitutional pageant, though, the contenders have a slightly different twist on this refrain. "All I want is for everyone to be equal."

Equality — big and small provinces were supposed to be equal in the Senate. Equality — the aboriginal people fought for the right to be an equal nation to Quebec or the rest of the country. Equality — women wanted it in every part of the constitution. Equality — the Reform Party wanted it for all citizens. Equality — Quebec wanted its place assured as an equal partner to English in Canada. Equality — former prime minister Pierre Trudeau said it had to be sealed and inviolable in the Charter of Rights and Freedoms.

In 1992, every single interest in Canada's national-unity business had laid its own private claim to the value of equality. The constitutional battle was about which kind of equality could win; or if all these kinds of equalities could live together, side by side, in the Canadian nation. By the end of 1992, that was still an impossible dream. In fact, the great mistake of the national-unity mission of 1992 was its failure to reckon with the huge power of equality; the same power that stirred most Canadians to vote No to the politicians' Charlottetown accord on October 26.

The passion for equality was a sign that Canada was coming of age as a nation in the latter half of the twentieth century. The idea of equality is often said to have radiated northward into Canada from the United States, where the 1960s civil-rights protests fed the North American imagination, especially among a generation of thirty-something television watchers who dominated the Canadian electorate. That is part of the reason. It also emanated from deep within the Canadian identity — the way Canada had come to be known as the peacekeeper and mediator in international disputes, treating each side equally. It thrived in a nation made up of people from different cultures, who knew that equality was the slender thread that bound diversity together.

But the passion for equality was only truly consummated in 1981, when Trudeau patriated the constitution and introduced the Charter of Rights and Freedoms to Canadians. From then on, Canada's entire political culture was pitched headlong into its tempestuous relationship with the idea of equality. Canadian society was totally reshaped by the results of a flood of Charter cases in the courts over the first ten years after the constitution was patriated. Rulings on everything from abortion to mandatory retirement to adoption radically changed the way Canadians viewed and enjoyed their rights. And in almost all cases, the common denominator was the assertion of the rights of the individual — that all Canadians are equal when it comes to basic rights.

When a Canadian says, "All I want is for everyone to be equal," he or she knows that the courts and the law and the constitution are nodding in agreement. But no matter how universal this value of equality appeared to be in the national-unity battle of 1992, all the equality seekers were bickering among themselves. The equality seekers, dubbed "Charter Canadians" by political scientist Alan Cairns, each tried to make themselves heard over the din of voices calling for different kinds of equality.

On June 10, 1992, one of these equality-seekers was at the microphone in the Pearson Building in Ottawa, where the constitutional negotiators were meeting in yet another vain attempt to get a new deal.

Judy Rebick, a fixture of media commentary over the year leading up to this day, was explaining how her group, the National Action Committee on the Status of Women, had been let down by the people who were building a new constitution behind closed doors. Less than ten metres away, the camera lights were turned on another spokesperson for equality — Reform Party leader Preston Manning, who had swung by the Pearson Building to light a fire under the West's campaign for equality in the Senate. Meanwhile, inside the various delegation rooms upstairs in the same building, the fax and phone lines were buzzing with calls from people such as Manitoba Liberal leader Sharon Carstairs and British Columbia Liberal leader Gordon Wilson, who were busily trying to ensure that the equality rights hard-earned in 1981 weren't bargained away in 1992.

That day was a vivid reminder that equality was banging on every door of the Pearson Building. But all the equality-seekers weren't knocking together — they really didn't agree at all about what equality meant in 1992.

Judy Rebick is a sharp-thinking, left-leaning, American-born feminist whose entire political consciousness is steeped in 1960s-style activism. As head of NAC from 1990 to 1993, she was an omnipresent and very vocal figure in Canadian politics. Rallies, demonstrations and protests are Rebick's forte, and she thinks nothing of making herself and her group into a spectacle to gain public attention. No one would ever accuse Rebick or NAC of fading away into the background. The entire feminist movement, in fact, appeared to revolve in 1992 around Rebick's frequent appearances on CBC's all-news channel, Newsworld. She is more than a media hound, however. Her views of the state of discontent in Canadian politics are sophisticated and well-considered.

As the country was settling into its ten-year-old familiarity with the Charter of Rights, Rebick was on hand constantly, reminding politicians and voters that women's equality was an enduring demand on the system. One day she would be in the press room in the basement of the Parliament Buildings, condemning the actions of the government's Royal Commission on Reproductive Technology. Another day, she would be speaking out on proposed new rape laws being drafted by Ottawa. Still more often, she would be talking to the cameras about the need for women's equality to be guaranteed in the constitution, whether it was in the Senate or in the so-called Canada clause. No matter what the issue, the underlying theme was the same — women must be equal, strong partners in Canada.

She had come to the Pearson Building on June 10 to protest that women's equality was sliding off the table as the Canada clause was being drafted. Rebick claimed that women had been forgotten, marginalized in the mad rush to get a deal. She was particularly impatient with all the fuss over the Senate, and the provinces who were digging in their heels for an equal Senate. Rebick called the Senate dispute a mere men's diversion and a game.

But wait a minute — shouldn't a woman who was committed to equality be able to understand the small provinces' quest for that same, elusive goal? Weren't they both asking for the same thing, in different ways? And what about the Reform Party? If it was so committed to the idea of equality, why didn't Reformers link up with the feminists and form a united front to demand it? Why didn't Manning join Rebick at the microphone for a tag-team assault on the constitutional negotiators that day at Pearson?

The answer is simple. Rebick had one idea of equality. Manning had another. They were radically different. And in turn, those two ideas of equality were completely at odds with the equality of former prime minister Pierre Trudeau. In 1992, those three equalities were irreconcilable.

Prime Minister Brian Mulroney was fond of saying during the referendum that the No side could never agree on anything. With a sarcastic guffaw, he would ask his audience to imagine all the No forces sitting at the same table, incapable of reaching any kind of agreement. "Can you imagine them around a table? Preston Manning, Sharon Carstairs, Jacques Parizeau, Pierre Trudeau, Judy Rebick, Lucien Bouchard?" Mulroney asked a Quebec audience during one of his campaign appearances during the referendum. "What unanimous commitment do you think the No leaders would give to Canada?"

He was right. Manning, Rebick and Deborah Coyne, a self-appointed spokesperson for Trudeau-style Liberalism, were the three leading voices for the

No campaign in English Canada. And they did not agree at all on how to protect the principle of equality in the constitution. The only time they could agree, in fact, was in their decisions to mark an X beside the word No on the October 26 referendum ballot. That, to Mulroney's dismay, was agreement enough — it sunk the Charlottetown deal.

Rebick would never share a stage with the Reform Party. She would wage her battle for women's equality on one side of the tracks, and the Senate equality crusade would run down the other side. They would never meet, though they travelled with the same locomotive force across the nation, with Trudeau's equality as the engine that steamed along the tracks. In the 1800s, the great Canadian dream was realized by joining the country with the steel rails of the railways from coast to coast. In the 1990s, the great Canadian dream was a train track of ideas — not steel, but Rebick's track of equality, Manning's track of equality and Trudeau's equality engine.

In Rebick's view, the Canadian crusade for equality of the provinces is actually "anti-equality." It rests on the demand that everyone be treated the same, she says, and that just does not produce a country where everyone is equal.

"If everybody is treated the same, what you have is to the benefit of people who are privileged in society," Rebick explains. "You don't have pay equity or affirmative action, you don't have grants for people with disabilities..."

Those who led the charge for equality in the Senate are the same people who place all their political stock in the notion that everyone must be treated equally. Look at where the Triple E Senate crusade took root. In Alberta and in Newfoundland — not exactly the places famed in Canada for affirmative action policies or social-rights revolutions.

Manning, as the voice of the Reform Party and populist discontent out West, agrees that the key to Canada's future as a political society is treating everyone equally. He knows that the idea of special treatment for anyone is anathema to many of his supporters. But he isn't blind to Rebick's notion — he sums up the debate as one between "equality of treatment" and "equality of outcome."

"Yes, I'm arguing for equality of treatment first of all. I think that's your base line. But secondly, I'm recognizing that equality of outcome is a desirable objective as well. Not everybody starts at the same place, so you've got to provide special help to certain people."

And that's where yet another voice of equality weighs into the dispute. Deborah Coyne, the founder of the Canada for All Canadians committee in the No campaign, says that the basis of the country has to be "equality of opportunity." With the Charter, says Coyne, the country has a solid base to ensure Rebick's equality of outcome and Manning's equality of treatment. Don't mess with it, Coyne says.

Coyne believes she speaks for a majority of Canadians who take this "don't mess with success" view of the Charter. The Charter rights endure, she says, because it is the pillar on which any healthy liberal democracy can stand.

"I don't buy all these arguments that it's just Americanizing us because of the bill of rights. It's a very different document from the [American] Bill of Rights. It has, for example, that affirmative-rights section. It already has the reasonable limits clause which, in fact, . . . the Americans didn't have and had to develop . . . It's totally different. It's more suitable to a liberal democratic state in the twentieth century because it talks about government action."

All kinds of people are anxious to jump on the
Charter and blame it for the country's woes, she says.
Canadians have gone rights-crazy, they say. Canadian
courts are tied up needlessly with people who are using
the Charter to guarantee their own selfish interests.
Canada has been infected with the American disease of
equality over all, which has led to the collapse of faith
in the system.

Nonsense, says Coyne. "Sure, we're becoming a bit
more litigious. You sense that you can challenge things.
But I don't think it's excessive."

Coyne was a law student in the 1970s, when the
debate was raging in Canadian politics about the need
for rights in the constitution. Ten years later, she was
teaching law school at the University of Toronto and
her students accepted the Charter of Rights and Freedoms as a cornerstone of Canadian legal and political
thought. Her students, she said, regarded her as "pre-
historic" because she was graduated in the 1970s, B.C.
— before Charter, that is. For a mere document to take
such a hold of people in such a short time is proof that
the Charter is more than an invention of a politician or
a decade of politics; it speaks to a deep philosophy
within Canadians that always existed but was not articulated until Trudeau's time.

"I find that this group coming in understands the
Charter. They're growing up with the Charter and they
see how it interacts . . .

"We're going through cycles, and the court sometimes will seem fairly open, and at other times, it
won't . . . It depends on judges sometimes. And some-
time we're going to have to get around to reforming
the Supreme Court and the appointment procedures.
But this generation understands that. I think the difficulty is, there's still a batch of people out there who
aren't used to it yet."

The equality passion in Canada, in other words, is not just a Trudeau creation or a Charter creation, she says — it is a natural, noble step in the evolution of a liberal, democratic country.

Gordon Wilson, leader of the British Columbia Liberals throughout the referendum campaign, is a Trudeau Liberal who relied on the guidance of the former prime minister through frequent telephone conversations in the early 1990s. He believes that Canadians can thank Trudeau for equality fever.

"It stems back to the Trudeau years, where Trudeau talked about the just society and he talked about multiculturalism . . . And that we should celebrate our differences, recognize that we can be different but yet be equal."

Wilson even believes that Trudeau's brand of equality is what paved the way, ten years later, for the West to carry out its Senate-equality crusade. Sure, Trudeau didn't care about the Senate or the West, Wilson says, but the drive for equality in the 1990s is rooted in what he gave the country in the 1970s and 1980s.

Preston Manning has a lot of problems with that idea. He does not believe that Trudeau was the great innovator of equal rights for all Canadians. He believes, in fact, that the former prime minister set in place only the equality of two nations — French and English — and that it was Trudeau who really instilled the whole notion that Canada had to be a deal between racial or ethnic groups.

"Trudeau did more to entrench this equal partnership of founding races, cultures and languages," Manning says. "Trudeau's concept of equality was more the equality of founding groups than it was the equality of citizens before the law. Our Charter is just shot full of this founding-equality-of-the-racial-groups model. It's not strong on equality of citizens."

It goes even farther back than Trudeau, he says. Manning, the son of former Alberta premier Ernest Manning, remembers a day long ago in 1965 when his father received notice of the new Royal Commission on Bilingualism and Biculturalism that was being set up by Trudeau's predecessor, Liberal prime minister Lester Pearson. Ernest Manning looked at the marching orders for this inquiry. There it was, in black and white, this assumption that Canada revolved around two "races," French and English. The younger Manning saw his father fly into a rage. How could they use the word "race" so blatantly to describe Canada's political foundation?

"This is the old Upper Canada," Manning remembers his father saying. "And it will not fly out here."

Many years later, soon after the referendum campaign was over in 1992, the Mannings would receive surprising confirmation of their suspicion that Canada truly was on the road to a new idea of itself as ten equal provinces, not the old Upper and Lower Canada. A massive Decima poll, published in the January 4, 1993, edition of *Maclean's* magazine, showed that a full 68 per cent of respondents believed that the country was based on a relationship between ten equal provinces. Even among those who believed that the country consisted of two founding groups, 67 per cent of the respondents would still be prepared to accept an arrangement based on equality of the ten provinces.

But here was Canada, in 1992, still actively embroiled in the debate over how to protect the country as a pact between French and English, even as the political culture in the country was giving way to the idea of ten equal provinces. Manning believes that the country is ready to abandon this old Upper Canada–Lower Canada notion and move on to a bigger idea. Trudeau's Charter of Rights is actually part of the problem that needs to be fixed, he says.

That's the big flaw in the Charter for Manning and the political right wing. Rebick, as a voice on the left, sees another kind of flaw. The big problem with the Charter of Rights, says Rebick, is that it is focused far too much on rights for individuals, and not on rights for groups. You need both kinds of rights in the politics of the 1990s, she says.

The rights of groups versus the rights of individuals. That's where everyone thought the big national-unity debate would take place when the hard bargaining started on the constitution in 1992. The rest of Canada, the ROC, had embraced the notion of individual rights by 1992. How did you define civilization in the rest of Canada? Running water, public roads, access to television and individual rights under the Charter. But in the confrontation between the ROC and Quebec, or between the ROC and aboriginal people, the issue was the rights of groups. Quebec wanted rights as a francophone group, not as a collection of French-speaking individuals. Native people wanted the same thing — a group right to self-government. If this great Canada round was to reconcile Quebec, the aboriginal people and the rest of Canada under one big banner, the major conflict was going to be between collective and individual rights.

Assembly of First Nations chief Ovide Mercredi would constantly insist that Quebec and native people had to be seen as groups with the same dreams. In moments of high drama, the rhetoric would be stirring, the common cause would be emotional: a story of two "vanquished" nations trying to make their place in a larger nation. In other, more petty moments, Mercredi's rhetoric would seem almost churlish. If Quebec gets it, natives get it too. Quebec gets distinct society; natives get distinct society. Quebec gets to protect its culture, natives have culture too. If Quebec is the dinner-time topic at multilateral talks in Halifax, then native people will be the dinner-time topic in Saint John. And so on.

It was not petty, though. It was a real phenomenon and a real debate. In 1992, the constitutional negotiators had to decide whether they were ready to build a Canada with two different kinds of rights — one set for individuals, one set for groups.

The time was ripe for group rights to make their debut on the constitutional scene. After years of debate on Meech Lake, Quebec had made a strong case for itself as a society with group rights. People in the rest of Canada, even those who may have once opposed it, were almost worn down to the point of assent on Quebec's need for group rights. Even Newfoundland premier Clyde Wells, for instance, had softened his Meech Lake stand in 1992 and shrugged off the absolute need for the Charter to reign supreme in Quebec.

"If that's what the majority of the people of Quebec want, then okay, I can't quarrel with it," Wells told reporters after a significant, history-making meeting with Bourassa in Montreal in May 1992.

In the meantime, the pictures of the 1990 native revolt at Oka, Quebec, and other places across the country had stirred up a sense that the country owed some group rights to aboriginal people as well. And Ovide Mercredi, as an articulate, charismatic spokesperson for the natives, was poised to earn some powerful credibility among Canadians and the politicians. Add to this the presence of three New Democratic Party governments at the constitutional table, and you had a fertile breeding ground for group rights.

The left wing, whether it was Judy Rebick or Bob Rae,

or any of the NDP politicians, had their own well-considered case for group rights. They are, after all, socialists, and any first-year political science student could explain how socialism revolves around the interests of the collective, or the group. And true to their socialist theory, every one of the New Democrats in this 1992 national-unity business had come to the table with their credentials firmly established in the demands for group rights.

Rebick, of course, had a vested interest in the case for group rights. She was the leader of a group claiming to represent women, and she saw women's interests as a collective interest. This was by no means a view shared by all women. During the referendum campaign, a strong anti-NAC mood took hold among many Canadian women, who wore buttons with the disclaimer: "NAC doesn't speak for me." Translation: even among women, there is an ideological tug-of-war over whether they are part of a group or individuals. Rebick would argue that they were a group, just as she would argue the case for group rights in Quebec, for aboriginal people and other constitutional collective interests, such as the campaign for group rights under a social contract in the constitution. This triple-Crown concept of group rights came to be known as the "three nations" idea, and it had picked up some force in the 1990s.

Rebick, in fact, was aligned with another left-wing group, the Council of Canadians, when it was pushing its "three nations" idea of Canada in the fall of 1991. Maude Barlow, head spokesperson of the group, was out on the road continuously in those months, pushing this idea that Quebec was one nation in Canada, the aboriginal people were another, and the rest of Canada was also a nation. Barlow insisted that any new constitutional deal had to be a pact between the three nations. She reported that Canadians, judging from their response to her speeches, were ready for such an idea. Try it, she said.

Rebick was certainly open to the three nations idea. She made her own speeches in advocacy of three nations, and told Canadians that NAC was willing to make such a pact to ensure constitutional peace. The women's group, in other words, was happy to make way for other groups in the country. It was time for group rights.

Maybe Rebick did end up on a different side of the referendum campaign from her fellow NDP partisans in the Ontario government. This made for a bit of tension. Once, she had been a political comrade-in-arms with Ontario premier Bob Rae; she ran unsuccessfully as an NDP candidate during the 1987 Ontario election, when Rae became opposition leader. She had a long history of NDP ties, and a good working relationship with the Ontario government. So this head of NAC would become very, very angry with Bob Rae in the referendum campaign when he dismissed her as a "special interest." It was a stunning dismissal from an old ally.

Rebick's anger came from her feeling that Rae had let her down. He said he understood group rights, but he had dismissed her group, women, as "a special interest." That was the heat of the campaign talking, though. Bob Rae was as solid as Rebick on the idea of group rights, and so was his deputy of intergovernmental affairs, Jeff Rose. They had long believed that Canada was missing something vital when it promoted only individual rights in the Charter.

Rose, long before he joined Rae's government, had made his name as a labour leader at the head of the Canadian Union of Public Employees. Labour was his job, but he also wore his constitutional interests openly on his sleeve. Just before he took over as deputy for his friend Bob Rae, in 1990, he put out a collection of his thoughts on everything from trade to the GST. There, among many other clues to Rose's future manoeuvrings, is his declaration on the failings of the Charter of Rights and Freedoms. In 1987, Rose and his Canadian Union of Public Employees published a policy paper. It said: "The Charter fails to provide the proper balance between collective and individual rights. Such a balance is essential in a modern democratic society. Yet the dice are now loaded."

Rae, for his part, brought his own group-rights theory to the table. His antipathy to Trudeau was no secret. The two joked about it when they met at the University of Toronto's Hart House in early fall of 1992. But Rae's problems with Trudeau are not just personal; they are deeply philosophical, and they rest on Trudeau's refusal to acknowledge the need for group rights. The conflict also has a long, long history. In fact, Rae and Trudeau clashed on this issue long before Rae became premier. It was over the debate on aboriginal rights in Ottawa in the early 1980s, and Rae, as a young up-and-comer among the New Democratic MPs, was making the case for native rights.

"He just couldn't get it. He didn't get it, never got it," Rae said.

Rae had his own pet project for getting group rights for everyone into the constitution. It still came in a clump of three, but it wasn't the three nations idea of his other left-wing friends in Canada. Here was Ontario's way to get three sets of group rights in the constitution:

1. Quebec would get its distinct society.
2. Aboriginal people would get native self-government.
3. The rest of Canada would embrace a "social

charter" — a group of collective rights on everything from medicare to housing to welfare.

Some of these social rights actually made it into the
Charlottetown deal, but not without a bit of political
finesse-work. Cleverly, the left wing and right wing at
the table put their demands in pairs and filed them, in
orderly fashion, into the new deal for Canada. A type
of Noah's ark was created, called the "social and economic union." Ontario's demand for medicare guarantees, for example, was paired off with Ottawa's
demand for freer trade within the provinces. Both were
installed in the social and economic union. Ontario's
demand for the right to housing was twinned with
Ottawa's demand for greater mobility of goods, services
and capital. And so it went. This social and economic
union was not the new constitutional powerhouse that
either side wanted. For instance, as we have seen, the
courts were not going to have any authority to enforce
it — that would be left up to an independent tribunal.
But it was a step in the direction of a new type of group
rights in Canada, covering collective goals of the
society.
    The deal-makers liked to refer to this as the social
and economic "covenant." So maybe it wasn't really
Noah's ark; maybe it was more like the famed "Ark of
the Covenant" that Harrison Ford was looking for in
the adventure movie *Raiders of the Lost Ark*.

But that social and economic ark really only bobbed
around on the surface of the great debate over equality in 1992. It was only when the talks turned to the so-
called Canada clause that the real basics of equality
were tossed onto the negotiating table. Here, it was New
Brunswick that stirred up the debate between group
rights and individual rights.

New Brunswick premier Frank McKenna, as the leader of Canada's only officially bilingual province, was keen to get the rights of language minorities into the constitution. His province's French-speaking Acadian community had been vocal opponents of the way the Meech Lake accord had dealt with them from 1987 to 1990. This time, McKenna was going to make sure that any new constitutional deal protected French people outside Quebec as well as inside Quebec.

He had a political fact of life to consider as well. A disturbing new political party had risen up to opposition status in New Brunswick since 1990. The Confederation of Regions Party was posing an angry challenge to bilingualism. McKenna wanted to find a way to seal the French–English fact of New Brunswick into the constitution, out of the reach of the COR party.

The two kinds of equality were barrelling down the two tracks all over the country, even in quiet little New Brunswick. McKenna's idea of equality was very much the same as Rebick's, because it made room for group equality too. The COR party's equality was like the Reform Party's — everyone had to be treated equally; equality of citizens above all.

Long ago, Frank McKenna was a devotee of Pierre Trudeau's vision of Canada. As a young Liberal, he was devout in his admiration of Trudeau's ideals and the "just society." But as he grew older, and as he came to sit as the head of government in New Brunswick, McKenna started to do some serious rethinking about the dilemma over group and individual rights. Once he had shared Trudeau's fervent conviction that individual rights were all you needed in Canada. Now he knew that wasn't enough.

"I've now started to balance idealism with realism," McKenna says. "I now reject the purity and idealism of the Charter Canadians."

Many people would like to think that Frank McKenna simply sold out during the Meech years, when he turned from Meech foe to Meech supporter. His former friend, Manitoba Liberal leader Sharon Carstairs, said bluntly that he had been co-opted by his province's economic dependence on Ottawa. And it is true that McKenna was a good pal of Brian Mulroney and Quebec premier Robert Bourassa.

But it wasn't that simple. McKenna's change of heart was a result of serious rethinking about groups and individuals. Many other Trudeau-style Liberals have taken this journey with him. By 1992, McKenna had revised his thinking about the dreaded "notwithstanding clause" in the constitution. Once he had believed that it was an evil impediment to the rights of individuals. Now he saw where you might need to opt out of individual rights every now and then to protect the rights of groups.

In early 1992, he told reporters about his evolution. "I've looked almost a little wistfully at the province of Quebec, where they've managed to have a sense of collective identity. . . . Yes, individual rights are important, and yes, the Charter of Rights was an enormous accomplishment. But let us not worship at that altar to the exclusion of a sense of collective identity."

Frank McKenna had moved away from Trudeau Liberalism.

The two friends at the constitutional table in 1990 were Frank McKenna and Ontario premier David Peterson. In 1992, with Peterson gone, McKenna found a new buddy — Saskatchewan premier Roy Romanow. They shared a sense of fun, a fondness for dining together and doubts about the Charter of Rights and Freedoms. Neither really believed that the Charter embraced every kind of right that was needed by Canada in the 1990s.

Romanow had been at the constitutional table in 1981 when the Charter was designed, and he was always a sceptic. He remained sceptically supportive in 1992, when the Charter was ten years old and he was back at the unity discussions. Romanow, like McKenna, believed something was missing in the world of Canada's rights.

In the early 1980s, Romanow co-authored a book, called *Canada Notwithstanding*. Its final line is a warning: "We have renewed Canada. Did we lose its soul?" Ten years later, Romanow would answer yes to that question. Something of Canada's soul was missing. Yes, the country now had a firm sense of individual rights, but where was the sense of community, of collective good? The biggest balancing act for society is between rights and responsibilities. With every right comes a responsibility. With every responsibility comes a right. Canada, in the 1990s, seemed well grounded in rights, and not so grounded in responsibilities.

McKenna, echoing Romanow, would talk about this Canadian fixation with rights and the amnesia about responsibilities. "If we're blindly loyal to the notion of individual rights, we lose the very fabric of the nation we care about." It's another way of saying that Canada is in danger of losing its soul. "People are detached from the responsibility. A right is something they want to cling to," McKenna says.

This cry for responsibility was coming in from all quarters in Canada in the 1990s. Reform Party leader Preston Manning was giving eloquent, profound speeches about the need for responsibility in society to balance off the Canadian craze for rights. Even Prime Minister Mulroney, in the final, year-end interview he would give in his political life, talked about the need for a new sense of responsibility among the Canadian people.

"You can't always blame politicians," Mulroney told CBC television interviewers Peter Mansbridge and Pamela Wallin late in December 1992. "You can't always blame your leaders. At some point in time, you have to look at yourself in the mirror and say: 'I am a very privileged person. I am a Canadian. I have been given the greatest country in the world. To keep it together requires generosity from me, openness and vision from me. When am I going to stop blaming my neigbours and leaders and say that I, too, have a personal responsibility?'

"This is not only a country of rights. People talk about our Charter of Rights. Where is our charter of responsibilities to one another, to our province, to our country? I think Canadians are going to have to reflect seriously upon their responsibilities to each other and to Canada."

It was Mulroney's clearest, most passionate statement on the dangerous drift between rights and responsibilities in Canada. But he would not be around to help heal the rift; he would resign from politics just two months later.

Other politicians were also starting to put their finger on this dangerous absence of a sense of responsibility in Canada. Former Conservative leader Robert Stanfield talked about the "sick society" in Canada. Ontario's Bob Rae was ending the referendum with a plea for people to look at their own responsibility for the national-unity dilemma.

The Canadian public were talking, for instance, about their right to vote in the referendum and their right to information about the deal. But they weren't rallying in the streets, talking about their responsibility to vote, or their responsibility to make an informed vote. As Mulroney pointed out, the media and the politicians were blamed for the failure of communication in the national-unity mission of 1992. But maybe, just maybe, the public had to bear some responsibility too.

There was hope, though, that responsibility hadn't gone completely missing in 1992. In fact, there were signs that maybe rights and responsibility had just become strangely separated. Rights were shoved off in one direction, responsibilities in another. In Canada in 1992, the people seemed to be hoarding all the rights, and the politicians seemed to be hoarding all the responsibilities.

What was all the fuss over the perks and privileges of politicians? It was rooted in the public's jealous hold on rights. Every right a politician exercised was a right taken away from them. The notion of equality had sunk in so deep that people believed that politicians should be treated to exactly the same rights as individuals. It didn't matter that they had additional responsibilities. Once upon a time, politicians were regarded in the same light that any worker in Canada would be judged — as someone with rights and responsibilities. Just as teachers or nurses had to balance their right to strike with their societal responsibilities, so were politicians seen as balancers of the two values. When Canadians had a healthy view of politicians, they understood that a political right equalled a political responsibility and vice versa. But that equation simply did not compute in Canada in the 1990s.

Similarly, the politicians were jealously guarding their responsibilities. Every cry for the public to seize responsibility for decision-making or the social good was regarded suspiciously by politicians wary of handing over responsibility to the chaos of the public arena.

Rights and responsibilities were separated in yet another way. Canadians looked to the big arenas of politics for their rights, and to the smaller, local arenas for responsibility. Canada-wide politics was all about rights. Local politics was steeped in responsibility. While more and more Canadians were demanding rights from their federal politicians, they were accepting more and more responsibility at the local level. Community activism was on the rise at the local level in the 1990s. Food banks, though a horrible sign of the country's poverty, were also a sign of the richness of responsibility of people. The food banks were functioning in the 1990s because people were going out and exercising local responsibility, not rights. The challenge for the future is to get responsibilities and rights working together again.

Why are Canadians so seized with rights and so unclear on the nature of responsibilities? Frank McKenna and Roy Romanow would answer that the fault lies with the Charter of Rights and the great social forces it set in motion in the early 1980s. But there's another factor at work too. Some of the leading spokespersons for equality rights in Canada — equality over all — have received their apprenticeship in rights by watching other countries. B.C.'s former Liberal leader Gordon Wilson was born in Kenya, and traces his respect for rights to his experiences there.

"I grew up in a country where I've seen the state remove civil liberties. I've seen people been 'disappeared,' never to be seen again," he said. "There's a very fine line that keeps democracy in check." That line, in Wilson's mind, is drawn with rights.

Deborah Coyne has learned a lot about rights by travelling and learning about Third World countries. If you want to see the danger of group rights, she says, you don't have to look any farther than the world's trouble spots in 1992 — Yugoslavia and Somalia, where tribalism and ethnic nationalism bred strife and violence. Group rights only splinter society, according to Coyne.

If you tuned in every night to the TV news in 1992, you could see the consequences of warring nationalism in Yugoslavia. You could see Somalia, a country splintered among tribal warlords, battling for control. "You realize," said Coyne, "in a civilized country such as ours you respect the individual as the basic unit." She was struck by a report on Somalia in which the children were described as being taught to dispense with tribalism and see themselves as one country, part of the world at large. Thousands of miles away from Canada, the warnings against group rights were being taught to the Somali children. Canada should be taking a lesson from this primer in the importance of individual rights, she said, starting its own children on the right path.

Wilson and Coyne are intent on building a Canada where no rights are conferred because of race or nationalism. Yes, people will have different rights and different responsibilities, but those values will be determined by what a person *does*, rather than what this person *is*. That's what led Wilson to oppose aboriginal rights too — he saw them as setting up a ranking of rights, depending on who had been in Canada the longest. "Immigrants with seniority," in a country of immigrants. (Naturally, aboriginal people would bristle at the suggestion that they are immigrants like other Canadians. Their treaty rights, the very basis of the relationship between native and non-native Canadians, are conferred on individual aboriginal people because of their place in a group.)

All over the country, worries are being expressed about race-based rights. The Reform Party, for instance, likes to talk about the importance of a "culturally neutral" society, where a person's culture is not a consideration in how many rights or responsibilities are held. These adherents of absolute equality see the waves of immigrants coming into Canada, and the transformation of the country into a multi-ethnic society. If you've got rights based on race, and all kinds of races making their way here, you've got big trouble, they say.

"We are on the verge of the next major global migration," says Wilson. "As sure as we're sitting in this room, Canada is going to be the most favoured destination, as the next major global migration occurs. And if we don't have a constitution that recognizes equality among individual Canadians, then when that migration occurs, we're going to have all kinds of fractured groups of people, based on language, culture, race, religion. We're going to end up with tremendous conflict in this country."

But there's a fine line between being blind to cultural differences and being ignorant of them. Crazies and racists have a way of hearing that "culturally neutral" line and believing that the equality-seekers speak for them. The idea of "neutralizing" the cultures has disturbing echoes for people who believe that Canada should celebrate diversity, not extinguish it.

Wilson and Manning have both been plagued by the fact that their equality crusades attract known racists.

The Reform Party leader dismisses this with a quip: "When you shine a bright light, you attract a lot of bugs." But the equality-seekers spent a lot of time in the referendum campaign insisting that they didn't speak for the crazies or the racists. They also were accused themselves of being crazies or racists. Many people on the opposite side of their arguments were eager to dismiss them.

Rebick, for instance, was certain by the summer of 1992 that she was being written off as a crazy person, and that her demands were not being taken seriously. She was right. The mere mention of her name around the constitutional talks at the Pearson Building would

prompt politicians and bureaucrats to roll their eyes
and dismiss her. On that June day when she showed up
at the microphone at Pearson, Rebick was viewed with
anger and impatience by the provincial negotiators. Joe
Clark even made a few public digs at her later in the
day for monopolizing the microphone. Reporters were
tired of seeing Rebick make her frequent complaints,
and scurried around looking for more information on
the Senate dispute. The clock on her fifteen minutes of
fame had long ago run into overtime at the Renewal of
Canada conferences.

Rebick's concerns had dropped off everyone's priority list. She just couldn't make anyone understand
that she had a new, urgent worry. Group rights had
made it into the Canada clause, she learned. But that
didn't upset her. What did make her angry was that New
Brunswick's language minority had been singled out
for special protection in this clause — not women, not
racial minorities, and not the disabled.

"They needlessly created the impression that collective rights undermined individual rights. And set up a
hierarchy of rights," Rebick said.

There they were, the three words that Pierre
Trudeau used to great effect in his explosive expression
of No — "hierarchy of rights."

But Rebick wasn't afraid of a few group rights, as
Trudeau was. She just wondered why there was no
attempt to protect individual rights from these new
group rights. If the new Canada clause singled out
language minorities for special protection, and aboriginal people under self-government, then why
couldn't women's rights be singled out too? This was
the same worry that led to the court challenge later
that fall by the native women, who feared that their
individual rights would be overtaken by aboriginal
self-government.

A furious scramble started to find a solution. Rebick and her allies came up with a plan that would have protected group rights. Joe Clark promised her that Ottawa's lawyers would sit down and work it out with them. The discussion did not take place until September, long after the Charlottetown deal was signed. Rebick was then sure that she had been dismissed, written off. By summer, she believed, the constitutional negotiators simply decided that women's group rights, as demanded by Rebick and her organization, were just not important enough to protect in the Canada clause.

"We never got a satisfactory explanation of why they wouldn't do that. It would have solved the problem for a whole group of people . . . It might have solved the problem for native women. It would have solved the problem for people with disabilities, gays and lesbians, all the equality-seeking groups. It would have solved the problem, but they wouldn't do it."

"Hierarchy of rights" would become a rallying cry for the No forces in the referendum campaign. The native women would make the case in court. Judy Rebick would make her protest on television. Pierre Trudeau made his protest at the Maison Egg Roll. The phrase immediately stirred up that fierce, intense need for equality in Canada. What? All rights aren't equal in this accord? And people like Pierre Trudeau say that equality is affected? It was enough to mobilize an army of No voters, all moved by that one sentiment: "All I want is for everyone to be equal."

When it was all over on October 26, the wish was answered. Charlottetown was dead, and Canadians had united, equally and fairly, in massive rejection of their politicians' deal. The winning equality in Canada's constitutional pageant was the equality of rejection.

10

Leap of Respect,
Leap of Faith

The happiest times in Canada's national-unity crusade took place in mid-air; but not on the fleet of airliners that shuttled the travelling talks all over the country, and not on the Challenger jet that Ottawa would loan the provinces from time to time for extra-special occasions. The joy in mid-air happened when someone was pulled aloft into a leap of faith, or a leap of respect. When that happened, the national-unity mission worked very well. When it didn't work, it was horrible.

It was about 10 p.m. in Halifax, on January 18, 1992. Constitutional Affairs Minister Joe Clark was getting ready to go out. He had an ear cocked to the goings-on across the hall in the hotel suite. His wife, Maureen McTeer, was in another room, talking to Judy Rebick about the chaos that plagued Ottawa's Royal Commission on Reproductive Technology. Clark walked into the room, preparing to pick up McTeer for a late event. On the television, a voice on the news was complaining

391

that Ottawa's set of Renewal of Canada conferences, starting that weekend in Halifax, amounted to an expensive farce. The 200 participants were co-opted, the discussion staged.

Rebick shook her head, refusing to believe this abuse being hurled against the Halifax conference. "No," she said, "They're wrong. These discussions are real." Rebick was swept up in the incredible experience of this conference, where ordinary and not-so-ordinary Canadians locked themselves in a room and sorted out the major philosophical debates facing the national-unity mission. And she was ready to shout it from the rooftops — Ottawa is really listening to us.

The next day, she did just that. Rebick, taking a familiar spot in front of the microphones, proclaimed to the 200 people at this conference and to the television audience: "It is real."

Newfoundland premier Clyde Wells was elected in April 1989. Two months later, a *Globe and Mail* reporter was sitting in the office of the federal–provincial relations minister, Senator Lowell Murray. The subject was the future of the Meech Lake accord, which had only one year left to become reality. All through the interview, the stiff, repressed Murray was making paper airplanes out of his pink telephone messages. By the end of an hour, a small fleet of pink paper aircraft was lined up on his desk.

"What are you going to do about Clyde Wells?" the newspaper interviewer asked, almost as an afterthought. The problem provinces were Manitoba and New Brunswick — the objections of Wells were a new, nearly unexamined phenomenon. He had only been elected as premier about a month earlier.

Lowell Murray picked up one of his paper jets and launched it into the air. "Nothing," he said, watching the little airplane sweep into the air, and then hurtle to the ground.

"What?" the interviewer asked, somewhat baffled.

Murray picked up another tiny jet. "Nothing," he said. It would be another five months before Lowell Murray even introduced himself to the Newfoundland premier.

Three years later, with Meech Lake dead and Clyde Wells vilified by the Mulroney government for helping in its demise, every word of the Newfoundland Premier was gauged, heard and measured. He was recognized as a formidable voice on the subject of the constitution. On August 28, 1992, Clyde Wells would stand with Mulroney, all the provincial premiers and leaders of the native and territorial organizations in Charlottetown. He could announce that he had been heard and that he had received an answer. Wells was one of the euphoric premiers standing in the wings, waiting to tell the nation about the important national-unity deal known as the Charlottetown accord.

At Toronto's Airport Hilton Hotel on July 3, 1992, the target was Ontario premier Bob Rae. As the meeting began, Manitoba premier Gary Filmon told the reporters that the real obstacle to a national-unity deal was Ontario. He was unrelenting in his criticism, portraying Ontario as a destructive force in the federation.

Bob Rae was steaming as he entered the private talks at the Airport Hilton. He had been standing in the background, waiting for his chance to talk to the assembled, full-court press. He heard every word Filmon said; he watched incredulously as his NDP colleague, Saskatchewan premier Roy Romanow, singled Ontario out for stubbornness.

The first hours of that meeting at the Airport Hilton were decidedly cool. Rae was miffed at the televised

attack on him. Filmon wasn't backing down. The two
were not even on speaking terms.

But as the day wore on, Filmon came to realize that
Rae was starting to understand the cries for an equal
Senate. Maybe he didn't embrace the idea of Senate
equality, but he was prepared to take the Triple E convictions on faith. For the next two months, Filmon
would look on Rae with a new respect. If this Ontario
premier could put aside his reservations to understand
the West, then he truly was an honourable politician.

It doesn't take a doctorate in political science to understand what was happening in all the above high points
of the national-unity mission. When it worked, it
worked well, and it was the result of a simple human
virtue known as respect. When it failed, it would fail
because that respect was missing in some vital relationships. The most crashing failure of the 1992 constitutional exercise took place on October 26, 1992,
and that was because respect had broken down at the
most basic level of democracy — between the public
and the politicians.

Another vignette from these days shows just how
badly the public and the politicians had fallen out of
step.

On October 27, 1992, the day after the referendum,
Manitoba's Liberal leader, Sharon Carstairs, was watching television. She should have been happy. As a
leading voice on the side of the No campaign, she had
waged an energetic fight. She should have been smiling
as a local Winnipeg television crew went out on the
streets, asking the public to take one more kick at the
Yes carcass, looking for day-after reaction. But a heavy
gloom descended over Carstairs as a local Winnipeg
woman was asked about the contribution of Carstairs
to this referendum campaign.

"She knew how we were going to vote," the woman said. "So that's the position she took."

Carstairs, by that time, had already decided that she was going to quit as Liberal leader of Manitoba. But if that decision hadn't already been made, she might have quit that day anyway — just to prove to this cynical Winnipeg woman that politicians could act on their principles. She wanted to show this ordinary Canadian that politicians didn't do everything for votes. But that was a hard message to sell to the Canadian public in 1992. This was a population that didn't have much respect for politicians. Poll after poll would show that politicians were held in very low esteem, regarded as crooks, snake-oil salesmen and opportunists. And in turn, it was very difficult for politicians to respect a public that hated them so much. The Canadian political system worked in 1992 when this antagonism was put aside, if respect made even a tiny appearance. The system failed very badly when disrespect was allowed to fester.

Rebick was one of the Canadians who saw it work both ways in 1992. In Halifax, she felt respected, heard — that she could make a difference. "This is real," she would tell Clark and McTeer and the whole television viewing audience. Later that year, as daily reports emerged about the progress of the multilateral negotiations, she felt that everything she said had been ignored or forgotten.

The pictures of Rebick scorned in the summer were very different from the snapshots that emerged of her at the weekend conferences in the winter. Angry, bending over the rope barriers at Charlottetown, she and her fellow feminists would be chanting, shouting, singing — anything to get the politicians' attention. That was no way to build respect. The politicians would just see it as abrasive petulance — special-interest groups insisting that they had as much right to represent the public as the premiers.

Rebick wasn't looking to join the politicians at the table — women just wanted to know they were being respected. Where once they had been invited to stand and speak at the national-unity microphone, now they were interlopers. Respect had given way to exasperation, on both sides. "I'm not saying it would have been better, that the way to do it was to have us at the table," Rebick said. They just wanted to have a chance for open debate; the same type of open debate that was held at the conferences. But in an atmosphere of broken-down respect, debate is simply dangerous.

It certainly seemed to Ontario, similarly, that there was a rampant fear of debate in the federal government. Why was Ontario such a thorn in the side of Ottawa? Because Bob Rae and Jeff Rose were becoming convinced in early 1992 that Prime Minister Brian Mulroney was not going to respect the provinces, that his Meech experience had made him regard his fellow first ministers as a pain in the neck. So, like the women in Rebick's group, they pushed and pushed and pushed to the point of being obnoxious — and the result was Ontario–Ottawa confrontation on March 12 over the style of negotiations.

Respect shows up in the way the No forces still talk about the Canadian people, and it isn't just a case of mutual congratulations all around. Almost reverentially, the leading spokespeople for the No side insist that Canadians can be trusted with the great debates of the nation. It's not a sentiment that turns up as frequently in the rhetoric of the politicians who fought for the Yes side.

Deborah Coyne speaks with awe about the instinctive sense of public justice. "I have a big belief in people's understanding of the issues," she says. You don't need to read Aristotle or John Stuart Mill or sit at the first ministers' table to make a judgment on the national debate, she believes. "The majority of people who voted No in the referendum understand this issue of individual and collective rights."

Reform Party leader Preston Manning has the same trust in the people. "My concern with the Canadian élite is that they never indicate any faith that maybe even the rank-and-file guy could understand the problems . . . Well, they understand a heck of a lot more than people give them credit for."

Late in the referendum campaign, when the Charlottetown accord was already making its plunge into ignominy, Joe Clark was out in Winnipeg, wearily going through the motions of the final days of selling the doomed agreement. He was tired, fed up, exhausted. He was trying to leave, to catch a little sleep before he dragged himself out to yet another Yes event the next day. A cluster of people stopped him at the door. They were environmentalists, feminists. They had come to this meeting with their arms folded suspiciously; they departed with their arms extended for warm handshakes with Joe Clark.

"You showed us such respect," they told the constitutional affairs minister. The word stuck in his very busy mind. After the referendum was over, Clark gave an interview to the *Toronto Star,* and he mentioned the notion of respect over and over again. He remembered a woman in Fort McLeod, Alberta, who approached him to point out that she was not uneducated, that she had opinions to express. "She's the kind of person who wants to have her voice respected, rather than taken for granted."

It was strange that politicians such as Clark, who had learned the importance of respect in their dealings with each other, were only just beginning to reckon with this concept of respect for the public — at the tail end of the referendum campaign. Respect worked for Filmon and Rae. Respect worked between Ovide Mercredi and Joe Clark. It worked in the effort to build a deal with Clyde Wells. It didn't quite work when it came to the public and politicians.

"People do listen to debate," says Rebick. "They changed their minds. And that's a notion that these guys don't seem to have. They have this notion of manipulation. They don't have a notion that you can actually openly, honestly say what you think and have somebody openly, honestly say what they think, debate it, and that people will make an intelligent choice."

Once upon a time in Canada, politics was the art of finding solutions in the heat of debate. It's a concept as old as the teachings of Socrates, but it was not an idea that seemed to be working in the Canada of the 1990s. First, debate withered away in the House of Commons itself. The performances for television, the incredibly lop-sided relationships between government and opposition, made the House of Commons look like a charade. Rigid party discipline made votes into non-events. The only time any attention was focused on the Commons votes was when MPs were released from party discipline, and allowed to vote according to their conscience on matters such as abortion or capital punishment.

Then debate withered away in the Commons committees, where the "real work" of the politicians was supposed to be done. Television, again, didn't help. The more committee hearings that were televised, the more partisan the performances. The more attention that was paid to the political process, the more the constructive debate faded away.

Two important parts of government are still closed

to public scrutiny. The federal cabinet is cloaked in secrecy, and hard decisions are still being made there. However, there are hints that the cabinet ministers of the 1990s are far more concerned with reinforcing the decisions of the leader than in actually debating the wisdom of the leader. That was evident in July 1992, around that sad, sombre cabinet table, where Joe Clark was pitied for the deal that put the prime minister in such political trouble with Quebec.

One more place on Parliament Hill is closed to inquiring eyes. The magical, mysterious caucus meetings, where an unpopular prime minister was able to rally extraordinary loyalty among his MPs. How did he do it? Did he hypnotize them? No, in Tory caucus, every Wednesday in the magnificent Reading Room on Parliament Hill, the unpopular Mulroney managed to show his fellow Conservatives that they could all express different ideas and be part of the team. Club membership was not denied to dissenters. Throughout the years, Tory MPs would emerge from these meetings with their chests puffed out, their pride enhanced as Mulroney cultivated respect for the team. Even as he resigned in February, Mulroney made it clear that he regarded himself as a Conservative above all — when he laid out his legacy, he compared himself to other leaders of the party, not the country. This was a prime minister who held on to his caucus in difficult times because he did not waver in his respect and reverence for his own party. Unfortunately, he would never show the same reverence or respect for his opponents outside the Conservative party.

It would be easy to point a finger at the television cameras as responsible for the destruction of debate in Parliament. But it's not the presence of the TV cameras; it's how the politicians react to television, the portrayal of themselves they choose to offer. It's what the politicians feel they have to present under the glare of those television lights, when they all link arms and deny that they disagree. It's the fear of debate itself — once the very essence of democracy.

Canada's history books are filled with struggles between dissenters. Parliament itself once rested on the notion that there was a role for one idea in government and another idea in opposition. The opposition leader isn't called Her Majesty's Loyal Leader of the Opposition for nothing. But by 1992, Canadians would see politics as the expression of one, headstrong idea bouncing stubbornly around the corridors of Parliament Hill. The Tories would take their one idea, whether it was the goods and services tax or free trade, and wrestle it through those corridors. The Liberals and New Democrats would be involved in their own wrestling matches, trying to find their one good idea to bounce through their hallways. On the crucial matter of national unity, they would all line up together, arms linked, united with their one good idea of a constitutional deal.

In the 1990s, if you wanted to find a place where discussion involved more than one good idea, it was in the halls of the schools, the education system. That was where everyone looked for credible dissent. Consider, for instance, the line-up of television commentators. When it was time for intelligent debate, the academics were pulled out. Television commentary by professors was a growth industry in the 1990s. Was it any wonder, then, that the No forces imitated teachers instead of politicians to build their case with the public?

Sharon Carstairs, a teacher-turned-politician, found herself picking up her first career when she hit the campaign trail in the 1992 referendum.

"I decided that I wasn't going to do this as a politician.

I was going to do this as an educator, as a teacher. . . . I was going to go out, and I was going to dissect the deal, and the speech was the same." *Globe and Mail* columnist Jeffrey Simpson would write in the referendum campaign about a "purring" Carstairs, gently nuzzling her audience into the No camp.

"Look," Carstairs the teacher would say, dispatching her students to do some referendum homework. "I want all of you to go and hear somebody on the Yes side. I am going to talk to you about the No side. But if you're going to vote, you have to hear both sides."

Something in this appeal touched the public. Here was a politician who was not afraid of different ideas. And the Reform Party's strategy, too, was to teach, not preach. "You know, if you're in the political business, and you studied the constitution backwards and forwards, they'd like to believe that what you're telling them is probably the way to go. But they have to get the sense that you actually do care about what they think," Preston Manning says.

Respect can make people change their minds. Respect can make people take each other on faith. There was one magical phrase that opened the door to a deal among politicians, a phrase that ushered in a sense of euphoria, pride and satisfaction in that ballroom in Charlottetown on August 28, 1992: "I don't believe what you believe. But I believe what you say." Whenever this phrase was uttered, in one form or another, the politicians broke through their difficulties.

When Bob Rae agreed to an equal Senate, this is what he said to his Western friends. When Joe Clark accepted the need for native people's treaty rights in the constitution, this is what he said to Ovide Mercredi. When Clyde Wells decided that Quebeckers might think that group rights were sometimes more important than individual rights, this is what he told the nation. And, in those terrible days of July 1992, when Clark and Mulroney were locked in their own climactic struggle, this phrase pulled them back from the brink.

"I don't believe what you believe. But I believe what you say."

It's called the leap of faith. The politicians were ready to make the leap of faith among each other, repeatedly bounding through an abyss of misunderstanding. But when it came to the rift between politics and the public, the jump couldn't be mimicked. The No vote on October 26 might well have been subtitled as this message to the politicians from the public: "We don't believe what you believe. And we don't believe what you say."

Judy Rebick had to make her own leap of faith during the debate over the Meech Lake constitutional accord. Women from English Canada were sure that Quebec's distinct-society clause was going to hurt the cause of women's equality inside Quebec. But Quebec women were telling NAC that distinct society was okay with them. What else could Rebick say? She didn't believe what they believed, but she had to believe what they said.

"I supported distinct society for political reasons," says Rebick. The women's movement was not happy about distinct society — they believed it would undermine women's rights. "But if women in Quebec whose rights it would undermine, if they're saying it's not undermining rights, then we have to accept that. It's the same argument we made for aboriginal women in this round, which is if they're saying it is undermining their rights, we have to respect it."

It was the very same logic that Clyde Wells used when he decided to give Quebec a little leeway on the issue of individual rights. Yes, maybe Clyde Wells didn't believe in the group rights that Quebeckers embraced, but he had to believe they were important to them.

Still, in 1992, when Rebick and other equality-seekers were getting nervous about the Canada clause, they were met by an absolute refusal by the politicians to budge. These same politicians who would make the leap of faith with each other would not make the leap of faith with Rebick. Rebick and Deborah Coyne and Manitoba's Liberal leader Sharon Carstairs were all told, in effect, "We don't believe what you believe. And we don't believe what you say." Hundreds of other Canadians, dozens of interest groups, were told the same thing when they raised concerns about the Canada clause and its treatment of precious equality rights.

A modern, mature system would have tried to deal with this opposition, says Rebick. True democrats would try to address dissent rather than ignore it. But the concerns of all these equality-seekers were written off. They were told they were wrong. They were told that the Charter issues were open to "interpretation" and that their interpretation was misguided. Rebick and the others weren't looking for the politicians to believe what they believed, but they wanted the politicians to at least believe what the equality-seekers said. "The fact that every equality-seeking group in the country felt threatened should have been enough of a political reason to do something about it. So then I say, well, why didn't they?"

It goes back to the fear of dissent, says Rebick — the same fear that made Ottawa and the provinces back away from any consideration of the idea of asymmetry for Quebec. Asymmetry would have given Quebec one set of powers, and the rest of Canada another. It would have met Quebec's demands for a decentralized government while satisfying the rest of Canada's demand for strong central government.

In Halifax, Rebick had taken her own leap of faith to understand that Quebeckers needed different powers from the rest of Canada. That's not what we want in the rest of Canada, but we can accept that you want them, she said. Rebick believes that if she could make this leap of faith, other Canadians could make it as well.

"If you explain that people in Quebec want more power for their province — we don't want that, we want a strong central [federal] government — it takes the emotion out of it. Then it becomes a rational discussion."

Rebick saw the rational discussion take place at that Halifax conference, and believed it could be duplicated on a much larger scale, through the whole Canadian nation. Joe Clark had hoped she was right. It would solve a lot of problems on that difficult issue of powers in the constitution. But after the Halifax conference, Clark got on the telephone, doing his own little reconaissance mission for the idea of asymmetry. And he didn't see it going anywhere.

"I could not find an elected person, including the leader of the opposition anywhere, or even a third party, who seriously thought we could get asymmetry through any legislature in Parliament." But that was just the elected people in Canada. Maybe the electors and the elected are far, far apart on what's possible and what can be sold to the Canadian public. That's what Rebick believed. It was not what Clark believed.

"I think she's very much in the minority on this. One of the difficulties of running an interest group, one of the few advantages of being in so-called organized politics is that you're forced to go back to a constituency that's larger than something you control. And then you hear from other people. Most interest groups, no

matter how much outreach they practise or intercon-
nection with others or things like that, are protected
against that sort of public."

This was the never-ending tussle in Canada in 1992
— the electors versus the elected. Most of the leading
voices for the No side were unelected people. Most of
the leading voices on the Yes side were elected. As a way
to describe this phenomenon, it came to be known as
the non-élites versus the élites. But that doesn't really
explain what was at work here.

"People say it was this anti-élite thing," says Rebick.
"That's a ridiculous notion. I mean, Trudeau is the
most élite person in the world. What do you think he
is? Some grassroots activist? It's nonsense saying it's an
anti-élite thing. That got totally confused. It was a rejection of what the élites were saying; not because they
were élites, but because people didn't agree with it."

Indeed, the so-called "élites" would be quite perplexed to find themselves with that label. On the last
Saturday night of the referendum campaign, Mulroney
was in Lloydminster, Saskatchewan, sharing a stage with
Yes politicians of all stripes, one last gasp for his
doomed deal. Mulroney looked ruefully at Premier Roy
Romanow, shook his head, and wondered how all these
Canadian men, from very modest roots, had suddenly
become "élites." Yes, they were the white men in suits
who held power in Canada, but there was once a time
when their rise to power would have been viewed as a
vindication of democracy, not a repudiation of it. All of
them, in their own ways, were local boys made good,
who came to power not on family connections or upper-
class privilege, but through work at the grassroots.

There was Romanow, a West-side boy from Saska-
toon, Saskatchewan, son of Ukrainian-born parents
who lived and died knowing 102 words of English.
There was Brian Mulroney, the electrician's son from

Baie Comeau. There was Deputy Prime Minister Don Mazankowski, the Polish car salesman from Vegreville, Alberta. And there, at the same table, was Agriculture Minister Bill McKnight, a farmer. "So we're the élites, eh?" Mulroney asked his fellow Yes campaigners at the table where they were dining.

The "élite" thing drove Manitoba premier Gary Filmon crazy. "If there's anything that can make me bounce off the walls, it was being called élitist by Preston Manning and Sharon Carstairs, both of whom are children of former premiers and former senators," says Filmon. "I'm a poor kid who grew up the son of a garment worker in north Winnipeg and I'm the élitist! And then on the night of the referendum, when [Global TV owner] Izzy Asper, one of the wealthiest men in Canada, said I'm an élitist and he's an ordinary guy who speaks for the people, I mean that drove me crazy."

Preston Manning is fond of making the distinction between the élites and the non-élites, and he believes it was a useful distinction on this issue.

"I do think at least on this issue, where your people, you know, your business leaders, your traditional political leaders, and your big national media, were all on one side and promoting a view that your rank-and-file of citizen just didn't buy. Like, there really was a gulf there. A political party like ours, we'd say, if you want to decide whether we're populist or not, you've got to go a little deeper as to whether I'm the son of a premier or not."

Who are the élites, in Manning's view? "I'm really talking about the top decision-makers in the public and private sectors. And I'm not denying that there has to be people that have to make decisions, that they're going to have more authority over other people than the people lower down. That's necessary to get things done." You don't judge this élite solely by his or her position — you judge them by their ability to listen. The description "élite," when Manning uses it, means someone in power who just doesn't listen; who believes that his or her power is justification enough for a belief or decision.

It was listening, in fact, that made Newfoundland premier Clyde Wells into such an anti-politicians' hero during the Meech Lake years. It wasn't just that he stood up to the unpopular Brian Mulroney; it was that he kept talking about respect for the people. While the Meech proponents were insisting that there were no "egregious errors" in Meech, that it was a seamless web, Wells was insisting that his concerns, and those of the public, be addressed. He was pleading: "I know you may not believe what I believe. But couldn't you believe what I say?" The politics of Brian Mulroney, braced against dissent from his opponents and critics, regarding every different opinion as a challenge, could not accept Wells as anything but a threat.

The perception of dissent as a dangerous notion was filtering down to the public, too, in subtle ways. They would applaud dissent, mainly because they were hungry for the expression of different ideas. Wells was praised by the public for having the "courage" to dissent in 1990; the allegation in 1992 was that he buckled under Mulroney's politics of fear. The Reform Party and the National Action Committee on the Status of Women was inundated with letters of support after they took their No stand in September 1992, being commended for "bravery" in saying No.

What does it say about the nation's politics when the bravest political act is to politely raise a hand and say: "I disagree"? Preston Manning and Judy Rebick would answer: "Welcome to Brian Mulroney's Canada."

The executive of the National Action Committee met

one Sunday afternoon early in September to figure out
their referendum position. It didn't take long for the
women to decide that they had to say No. It took a long
time to decide whether they had the courage to say No.
Inside the meeting, the NAC executive members talked
about the consequences they could face for taking the
No side. "Our funding could be cut," some suggested.
The government wouldn't do that, would they? NAC
thought they could.

"It was definitely a risk. Because the last time they cut
our funding, it was completely political. It was the year
after we opposed their budget," Rebick said.

The women decided to take that risk. They couldn't
have budgets slashed much more. Another worry
popped up: "What about all our allies, the labour
groups, the NDP governments and everyone?"

Up until about two years before the referendum, the
women's movement and the labour movement had not
been close friends. But between 1990 and 1992, a new
alliance had been built up, providing money and political support to the women. Now, that young alliance was
about to be rattled by the referendum. The Canadian
Labour Congress was voting Yes. NAC was going to vote
No.

"How can we take on every political party in the
country?" the women wondered. As Rebick says: " You
know, we are a lobby group . . . and we had made
progress in the year with the Tories. And this was going
to blow it completely."

They sat around that afternoon, mulling over the
threat, the danger of saying No. But then, says Rebick,
it struck them. "If we make the decision on this basis,
then how are we different than what we're criticizing
opportunist political parties for? If we're going to
decide not to fight this because it's saving our own
hides, then how are we different?"

The women sat and thought: "What if we lose the organization?" It was an extreme, maybe melodramatic thought. But the answer was equally dramatic: "Well, we've operated without a national organization before."

And so Rebick went out to face the cameras and explain that NAC had put itself on the list of foes of the Charlottetown deal. They had done so because they had put all their time and energy into this constitutional round, and they did not feel they were part of the end product. They had done so to show that dissent was alive and thriving in the politics of fear.

"We knew that constitutional deal better than anybody else. And if we opposed it, and we were not willing to say No, where was democracy in the country?"

The National Action Committee was immediately and universally criticized or condemned by almost every politician — especially women politicians — in the country for taking the No side. But in the NAC offices, the phone calls of support were flooding in. Eighty per cent support was logged on the phone records the first day, 85 per cent support the second day, 90 per cent the third day. It was a stark illustration of the politicians saying one thing, the people saying another. NAC was being told, over and over again, "thank you" for expressing dissent.

Around that same time, the Reform Party of Canada opened up its hotlines, fulfilling its promise to consult its membership before it took a national-unity position. (The hotlines were ridiculed as an escape from leadership by the country's politicians.) As the calls came in, the overwhelming sentiment was No. But again, the question was not whether to say No, but how to find the courage to say No.

"Could we take the No position and communicate it in a way that didn't just allow us to be caricatured as anti-Quebec or anti-French or anti-Confederation?"

Preston Manning wondered. "That was the box that the
Mulroney people wanted us and the BQ (Bloc Quebecois) to be in."

This climate of politics surrounding the referendum,
where Reformers and NAC activists had to be brave to
be on the No side, is linked to Mulroney's style of politics, as Judy Rebick sees it. "There's a notion of conse-
quence if you dissent. That you'll get punished in some
way, right? And I think that's frightening. Because, you
know, ruling by fear is not a quality of democracy. It's
a quality of dictatorship. And there is a fear of the con-
sequence of dissent in this country.

"That I put right at Mulroney's door. Because that's
how he leads. His leadership is the politics of fear. And
if you look at Meech Lake, if you look at the free-trade
agreement, everything he has sold he has sold through
fear. 'What will happen if we don't do it. There'll be
catastrophe.' It's always catastrophe."

There were many people in Canada in 1992 who
blamed Brian Mulroney's style for creating this us-
against-them mentality with regard to dissent. Certainly
his battle cry against the enemies of Canada mobilized
another call-to-arms among the No voters.

Jeff Rose, deputy to Bob Rae throughout the
national-unity negotiations, and a fierce combatant of
Mulroney-style politics, has given a lot of thought to the
way public debate changed under this prime minister.
Put simply, he says, Mulroney's politics were all about
imposing his personality on the nation, the "divine
right" of leadership. And once Mulroney started
running the constitutional show during the referendum campaign, his politics shattered the careful bridge
of respect and compromise that had been built in the
months leading up to the Charlottetown accord.

Rose is worried about politicians such as Mulroney
who believe that it is dangerous to give people the right

to decision-making, "who think that the problem with democracy is the people won't make the right decision." He sees Mulroney as the type of leader in the tradition of former British prime minister Margaret Thatcher, who believed power was the right to force the leader's ideas on the voters, the type of leader who would say: "Once you get power, you've got it for five years. Use it no matter what the public thinks about your policies. It's not like other systems of accountable government — it's a parliamentary dicatorship. Don't accommodate different points of view. This five-year blank cheque is a delightful thing for you, because you can use it secure in the knowledge that the people can't defeat you until five years are up." As a labour leader, Rose spoke out against Mulroney using this approach on the goods and services tax, on free trade. It was more than the politics of fear, or the threat of catastrophe, he said. It was simply the Mulroney government saying to the people: "We're right. You're wrong."

Indeed, in his final years in office, Mulroney would regard popularity and leadership as mutually exclusive notions. The good leader made tough decisions. The good leader didn't do things because they were popular, but because they were right. After Mulroney resigned, many people were reconsidering this notion, even members of his own party. During the race to replace Mulroney, the Tory contenders were constantly wrestling with the problem of reconciling Canadians' demands for "new politics" and "politics of inclusion" with the public's need for governance and leadership.

Rose, for his part, believes that Mulroney's unpopularity is a verdict on his style of "parliamentary dictatorship," a term coined by political scientist Richard Lipsey in a 1990 article, justifying Mulroney's risk in defying the public. Yes, Mulroney may have got things done, but he alienated Canadians in the process. Surely there must be a way to be a strong leader and stay in touch with the public — that's the biggest challenge of any "new politics."

The word "respect" pops up in Rose's analysis of the problems too. "I don't think that the *people* were out of sync with the *politicians.* I think that for the last few years, democracy has been in danger from a political style that doesn't respect the people. In the Canadian system of democracy, elected leaders are expected to make compromises, while in office, with points of view which aren't identical to their own. You don't back off your policy direction, but you must integrate people or they will lose faith in institutions. That used to be described as the 'Canadian political genius' — accommodation and compromise. But in the last few years, under Mulroney, Canada has not witnessed that kind of democratic accommodation."

Maybe this is the way to get things done in business or in the corporate world, says Rose, but it's not the way to get things done in politics. When he left office in February 1993, Mulroney would be praised as a radical politician. Even his opponents had to grudgingly admit that the Mulroney government's policies on free trade, tax reform and changes to national institutions had truly been a radical departure for the nation. Mulroney had come to office promising that Canadians wouldn't recognize their country after a few years of his rule, and he was correct. Rose applauds the politician who believes that change is necessary, but he doesn't think that change has to constantly fly in the face of the people.

"At the heart of Mulroney-style politics is the belief that radical policies can only be implemented against the people's will, because the people are wrong. That's really deplorable in my view, because it's so undemocratic."

The referendum was proof of this — the enormous effort that went into overwhelming the electorate, with fiery rhetoric, with massive campaign organizations, with all the political fireworks that were at the country's disposal. Being a leader is not about being a forceful personality, says Rose, it has to be about respecting the public. "If personality is what you think it's all about, you should be a rock singer. You shouldn't be a politician."

Out in the far reaches of British Columbia, the provincial Liberal leader, Gordon Wilson, was discovering as well that the politics of the 1990s was not about big-time campaigns or crowded halls or large, impersonal speeches to the crowds. Politics, 1990s-style, was all about going to tiny meeting rooms and listening to small groups of people. Granted, this was a circumstance forced on Wilson because of the dismal state of the Liberal Party of British Columbia when he assumed its leadership in 1987. But he was realizing that the route to the grassroots involved a massive detour around all those larger-than-life politics, all the huge campaign techniques that had been perfected in the past decades by politicians such as Brian Mulroney.

"When you're building a grassroots party, you're going into town-hall meetings where you get half-a-dozen people show up, and you go out and talk to a group of farmers, or you have to be out talking to some loggers in a logging camp." Could you put five people in a meeting room? Wilson would be there to talk to them. Could you gather up a university class or a high-school group for a political discussion? The leader of the tiny B.C. Liberal party would be there.

"I had the benefit of that because I wasn't locked into the legislative assembly. In fact, my biggest fear is that now that we're here, I'm losing those connections. The conventional wisdom was that if you can't put 100 people into a hall, don't go. Wrong. If five people go, [you] show up, because they're five people that want to talk to you, that have something to say. You're getting five people that are committed. Because if you have five people, you're better off than if you have 100 people that simply go out saying 'nice speech.' Because those five are going to convert ten who are going to convert ten. And the next thing you know, you've got a major movement happening."

It would be wrong to depict Canada's prime minister in 1992 as a man who only knew politics as the act of overwhelming dissent. Actually, there were two Brian Mulroney styles. One he reserved for the public, the one so condemned by Jeff Rose. But actually, there was another Brian Mulroney, too, who practised Wilson-style politics within his own party. His nine-year success in holding a huge Tory caucus together was largely due to the way he encouraged his fellow Tories to speak their minds: his willingness to listen and learn from them. The difference between the two approaches? Respect.

Many of the No people, such as Sharon Carstairs, thought that it was important to keep Brian Mulroney out of the debate. "Don't vote No because you don't like Brian Mulroney," she would tell her audience. "I can't stand the man, and as soon as I'm given the opportunity in the next election, I will do everything I can to make sure he's no longer the prime minister. But this isn't about Brian Mulroney. This is about what kind of a country you want."

Carstairs calls this one of her best lines; the one that spoke to the public's weariness with personal attacks and personality politics. "First of all, they didn't want to be told by politicians what to do, and also, they didn't want to have it a personal attack on another politician, even on Brian Mulroney, as much as they despised him.

They wanted somebody who talked to them about the issues."

Respect — there it was again.

But Deborah Coyne says that the No vote had to be seen as an indictment of Brian Mulroney — not just the man, but his brand of deal-making and constitutional horse-trading. "Certainly a lot of people did vote against Mulroney, there's no doubt about it. But if you followed Mulroney and his conception of the consensual-politics idea, his whole method of politics over the last eight years has been brokerage politics, special-interest groups, and that's what people were voting against. So I would tie the two together."

What could be said about Canada in the 1990s was that there was a tremendous quest to seize on that "one good idea" brand of politics. Find your position and then make all who disagree into enemies. It takes an enormous leap of faith, a different type of leap from the constitutional kind, to accept that there could be two good ideas, or three, or four. That's why Preston Manning doesn't like to characterize any disagreement as a battle between "consent" on the government side, and "dissent" on the other side. There is something called an "alternative," says Manning. Or you can call it a different opinion.

Canada, by 1992, was filled with frustrated voices of "alternatives" or "dissent," struggling to get out. There was no room in the federal Parliament for dissent except in caucus meetings; most real dissent on the constitution had been drummed out by party discipline and the search for three-party consensus. There was no room in the provinces; they had linked arms in the great national-unity struggle as well. That gigantic No vote on October 26 was, if nothing else, a huge release of this force that simply wanted to say: "I don't agree." Thwarted at every turn when it looked for a polite outlet, the No burst forth with an anger built out of frustration.

Canada's media have played into the hands of this notion of one good idea. Conflict, the essential element of news, has a tendency to pit ideas against each other as enemies. A different opinion is often seen as a challenge to government, not part of governing. The media, in turn, are seen by the politicians as an open challenge to good government. The image of the reporter is one of a combative, cynical crusader, out to reveal the weaknesses of politicians. The image of leaders, for reporters, is of a group of people intent on hiding their own deeds and actions. It takes an enormous act of will from both sides to overcome this abyss between the media and politicians.

Joe Clark, to his credit, gave it a try in the constitutional talks of 1992. He was not going to preside over an Ottawa that gave its information to reporters in a web of spinning and background briefings by unnamed officials. This tactic was one imported to Ottawa by the American example, and it had merely bred American-style antagonism between the elected people and the media. So Clark tried something new — or different, at least. He decided that he would come out each day and give a point-by-point rundown of what had been discussed at the talks. He would say where there were differences. He would explain why he was giving some information and not other facts. He would give details of the progress of negotiations.

It was, put simply, a gesture of respect, intended that way. Clark was employing a simple bit of common sense he had learned while he was external affairs minister. Two incidents, in faraway lands, taught him how respect breeds respect, even among traditional adversaries. First, he was leading a delegation to the Ukraine for a formal meeting with the president. It was a state affair, to be convened in a large, ornate meeting room in Kiev. The crowd of Canadians shuffled into the room — reporters, officials and clerks, all in tow. The president of the Ukraine announced the start of the meeting. Clark looked up beside the president and saw, to his utter disbelief, the face of Claire Hoy, a rebellious, cynical reporter for the *Toronto Sun*, the bête-noire of the Tory government for his tirades against Mulroney.

Clark cleared his throat. "We very much enjoy and appreciate your hospitality, the fact that you've extended it to all my delegation. It's naturally your choice, but in our country, at this stage, I would invite the journalists to leave." The president recoiled, then thundered: "We have nothing to hide."

Clark remembers how the Canadian reporters, including Hoy, responded to this rare gesture of inclusion in the world of diplomacy. There was even a spat between Canada and Ukraine, and it was treated with stunning delicacy, Clark remembers. "The journalists who were there in Kiev, acted with a sort of Canadian responsibility that they would not have if that had happened in Kingston."

On another occasion, Clark was in Budapest, Hungary, for some key meetings. This was an important time in history. Europe's Eastern bloc was in the grip of monumental changes, throwing off the shackles of communism. The meetings in Hungary were sensitive.

During his foreign trips, Clark often brought along a group of MPs from all three parties. But if there was a particularly touchy meeting, he would ask that a Tory come along with him, rather than a Liberal or New Democrat. Such was the case at this meeting. Clark had expected a fellow Tory to show up at the Budapest meeting. But at the last minute, the Tory had switched spots with an opposition member. Clark arrived at the meeting in a flurry of preparation, barely looking up from his notes as the delegates settled into their chairs. The meeting was called to order. He looked over, and there was John Nunziata, a Liberal MP, one of the famous "Rat Pack," whose anti-Tory tirades had made him as popular with the Conservatives as Claire Hoy.

Again, Clark marvelled at how Nunziata handled his entrée into this world. "There were some things that were discussed there that could have been very difficult, they could have been embarrassing if they had broken too early. And Nunziata respected that."

Clark could not take the political risk of inviting the journalists into the meetings. He wasn't worried about what they would do; he was worried about the effect of the media on the negotiators. Suddenly, everything would be a performance. If you want to get on the news as a politician, you have to talk the hostile language of conflict. There is little drama in compromise and tiny steps of progress. There's lots of drama in stand-offs. Witness all the attention paid to the Senate dispute, the way it was turned into a David-and-Goliath struggle between big provinces and small provinces. So Clark did the next best thing. He tried to provide a running commentary for the journalists, and he was surprised by the results.

"I was just amazed. I thought I was going to get mugged. . . . Because it was so dull." Dull it was, but the respect paid the journalists made them think twice about making cheap shots, or exploiting differences, or playing adversaries off each other — all approaches used by the media in more adversarial encounters with politicians.

Jim Horsman's diaries are also filled with his evolving attitude towards the media. Like Clark, Horsman was realizing that if you are straight with reporters, they

will return the respect. Horsman was one of the negotiators viewed with the most affection and respect by
the reporters at the end of the negotiations; so was Bob
Mitchell, another direct politician who didn't try to
play games. Moe Sihota would be respected, too, for
saying what was on his mind, and giving straight
answers. Of course, Clark's esteem was assured by his
show of rare political respect for the media adversary.

Clark would take the lesson back to his riding of Yellowhead, after the referendum and before he resigned
from politics. He tried something new on his riding,
late in 1992. He summoned a bunch of local people
together, a cross-section of all kinds of interests in Yellowhead. The subject was one of the burning political
issues for Canadian society in the 1990s — law and
order, and young offenders. The rise of populist discontent was feeding off the corresponding rise in
young crime in the 1990s, and governments were being
blamed for their failure to deal with the elemental
concept of justice — for criminals and victims. Clark
borrowed some pages from his constitutional hand-
book, and opened up the subject for a free-wheeling
debate.

Something surprising happened. As all these people
started talking about what governments could do, they
also started talking about what they should be doing.
The conversation turned away from what the system
could do for them, and on to the question of what they
could do for the system. Clark had stumbled on the
equation that could help Canada out of this terrible
breakdown in the political system. Respect equals
responsibility. And responsibility is a test in learning
about equals.

Canada, by 1992, was in desperate need of some new
politics. The referendum was not a rejection of change.
In fact, it was a cry for help from a tired, beleaguered

nation. The primer for this new politics is already written in the messages of the referendum. A new politics has to be found, one that embraces respect and is not afraid of dissent.

The lesson of the referendum was not for politicians to carry on with their old ways on a new subject, the economy. The lesson of the referendum was not that people simply hated Brian Mulroney or politicians or "élites," whatever they are. The lesson is that both sides in the referendum campaign must learn to get past No, with respect.

11

Getting Past No

How would you etch the tombstone that marks October 26, 1992, in the Canadian history books?

How about: "Here lies the political fate of Brian Mulroney and Joe Clark"?

Or: "Here lies the constitutional obsession that dominated Canadian political life"?

Or would you simply mark it: "No"?

None of these epitaphs truly describe what was buried in the national referendum of 1992. The most accurate epitaph for this date is summed up in these words:

"Here lies the old style of politics in Canada."

Something did indeed die in Canada in the fall of 1992. All of that constitutional wrangling was really the death throes of traditional politics in Canada, which revolved around compromises by the leaders and blind observance by the led. In its place has come a new, vaguely worded recognition of the need for "new politics" in the country.

Mulroney's successor, Kim Campbell, was talking

about it throughout her campaign to become Canada's
first woman prime minister.

Early in May 1993, Campbell arrived in Alberta for
the third of the Conservative leadership debates. Here
was a province heavy with the air of new politics, and
the demand for a new, populist era of governing. In the
wake of the referendum, the discontent with government had not abated. It had grown even larger, in fact.
The cry from the West for Senate reform had given way
to an even bigger demand for radical changes in the
country's system of government. Now Albertans
weren't looking for just one institution to be over-
hauled on Parliament Hill — they were doubting every
attitude, every assumption that fed representative government and Canadian democracy. The prevailing
wisdom among Albertans was that no one in Ottawa
could represent them; only the people could speak for
themselves.

On the very day of the Calgary debate, Alberta
premier Ralph Klein was abolishing pensions for
politicians — a response to the public's perception
that elected people cared more about the perks of
power than the duties of office. Hours earlier, Reform
Party leader Preston Manning had called a news conference to proclaim that the Tory leadership candidates were not giving concrete answers to the
Canadian public and that the country was really interested in radical changes in Ottawa's way of running
the economy. "The people are way ahead of their
elected representatives on this," Manning kept saying.
And at the Calgary debate itself, all six leadership contenders were vying to demonstrate their commitment
to a new style of governing. Clearly, by the spring of
1993, Alberta had become the test ground for all the
promises of "new politics" that sprung up in the wake
of the 1992 referendum.

Campbell touched on the dilemma for any Canadian political leader in this era — how does a leader lead, with a public so unwilling to follow?

"You hear a lot about strong leadership," Campbell told her Calgary audience. "But I think there's a difference between strength and bravado. Canadians are tired of being shouted at. They want to be respected and they want to be persuaded. And leadership is the capacity not just to know where you're going, but to know how to get there — to be able to mobilize people, to rally them to a sense of common purpose."

Though Campbell was a loyal cabinet minister to Mulroney, she and every other politician in Canada knew that it was not simply enough to heed Mulroney's advice that a leader must lead, and that unpopularity was a badge of honour, a proof of accomplishment for any politician. Such was the advice that Mulroney gave U.S. President Bill Clinton on his last official visit to Washington.

"I have read stories saying, 'Mr. Clinton has a broken presidency; Mr. Clinton is going down the tubes,'" Mulroney told reporters after he met the U.S. president, whose popularity was plummetting after his first 100 days in office.

"All of this, of course, is nonsense. It bears no relationship to what will happen to him in four years. He's elected for four years, and he should wear unpopularity as a badge of honour."

Such was the advice, however, that also put him out of touch with a public that sought more from its leaders than dismissal and a damn-them-anyway approach. The end of the Mulroney regime in Ottawa was greeted by relief from Canadians who were tired of being told that they were wrong and the government was right.

In her speech to the Tory delegates who elected her to replace Mulroney in June 1993, Campbell stressed the same message about the importance of a leader's style of governing, using the word "respect" several times throughout her appeal.

But was this a message that really sunk in with Campbell? In the many profiles of Kim Campbell that surfaced during her leadership campaign, little snippets of disrespect for the public kept peeking out from behind her promises of new politics. This was the same woman who called proudly apathetic voters "condescending S.O.Bs." This was the same politician who said she had little in common with the beer-drinking public who watched TV in their undershirts. This was a politician like many others in the country, whose words betrayed her difficulty in respecting Canadians who refused to show their own respect of elected leaders.

Politics and politicians were under siege everywhere in Canada in the wake of the referendum. No one dared mention the dreaded "c-word" — the constitution — in polite company, yet the country had really not stopped talking about radical change in the way Canada was governed. In 1993, though, the change was going to come through attitude, not multilateral negotiations, and not horse-trading around the first ministers' table.

Liberal leader Jean Chretien was fond of telling a story about a Quebecois who promised that if Chretien never mentioned the word "constitution" again, he could be prime minister forever. New Democratic Party leader Audrey McLaughlin put out the same message, vowing that the NDP was more worried about jobs than legal dances on the head of a pin. The Liberals and NDP, by virtue of their long experience in opposition, had vowed that they would be the parties that listened and respected the public, in a way that the nine-year Mulroney regime never did.

By 1993, however, the country had moved through the alphabet from the "c-word" to the "d-words" — deficit and debt. And the ghosts of the discredited old politics kept haunting the rhetoric of all parties, as the politicians talked about the tough decisions they would have to make and Canadians would have to swallow. The politics of fear were simmering to the surface again. Now it wasn't the fear of the country falling apart that was held over the public's head. It was the fear of crippling debt for future generations and the spectre of the International Monetary Fund moving in to take control of Canada's economy. The same message was out there: "Accept what we say — or else."

Maybe, if the constitution was not such an off-limits conversation and if the referendum was not such a black mark on the psyche of Canadian political leaders, the 1992 experience could be a guidepost for the future. In all that wrestling over the fate of the federation, there are lessons to be learned for any politician who wants to get past No and into the twenty-first century with the practice of governance intact.

Many of the country's politicians are hovering around the fringes of this revelation. Saskatchewan Premier Roy Romanow is one of them. He wasn't blind to the motivations of pride and ego that threw him twice into the no-win debate over the constitution. Nor was he blind to the message that Canadians sent him when they voted No to his efforts to grapple with the "big stuff" of Canadian government.

Canada's politicians were lured to the constitutional table by the chance to talk big issues under the glare of the television lights; to talk about all the principles that had brought them into politics; to try to shape the nation. All of them would talk about the mystical aura that surrounded the unity discussions for a politician, the lure and temptation of big ideas.

No one would articulate it more clearly than Romanow, who fell twice into the political temptation of the constitution.

"You're talking big issues. You're talking issues of equality, and fairness, and Canada, statehood. This is big, big stuff," Romanow explained, one cold December day, with the referendum behind him and a pot of tea in front of him. The tea, an herbal variety, was fittingly called "Constant Comment." Romanow, coincidentally, was explaining the politicians' penchant for constant comment on national unity.

"All of us get into public life because we want to do good things for people on day-to-day matters. But we also want to, you know, change the world."

He vows that for him there will never be a third time on the constitutional front. He sees now that the politicians are going to have to fight for their big principles on smaller, more stable ground. First, they have to prove that they can champion the values of equality and fairness at home, on the smaller matters, before trying to fiddle with the fundamental law of the land.

The public has every right to challenge their leaders to make good on all their high-sounding statements of 1992, Romanow says. Canadians have every right to expect that the politicians who trumpeted the virtues of accommodation, equality, fairness and compromise will show those virtues in the day-to-day life of the country.

"We need positive demonstrations of that kind of accommodation and compromise," he says.

"Put us in front of the television lights, expose our actions and our thoughts. We have to come up with answers for the Canadian public. I just don't think they'll tolerate any one of us until we come back to that accommodation." The route to getting past No, in

Romanow's eyes, is getting the politicians to make good on their constant comments of 1992.

Of course, if that is to happen, the politicians and the people have to find the starting ingredient of respect. As all the events of 1992 demonstrated, when respect is the basis of the relationship between political players, everything else can flow from it. When it's not there, everything fails.

How do you find that respect, though, in an era where everyone is talking about rights and not a lot of people are talking about responsibilities? Since the advent of the Charter of Rights and Freedoms, the Canadian public has become incredibly attuned to the measure of their own rights and the rights of others. The entire Canadian political relationship has come to be seen as a trade-off of rights. When a politician exercises a right or a privilege, Canadians tend to see it as a right that's gained at their expense. The public figure who takes a first-class airline seat is reviled for taking that seat away from someone more deserving, namely, an ordinary citizen.

But the whole rights-versus-rights argument was never the basis of the political relationship. Every right bears a responsibility — that's the real trade-off. Politicians get rights that ordinary people don't have, and they also have responsibilities that ordinary citizens don't have. Politics works when rights and responsibilities work together. The right to vote carries the responsibility to make an educated vote. The right to assemble peacefully carries the responsibility not to riot in the streets. A free press has to be a responsible press.

But in the Canada of the 1990s, rights and responsibilities are estranged partners, living distinct and apart, as separate as Quebec and the rest of Canada. Rights are locked in the embrace of the public.

Responsibility, and all the blame that goes with it, is in the grip of the politicians.

Romanow mourns this estrangement as the loss of Canada's collective soul. New Brunswick Premier Frank McKenna worries about the fraying of the fabric of the nation. Ontario Premier Bob Rae laments the breakdown of mutual trust between the leaders and the led in Canada. A new political philosophy called "communitarianism," which stresses the individual's responsibility to society, is rising up in pockets across North America.

At the heart of the breakdown of the Canadian political relationship is the drift away from the partnership of rights and responsibility. People point their fingers at the Charter of Rights and Freedoms, and wonder whether it really tells the whole story of Canada.

Some people want to temper the charter with group rights or social goals. Some people, such as Brian Mulroney, talked about balancing the charter of rights with a charter of responsibilities. Other people, such as Deborah Coyne and Pierre Trudeau, would say: "Leave the charter alone."

The Canadian people are smart enough to exercise the collective good and responsibility all on their own, without any help from the constitution, says Coyne. Look at food banks. Look at how Quebec has flourished as a distinct society without the guarantee of group rights.

Something has to happen, though, to bring them back together.

Is the Canadian public willing to take on some responsibilities, along with the rights so eagerly attained in Trudeau's constitution-making?

The 1992 referendum was an experiment in handing responsibility to the people. Bob Rae would argue that the experiment wasn't successful.

The folly of a referendum is pretty clear in Rae's mind. "All I can say is that I wouldn't do a referendum campaign, or the same kind of referendum as we did. Because it obviously didn't work." The Ontario Premier saw the referendum as the key to a Pandora's box of distrust and animosity and cynicism among the Canadian public. It was a no-win situation for Canadian politics.

On the other hand B.C. Premier Michael Harcourt sees something strangely unifying in this referendum. He is not sorry that his province, as one of the only ones required by law to hold a constitutional vote, essentially forced all of Canada to go along for the referendum ride.

"This is one area where a referendum is important," Harcourt says. "What was important about the outcome on the 26th was that it was a decisive No."

Something was stirred in Canada by the referendum. Governments were flooded with requests for information. The public was turning out in droves at information sessions, underlining their dog-eared copies of the Charlottetown accord, asking earnest and thoughtful questions of their politicians.

When they were treated with respect, they were grateful. Constitutional Affairs Minister Joe Clark was thanked over and over again for really listening to people. Judy Rebick was applauded for not speaking down to voters. Sharon Carstairs was appreciated for urging her audience to pay attention to the Yes and No side; for saying that the referendum wasn't about hatred of politicians.

Clearly, by 1992, the Canadian public was ready to play a responsible role in political decision-making. People were hungry to make an educated choice. The "Know More" of Preston Manning's referendum slogan had far more resonance than its synonym, "No More."

The same hunger for information was showing itself in the new Canadian obsession over the deficit and debt in 1993, when the public was demanding answers from the politicians about how each and every Canadian could play a part in getting the economy out of the red. On the federal political scene, politicians were finding that the public was willing to think about cost-cutting measures that had been unthinkable only ten years earlier: user fees for medicare, an end to universality in social programs, and so on.

For some time now, the Reform Party of Canada has been demanding a greater role for the public in government. Reformers would like to see the public paid greater respect, invited to start legislation, to have the right to recall politicians, and to hold more referenda on key issues.

Deborah Coyne, no ally of the Reform Party, nonetheless agrees that people are eager to take a more responsible role in government. The food banks, the surge of interest in parent-teacher co-operation in education, show that it's starting on a local level, among the generation that spent the 1980s in material pursuits.

"It's all there," Coyne says. "What we need is for that to happen more at the federal level."

Joe Clark, looking over the wreckage of his failed constitutional mission, would also agree after the referendum that some way had to be found to bring the public into the responsibility of government.

"I do think we have to look at some devices that give some comfort. I don't like any of them. The recall thing. The referenda. I don't like any of them. . . . They're all ways of saying No. But I think we have to look at them. Just because, if we keep saying No to every proposal that comes up, then that simply causes people to say No to us."

The idea of direct democracy is something that unnerves Alberta's Jim Horsman. Fuelled by the Reform Party's cries for these devices in the West, Horsman has spent a lot of time looking at the result. He sees California, where voters are flooded with tons of silly, complex questions every time a ballot box is set up.

Manning has a very Canadian answer to this: Why do we always look toward extremes? Canadians are not extreme people.

"Why not go to the Swiss? Why not go to the Australians? There are dozens of other states that have a more balanced approach than California. . . . There's one characteristic of our people: if there's three roads and there's a middle one, we'll take it. If the earth was flat, Canadians would run to the middle. They don't want to fall off any kind of edge," says Manning.

Underneath that same mild Canadian temperament, however, is a simmering anger over the way government has been practised. It creeps out in polls, when politicians are described as dishonest, unethical and deceitful. It shows up in the apathy and cynicism that run rampant among the voting public in Canada. At the root of this anger is the sense that government revolves around finding one good idea, and sticking to it despite the criticism. In the constitutional debates, the virtues of "control" and "strong leadership," as practised by the politicians, seemed dedicated to the notion that there was only one good idea in the world, and every possible effort must be made to make that idea into a reality.

The most eloquent voice on this issue is Judy Rebick. As a feminist, Rebick thinks that men in politics bear a lot of the responsibility for the idea that dissent has to be conquered, not accommodated. But whether or not the problem is rooted in the war of the sexes, there

is no denying the symptom. There is very little tolerance in Canadian politics for expressions of diverse
opinion. Dissent within political parties is punished.
Dissent within government is a sin.

"It's this notion that there's only one right idea," says
Rebick. "It's the notion that gives rise to threats and the
politics of fear." Nothing good comes from this kind of
government, says Rebick.

"You see, to me, democracy is the conflict of ideas, a
creative process that will bring you to better solutions
than any one good idea. To me, that's the essence of
democracy."

One need only look at the record of minority
governments in Canada, and their reputation for being
far more progressive than big, cumbersome majorities.
Ironically, it is the minority Liberal government in
Ontario from 1985 to 1987, with the partnership of Bob
Rae's New Democrats, that has been cited as the most
effective government Ontario ever had.

And yet it was Bob Rae, as part of this revolution in
government, who would not tolerate the idea of deadlock in Parliament as the provinces designed a new
Senate. Rae saw it as paralytic for Parliament, and yet
the clash between two strengths in Ontario had proved
to be unquestioningly successful.

So the question is how to soothe the phobia about
dissent that has risen up in Canadian politics. No
one has tried to erase this phobia in federal politics.
In fact, the art of a politician revolves around avoid-
ing dissent or handling dissent or putting down
dissent.

What's the best answer for a politician? A non-answer.
Whose style of politics was the most envied among
Canadian politicians in the 1990s? Robert Bourassa, for
his elegant way of straddling the fence and saying
nothing.

For nine years in Canada's Parliament, one voice of dissent was not allowed to be heard in the halls of power. In 1984, as Pierre Trudeau left Ottawa, his ideas and his legacy were buried by his successors — who were also his visceral ideological rivals.

Brian Mulroney's politics were steeped in deep distrust of Trudeau Liberalism. John Turner, who took over the Liberal helm, was also no fan of the Trudeau legacy. There was no room in this Ottawa for Trudeau's Liberalism, so it went underground, feeding a subterranean well of politics at the provincial and grassroots level. Barred from expression by any of the mainstream parties in Ottawa for most of the Mulroney years, Trudeau Liberalism became almost a rebel doctrine, fed and nourished by its forbidden status. It's reasonably safe to say that until it resurfaces in Ottawa as a legitimate, credible force again, it will keep bursting forth in little geysers of protest across the country.

How will Trudeau's Liberalism get back into the mainstream of Canadian politics? First, the federal Liberals have to give it a home and a place to flourish in open debate in their party. Deborah Coyne, along with several other like-minded Liberals, has been quietly working on setting up a pocket of Trudeau ideology inside the Liberal Party.

"We want to reach out to the people who have felt alienated, who want to be involved . . . And you can do that within a political party," Coyne insists.

The test for the Liberals' commitment to the new politics will be whether Coyne's group is seen as unhealthy dissent or healthy democracy. Liberal leader Gordon Wilson, his own career sidelined by personal problems in British Columbia in early 1993, believed that Trudeau Liberalism would first find its renewed strength in the provinces, not Ottawa.

But it isn't just the Trudeau vision that has to be given a voice. It's only the most powerful of a number of voices that have been silenced by the fear of dissent. Clyde Wells, another student of Trudeau-style Liberalism, has been calling for a constituent assembly on the constitution for a number of years. So has the Reform Party of Canada. Their calls were dismissed in the past. What they were trying to do, however, was reintroduce the notion that it's okay to express different ideas in Canada. Gordon Wilson says, "The next time, the people are going to take command."

But when the people actually do take command, they may soon learn the lessons that politicians learned when they tried to sit down and rebuild the country. Sometimes, you can't find a deal that embraces the rock-solid convictions of each person at the table. Sometimes, you have to take your opponents on faith rather than conviction. Bob Rae learned that on the Senate question. Clyde Wells learned that in the fuss over collective rights for Quebecois and aboriginal people.

The most joyous experience for politicians in the national-unity mission of 1992 came when they went soaring aloft in a leap of political faith. If people were allowed to leap with the politicians, some of the joy and euphoria might rub off on them too. But that will be difficult in the Canada of the 1990s. There are even more obstacles to the leap of faith than there were in past decades. The climate of disrespect and distrust is a daunting challenge for any deal made with faith.

In Bob Rae's view, isolation is the price Canada is paying for the loss of important national symbols and the economic fragmentation of the country during Brian Mulroney's years.

"Meech, I think in some ways, encouraged greater

isolations," he says. "The atmosphere after Meech, with French in one camp and English in the other, became an obstacle to understanding." Many of the national institutions which built bridges between Canadians have also been eroded in the tough economic and political climate of the late 1980s and 1990s, too.

"Those things have not been strengthened. And I would argue — and this is, I suppose, a political point, but I feel it very strongly — the last eight years we've seen a lot of national institutions significantly undermined. This notion of nationhood undermined, even by free trade itself, has deprived the country of a sense of having a national economy, of having a lot of things that are shared in common. And I think that's encouraged all the tendency to distance and to people taking exclusive positions."

Long ago, a former prime minister named Joe Clark talked about Canada as a community of communities. In 1991-92, as Clark criss-crossed the country, he would see a stark illustration of the isolation of Canada's communities. Nobody seems to know or care much about the other parts, he says.

But Clark, an optimist, also sees signs that this is changing. The key to ending the sense of isolation, according to him, is more travelling of the country. He would like to see government get out of Ottawa and he would like to see the people making a better effort to get out and understand other parts of the country. His heartfelt speeches as constitutional affairs minister were filled with calls for an end to this isolation, pleas for patriotism that were active, not passive.

The answer is to make Canada bigger, as Bob Rae wanted, to make Canadians realize that the country is made up of more than they can see out their front doors.

Is there room in this Canada for a Trudeau equality, a Rebick equality and a Manning equality? Can all of them live together?

Yes, Bob Rae says.

"Absolutely there's room. There has to be room. But I think the key is to find a constitution which allows principles to be reconciled. I think, again, the key to maturity in the country, is the willingness to be a really mature political system, where your people recognize that even on matters of principle, there's nothing wrong with reaching accommodation or less than perfect embodiments of the principle, in order to move, to make progress, in order to reach some kind of understanding. Otherwise life would be unbearable."

Rae is talking about the need for a leap of faith.

Much has been said about the virtue of "consensus politics," of having everyone agree to one idea. A unanimous deal is billed as a wonderful deal. In fact, in the Canada of the 1990s, a deal with no dissent is seen as the ultimate goal of politicians and statesmen.

It is also very difficult to obtain. Prime Minister Brian Mulroney knocked himself out to get two unanimous national-unity deals in his years in office, and yet these agreements were crushingly defeated. Still, most of the premiers and politicians agreed that Mulroney's strategy was the right one. The last thing Canada needed in its fractured, cynical climate was to have the provinces and Ottawa warring with each other on something as fundamental as national unity. When the Senate dispute threatened to isolate Alberta and the West, Saskatchewan's Roy Romanow used this spectre to put consensus politics back on track.

He would ask: can you imagine Don Getty and

Preston Manning and the rest of the West, campaigning against Ottawa, Ontario and Quebec? The thought was spooky enough to put the all-for-one team back together in the Senate dispute.

Reform Party leader Preston Manning agrees that consensus politics are still the best way to reach a decision. But it has to be a slow, gentle consensus. This is the whole debate that's raging beyond politics, he says, in the argument about the American style of management versus the Japanese style of management.

The U.S. style has been nicknamed "practice for defeat," and it revolves around the notion of strong management and authority. It's fast and effective, say the people who preach this management.

The Japanese style, however, delicately walks up to change, bringing everyone along in consensus. The followers of this style argue that it's faster than American management. Yes, the decision takes longer to make, but it's a lot quicker to implement, because you're not dragging people kicking and screaming into a new approach.

Manning thinks Canada is a lot more comfortable with the gentle form of consensus, real consensus politics as practised by Ovide Mercredi. Not given to extremes, Canadians will go a long way down the road to consensus. But push them, as they felt pushed in the referendum, and look out, says Manning.

"They get their back up and then there's all sorts of ways of not co-operating."

Meanwhile, in the era of consensus, the media is a great enforcer of hard-line consensus building. The politicians with different opinions in party caucuses are branded as rebels or mavericks. A House of Commons committee that dares to issue a minority report is seen as a sign of breakdown in political co-operation.

It's hard to accept the idea that people can disagree and co-operate at the same time. Slowly, the politicians are working to detour around the media, believing that the people have more tolerance for dissent than the media. In the U.S. presidential election of 1992, Democrat Bill Clinton and millionaire-populist Ross Perot showed that the new trick for public figures was to waltz past the reporters' questions and wade right into the free-for-all of a public discussion.

By early 1993, Canada's political junkies were looking down to the States to see whether this approach could be mimicked in the next election. Senator Lowell Murray, a key communications adviser to Mulroney and to Kim Campbell, acknowledged in the spring of 1993 that he was telling all federal government politicians to detour around the confrontational style of the Ottawa press gallery and to seek ways of getting messages to Canadians without the media's antagonistic filter.

"We've told ministers not once, but a hundred times, if you've got an announcement to make, don't go over to the bloody press theatre and sit there while they have at you . . . Go to a high school, go to a plant, go to a hospital, go out of Ottawa as far away as you can get."

Clearly, the Clinton victory in 1992 in the United States also showed that people were eager to talk about ideas, not personalities. Clinton's extra-marital affairs were forgotten in the demand for new leadership. His apparent respect for the voters was more influential than doubts about his morality.

The referendum campaign of 1992 demonstrated the public hunger for ideas over personalities. No matter what famous or notable Canadians were dragged out on stage by the Yes campaign, the Cana-

dian public kept asking to see the legal text of the agreement. People were tired of larger-than-life politics and
larger-than-life leaders.

More than anything else, too, people were tired of
politicians' egos. Whenever the great Canadian
national-unity debate got mixed up with someone's
ego, there was trouble.

Very early in the spring of 1992, the negotiators at
the table realized this. They were all politicians; all of
them knew the lure of the lights and the "big stuff,"
as Romanow called it. But they soon realized that
when they played for the cameras, they didn't get
anything done.

No matter how much time was spent at question-
and-answer sessions with the media before, during
and after the meetings, much of the inside business,
in the wake of these encounters with reporters,
revolved around getting people to justify what they
said at the microphones, or to summon up the
courage to back off. If a politician tried to score
points in the media by setting out a hard line, the
negotiations got bogged down.

Moe Sihota says he quickly learned that ego had to
be put away in this business. Look at Joe Clark, he says.

"You know, Clark operated in as ego-less a fashion as
I've seen anybody operate through a process." Clark
would be the one to swallow his pride or put aside his
ego to make room for others, whether it was in taking
the blame for Quebec's misjudgment of opinion, or
stoically accepting the prime minister's non-support of
him in July.

When Sihota talks about the danger of ego, he is
talking about Brian Mulroney. "I pleaded with Clark on
several occasions to keep Mulroney out of the process,
in the talks and in the campaign. It was his ego."

Any time a politician's ego intruded, as Mulroney's did, the public radar immediately spotted it, Sihota says. He also saw the ego problem surface in the actions of Romanow, who was keen to save the day with his deal from New York and his suggestion of the 25-per-cent guarantee for Quebec. "He wanted to be the guy to cut the deal," says Sihota.

Every ego-inspired intrusion was pounced upon by the public, "You can't let your ego drive decisions for you. . . . You know, I'm one of these guys, I've never met a microphone I didn't like. So I understand all that stuff. But this was not the time and place for it. I felt very strongly about that. It just wasn't the time and place to do that."

Egos were definitely bruised in the national referendum debate. Politicians who strutted their egos are either gone from power, like Mulroney, or considerably quieter, like Romanow. So it likely won't be the politicians who attempt to make the first step toward reconciliation with the cynical public — it will have to be Canadians themselves.

In 1992, the public would find a thousand different ways to protest that it had been ignored. The irony is that government was listening to the public, but people weren't listening to government.

The politicians would point to all their hearings, all their long hours of concentration on what they could "sell" at home. Incredulously, the Western premiers would say to their public after the referendum was over: "But we thought you wanted an equal Senate. That's what you told us you wanted."

Quebec's politicians would be shaking their heads too. "Didn't the people want Meech back? Didn't we get them that and more?" It was the ultimate experience of bewilderment for these politicians, who truly thought they had taken the public's best interests to the table.

Millions of dollars — as much as $300 million according to some estimates — were spent by Ottawa on the national-unity crusade that ended in failure on October 26, 1992. Millions more were spent by the provinces and all the business, labour and social groups that conducted their own constitutional hearings and seminars. What's the return on this investment?

Undoubtedly the Canadian public knows more about the constitution. We are arguably the most literate society in the world when it comes to the technicalities of constitutional law.

But Joe Clark would say that we still don't know much about each other. The isolation and ignorance and misunderstanding plaguing the nation are serious. Quebec and the rest of Canada are no closer to understanding each other, though now they are united in their rejection of constitutional compromises.

The rift between the politicians and the public is the real threat to national unity now. The country is split between the electors and the elected, the represented and the representers. The next national-unity mission will have to heal this breach.

There's no sense looking out the window, waiting for a new national-unity team. No travelling road show will lumber into town for limited engagements. No 1-800 numbers will be set up to monitor the public. Want to talk about the constitution? You'll find the politicians under the table.

The politicians thought they had been listening to the public all through 1992. Now, they're not so sure. But they are certain they were listening on October 26, 1992, when the answer was No. They've given the public the last word.

As the holders of that last word, though, it will be up to the public to initiate any reconciliation with the politicians. The next move belongs to the Canadians who want to get past No. United, the politicians fell. And they won't get up again until the public reaches out a hand to help them up.

Chronology

May 1987: Meech Lake accord is signed by all first ministers.

June 4-9, 1990: Marathon talks at Government Conference Centre in Ottawa to save the Meech Lake accord.

June 22, 1990: Meech Lake accord dies after Manitoba, Newfoundland fail to ratify deal in their legislatures.

Nov. 1990: Citizens' Forum on Canada's Future is established, headed up by Keith Spicer.

Dec. 17, 1990: Commons-Senate committee is struck to examine amending formula for Constitution.

Jan. 26, 1991: Quebec Liberal Party issues Allaire report, calling for sweeping list of 22 powers to be transferred to Quebec.

March 27, 1991: Quebec's Belanger-Campeau Committee calls for a referendum on sovereignty to be held no later than October, 1992, if an acceptable deal is not offered by the rest of Canada.

April 21, 1991: Joe Clark is named Constitutional Affairs Minister.

Summer, 1991: Unity committee of cabinet conducts deliberations all over the country — Winnipeg; Niagara-on-the-Lake, Ont.; Iqaluit, NWT; Quebec.

September, 1991: Federal government introduces set of 28 constitutional proposals, titled Shaping Canada's Future.

September, 1991: Federal government finances four aboriginal organizations to hold national hearings on the constitution.

October, 1991: Special Joint Committee of the House of Commons and Senate begins hearings into federal proposals.

November, 1991: Special joint committee collapses in disarray; Senator Claude Castonguay quits as chairman; federal government sets up series of Renewal of Canada conferences as alternative plan.

December, 1991: Special joint committee restarts hearings in Ottawa.

Jan. 17-19, 1992: Renewal of Canada conference on division of powers in Halifax.
    Conference urges governments to look at "asymmetry" of powers; different powers for Quebec and the rest of Canada.

Jan. 24-26, 1992: Renewal of Canada conference on Senate reform in Calgary.
Clark says equal Senate is as likely as "another virgin birth."
Gender equality demanded by women.

Jan. 31-Feb. 2, 1992: Renewal of Canada conference on economic union.
Federal proposals on economic union deemed unacceptable.
Groups call for social charter in the constitution.

Feb 5, 1992: Ontario Constitutional Committee releases its report.

Feb. 7-9, 1992: Renewal of Canada conference on distinct society in Toronto.

Feb. 14-16, 1992: Final wrap-up of Renewal of Canada conference in Vancouver.

March 1, 1992: Special Joint Committee issues report, known as Beaudoin-Dobbie report after furious, last-minute scrambling among Conservatives, Liberals and New Democrats.

March 10, 1992: Alberta issues its constitutional report.

March 11, 1992: Quebec National Assembly votes overwhelmingly to reject the Beaudoin-Dobbie report.

March 12, 1992: Clark convenes special "multilateral ministerial conference" on the Constitution.
Native organizations, territories are accepted into the talks.
Ontario advocates and wins a new multilateral

process for Ottawa, provinces to come up with constitutional offer to Quebec.

March 13-15: Special renewal of Canada conference is held on aboriginal issues in Ottawa.

March 31, 1992: Prime Minister Brian Mulroney says Ottawa could move on its own if constitutional deal can't be reached by deadline.

April 8-9, 1992: Multilateral talks take place in Halifax.
  • Negotiators agree on principle of inherent right of self-government.
  • Western ministers meet; alliance for Triple E Senate begins.

April 14, 1992: Multilateral talks take place in Ottawa at Government Conference Centre — one-day meeting.
  • Clark says equal Senate is possible.

April 29-30, 1992: Multilateral talks in Edmonton.
  • Native people come close to walkout; win promise of special sessions in coming weeks.
  • Four of five parts of Meech Lake are revived.
  • Triple E group has expanded to five provinces — Alberta, Newfoundland, Manitoba, Saskatchewan and Nova Scotia.

May 3-7, 1992: Quebec Premier Robert Bourassa and Intergovernmental Affairs Minister Gil Remillard tour four Western provinces.

May 7-8, 1992: Multilateral talks in Saint John, N.B.
  • Principle of equalization expanded in constitution.
  • Triple E group wins time to prepare proposal.

May 11-14, 1992: Multilateral talks in Vancouver.
- Native groups win right to describe, not define self-government with "context clause" in Constitution.
- Negotiators feel clock ticking; pressure builds to get a full deal before turning over issue to the first ministers.

May 15, 1992: National referendum bill tabled in the House of Commons.

May 16, 1992: Four Western premiers meet in British Columbia.

May 19-22, 1992: Multilateral talks in Montreal.
- Quebec government hosts reception for negotiators.
- Discussions finally deal with division of powers; agreement is reached to clarify six powers as provincial — tourism, mining, forestry, housing and municipal affairs. Agreement is reached to make culture and job training exclusive areas of provincial jurisdiction.
- Triple E group produces document — puts pressure on Ontario.

May 25-31, 1992: Multilateral talks in Toronto.
- Senate impasse deepens — big provinces against small provinces.
- Native groups win guarantee of treaty rights in the Constitution.
- Deadline missed, negotiators agree to 10-day pause in talks.

June 8-11, 1992: Multilateral talks at Lester B. Pearson Building in Ottawa.
- Negotiators hold "terrible" dinner.
- Saskatchewan Premier Roy Romanow flies up from

New York to help solve Senate impasse; introduces his new Romanow proposal.

June 24, 1992: Prime Minister Brian Mulroney announces that he will recall Parliament on July 15, 1992 to consider constitutional impasse.

June 28, 1992: Leaders of four aboriginal organizations meet Prime Minister Brian Mulroney at 24 Sussex Drive.

June 29, 1992: All premiers, except Quebec Premier Robert Bourassa, meet Prime Minister Brian Mulroney at 24 Sussex Drive. The Senate impasse is described as a provincial one, to be worked out by the premiers on their own.

July 3, 1992: Premiers meet at Toronto's Airport Hilton Hotel, work Senate impasse down to one, equal proposal.
   • Ontario Premier Bob Rae says he will consider equal Senate, Clyde Wells says he will consider veto for Quebec.

July 6, 1992: Multilateral group reconvenes to resolve outstanding native issues.

July 7, 1992: Premiers reach new national-unity deal, featuring equal Senate.
   • Clark praises "historic" agreement.

July 8, 1992: Clark briefs cabinet colleagues on the premiers' agreement. Mulroney, in Europe, has only faint praise for deal.

July 9, 1992: Quebec Premier Robert Bourassa holds

press conference on premiers' package. He is non-committal, but insists he is looking for the substance of Meech.

July 10, 1992: Prime Minister Brian Mulroney holds press conference to postpone recall of Parliament.

July 16, 1992: Yukon leader attacks Quebec's demands for veto over creation of new provinces.

July 28, 1992: Prime Minister Brian Mulroney invites Premiers to attend a "first ministers' lunch" at Harrington Lake on Aug. 4.

July 29, 1992: Quebec Premier agrees to attend Aug. 4 lunch, since it is not a negotiating session. Aboriginal and territorial leaders are not invited.

Aug. 4, 1992: First ministers hold meeting, only agreement is to hold another gathering on Aug. 10.

Aug. 5, 1992: Ovide Mercredi and Tony Penikett boycott briefing at Harrington Lake for native and territorial leaders.

Aug. 10, 1992: First ministers agree that next step is full constitutional conference.

Aug. 11, 1992: Prime Minister calls constitutional conference for Aug. 18 in Ottawa.

Aug. 18-22, 1992: Negotiations at Pearson Building produce tentative deal.
- Equal Senate is part of package
- Quebec gets guarantee of 25 per cent in the Commons.

• More Commons seats given to Ontario, Alberta, B.C. and Quebec.
• Number of extra B.C. seats still unresolved.

Aug. 22, 1992: Tentative agreement is announced, Prime Minister addresses Quebec caucus in Drummondville, Que.

Aug. 26, 1992: First ministers arrive in Charlottetown, PEI for final work on deal.

Aug. 28, 1992: Charlottetown agreement is reached. Prime Minister Brian Mulroney vows to wage referendum campaign against the "enemies of Canada."

Sept. 8, 1992: Prime Minister addresses House of Commons to announce Charlottetown accord.

Sept. 9, 1992: Alberta Premier Don Getty announces resignation.

Sept. 10, 1992: Reform Party announces it will campaign for No side in referendum.
House of Commons approves referendum question.

Sept. 12, 1992: Parti Quebecois launches No rally in Montreal; 1,200 people attend.

Sept. 13, 1992: National Action Committee on the Status of Women announces it will campaign on the No side.

Sept. 14, 1992: Quebec's senior civil servant, Diane Wilhelmy, goes to court at eleventh hour to stop a radio station from publishing a transcript of a telephone conversation.

Sept. 15, 1992: *The Globe and Mail* publishes transcript; shows that Quebec's senior civil servants believe Quebec "caved in" to the rest of Canada on constitutional deal.

Sept. 16, 1992: Quebec women's federation says it was threatened with funding cuts in exchange for Yes vote. Quebec National Assembly approves referendum question.

Sept. 17, 1992: Former Ontario premier William Davis speaks out for Yes campaign in Ottawa luncheon. Parliament adjourns to allow MPs to fight referendum campaign.

Sept. 20, 1992: Article by former Prime Minister Pierre Trudeau appears in *Maclean's, l'Actualité,* urging Canadians to "resist Quebec blackmail."

Prime Minister Brian Mulroney launches Yes campaign effort in Vancouver.

Sept. 22, 1992: The "Canada Committee" for Yes launches campaign in Ottawa high school with seven eminent Canadians, no French translation of Yes.

Sept. 24, 1992: Prime Minister Brian Mulroney and Quebec Premier Robert Bourassa campaign together at aluminum smelter.

Sept. 25, 1992: Royal Bank of Canada issues report, warning of dire consequences of No vote. An Angus Reid poll shows that No has slim majority and momentum.

Sept. 27, 1992: Quebec's Yes campaign officially begins.

Sept. 28, 1992: Prime Minister Brian Mulroney rips up

copy of Charlottetown accord during a speech in Sherbrooke, Que., to demonstrate how No vote will destroy
historic gains of the deal.

Sept. 29, 1992: Constitutional Affairs Minister Joe Clark
responds to outcry over legal text, promising that it will
be released before the referendum.

Sept. 30, 1992: Bank rate jumps 2 percentage points, to
8.25 per cent; referendum rhetoric on both sides is
blamed. Injunction is lifted on Quebec transcripts.
Prime Minister Brian Mulroney urges Canadians to put
aside their problems with him to vote Yes in referendum.

Oct. 1, 1992: Former prime minister Pierre Trudeau
speaks at Maison Egg Roll in Montreal; calls Charlottetown accord "a big mess."

Oct. 2, 1992: Quebec comedienne Diane Jules insults
senior citizens, hinting that they are too frightened to
vote No.

Oct. 3, 1992: Constitutional Affairs Minister Joe Clark
and Liberal leader Jean Chretien campaign for Yes side
together in Drayton Valley, Alta.

Oct. 5, 1992: Newfoundland Premier Clyde Wells
threatens to cancel Western tour if his concerns about
legal text are not addressed.

   New Democratic Party leader Audrey McLaughlin
takes on Reform Party leader Preston Manning in
debate at Guelph, Ont.

Oct. 6, 1992: Yes committee unveils television advertising campaign, featuring baseball player, a class portrait.

Liberal leader Jean Chretien debates Bloc Quebecois leader Lucien Bouchard on Radio-Canada's "Le Point" television program.

British Columbia's Constitutional Affairs Minister Moe Sihota insists that Bourassa lost at the constitutional negotiations.

Oct. 7, 1992: Newfoundland Premier Clyde Wells arrives in Calgary to start Western tour. Prime Minister Brian Mulroney flies to San Antonio, Texas, for a signing ceremony on North American Free-Trade Agreement.

Oct. 8, 1992: Newfoundland Premier appears in Vancouver to campaign for Yes side, appears on Rafe Mair's controversial talk show.

Oct. 9, 1992: Legal text of Charlottetown agreement is released.

Oct. 12, 1992: Quebec Premier Robert Bourassa debates Parti Quebecois leader Jacques Parizeau on television.

Oct. 13, 1992: Native Women's Association of Canada goes to Federal Court in bid to stop referendum, arguing that their rights were trampled in negotiations for self-government.

Oct. 14, 1992: The Canada Committee launches more aggressive advertising, issues challenge for Super Debate with leading No proponents.

Oct. 15, 1992: Prime Minister Brian Mulroney says it's only "boozed-up Tories" who are talking about revolt against him. Constitutional Affairs Minister Joe Clark speaks to meeting of Assembly of First Nations chiefs in Vancouver.

Oct. 16, 1992: More transcripts appear in Quebec, published in *l'Actualité* magazine, alleging that the province failed to achieve its objectives in Aug. 28 deal. Assembly of First Nations chiefs fail to endorse Yes vote in referendum.

Oct. 19, 1992: Prime Minister Brian Mulroney launches a week of editorial-board meetings and interviews, in bid to secure Yes vote. On radio program in Toronto, he says that Quebeckers don't want to be "Cajuns with banjos" in Canada. Yukon leader Tony Penikett is defeated in general election. Super Debate is rebuffed by No forces.

Oct. 20, 1992: Assembly of First Nations chief Ovide Mercredi, Ontario Premier Bob Rae and Prime Minister Brian Mulroney campaign together for Yes in Guelph, Ont.

Oct. 23, 1992: Constitutional Affairs Minister Joe Clark heads to Alberta for final days of campaign; Prime Minister Brian Mulroney in Saskatchewan for his final appearances of referendum.
Toronto Blue Jays win World Series.

Oct. 26, 1992: Referendum Day. Canada votes No to Charlottetown accord.

Index